# Facts On File

## BIOGRAPHICAL

## ENCYCLOPEDIA OF

# ARTISTS

### SIR LAWRENCE GOWING
GENERAL EDITOR

## VOLUME 2

ALBRECHT DÜRER – JAN LIEVENSZ

Facts On File, Inc.

Published in North America by:
Facts On File, Inc.
132 West 31st Street
New York, NY 10001

The Brown Reference Group plc
(incorporating Andromeda Oxford Ltd)
8 Chapel Place
Rivington Street
London EC2A 3DQ

Library of Congress Cataloging-in-Publication Data

LC Control Number: 2005040500
   Type of Material: Text
      Main Title: Biographical encyclopedia of artists / edited by Lawrence Gowing.
Published/Created: New York: Facts On File, c2005.
Projected Pub. Date: 0504
   Related Names: Gowing, Lawrence.
      Description: p. cm.
         ISBN: 0816058032
      Contents: v. 1. Alvar Aalto–Paul Durand-Ruel -- v. 2. Albrecht Dürer–Jan
         Lievensz -- v. 3. Limburg Brothers–Francisco Ribalta -- v. 4.
         Jusepe de Ribera–Francisco de Zurbarán.
      Subjects: Artists--Biography.
         Artists--Encyclopedias.
LC Classification: N40 .B535 2005
   Dewey Class No.: 709/.2/2 B 22


Volume 2 ISBN        0-8160-5805-9
Set ISBN             0-8160-5803-2


Facts On File books are available at special
discounts when purchased in bulk quantities
for businesses, associations, institutions, or
sales promotions. Please call our Special Sales
Department in New York at (212) 967-8800
or (800) 322-8755.

You can find Facts On File on the World Wide
Web at http://www.factsonfile.com

Cover design by Cathy Rincon

Printed in China

10 9 8 7 6 5 4 3 2 1

The publisher wishes to thank the following individuals and institutions for
their help in the preparation of this work:

INDIVIDUALS: Margaret Amosu, Professor Manolis Andronikos, Janet
Backhouse, Claudia Bismarck, John Boardman, His Grace the Duke of
Buccleugh, Richard Calvocoressi, Lord Clark, Curt and Maria Clay, James
Collins, Bryan Cranstone, Mrs E.A. Cubitt, Mary Doherty, Judith Dronkhurst,
Rosemary Eakins, Mark Evans, Claude Fessaguet, Joel Fisher, Jean-Jacques
Gabas, Dr Oscar Ghez, Paul Goldman, G. St G.M. Gompertz, Zoë Goodwin,
Toni Greatrex, A.V. Griffiths, Victor Harris, Barbara Harvey, Maurice
Howard, A.D. Hyder, Jane Jakeman, Peg Katritzky, Moira Klingman,
Andrew Lawson, Betty Yao Lin, Christopher Lloyd, Jean Lodge, Richard
Long, Lorna McEchern, Eunice Martin, Shameem Melluish, Jennifer
Montagu, Sir Henry Moore, Richard Morphet, Elspeth O'Neill, Alan
Peebles, Professor Dr Chr. Pescheck, Pam Porter, Professor P.H. Pott, Alison
Renney, Steve Richard, Andrew Sherratt, Richard Shone, Lawrence Smith,
Don Sparling, Graham and Jennifer Speake, Annamaria Petrioli Tofani, Mary
Tregear, Jim Tudge, Betty Tyers, Ivan Vomáčka, Tom Wesselmann.

INSTITUTIONS: Ashmolean Museum, Oxford; Bibliothèque Nationale, Paris;
Bodleian Library, Oxford; British Library, London; British Museum,
London; Courtauld Institute of Art, London; Gulbenkian Foundation,
Lisbon; Louvre, Paris; Merseyside County Museums, Liverpool;
Metropolitan Museum, New York; Museum of Modern Art, New York;
Museum of Modern Art, Oxford; Oriental Institute, Oxford; Oxford City
Library; Petit Palais, Geneva; Phaidon Press, Oxford; Pitt Rivers Museum,
Oxford; Sainsbury Centre for the Visual Arts, Norwich; Sotheby Parke
Bernet & Co., London; Tate Gallery, London; Victoria and Albert Museum,
London; Warburg Institute, London.

The publisher wishes to thank the numerous individuals, agencies, museums,
galleries, and other institutions who kindly supplied the illustrations for this
book.

The publisher also wishes to acknowledge the important contributions of
Judith Brundin, Ann Currah, Bernard Dod, Herman and Polly Friedhoff, Juliet
Grindle, Jonathan Lamède, Giles Lewis, Andrew McNeillie, Penelope Marcus,
and Louise Pengelley.

# Dürer Albrecht 1471–1528

The German painter, printmaker, and theorist Albrecht Dürer is generally acknowledged to be the most significant figure in the history of European art outside Italy in the period of the Renaissance. His prints especially had an enormous influence on all forms of the pictorial and decorative arts both in northern Europe and Italy. A critical understanding of Dürer's art is facilitated by the large quantity of personal information that survives in the form of letters, theoretical writings, and carefully annotated drawings. This constant comment on his work is more sustained than that of any other north European artist of the period.

Dürer was born at Nuremberg, the son of a goldsmith of Hungarian origin in whose workshop he originally trained. At the age of 13 his precocious talents were sufficiently developed to produce the earliest of many self-portraits, the accomplished silverpoint drawing in the Graphische Sammlung Albertina, Vienna. His apprenticeship, in the strict sense, was in the workshop of the Nuremberg painter Michael Wolgemut; he gained his general artistic education through years of travel from 1490 to 1494.

It is significant, in the light of Dürer's mastery of the graphic arts, that the aim of one of his journeys was to reach the workshop of the leading German engraver of the day, Martin Schongauer of Colmar; but in this he was frustrated by Schongauer's death. Dürer was already gaining a reputation as a designer of woodcuts for printed books; while at Basel in 1492 he designed a *St Jerome in his Study* for an edition of the saint's letters. Many copies of this print were duly painted, following the contemporary tradition of treating the woodcut as a network of lines demanding filling-in of color to resemble the effect of stained glass. But Dürer's attempt to render interior space, and his careful hatching of light and shade, point the way to a freeing of the woodcut from dependence on applied color.

Dürer's earliest knowledge of Italian art was through prints; by 1494 he was copying the mythological engravings of Mantegna. His desire to travel south was not curbed by his marriage to Agnes Frey in Nuremberg in 1494. Shortly after this, he left alone for his first visit to Italy. The watercolors that survive from his journey across the Alps are some of the earliest evidence of Dürer's curiosity about the world around him. Many of them are rapid sketches of broad areas of color, conveying not only the landscape of mountains of Alpine towns new to him, but also the effects of atmosphere and light, as in *The Pond in a Wood* (British Museum, London). From comments made on a second visit to Italy ten years later, it is clear that Dürer reached Venice on this journey; but where else he may have traveled in Italy remains speculative. By the spring of 1495 he had returned to Nuremberg.

In the following years, Dürer established a workshop in his native city and received commissions from several German patrons, including Frederick the Wise, Elector of Saxony, for portraits and religious works. One of the most significant of the latter was the Paumgärtner Altar of 1503 (Alte Pinakothek, Munich), the central panel of which reflects a blend of northern and Italian ideas. The tiny donor figures with their armorial devices are placed in the foreground of a ruined courtyard, with plunging diagonals towards a background landscape. Portraits of this period include the tense characterization of *Oswolt Krell* (1499; Alte Pinakothek, Munich) and two self-portraits which show Dürer's highly self-conscious approach to his status as an artist. The 1498 *Self-portrait* (Prado, Madrid), though indebted to Flemish portrait conventions in format, is also highly Italian in its use of modish dress and in its relaxed elegance of pose. Here Dürer seems to wish to present the artist as a cultured gentleman. The 1500 *Self-portrait* (Alte Pinakothek, Munich) seeks to elevate the position of the artist, in a religious rather than social sense: the physical equation of Dürer with the image of Christ suggests the artist as creator, as a unique figure with God-given talents.

It was, however, with the production of woodcuts and engravings that Dürer was chiefly preoccupied at this time, and it is here that the lessons of Italy are most manifest. He not only designed but published his own graphic work, thus establishing a link between his artistic judgment and the market for prints. He was therefore able to risk the unusual, as when he issued the *Pig with Six Feet*, depicting a freak of nature that he himself had seen. The *Men's Bathhouse* woodcut of 1496–7 shows an effort at classicism. Half-length figures in the foreground are placed to show the back and front views of the same human form; the composition is centered

Albrecht Dürer: Large Piece of Turf; watercolor; 41×32cm (16×12½in); 1503. Graphische Sammlung Albertina, Vienna

on the figure of the flautist, who provides a point of stability. As in his religious paintings of this period, Dürer adds a northern landscape, again evoking the direct contrast between his local artistic origins and the Italian style.

The engravings of these years are increasingly refined in style and detail, achieving effects in tone and texture not possible in woodcuts. By working slowly on one small area of the copper plate at a time, Dürer transformed the engraving technique of his day. He replaced the current rigid linear style with a fine but repetitive method of hatching. Using flexible draftsmanship, he varied the length and pressure of his incision with the engraver's tool, the burin, to produce a multiplicity of curved lines and cross-hatchings. *The Fall of Man* of 1504 demonstrates this achievement in the fine detail of animals and trees which are symbolic allusions to the main figure-subject. The figure of Adam is indebted to the Classical sculpture of the *Apollo Belvedere*.

Dürer's most influential work in the period between his two visits to Italy was probably the series of woodcuts illustrating major biblical themes; at this time he began the *Great Passion* series and finished the *Apocalypse* (1497–9). The latter consists of 14 full-page woodcuts issued as a book. For the first time, the text in German and Latin is clearly aligned with the illustrations. He appears to have worked on two or more of the woodcuts simultaneously, so that there is a close interrelation between the development of subjects. Nevertheless, certain works of the 14 stand out as being

Albrecht Dürer: St Michael from the series of woodcut illustrations of the Apocalypse; 39×28cm (15×11in); 1498

**Albrecht Dürer: The Painter's Father; panel; 51×40cm (20×16in); 1497? National Gallery, London**

exceptionally powerful: for example, *The Four Horsemen*. Here the narrative is most forceful in the depiction of the irresistible forces of Death, War, Famine, and Pestilence. More than any other work of this period, the *Apocalypse* series spread Dürer's fame throughout Germany and Italy. As visionary subjects, they echoed the troubled mood of the close of the century. And, on an artistic level, the fact that they are related to earlier woodcuts on the same theme only underlines the superiority of Dürer's skill and narrative power.

The first published reference to Dürer is in a German chronicle of 1505 which confirms the profound impact of his prints upon Italian artists; it is interesting that he paid his second visit to Italy in this year. His stay at Venice is well documented by letters home to his friend, the humanist Willibald Pirckheimer. In these he contrasts the respected position of the Italian artist with the lower social status of the artist in Germany.

During the visit, he consciously tried to equal the painterly skill of the leading Venetian artists of the day. *The Feast of the Rose Garlands* (1506; National Gallery, Prague) was painted for the German national church in Venice. Thematically, it combines the cult of the rosary with the idea of the universal brotherhood of Christianity—showing Pope and Emperor leading the spiritual and temporal worlds in adoration of the Virgin and Child. Its centralized composition and richness of color, much subdued in its present damaged state, are reminiscent of Venetian altarpieces. A tribute to Giovanni Bellini, who befriended the artist on this visit, is found in the single music-playing angel at the base of the throne. The *Portrait of a Young Woman* (c1506; Staatliche Museen, Berlin) shows Dürer attempting to emulate contemporary Venetian portraiture; the figure is placed against a blue background and her features, though Germanic in character, are modeled in light and shade rather than in his usually incisive drawing style.

After his return to Nuremberg in 1507 Dürer appears to relinquish the freedom of brushwork and color that marked his Venetian works, perhaps under pressure from northern patrons. The altarpiece he painted for the Frankfurt merchant Jacob Hellar (1508–9; now lost; copy in the Historisches Museum, Frankfurt am Main) was executed with meticulous care

for detail, as is made clear in Dürer's letter on the subject. His *Trinity Adored by Saints* (1511; Kunsthistorisches Museum, Vienna) is also painstakingly finished. At this period Dürer's initial inspiration is reserved increasingly for the preparatory stages of the painted work, in many drawings in a variety of media, including chalk or brush on prepared ground. Throughout his life, his skill and reputation as a painter and his conscious attempt to equal his contemporaries in this field was a hardwon triumph; whereas in the graphic arts his supremacy was unchallenged.

More woodcut series, such as the *Life of the Virgin*, were completed in succeeding years. But the period 1511 to 1514 is most remarkable for Dürer's successful "Master" engravings, which exhibit his most mature graphic style. *Melencolia I* of 1514 is the representation of reason reduced to inertia by the melancholy spirit; its counterpart, the *St Jerome in his Study* of the same year, presents the security, comfort, and fulfillment of scholarship. The latter engraving especially shows the refined technique of the late works, in its depiction of surfaces, and of light passing across them through multiple variations of cross-hatching.

Dürer worked in his later years for the Emperor Maximilian and designed the enormous print of a *Triumphal Arch* (1515–17) made up of 192 blocks of woodcut and standing more than 27 ft (9 m) high (one example in the British Museum, London). Its exceedingly complex design detracts considerably from the visual impact, suggesting that here the artist was not working on his own initiative. His inventiveness was still reserved for the curious, the everyday details of life as he viewed it. From his journey to the Netherlands of 1520–1 his drawings include, alongside highly finished portraits in charcoal, a single pen sketch of the *Harbour at Antwerp* (Graphische Sammlung Albertina, Vienna) and the *Head of a Walrus* in pen and watercolor (British Museum, London) drawn from a real animal specimen washed up on the shore.

His last years were troubled by the coming of the Reformation. There is considerable evidence that he turned Protestant; he certainly held great faith in the teachings of Luther. Luther's translations of writings by the apostles are found at the foot of his panels of the *Four Apostles*, presented to the town council of Nuremberg in 1526 (now Alte Pinakothek,

Munich). Significantly, the quotations refer to the dangers of excessive religious zeal, reflecting the mood of uncertainty created by extremism on both sides of the controversy. These are among Dürer's last painted works; the monumental forms of the Apostles fill the picture-space, and the bold simplicity of their drapery underlines the powerful message of the panels.

Dürer was also preoccupied at this time with preparations for his books on measurement and proportion. His treatise on measurement appeared in 1525 and his books on human proportion were published posthumously, following his death in 1528. His books are attempts to rationalize his approach to art, based on knowledge of Italian forerunners in the field of artistic theory. Yet perhaps Dürer's ultimate importance lies not so much in his theories as in the general attitudes to art he displayed in the practice of his profession. It lies, too, in his many-sided impact on the work of his contemporaries both north and south of the Alps. The degree of selfconsciousness apparent in everything he undertook, from commissioned works to self-portraits to spontaneous drawings, suggests an artist convinced of his unique gifts and their value to posterity. In the Germany of his day, his belief that originality and inventiveness were worth more than simple diligence and traditional craftsmanship was revolutionary.

**Further reading.** Kurth, W. *The Complete Woodcuts of Albrecht Dürer*, London (1927). Levey, M. *Dürer*, London (1964). Panofsky, E. *The Life and Art of Albrecht Dürer*, Princeton (1955, reissued 1971). Strauss, W. *Albrecht Dürer: the Complete Engravings, Etchings and Drypoints*, New York (1971). Streider, P. *Albrecht Dürer: Paintings, Prints, Drawings*, New York (1990). White, C. *Dürer, the Artist and his Drawings*, London (1971). Wölfflin, H. (trans. Grieve, A. and H.) *The Art of Albrecht Dürer*, London (1971).

## Dyce William 1806–64

William Dyce was a Scottish painter and art educationalist. Born in Aberdeen, he trained in Edinburgh and London; he then visited Italy from 1825 to 1829, studying early Italian painting and meeting the Nazarene group of artists. On his return he produced works based on the manner of the Italian masters (for example, *Madonna and Child*, c1840; Tate Gallery, London).

William Dyce: A scene on Arran; oil on board; 35×50cm (14×20in); 1858–9. Aberdeen Art Gallery

He evolved a precise style which resembled but predated Pre-Raphaelitism, painting religious, historical, and modern subjects, often in landscape settings (for example, *Pegwell Bay*, 1859–60; Tate Gallery, London). He was involved in the attempted revival of fresco painting in the 1840s and was Director of the Government School of Design at Somerset House (1838–43).

# Dyck Anthony van 1599–1641

Sir Anthony van Dyck holds a special place in 17th-century art as the creator of the Baroque court portrait. He had a highly developed sense of elegance and refinement, and made from his courtly sitters an image of ideal aristocracy that has retained a lasting hold on the European imagination.

Born in Antwerp, he was apprenticed in 1609 to Hendrik van Balen. He was a precocious artist, endowed with a remarkable fluency in the handling of paint. By *c*1616–18 he already had his own studio and assistants; at that date he was creating a series of paintings of Christ and the Apostles. Between 1618 and 1621 he worked as principal assistant to Rubens. Under that master's influence he modified his harsh, robust early style, and began to

use smoother paint and delicate, silvery tonalities. There are sketches and copies of figure-subjects, both after Rubens and from prints by Renaissance masters, contained in van Dyck's Antwerp sketchbook; these provide evidence of the thoroughness and breadth of his education as a religious and historical painter.

The ambitious figure-compositions of his first period in Antwerp (1599–1620) already reveal a profound debt to Rubens and Titian that was to last throughout his life. Yet his *Samson and Delilah* (Dulwich College Picture Gallery, London), *The Betrayal of Christ* (*c*1617; Prado, Madrid), and *The Continence of Scipio* (*c*1620–1; Christ Church Picture Gallery, Oxford) also show a highly personal preference for shallow space and frieze-like designs, for a sophisticated grace of gesture and expressions, and for decorative surface patterns of light and shade. Van Dyck's early self-portraits are of astonishing quality; they combine informality with elegance and their rich clothing and slightly narcissistic appeal seem to demonstrate his claims to be considered a prince among painters. By *c*1621–2 his portrait style had moved away from the conventional designs of his earliest years towards a new naturalness and freedom of pose.

In 1621, after an abortive visit to the

court of James I in London in 1620, he left for Italy; he spent longest in Genoa and Rome but also traveled to Florence, Venice, and Sicily. His Italian sketchbook (British Museum, London) shows how deeply he studied the works of Titian in these years; he responded to his glowing color, the openness of his compositions, and the lyrical poetry of his early allegories. His own most Titianesque work is the *Four Ages of Man* (*c*1622–7; Museo Civico, Vicenza). He was also influenced by Bolognese art, particularly by Guido Reni's expression of intense religious feeling.

In Genoa van Dyck painted a magnificent series of portraits of the aristocracy; these were often full-length, some of them equestrian. Rubens, in Genoa 15 years earlier, had already created the new *mise-en-scene* of the terrace or palace. Now van Dyck transformed Rubens' robust power into grace and elegance. In his spectacular *Marchesa Elena Grimaldi* (1625; National Gallery of Art, Washington, D.C.) the reticent majesty of the figure is enhanced by the magical beauty of the terrace setting, by the Italian light on the distant hills, and by the luxurious, almost ceremonial, dress. The painting seems to capture the essence of aristocracy.

In 1627 van Dyck returned to Antwerp; in 1630 he was made court painter at

Anthony van Dyck: *Mountjoy Blount, Earl of Newport*; oil on canvas; 215×130cm (85×51in); c1633. Private collection

Charles I was a learned patron of the arts who shared van Dyck's love of Titian. Van Dyck's portraits of the King and courtiers show how sensitive the artist was to the ethos and aspirations of the Caroline court. He painted shimmering, silvery portraits of the Queen and the ladies of the court, and within the formal trappings of the state portrait he managed to convey the restless charm of Charles' five children. Above all, he painted Charles I in many roles which interpret with poetic beauty Charles' vision of the monarchy. In 1633 he painted him as king and warrior in the equestrian portrait (National Gallery, London) based on Titian's *Charles V* (Prado, Madrid); and again in the *Charles I on Horseback, with M. de St Antoine* (Collection of H.M. Queen Elizabeth II). This work, which shows the King riding through an archway, gave scope to van Dyck's thwarted ambitions as a large-scale designer; it is his most magnificent use of Baroque illusionism. *Charles I Hunting* (1635; Louvre, Paris) shows the king as the perfect cavalier. In 1636 he painted him as a robed monarch (Collection of H.M. Queen Elizabeth II). He also painted Charles' head from three different positions on one canvas (c1637; Royal Art Collection, Windsor). This triple portrait was intended as a model for the sculptor Bernini, who is said to have exclaimed over Charles' melancholy expression.

Van Dyck's portraits of the English aristocracy revolutionized English painting. He brought to the art of portraiture a wide new range of designs, a rhythmic elegance of composition, and a nervous, flickering beauty of touch. The influence of his brilliant painterly surface and his landscape settings may be seen at its best in full-length portraits by Gainsborough. Van Dyck also did some unusually spontaneous watercolors and drawings of the English countryside. One or two subject paintings from his late period survive; the delicate voluptuousness and light coloring of the *Cupid and Psyche* (c1639–40; Collection of H.M. Queen Elizabeth II) seem to anticipate the Rococo.

**Further reading.** Cust, L. *Anthony van Dyck*, London (1900). Gerson, H. and Kuile, E.H. ter *Art and Architecture in Belgium: 1600–1800*, Harmondsworth (1960). Glück, G. *Rubens, van Dyck, und Ihr Kreis*, Vienna (1933). Jaffé, M. *Van Dyck's Antwerp Sketchbook*, London (1966).

Brussels by the Archduchess Isabella Clara Eugenia. In his second Antwerp period he painted many portraits of collectors, fellow artists, and of the Spanish court in Brussels, and he fulfilled several great commissions for churches. Van Dyck's Flemish sitters wear black, and the cool blacks and whites are relieved only by the brilliant reds of the studio properties. His portrait style became more severe and monumental. He developed superb mastery over the double portrait, creating subtle composi-tional links that are full of psychological significance. He also began to work on the *Iconography*, a collection of engravings after portraits of celebrated persons. The religious works he painted at this period are deeply indebted to the heightened emotionalism of Guido Reni. In 1632 van Dyck moved to London where he was knighted by Charles I, named Principal Painter, and granted a house at Blackfriars. He visited Antwerp in 1634 and 1640, but died in London in 1641.

# E

## Eakins Thomas 1844–1916

Thomas Eakins was possibly the greatest of all American artists. Masterpieces such as *Max Schmitt in a Single Scull* (1871; Metropolitan Museum, New York) mark a high point of psychological realism in 19th-century art, displaying brilliant control over perspective, anatomy, mechanical drawing, and the study of the human form in motion. In all Eakins' art the human figure is central; his composition is enlivened by a use of light that derives from Rembrandt (1606–69) and Velazquez (1599–1660) and yet is wholly personal and American in execution and feeling.

Eakins worked in Philadelphia, where he

Thomas Eakins: Portrait of Louis N. Kenton (The Thinker); oil on canvas; 208×107cm (82×42in); 1900. Metropolitan Museum, New York

studied art at the Pennsylvania Academy of the Fine Arts and anatomy at Jefferson Medical College. From 1866 to 1869 he studied under Jean Léon Gérôme in Paris, and went to Spain to see the works of Velazquez and Ribera. Returning to Philadelphia in 1870, he began a series of family portraits; he also painted scenes of sporting and outdoor life such as *Max Schmitt*. Eakins' second masterpiece, *The Gross Clinic* (1875; Jefferson Medical College, Philadelphia), painted for the Philadelphia Centennial, was rejected for the art exhibition because of its depiction of blood and was shown in the medical section instead.

Eakins was also a great teacher, and the study of the nude was the pivot of his teaching method. He taught at the Pennsylvania Academy of the Fine Arts from 1876, became its head in 1879, and resigned in 1886 because of opposition to his insistence on the total nudity of the model. His students followed him, and he thus became a decisive influence on the realism of the so-called Ash Can School. Eakins' interest in motion led to his making wax and bronze figures to help in compositions such as *The Swimming Hole* (1883; Fort Worth Art Museum). His enquiries paralleled, and were aided by, the photographic studies made by Eadweard Muybridge of the human body and the horse in movement. The climax of Eakins' art was his series of late portraits of artists, musicians, and other prominent figures. The excellence of works like *Mrs Edith Mahon* (1904; Smith College Museum of Art, Northampton, Mass.) elevates Eakins above all his American contemporaries.

**Further reading.** Carter, A. A. *The Essential Thomas Eakins*, New York (2001). Homer, W. I. *Thomas Eakins: His Life and Art*, New York (2002). Sewell, D. (ed.) *Thomas Eakins*, New Haven (2001).

## Eastlake Charles 1793–1865

The English painter Sir Charles Eastlake was also a scholar and administrator. Born in Plymouth, he trained in London at the Royal Academy Schools and under B.R. Haydon. In Italy from 1816 to 1830, he painted landscapes and genre scenes, and successfully continued these on returning to England. Historical (for example, *The Escape of the Carrara Family*, 1849; Tate

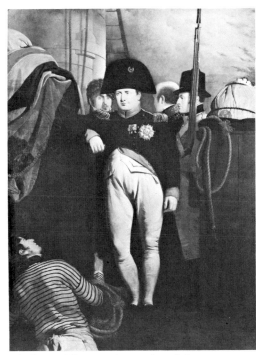

Charles Eastlake: Napoleon on board the "Bellerophon" in Plymouth Sound, 1815; oil on canvas; 259×184cm (102×72in); 1815. National Maritime Museum, Greenwich, London

Gallery, London) and less specific (for example, *Haidée: A Greek Girl*, 1827; Tate Gallery, London) they embody refined sentiment and warm, Venetian-inspired coloring. Eastlake's wide and discriminating knowledge of art brought many professional commitments—Presidency of the Royal Academy, first Directorship of the National Gallery—which he outstandingly fulfilled.

## Egas Enrique c1455–c1534

The Spanish architect Enrique Egas was the nephew of Anequin Egas of Brussels and Toledo; he was one of the first architects to give a distinctive character to the Plateresque style. Several attributions to the early years of his career are dubious, but it is certain that between 1499 and 1515 Egas planned and directed the works of the three Royal Hospitals founded by Isabel the Catholic. These were cruciform buildings based on a central chapel, at Santiago de Compostela (1499–1511), Granada (1511), and Toledo (by 1514). He subsequently carried out extensive work in the cathedrals of Toledo and Jaen and designed the Chapel Royal of Granada, the burial place of Ferdinand and Isabella now incorporated in Granada Cathedral.

## Eiffel Alexandre-Gustave
### 1832–1923

A French structural engineer, Alexandre-Gustave Eiffel is famous for the 984 ft (300 m) tower that bears his name. The Eiffel Tower, largely responsible for the integration of steel into the language of architecture, was built for the 1889 Paris Exhibition. It is a masterpiece of intricate rolled iron and steel construction and was greatly admired by later artists and architects for its unsurpassed variety of exciting spatial experiences. It was developed from Eiffel's bridge building in steel lattice-work (Douro Bridge 1877; Garabit viaduct 1880–4), which displays a similar talent for combining technical skill with formal daring. After 1910, Eiffel became a specialist in aerodynamics.

## Eilbertus of Cologne *fl. c1220–60*

The goldsmith Eilbertus is known only from an inscription on the base of the portable altar in the Guelph Treasure, now in the Kunstgewerbemuseum, Staatliche Museen, Berlin. The altar, one of the finest examples to survive, is decorated with champlevé enamels on its top and sides. On the top the enamels show scenes from the life of Christ with gilt figures against blue and green backgrounds. Plaques with the 12 apostles surround a transparent rock crystal altar stone mounted in the center over an illumination showing Christ in Majesty, with symbols of the four Evangelists. On the sides standing figures of 18 Old Testament Prophets (one is missing) are shown on a gilt ground in imitation of Byzantine gold cloisonné enameling. The date of the altar is not recorded, but is likely to be between 1130 and 1160. The central illumination is by the same hand as a *Christ in Majesty* in a gospel book from St Vitus, Gladbach, now in the Hessisches Landesmuseum, Darmstadt (Cod. 508), which has been dated to c1140.

A number of other goldsmiths' works have been attributed to Eilbertus on the basis of style, including parts of the shrine of St Victor, Xanten (soon after c1129) and *The Cardinal Virtues*, a portable altar, also in the Guelph Treasure (Kunstgewerbemuseum, Staatliche Museen, Berlin). His lively, sketchy drawing technique and his fine sense of color were influential both in Rhenish metalwork, and in east German workshops in Hildesheim and Brunswick, throughout the second half of the 12th century.

Alexandre-Gustave Eiffel: The Eiffel Tower; steel; height 300m (984ft); finished in 1889; Paris

## Eitoku Kano 1543–90

The Japanese painter Kano Eitoku was the son of Kano Naonobu (Shoei) and grandson of Kano Motonobu. He was a pioneer of decorative screen painting of the Momoyama period. The sliding doors of the Jukoin of the Daitokuji Temple, Kyoto, done in 1566 with his father, show the arrival of a bold new talent. Across four doors spreads a gnarled plum tree, overhanging a stream with ducks and rocks of bold triangular shape. There is hardly any background, all attention being on the dynamic shape of the tree. There are touches of color and extensive gold washes. These are in great contrast to his father's gentle landscapes, though they are still in the ink-painting tradition.

His full-scale adoption of gold-leaf backgrounds, which led to the Momoyama style proper, probably came from the influence of the *Tosa* School. They can be seen in the 1574 screens of scenes in Kyoto, where numerous glimpses of the city and its people are seen through gaps in thick, gold-leaf clouds. The logical step from this was a combination of *Kano* brushwork with *Tosa* color and gold. We can see this in the six-fold screens of c1582, *Kara-shishi* (Imperial Collection, Tokyo) portraying the two lion-dogs, peace and dignity, and *Cypress Trees* (Tokyo National Museum). This is a masculine style of pure decoration, which must have been used in the Azuchi Castle (now destroyed) of the dictator Nobunaga. Eitoku was invited to decorate the Castle in 1576; it was the first of the huge commissions that are said to have caused his early death from overwork. His great pupil was Kano Sanraku.

## Elsheimer Adam 1578–1610

Adam Elsheimer's surviving works are few, but his art opened up new possibilities to the 17th-century painter. He worked mostly for private patrons and painted on copper panels of extremely small dimensions. Minute details of plants and costumes are shown with miraculous precision, yet his works retain the power of large-scale art. He brought a fresh simplicity and truth to landscape painting, and he depicted the moods of nature, whether idyllic or dramatic, as reflecting a human emotion. Revolutionary in his use of light, he studied the natural effects of sun and moon, fires and torchlight, and the mysterious shadows cast in dark interiors by oil lamp and candle. He brought to the interpretation of biblical and mythological scenes a tenderness, intimacy, and directness that leads to Rembrandt.

Elsheimer was born in Frankfurt am Main and probably studied under the local painter Philipp Uffenbach. His roots are in German art; his treatment of landscape evolves from the work of artists of the Danube school, and his tenebrism is indebted to Altdorfer's nocturnal world. His figure-style is based on Schongauer and Dürer.

In 1599 he arrived in Venice where he worked with the group of artists influenced by the German painter Hans Rottenhammer. *The Baptism* (National Gallery, London) shows how he responded to the complex rhythms, glowing colors, and rich draperies of Bassano and Veronese. By 1600 he was in Rome, where he became famous for his rendering of night scenes and use of several sources of illumination. *The Burning of Troy* (Alte Pinakothek, Munich) and *St Paul on Malta* (National Gallery, London) explore the dramatic potential of flood and fire, while recording the events with deeply human realism. In *St Paul on Malta* shipwrecked travelers cluster naked around fires and attempt to dry their clothes; his narrative style avoids the grandiloquent and depends on vivid detail.

Elsheimer's best documented work was a seven-part house-altar of *The Story of the True Cross* (c1603–5) once owned by the Grand Duke of Tuscany (panels now in

Adam Elsheimer: St Paul on Malta; oil on copper; 17×21cm (7×8in); c1600. National Gallery, London

the Städelsches Kunstinstitut and in the Städtische Galerie Liebighaus, both in Frankfurt am Main). The scenes are presented with touching realism.

Elsheimer's late landscapes show a greater emphasis on mood; their delicate light and tender melancholy which so perfectly capture the essence of the story were later to inspire Claude. *The Flight into Egypt* (1609; Alte Pinakothek, Munich) is an astonishingly naturalistic rendering of the Milky Way and the constellations of the northern hemisphere; yet it is also an intensely poetic work in which the tiny figures are sheltered by the dark and infinite spaces of nature.

The painter was a withdrawn character, subject to melancholy. His small output became widely known throughout Europe, however, largely through the engravings of his pupil, Hendrick Goudt. He was admired by the Dutch landscape artists, by Rubens and Rembrandt; Claude understood and developed the idyllic element in Elsheimer's art.

**Further reading.** Andrews, K. *Adam Elsheimer: Paintings, Drawings, and Prints*, Oxford (1977).

## Ensor James 1860–1949

James Ensor was a Belgian painter, printmaker, and writer. He was born in Ostend, of an English father and a Belgian mother; his parents ran a souvenir shop, selling seashells, puppets, toys, and carnival masks. His childhood was unhappy: his businesslike mother dominated his well educated and artistic father, who died of alcoholism in 1887. Ensor studied at the Brussels Academy from 1877 to 1881. His early works—landscapes and still lifes—were influenced by Courbet and Manet, but by 1882 his *Woman Eating Oysters* (Royal Museum of Fine Arts, Antwerp) showed a competent handling of Impressionist light and color.

His submissions to the Brussels Salon of 1883 were rejected: the following year he joined the avant-garde group called Les Vingt. But even there, his most important single work, *The Entry of Christ into Brussels* (Casino Communal, Knokke-le-Zoute, Belgium) was refused in 1888. Ensor imagines Christ's entry on a new Palm Sunday. It becomes an indictment of modern society: Christ, a minute figure in the center mounted on an ass, is dwarfed by a strident mob waving banners; towards the front, faces harden into masks.

Ensor's use of masks continued in a series of paintings attacking the hypocrisy of society. His attacks on the social order were even more vitriolic in a set of etchings of the seven cardinal sins (1892 and 1904). After 1900 his fury subsided; his later pictures were often bland reworkings of his earlier ones. He spent his life in Ostend: some of his seascapes are reminiscent of J.M.W. Turner's late work. An idiosyn-

James Ensor: The Fall of the Rebel Angels; oil on canvas; 108×132cm (43×52in); 1889. Museum of Fine Arts, Antwerp

One of the most pleasing of these depicts two revelers (British Museum, London; E.137). In the foreground stands a youth playing the pipes, his pipe-case over his arm; in the background a bearded reveler stoops to set on the ground his huge *skyphos*, probably full to the brim with wine, before beginning to dance. Around these graceful figures runs the painter's signature, binding the whole composition together. On his later pieces he displays a knowledge of the new researches of Euphronios and Euthymides but he never lost himself in the exploration of anatomy as they did. It is possible that he continued to paint in his own fashion into the second decade of the 5th century BC, although he does seem to have been influenced by Douris, the most graceful cup-painter of the next generation.

## Epimenes  *fl. c*500 BC.

Epimenes was a Greek gem-engraver of *c*500 BC. There is one signed gem in Boston (Museum of Fine Arts), showing a youth restraining a restive horse. A gem in the Metropolitan Museum, New York, with a young archer testing his arrow has been attributed to him; so have another gem in Boston, with an archer crouching to draw his bow, and a gem in Lausanne (private collection) with an athlete. He belongs to a period when the best Archaic work was done on scarab-shaped gems and scaraboids of carnelian or chalcedony, most of it produced in the east Greek world or on the Greek islands. Generally this work presents conventional Archaic motifs rendered with precision and subtlety but without ambitious modeling.

Epimenes is exceptional in attempting miniature sculptural poses; he rendered figures barely $\frac{1}{2}$ in (1 cm) high in intaglio in poses that at that date were rarely attempted by sculptors of larger reliefs. His best are the first two named above, with studies of youths in a twisting three-quarter back view, and the last, where a plausible profile view of a stooping figure is achieved. In many respects these *tours de force* are inappropriate to the scale and nature of the medium, and their sculptural qualities are not seen again in Greek gem-engraving until the 4th century BC.

## Epstein Jacob  1880–1959

The sculptor Sir Jacob Epstein was born in New York, the son of Russian-Polish im-

cratic Expressionist and Symbolist, his work influenced the Dadas and Surrealists and, later, the work of Jean Dubuffet.

Further reading. Croquez, A. *L'Oeuvre Gravé de James Ensor*, Geneva (1947). Haesaerts, P. (trans. Guterman, N.) *James Ensor*, London and New York (1959). Tannenbaum, L. *James Ensor*, New York (1977).

## Epiktetos  *fl. c*520–490 BC or later

Epiktetos (or Epictetus) was a prolific cup-painter in Athens who also potted some of his own pieces. He frequently signed his name, though his late pieces are unsigned. Like those of his contemporary, Oltos, a number of his early cups are decorated in black-figure technique on the inside, but in red-figure technique on the exterior. One such early cup (British Museum, London; E.3), is signed by Epiktetos as painter, by Hischylos as potter. It has a black-figure mounted horseman on the interior, and on each side of the exterior—between evil-averting eyes—a satyr armed with a shield. Instead of spears, one satyr has a jug, the other a drinking horn. (The basic shape of

the cup and the use of eyes were innovations of Exekias.) Epiktetos' drawing is clean and delicate, his figures spruce and energetic. He used only a minimum of internal markings, his drawing relying solely on the sureness of his outlines.

Epiktetos also painted a series of plates which demonstrated his unsurpassed mastery of compositions in a circular field.

Epiktetos: Archer in Scythian Costume; diameter 20cm (8in); late 6th century BC. British Museum, London

migrants. He studied briefly in New York at the Art Students League in the mid 1890s, and decided to become a sculptor *c*1900. In 1902 he moved to Paris, studying at the École des Beaux-Arts and the Académie Julian until 1904. After traveling on the Continent and visiting Florence, he moved to London in 1905. He was commissioned by the architect Charles Holden in 1907 to carve 18 figures for Holden's new British Medical Association building. They were completed in 1908, and caused much controversy in the press. This early incident gave Epstein such notoriety that none of his subsequent public sculptures escaped noisy press comment, which embittered the artist and may have had a bearing on his subsequent development.

In 1910 he received the commission for the tomb of Oscar Wilde; this was eventually erected in the Père-Lachaise cemetery in Paris in 1912, at which time Epstein met Picasso, Brancusi, and Modigliani. In 1913 he settled at Pett Level, Sussex, and during a period of intense activity executed *The Rock Drill* (Tate Gallery, London). This jagged work, which integrates a robot-like figure with a real rock drill, represents Epstein's closest identification with modernism, both in form and conception. While *The Rock Drill* is a unique achievement its origins are in Cubism and Futurism: it has affinities with works by Boccioni, and with the "Ready-mades" of Duchamp which originated in the same year. *The Rock Drill* coincided with the beginnings of Vorticism in England; Epstein contributed drawings to the periodical *Blast*, but did not otherwise align himself with the Vorticists, in spite of similarities of style and attitude. *Rock Drill* was not publicly exhibited until 1915; the following year, a truncated version—minus drill—was exhibited, signaling Epstein's abdication from a pioneering role. Other notable works of this brief phase are *Female Figure* (1913; Tate Gallery, London), *Venus* (1913/14; Yale University), and *Doves* (1915; marble version in Tate Gallery, London).

From the beginning, however, Epstein was a portraitist; throughout his career, and during his spasmodic preoccupation with carving, he sought human likeness in clay. His best portraits, such as *Head of a Baby* (1907 version, Scottish National Gallery of Modern Art, Edinburgh), *Jacob Kramer* (1921; Tate Gallery, London), *Paul Robeson* (1928; Museum of Modern

Jacob Epstein: Oriel; bronze; height 55cm (21in); 1931. Aberdeen Art Gallery

Art, New York), *Ernest Bevin* (1943; Tate Gallery, London) entrap likeness and expression in a mobile and "unfinished" surface. But there are many other commissioned busts that lack vitality.

From *c*1917 when he began *The Risen Christ* (1919; Scottish National Gallery of Modern Art, Edinburgh), Epstein regularly sculpted thematic works, often with a religious content, either in response to a personal compulsion or as a result of commissions. These figures and groups, particularly the carvings, are often awkward in form while possessing a strong emotional content. For example *Genesis* (1930; private collection) displays a combination of delicacy and primitivism. *Ecce Homo* (1935; Coventry Cathedral) is crude yet dignified. Other works of this kind include *Adam* (1938; Collection of the Earl of Harewood), the massive *Jacob and the Angel* (1940; private collection), and *Lazarus* (1948; New College Chapel, Oxford). Epstein died in London in 1959. To younger English artists such as Henry Moore, Epstein was both the representative of modernism, and also the man who smoothed their path by drawing the fire of the Philistines. His *Madonna and Child* (1950–2; Convent of the Holy Child Jesus, Cavendish Square, London), is one of his finest works.

**Further reading.** Buckle, R. *Jacob Epstein, Sculptor*, London and New York (1963). Epstein, J. *Epstein, an Autobiography*, London (1963) and New York (1975). Epstein, J. and Haskell, A.L. *Sculpture Speaks: a Series of Conversations on Art*, New York (1976).

## Ernest John 1922–1994

John Ernest was born in Philadelphia in 1922, but since studying sculpture at St Martin's School of Art in London (1952–6) he has lived and worked in Britain, teaching at the Chelsea School of Art. A leading British Constructivist, he has worked in various media, including wood, metal, and formica, since 1956. His work is based partly on conceptual or theoretical models which are usually mathematical, but also on topological figures such as the Möbius strip. Works such as *Relief Painting: Iconic Group Table* (1977; artist's collection) illustrate his continuing interest in the structure of groups.

## Ernst Max 1891–1976

The German painter and sculptor Max Ernst was the cofounder of the Cologne branch of Dada, and later became a leading Surrealist artist. He was born in Brühl, near Cologne. His father was a teacher of the deaf and dumb, but also a painter with a local reputation. In 1909, Ernst enrolled in Bonn University where he studied philosophy, psychiatry, and art history, while painting small landscapes in the manner of Van Gogh. By 1910 he had decided to devote himself to painting—though he never received any formal training.

In 1911, Ernst joined *Das Junge Rheinland*, a group of liberally minded painters and poets which included August Macke. Through Macke he became associated with the *Blaue Reiter* group in Munich; in 1913 he exhibited in the *Der Sturm* gallery in Berlin beside Kandinsky, Klee, Macke, Chagall, and Delaunay. His work both at this time and during the First World War, when he served in the artillery, shows the marked influence of these contacts and of Futurism. It is characterized by the qualities that persisted throughout his career: fantastic, dream-like imagery, whimsical humor, and an emphasis on poetic content rather than plastic form.

The war over, Ernst—who was fully informed about the Dada group in Zurich—founded a Dada group in Cologne with the left-wing activist, Johannes Baargeld (1891–1927). They were joined by Arp. In 1919, Ernst published *Fiat Modes*, eight lithographs which, with their imagery of bizarre stuffed dummies and impossible perspective systems, revealed the influence of de Chirico. Among his other Dada works were pictures of unstable semimechanical, semiarchitectural

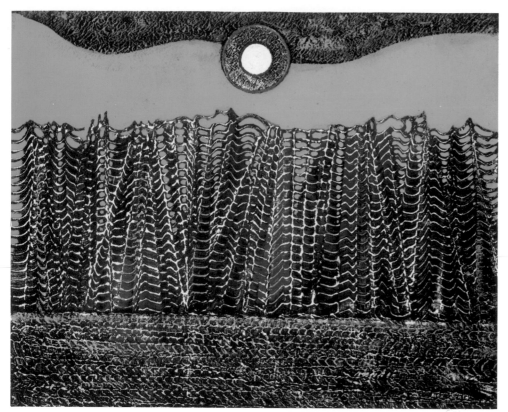

Max Ernst: The Edge of a Forest; oil on canvas; 1926. Private collection

structures, which were created from rubbings taken from large wooden printing
type. In his collages, some of which were
made in collaboration with Arp, Ernst
combined cutouts from wallpaper, advertisements, illustrations in scientific text-

books, and photographs, evoking monstrous and fantastic landscapes, interiors,
animals, and anthropomorphic beings.

Following the success among the Surrealist poets of an exhibition of his collages,
Ernst moved to Paris in 1922 and im-

Max Ernst: Stratified Rocks, Nature's Gift of Gneiss Lava, Iceland Moss, two kinds of Lungwort,
two kinds of Ruptures of the Perineum, Growths of the Heart (b) the same thing in a well-polished
Box somewhat more expensive; anatomical engraving altered with gouache and pencil; 15×21cm
(6×8in); 1920. Museum of Modern Art, New York

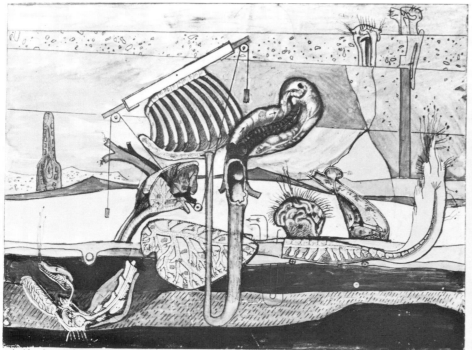

mediately began collaborating with the
Surrealists. He found himself naturally in
sympathy with their interests in hypnot-
ism, dreams, madness, and the subconscious, and he shared their admiration for
de Chirico. His paintings of 1921 to 1924,
such as *Oedipus Rex* (1922; private collection), are justly described as the first
Surrealist paintings, with their irrational
juxtapositions of objects, their allusions to
dreams, their Freudian-inspired symbolism, and their avoidance of visual
"beauty". With de Chirico's Metaphysical
paintings, they also provided the basis for
the resurgence of illusionism in Surrealist
painting in the late 1920s and 1930s.

In 1925, Ernst developed the *frottage*
(rubbing) technique. Taking rubbings from
such surfaces as floorboards, leaves, and
sacking, he found a pictorial equivalent for
the automatic-writing procedures of the
Surrealist poets, and answered Breton's
call for "pure, psychic automatism". A
collection of *frottages* was published in
1926 as *Histoire Naturelle*.

Ernst employed a related technique, *grattage* (scraping), in his paintings—placing
objects under a canvas covered with layers
of paint and scraping the paint from the
raised portions. In complete contrast to the
precise imagery of his earlier paintings,
these are spontaneous, full of movement
and flux—vague, expressionistic representations of birds, monsters, horses, forests
and flowers, which frequently convey the
uninhibited violence and passion that the
Surrealists recognized as fundamental to
human nature.

In 1929, he published the first of his
collage-novels, *La Femme 100 Têtes* (the
title is a pun in French: "The hundred-
headed Woman" or "The Woman without
a Head"). In this and subsequent "novels",
such as *Une Semaine de Bonté* ("A Week
of Goodness", 1934) Ernst subtly altered
popular 19th-century engravings through
the collage process, evoking dramas of
unparalleled fantasy, and implying that the
forces of desire lurk beneath even the most
respectable facade. It is in these collage-
novels, and in his *frottages*, that Ernst is
most original and provocative.

In 1934, Ernst made his first sculptures,
carving low-reliefs on large granite stones
and creating his first independent sculptures from modified *objets trouvés* such as
flowerpots. In the 1930s the imagery of the
*grattage* paintings tended to become more
clearly defined and the subject matter more
menacing: savage monsters and skeletal,

low-lying cities were among Ernst's favorite motifs. At this period he also reverted to conventional oil-painting techniques and an illusionistic manner in, for instance, the *Garden Airplane-Trap* (example in Centre Georges Pompidou, Musée National d'Art Moderne, Paris) series of 1935 and *The Angel of Hearth and Home* (private collection) series of 1937. In works like *Lust for Life* (1936; private collection), Ernst expressed his anxiety about the worsening political situation in images of a ruined Eden, overgrown with rank vegetation and inhabited by predatory creatures.

Interned by the French as an enemy alien at the outbreak of war in 1939, Ernst emigrated to New York in 1941. There, with Breton and Duchamp, he edited a new Surrealist review *VVV*. In the years of the Second World War his work became increasingly rich in color and in detailed, elaborate imagery. He now used to dazzling effect the *decalcomania* technique of the Surrealist painter Oscar Dominguez (1906–57). Ernst created impressions of coral reefs, seabeds, spongy vegetation, and rotting matter, in works like the apocalyptic *Europe after the Rain II* (1940–2; Wadsworth Atheneum, Hartford, Conn.). His most ambitious sculptural project was realized in his house in Sedona, Arizona, both in wall-decorations and in the monumental, freestanding group *Capricorn* (1948; bronze cast; Centre Georges Pompidou, Paris). In its hieratic image of a semihuman, semianimal "royal" family, *Capricorn* epitomizes Ernst's mythic concept of man.

In 1953 Ernst returned to France and in 1958 became a French citizen. His work after the War was varied in style and technique, becoming increasingly bright and lyrical in color and sanguine in mood.

Prolific and eclectic throughout his career, Ernst had the most significant impact on the painters who joined the Surrealist movement after c1927. His intelligence and wide culture undoubtedly also contributed to the development and the ever-broadening range of Surrealist artistic and philosophical thinking.

**Further reading.** Ernst, M. (ed. Motherwell, R.) *Max Ernst: Beyond Painting and Other Writings by the Artist and his Friends*, New York (1948). Russell, J. *Max Ernst: Life and Work*, London and New York (1967). Schneede, U. *The Essential Max Ernst*, London (1972). Waldberg, P. *Max Ernst*, Paris (1958).

Richard Estes: Bus Window; acrylic on canvas; 62×84cm (24×33in); 1969. Neue Galerie, Sammlung Ludwig, Aachen

## Estes Richard 1936–

The American Photo-Realist painter Richard Estes was born in Evanston, Illinois. He studied at the Chicago Art Institute (1952–6) and had his first solo exhibition in 1968 in New York, when he first came to public prominence. His paintings of urban scenery are based on color photographs that he takes himself (for example, *Food Shop*, 1967; Museum Ludwig, Cologne). Ever since his most important earlier works such as *Booths* (1967; Haigh Cundey Collection, New York) he has been attracted to images that include multiple reflections in glass and metal. His pictures are usually devoid of dirt and other evidence of people's lives, rather simplified and idealized, even in drug store scenes like *Ice cream* (1976; Allan Stone Gallery, New York).

**Further reading.** Arthur, J. *Richard Estes: Paintings and Prints*, Petaluma, CA (1993). Raymond, H. "The Real Estes", *Art and Artists*, London (August 1974).

## Etty William 1787–1849

The English figure-painter William Etty was a baker's son, born in York. After serving a printing apprenticeship, he moved to London in 1805, entering the Royal Academy Schools. On tours abroad he studied Rubens, Titian, and French Academic painting. He exhibited a succession of grand history pictures, such as *The Combat* (1825; National Gallery of Scot-

William Etty: Standard Bearer; oil on panel; 43×34cm (17×13in); c1843. Fairhaven Collection, Anglesey Abbey, Cambridgeshire

land, Edinburgh) and *Venus and her Satellites* (1835; private collection). A more marketable line, however, lay in nude studies, painted freely from the life. By 1847, when he finished his huge *Joan of Arc* triptych, which fetched 2,500 guineas, he had become England's most respected painter.

## Euphranor 4th century BC

The Greek sculptor and painter Euphranor came from Isthmia and was a contemporary of Praxiteles. He became an eminent member of the Attic school and carried out a number of public commissions in Athens, including the pictorial decoration of the Stoa of Zeus with historical and mythical scenes, and the cult statue of Apollo Patroos, patron of the city (Agora Museum, Athens). His grandiose style was particularly suitable for the representation of gods, heroes, and battles. He also wrote treatises on colors and on proportions. Among his most famous bronze statues were a *Paris* and the portraits of Philip and Alexander (a copy of his *Alexander* is in Glyptothek, Munich). The bronze *Athena* from Piraeus (National Museum, Athens) has been attributed to him.

## Euphronios *fl. c*510–465 BC

Euphronios was a Greek vase-painter whose name is known from about 20 vases. Some of these he signed as painter, the others, which are all later, as potter. His long career thus divides into two

Euphronios: Athenian Cavalryman dressed in a Thessalian Cloak on a red-figure cup; c510 BC. Staatliche Antikensammlungen, Munich

phases: until *c*500 BC he painted vases, thereafter he fashioned them. In this later period he was apparently the master of a flourishing workshop, able to afford a dedication to Athena, which has been found on the Acropolis.

His earliest works as a painter owe something to the Andokides Painter, but they have none of his mannered elegance. Instead, the figure of a running Amazon on his early cup in Munich (Staatliche Antikensammlungen; Inv. 8953) is so powerfully drawn that the circular frame scarcely seems able to hold her. Euphronios together with two contemporary painters, Euthymides and Phintias, looked beyond the simple silhouette technique of black-figure to a more detailed observation of the human body; they experimented with new poses and views as well as with rudimentary foreshortenings, and are considered pioneers in the development of the art of that period. Euphronios' mature works display inventive iconography and a fascination for the muscles of the body. A *kalyx-krater* in Paris (Louvre; G.103) gives us a splendid study of power and tension in the figures of Herakles and the giant Antaeus (Antaios) wrestling to the death. A fully mature work in New York (Metropolitan Museum) is a *kalyx-krater*, with the winged figures of Sleep and Death lifting the limp body of the hero Sarpedon from the battlefield. There a marvelously constructed composition is matched by remarkable observation of relaxed limbs. On his last preserved work his figures no longer interact. They are a mere lifeless procession, all tension lost.

At this point, when he was perhaps already well into his middle age and surrounded by a new generation of painters, he changed to potting. As a potter, specializing in cups, he continued to work for a further 25 years: his earliest pieces were decorated by Onesimos, and his latest by the Pistoxenos Painter, both of whom were the greatest cup-painters of their time.

## Euthymides *fl. c*520–500 BC

Euthymides was a Greek vase-painter who worked in Athens. Along with the other so-called pioneers, Euphronios and Phintias, he experimented with new poses and views of the body which incorporated rudimentary foreshortenings. In an inscription he wrote beside three dancing revelers on an *amphora* in Munich (Staatliche

Antikensammlungen; Inv. 2307), Euthymides boasted that his rival Euphronios had never painted better; the inscription reads simply: "as Euphronios never". More of the lively rapport between the "Pioneers" can be seen on a *hydria* by his friend Phintias (Staatliche Antikensammlungen, Munich; Inv. 2421) who both toasts and depicts him. Euthymides' figures, with their massive chests and shoulders, are like Nestor's heroes of an earlier age. One of his pupils was the Kleophrades Painter who became the greatest painter of large vessels in the next generation. The Berlin Painter also owed much to him.

## Eutychides
late 4th–early 3rd century BC

Eutychides, a Greek early Hellenistic sculptor from Sicyon, was a pupil of Lysippos. His art marks an advance in realism as he tried to capture the third dimension and imitate the texture of skin and draperies. His most influential creation was the colossal bronze group the *Tyche* of Antioch, in which Antioch is personified in the figure of Tyche, goddess of Fortune, and its river, the Orontes, is a youth emerging from the ground. The type survives in reduced copies in the Vatican Museums and in private collections: Fortune is a girl with a city-crown, heavily draped; seated on a rock, she leans above the swimming Orontes. Their poses are momentary and characterized by abrupt transitions.

## Eworth Hans *fl.* 1540–*c*74

The portrait painter Hans Eworth was born in Antwerp. He is now identified with the artist who signed himself HE and who worked in England. He is probably the "Jan Eeuworts" listed as a freeman of Antwerp in 1540 and working in England by 1549. Eworth is known to have painted Mary I (notably a portrait in the Royal Museum of Fine Arts, Antwerp) and to have worked for Elizabeth I on court festival designs from 1572 to 1574. He was patronized by both nobility and gentry. Portraits such as that of *Lady Dacre* (National Gallery of Canada, Ottawa) show that his style was derived

Hans Eworth: Portrait of Lady Dacre; oil on panel; 74×58cm (29×23in); 1540. National Gallery of Canada, Ottawa

from the work of Holbein the Younger, his predecessor in favor at the royal court. The allegorical portrait of *Sir John Luttrell* (Courtauld Institute Galleries, London) is a unique example of contemporary French influence on his work.

## Exekias *fl. c545–530 BC*

Exekias was an Athenian black-figure painter and potter. His name appears on 12 vases and fragments, usually as potter, but also on two *amphorae* as both potter and painter. He decorated a wide variety of shapes, and can probably be credited with the invention of the "eye-cup" and *kalyx-krater*.

His earliest vase is a neck-*amphora* in Berlin, signed in his meticulous handwriting as potter and painter. The *amphora* has the same compact and well-proportioned body as the powerful Herakles who wrestles with the Nemean Lion on the obverse. Herakles and his nervous nephew Iolaos are painted with steady, careful brush strokes whose sharp edges and deep sheen recall bronze statues. Equally clean and metallic are the slowly winding spirals and friezes of floral ornament above and below the main scene. The reverse shows two armed warriors standing quietly by their handsome steeds: horses and humans alike are given names. Exekias' devotion to horses was a lifelong passion, equaled only by the consummate skill with which he drew them. These early horses have all the dignity and good manners of his later thoroughbreds, and a statuesque elegance reminiscent of Archaic horses in marble and bronze.

A *kylix* in the Staatliche Antikensammlungen, Munich, signed by Exekias as potter, represents a new form of wine-cup, perhaps invented by this artist. He departs from Athenian tradition by filling the interior with a single picture, unrestricted by groundlines or borders: Dionysos reclining in his vine-laden ship sails freely across a sea alive with dolphins. The outside is decorated with scenes of combat which are forced around and under the handles by a broad, decorative scheme, new to Attic cups: graceful eyebrows, a nose and two large eyes. An apparent parody of the "eye-cup" by Exekias' rival, Amasis, suggests that the shape of the cup and the ornamental eyes were regarded as the property of Exekias. Under each handle sits a defecating hound and between them an enormous siren whose body consists of

Exekias: Dionysos on his Vine-laden Ship; black-figure painting on a kylix; c530 BC. Staatliche Antikensammlungen, Munich

the Exekian eye. Exekias lashed back at his rival on two vases: a neck-*amphora* (British Museum, London) with Memnon and his black squires, one of whom is named Amasis; and an *amphora* (Philadelphia Museum of Art) with Ajax lifting the dead Achilles, while a Greek pursues a scrawny black man who is named Amasos. Such amicably biting gestures anticipate the friendly jabs and greetings written on the vases of Euthymides, Phintias, and other red-figure "pioneers".

One of his finest works is the *amphora* in the Vatican Museums, Rome, signed as potter and painter. Achilles and Ajax sit absorbed in their board-game, in much the same composition as Cézanne's *Card Players* (c1890–2; Collection Pellerin, Paris). Their elaborately engraved hair, beards, and cloaks reveal a master in full control of his difficult technique. The heroes are thoughtful, well-bred men with the lordly bearing of Olympians. The mood of the picture exemplifies Exekias' preference for quiet, reflective figures en-

gaged in unhurried activity—a rare and unusually "classical" preference, in stark contrast to the lively action scenes beloved of Archaic painters.

The solemn mourners on his funeral plaques (Staatliche Museen, Berlin) show a rare delicacy of emotion that was seldom equaled in Greek painting. And his *Ajax* (Musée des Beaux-Arts et d'Archéologie, Boulogne)—who is depicted slowly and carefully fixing the suicidal sword in the earth—is portrayed with a grave inwardness, perhaps reflecting the painter's own personality.

Exekias represents black-figure painting at its finest hour. To a spirit of great sensitivity he joined faultless technical control, revealing to his contemporaries and all who followed that the upper limits of black-figure work were far higher than any of them had ever imagined. His latest paintings show no sign of influence from the new red-figure technique, and so his brief but brilliant career must have come to an end shortly before 530 BC.

## Eyck brothers
### 14th and 15th centuries

The brothers Hubert (1366/70–1426) and
Jan (c1390–1441) van Eyck were the
founders of the Flemish school of painting.
Jan van Eyck was undoubtedly the most
famous painter of his age; his paintings
broke completely with the art of the
Middle Ages. His supreme excellence lay in
his power to represent the visible world by
the patient observation of an endless variety of detail. Unlike his Italian contemporaries, van Eyck had no knowledge of
the laws of mathematical perspective, nor
of anatomy. It is his study of the fall of
light that gives reality to the objects and
unifies the scene. His creation of a convincing space was achieved empirically. A
feeling for the beauty of the surface and
texture of things, of flowers, rocks, jewels,
fabrics, and metals, remained characteristic of Flemish art. His technical mastery
was outstanding and he perfected the art of
oil painting: by enabling the artist to apply
the paint in transparent layers, the new
technique gave colors a fresh intensity and
made possible sparkling highlights and
subtle half-tones.

Jan's relationship to his brother, Hubert,
is one of the most difficult problems in the
history of art. In 1823 an inscription on
the *Adoration of the Lamb* altarpiece (St-
Bavon Cathedral, Ghent) was published.
The altarpiece was the most renowned of
all early Flemish paintings. The inscription—partly indecipherable and post-
dating the execution of the work—began a
controversy, which still continues, about
the share each of the two artists may have
had in the painting of the altarpiece. It
reads:

> ... ubertus eyck maior quo nemo
> repertus
> incepit pondusq johannes arte secundus
> ... iodici vyd prece fretus
> versu sexta mai vos collocat acta tueri

This may be translated:

> The painter Hubrecht Eyck, than whom
> none was greater, began this work,
> which his brother Jan, who was second
> to him in art, completed at the behest of
> Jodoc Vijdt, and which he invites you by
> this verse to contemplate on 6 May
> [1432].

Jan van Eyck: the Annunciation; oil on panel
transferred to canvas; 93×36cm (37×14cm).
National Gallery of Art, Washington, D.C.

The date is given by a chronogram in the last line.

We know almost nothing about Hubert (or Hubrecht); a 16th-century tradition suggests that both artists probably came from Maaseyck in Limborg. Their birth dates are unknown. Hubert died in 1426; no separate works can be attributed to him on external evidence. He is usually identified with a painter mentioned, in documents in Ghent, in 1425 and 1426 as "Hubrecht", "Ubrechts" etc.

By contrast Jan's career is well documented, and his artistic activity is known from a series of signed and dated works from 1432 to 1441. From 1422 to 1425 he worked at The Hague as *peintre et valet de chambre* of John Count of Holland. On John's death he entered the service of Philip, Duke of Burgundy. Philip also employed him as confidential agent and in 1426, 1428, and 1436 he was sent to Portugal to negotiate the Duke's marriage with the Infanta Isabella. He worked at Lille and Bruges and was patronized by the Burgundian court and by Italian merchants at Bruges.

The *Adoration of the Lamb* is the major achievement of 15th-century Flemish art and its new realism of figure and landscape mark the break with the art of the 14th century. This large polyptych, which consists of 20 panels, shows three rows of figures when the shutters are closed. At the top are figures of prophets and sibyls. Beneath them, spreading across four panels, is an Annunciation, set in a room with a view of a Flemish town from the window. The bottom row shows the donors, Josse or Jodocus Vijdt and his wife; and between them, in grisaille paintings that imitate stone sculpture, are the figures of St John the Baptist and St John the Evangelist. The color is a brownish monochrome though the portraits are in scarlet and green.

The brilliance of the interior is a startling contrast. The central panel of the lower row shows an Adoration of the Lamb. Processions of worshipers advance across a flowery meadow towards the altar of the Lamb. Before the Lamb is the Fountain of life, symbol of Redemption, and above is the Holy Dove. Twelve prophets gather on the left, behind them the Patriarchs. The Apostles are on the right, and behind them the martyrs. Further groups of saints gather in the distance. In the four wings on either side of the central panel the procession continues. The Just Judges and the

Warriors of Christ move in from the left, the Holy Hermits and the Holy Pilgrims from the right. In this row the figures are small and the five panels unified by one continuous landscape; in the distance are the spires of the Heavenly City.

In the upper row the figures are larger. In the center is God the Father, to the left and right the Virgin and St John the Baptist. On either side of them are angels making music, and on the outermost panels Adam and Eve.

In this interior the new technique of oil painting may be seen in all its splendor. The painting is deeply religious and its beauties seem a paean of praise to the glory of God. In the Paradisal landscape of the lower row the colors are brilliant, scarlets and blues against a startlingly bright green ground; there is a rich profusion of lovingly observed plants and trees, and wonderful effects of light falling on distant meadows and Gothic towers. The plants can all be identified, and the palms, cypresses, and orange trees must postdate Jan's journey to Portugal. Several of the buildings can also be named. The Knights and the Judges are richly dressed in shining armor and with decorated bridles; in the upper row jeweled crowns, robes, and lavish brocades create a still richer effect.

The love of delicate detail and gorgeous costumes and jewelry is already present in Gothic art—we are reminded of the early-15th-century *Très Riches Heures du Duc de Berry* by the Limburg brothers (Musée Condé, Chantilly). But Jan's observation is more scientific and his study of light gives the landscape a new unity. The nude figures of Adam and Eve create a startling contrast to the more hieratic figures in the center of the upper row. The nude is represented with an entirely new and almost harsh realism. Unlike the other figures in that row they were designed to be seen from below, and Adam's foot seems to jut out of the niche in which he stands.

No opinion has been generally accepted as to how much of the altarpiece Hubert had completed on his death in 1426. There are certainly discrepancies of style within the work as a whole. The most widely held view is that Jan, between 1430 and 1432, repainted an altarpiece that had been designed and partly completed by Hubert before 1426. Most authorities assign wholly to Jan the most "advanced" parts of the altarpiece, the Adam and Eve and the beautiful rendering of atmospheric

perspective in the upper part of the landscape in the lower row.

After the Ghent altarpiece we have a series of signed and dated works by Jan. His earliest portrait, dated 1432, is *A Young Man* or *Timotheos* (National Gallery, London); *The Man in a Turban* (National Gallery, London) was painted in the following year. The *Young Man* is shown against a plain background and behind a stone parapet; he holds a script in his hand. His plain features are unidealized; his face is turned towards a gentle light that falls from the left and models the features with great subtlety. The stone parapet, which is inscribed with the words *Leal Souvenir* ("loyal remembrance") and with the signature and date, is one of the marvels of Jan's art; the surface of the stone, cracked and pitted, is faithfully recorded. These works mark the beginnings of modern portraiture. The three-quarter view is new; so is the detailed description of the face—the wrinkles of the skin, the texture of the hair, the light in the eyes. The *Man in a Turban* looks out of the painting towards the spectator, thus creating a sense of lifelike immediacy; it is possibly the first instance in the history of painting of this connective gaze, and it has been suggested that the painting may be a self-portrait.

The most famous of Jan's portraits is the *Arnolfini Wedding* (1434; National Gallery, London). This shows the marriage ceremony between Giovanni Arnolfini and his wife Giovanna Cenami; the vows are taken within their own room, surrounded by their own objects; the marriage was witnessed by van Eyck himself, whose reflection appears in a convex mirror hanging on the back wall. His presence is confirmed by the inscription on the wall over the mirror, which reads, "Johannes de eyck fuit hic" ("was here") 1434. The small scale of the painting gives it a sense of magic. The nuptial chamber is full of objects—a small dog, cast-off shoes, fruit, a chandelier, a bed, a chair-back topped by a statuette of St Margaret—several of which contain symbolic references to marriage. There are beautifully controlled effects of light on the chandelier and on the wall. The technical supremacy of the convex mirror is a *tour de force*; around it are 10 small round panels showing, in minute detail, scenes from the Passion of Christ. This detailed description of a private and domestic scene, the creation of a convincing space, and the observation of immobility; the total effect is calm and remote, and this quality is characteristic of Jan's mature work. His later religious works, *St Barbara* (1437; Royal Museum of Fine Arts, Antwerp) and *The Madonna at the Fountain* (1439; Royal Museum of Fine Arts, Antwerp), tend to be less realistic, simpler, and more restrained. The unsigned *Madonna of Chancellor Rolin* (1435; Louvre, Paris) contains one of van Eyck's most wonderful landscapes, remarkable for its unparalleled breadth of vision. A river crossed by a bridge leads the eye from a town in the foreground through an extensive sweep of rich countryside to the blue of distant hills.

The van Eycks' early style is highly controversial. The problem works consist of five or six paintings and the illuminations in the Hours of Turin. The *Three Maries at the Sepulchre* (Boymans-van Beuningen Museum, Rotterdam) is usually agreed to be an Eyckian picture, often attributed to Hubert. In 1902 a group of miniatures were discovered in the Turin library which formed part of the Hours of Turin. A further series were found in the Biblioteca Trivulziana, Milan (now in the Museo Civico, Turin). Turin library and the miniatures were destroyed by fire in 1904, but the brief reappearance of these works had started a long argument as to their authorship. The manuscripts may almost certainly be dated to 1416 and anticipate in an astonishing way later developments in 15th-century art. They have a new feeling for light and atmosphere and show an ambitious attempt to set figures in space. It is possible that they show the Eyckian style as it moves towards the Ghent altarpiece. Some authorities have attributed them to Hubert on the grounds that they show a concentration on figures in action that we do not associate with Jan. Others have suggested the possibility of collaboration; others, that they represent the early style of the young Jan.

The van Eycks will doubtless continue to be the focus of controversies. Yet their supreme position in the history of Flemish art will remain unchallenged. All later Flemish artists were affected by them and later in the 15th century their achievement began to influence artists of the Italian Renaissance.

**Further reading.** Baldass, L. *Jan van Eyck*, London (1952). Hughes, R. and Faggin, G. *The Complete Paintings of the van Eycks*, London (1970). Whinney, M. *Early Flemish Painting*, London (1968).

Jan van Eyck: St Donation, a detail of the Madonna with Canon van der Paele; oil on panel; full size 122×157cm (48×62in); 1436. State Museum, Bruges

the fall of light lead on to 17th-century Dutch genre painting. Jan van Eyck's later dated portraits include the *Jan de Leeuw* (1436; Kunsthistorisches Museum, Vienna) and the *Margaretha van Eyck* (1439; State Museum, Bruges). With these may be associated the *Portrait of Cardinal Albergati* (Kunsthistorisches Museum, Vienna).

In the religious paintings of the mid 1430s, the *Madonna with Canon van der Paele* (State Museum, Bruges) and the *Dresden Triptych* (1437; Gemäldegalerie Alte Meister, Dresden), van Eyck was concerned with the problem of setting figures in space, and with the splendor of effects of light and surface texture. The former work shows the Virgin enthroned within the apse of a Romanesque church. The donor, one of van Eyck's most powerful portraits, kneels on the right with St George; on the left is St Donation. The massive figures are pushed back in space and the composition has a classical severity. There is an astonishing clarity, sharpness of detail, and contrast of textures—of carpets, tiles, brocades, armor, glass, and stone. The figures have a strange

# F

## Fabré Jaime *fl. c1300–39*

Jaime Fabré was a Spanish architect. A native of Palma in Majorca, he was appointed in 1317 as architect to Barcelona Cathedral, where work had begun in 1296 to a plan based on the plan of the cathedral at Narbonne. By 1321 Fabré was in charge at Narbonne itself and also at Gerona Cathedral, another Narbonne-influenced design which had been started c1312. However, Barcelona differs from Narbonne in not following the usual two tier, basilican spatial arrangement. Instead the heights of chapels and aisles are staggered in a way that recalls Toledo Cathedral, which was begun before 1224. The circular clerestory windows and low triforium derive from the inner aisles at Toledo. This so-called "spatial" Gothic achieved its finest expression at S. Maria del Mar in Barcelona, a church begun in 1323 by Berenguer de Montagut and Ramón Despuig.

## Fabritius Carel 1622–54

The Dutch painter Carel Fabritius was the most gifted of Rembrandt's pupils, and is historically important as a link between Rembrandt and Vermeer. After his apprenticeship in the early 1640s he followed Rembrandt in attempts at dramatic biblical narratives, also employing something of the freedom of his teacher's application of paint. Later, after settling in Delft, he turned instead to portraiture, genre, and still-life painting. His colors became paler and cooler, and he increasingly stressed purely pictorial effects rather than the projection of a particular mood. This is evident in his portraits (where personality is partially subordinated to the organization of shapes, colors, and tones). It is perhaps even more apparent in such paintings as *The Goldfinch* (1654; Royal Museum of Art, Mauritshuis, The Hague): a superb demonstration of balance in an asymmetrical composition.

Fabritius' interest in the abstract components of a design, the architectural character of some of his compositions, his study of the fall of light on objects, and of optical problems in general all reappear in the work of Vermeer—who was probably his pupil and certainly owned some of his

Carel Fabritius (attrib.): Portrait of a Young Man; oil on canvas; 63 × 51 cm (25 × 20in). Alte Pinakothek, Munich

pictures. Very few of Fabritius' paintings have survived; the Delft gunpowder factory explosion that caused his early death probably also destroyed many of his pictures.

## Falconet Étienne-Maurice 1716–91

The Parisian sculptor Falconet was trained first by his uncle, and then—like his later rival, Jean-Baptiste Pigalle—at the studio of Jean-Baptiste Lemoyne (1704–78). He was accepted at the Académie Royale in 1744 on the strength of his plaster model for *Milo of Crotona* (marble version, 1754; Louvre, Paris). From 1745 to 1765 he exhibited regularly at the Salon, and in 1783 became Professor at the Académie— a rare honor for a sculptor of that period.

Falconet was the favorite sculptor of Mme de Pompadour, mistress of Louis XV, and for her he created *L'Amour Menaçant* and *La Baigneuse* in 1757 (both

Étienne-Maurice Falconet: Louis XV; biscuit porcelain; height 33cm (13in). Musée Lambinet, Versailles

Henri Fantin-Latour: Roses and a Glass Jug; oil on canvas; 44×56cm (17×22in); 1889. Musée des Beaux-Arts, Lyons

now in the Louvre, Paris). The former was conceived in a Rococo spirit, while the latter had a more classical tendency. Through the influence of his patroness he was appointed that year as Director of the Sèvres Porcelain Factory, where many of his boudoir pieces, usually soft female nudes, were reproduced as statuettes in biscuit (unglazed porcelain), a recently-popularized genre.

The ambitious Falconet never actually secured a commission from Louis XV. In 1766, he was working on a large-scale marble of *St Amboise* destined for the Invalides, but since destroyed. Diderot offered him Catherine II's commission for a bronze *Equestrian Statue to Peter the Great* at St Petersburg. He finished this powerful and highly original piece in 1769, casting it himself, but he left Russia before the unveiling, dissatisfied with his fees.

He was a thinker, and unusually literate for a sculptor of the time. In 1761 he published *Réflexions sur la Sculpture*, ad-vocating realism and modernity as against servile copying from ancient prototypes. He himself never visited Italy.

## Fan K'uan *fl. 990–1030*

The Chinese painter Fan K'uan came from Hua Yuan; he lived a solitary life, roaming at first between Loyang and Yung but later living in T'ai-hua in Chung-nan. He is described as a man of stern and old-fashioned manner and appearance, a rustic and Taoist. Yet he seems to have had a warm character for which he was much respected. Fan K'uan apparently followed the Chinese artistic tradition, first studying Li Ch'eng closely and then developing his own style. The remark attributed to him, and echoed by many Chinese artists, sums up his attitude: "My predecessors have not yet tried to seize things as they really are; surely it is better to take the things themselves than men as teachers, and a still better teacher than material objects is the heart". This order of study is recommended repeatedly, but artists are always told to follow a thorough grounding in the techniques of painting by study of the Old Masters. Most of Fan K'uan's own painting seems to have been of classical mountain landscape. He apparently mastered the structure of his subject and then painted directly without self-conscious regard for brush stroke.

## Fantin-Latour Henri 1836–1904

The French painter Ignace Henri Jean Joseph Théodore Fantin-Latour was born in Grenoble and worked in Paris. His most ambitious works were allegories inspired by his love of the music of Berlioz and Wagner, with elusive figures evoked in feathery brush strokes achieving a Romantic rather than Impressionist haze. These paintings are an important link between the late Delacroix and the younger French Symbolist painters. His commercial success was gained by flower painting, a genre he found less congenial than the allegories. His flower pieces gave full scope to his skillful control of tone. Like his friend J.A.M. Whistler, he achieved this by the use of very thin paint which exposed the texture of the canvas.

## Feininger Lyonel 1871–1956

The American painter Lyonel Feininger was born in New York. He studied at the Hamburg School of Applied Arts, then at the Berlin Academy, and later in Paris. He worked successfully as a cartoonist for some years, but by 1909 was concentrating on painting. In 1911, during a visit to Paris, he discovered Cubism and began to use its formal qualities for his expressive aims. He met members of *Die Brücke* Expressionist group in 1912. Feininger has sometimes been categorized as an Expressionist, but his paintings are cooler in

Robert Feke: The Family of Isaac Royall; oil on canvas; 143×197cm (56×78in); 1741. Harvard University, Cambridge, Mass.

Lyonel Feininger: Yellow Street II; oil on canvas; c1917. The Montreal Museum of Fine Arts

color than most Expressionist works; they are also more contemplative in content, dealing with subjects like churches and the sea. He was appointed to the Bauhaus staff on its establishment in 1919, and directed its print workshop until 1923. He later joined the exhibiton group "Blue Four", with Kandinsky, Klee, and Jawlensky. Feininger returned to America in 1938.

## Feke Robert *fl.* 1724–c67

Robert Feke was an American portrait-painter who worked in the Colonial style. He has been described as the best American-born artist before J.S. Copley (1738–1815). Historically, Feke is a somewhat shadowy figure. The facts about his life are very sparse: he is thought to have been a mariner, and to have made several visits to England. Born between 1705 and 1710, he was, by 1741, an established portraitist based in Boston. His *Family of Isaac Royall* (1741; Harvard University, Cambridge, Mass.) is one of his earliest best-known works. He was married in 1742. In succeeding years he traveled between Newport and Philadelphia and disappeared from accounts until his death in Bermuda or the West Indies. His portraits are the first in the art history of the U.S.A. to achieve something that belongs distinctly to that nation.

## Ferrari Gaudenzio c1475–1546

The Italian painter and sculptor Gaudenzio Ferrari was a native of Valduggia. He worked in Piedmont and Lombardy, where his major works are still to be found. Between 1523 and 1528 he worked at the Sacre Monte in Varallo (where 45 chapels are grouped on a hill) where he did frescoes and sculptures in the chapels of the Crucifixion and Adoration of the Magi. His combination of fresco and painted terracotta resembles a *tableau vivant* and is reminiscent of German Gothic sculpture. His other major works are in S. Cristoforo, Vercelli (1529–32) and in Saronno (1534–6). In his painting, Ferrari reveals the influence of both Leonardo da Vinci and Perugino.

## Ferrer Bassa c1290–1348

Born at Sasgaioles, near Barcelona, Ferrer was the effective founder of a tradition of Catalan painting. Although it was at times subject to external pressures and international fashions, Catalan painting preserved its individuality from the early 14th century until the death of Jaime Huguet. The first phase of this tradition, represented at its best by Ferrer, was characterized by the combination of personal originality with marked Italian—particularly Sienese—influence. This had reached Spain by way of Mallorca but also through Simone Martini and the School of Avignon. By 1320 Ferrer was painting at the court of Jaime II where he also seems to have taken part in other activities. His association with the court continued for most of his working life: he subsequently worked for Alfonso IV to illuminate the *Usages of Barcelona and the Customs of Cataluña*—the so-called *Usajes*; the work has not survived.

In 1344 Ferrer was appointed painter to the court of Pedro IV, a post that carried with it the opportunity to travel in the royal service. Some time after 1335, possibly during this period of official travel, he went to Avignon, thereby fortifying the connection between Cataluña and the Sienese School. In 1344 he apparently painted the principal altarpiece of the Chapel Royal of Barcelona; this work was replaced in 1464, at the order of D. Pedro, Condestable of Portugal, by one painted by Jaime Huguet.

In 1344 Ferrer began the only work—fortunately an extensive one—that has survived to the present day: the decoration of the chapel of S. Miguel in the Convent

Gaudenzio Ferrari: The Flight into Egypt; fresco; 267×130cm (105×51in); c1511–13. S. Maria delle Grazie, Varallo

of the Nuns of St Clare at Pedralbes, near Barcelona. This is a narrative cycle of paintings with a largely didactic purpose, in accordance with the precepts of St Bernard on the education of the faithful. It shows the life of the Virgin Mary and the life and Passion of Christ. Though the effects of Florentine and Sienese painting (particularly of Giotto and Duccio) are clear, Ferrer's work is by no means without originality. The arrangement of figures

in formalized rows and the diagonal, slightly sly lines of the faces are unmistakably Sienese. In common with almost all Italo-Catalan painting, the series shows little interest in effects of depth, and the backgrounds are perfectly flat. The comfortable grace and the careful detail of the Sienese style are absent: greater simplicity is reinforced by a tension that sometimes characterizes later Spanish art almost to the point of melodrama. The faces have a harshness of expression amounting at times to distortion which suggests, if not outward beauty, a considerable inner turbulence.

As the most obvious Italian influences died away, or yielded before the pressure of new fashions, the sense of drama and spiritual tension introduced by Ferrer persisted. His immediate followers, before the weight of the International Gothic style was fully felt, were Ramón Destorrents and the Serra brothers.

## Feti Domenico c1589–1624

The Italian painter Domenico Feti (or Fetti) was born in Rome, where he was later taught by Cigoli. He was influenced by the realism and dramatic lighting of Caravaggio and his followers, but he did not himself become a Caravaggist. The work of Elsheimer, who was a painter of tiny highly realistic landscapes, also made an impact on him. His patron was Cardinal Ferdinando Gonzaga; on becoming Duke of Mantua in 1613, Gonzaga left Rome taking Feti with him to be his court painter.

In Mantua Feti became closely acquainted with the work of Rubens, who had been court painter to Vincenzo Gonzaga from 1600 to 1608, and also with the work of the Venetians, whose paintings were well represented in the ducal collection. Feti's best known pictures date from the beginning of his stay in Mantua. The combination of influences from Elsheimer and Rubens led Feti to develop a highly individual style of genre painting which was both rich in color and subtle in tone, and in which the action often conveyed melancholy. *The Pearl of Great Price* (William Rockhill Nelson Gallery, Kansas City) is such an example. Small in size, it is one of a set of 12 paintings of parables made for Ferdinando Gonzaga; it illustrates the parable in Matthew 13 and shows a market scene with dealers haggling over pearls. Other genre scenes are more explicitly tragic, for example, *The Blind Leading the Blind* (Barber Institute of Fine Arts, Birmingham, England). In 1621 Feti moved to Venice, and lived there until his death.

Domenico Feti: The Flight into Egypt; oil on canvas; 73×82cm (29×32in); c1621–3. Kunsthistorisches Museum, Vienna

## Feuerbach Anselm 1829–80

The German painter Anselm Feuerbach studied from 1845 to 1848 at the Academy in Düsseldorf, then the center of German Neoclassicism. A brief stay in Antwerp (1850–1) taught him the importance of realism; but it was between the years 1851 and 1854 in Paris, where he attended Thomas Couture's studio, that he achieved a balance between the intellect and the senses. This ideal, dear to his heroes Goethe and Schiller, seemed embodied in the works of the Italian Renaissance masters. When he moved to Rome in 1856 he, like other Deutsch-Römer (German-Romans), copied many of them for Count Schack. His art was profoundly influenced by this experience. He treated Classical subjects and portraits with increasing simplicity of line and color (usually subdued and chalky). His paintings often express a Roman *gravitas* through their monumental poses and frieze-like compositions (for example, *Iphigenie*, 1862; Hessisches Landesmuseum, Darmstadt).

## Filarete c1400–69

The Florentine sculptor and architect Antonio di Pietro Averlino was known as Filarete. He was trained under Ghiberti, a degenerate version of whose relief-style he used in the bronze door commissioned from him by Pope Eugenius IV for St Peter's in Rome (1433–45). Accused of stealing sacred relics and expelled from Rome by the Pope, Filarete traveled to northern Italy and in 1451 became architect to his protector Francesco Sforza, for whom he designed the Ospedale Maggiore in Milan (1456). It was to Sforza that he later dedicated his *Trattato d'Architettura* (1461–4), a diverting architectural treatise cast in the form of a project for the construction of an ideal city, Sforzinda, and its port, Plusiapolis.

## Finiguerra Maso 1426–64

Maso Finiguerra was a Florentine goldsmith. According to Vasari, he was the inventor of engraving, but the claim has no documentary proof. However, his fame as a craftsman in niello—a process very similar to engraving—suggests that the ascription to him of several engravings is probably correct. These, usually dated to the 1460s, are done in the so-called Fine Manner: for example, the series of *Planets* (British Museum, London). In 1463 Finiguerra was commissioned to make drawings for *intarsia* (wood inlay) panels for the north sacristy of Florence Cathedral. These drawings (now in the Museo dell'Opera del Duomo, Florence) are his only positively authenticated works.

## Fischer J.M. 1691–1766

The prolific South German architect Johann Michael Fischer claimed responsibility for no less than 32 churches, 23 monasteries, and "very many" secular works, according to his tombstone. He ranks with Balthasar Neumann among the greatest of the Germanic architects of the 18th century.

Born in the Upper Palatinate, the son of a municipal master mason, Fischer worked as a foreman in Moravia (c1715–16) before moving on to Munich. There he worked for Johann Mayr, mason to the city, before becoming a master mason himself in 1722. Thus at the outset of his long career Fischer was familiar with a wide range of contemporary architecture including the Austrian Baroque and, probably, the buildings of G. Santini and C. Dientzenhofer in Bohemia and Moravia.

His first independent commission was for the reconstruction of the choir of the abbey church of Niederaltaich (begun 1724). In the church of St Anna-am-Lehel in Munich (begun 1727) Fischer clearly reveals the impact of the designs of C. Dientzenhofer (for example Obořiště and Smiřice). Unfortunately the Asams' decorations in St Anna were destroyed in 1944.

In the abbey church at Osterhoven (1727–8) the Bohemian elements are more explicit and the convex gallery fronts are contrasted with the concave faces of the piers. This creates an undulating effect inspired, no doubt, by C. Dientzenhofer's nave of sv. Mikuláš, Malá Strana, in Prague. Again the immensely rich decoration was executed by the Asams (1728–35). In the abbey church of Berg-am-Laim, on the outskirts of Munich, Fischer was able to explore the possibilities of interlinked centrally-planned spaces on a considerable scale (1738–42).

Fischer's role as architect was generally confined to the structure of the building and during the 1720s and early 1730s he usually worked with the Asams as decorators. In the mid 1730s he turned instead to the teams of Wessobrunn *stuccatori* and painters working in the Rococo style. His designs for the abbey church at Zwiefalten (1744–65) were circumscribed by the reuse of existing foundations. The length of the church is undeniably excessive, but the stuccos by J.M. Feichtmayr and the swirling frescoes of F.J. Spiegler are highly successful.

Less rigid limitations applied to the huge abbey church of Ottobeuren where Fischer, from 1748, was again able to explore the possibilities of a large central vaulted space with equal emphasis laid on the nave and choir. The team of J.M. Feichtmayr moved on from Zwiefalten to decorate Ottobeuren together with the painters F.A. and J.J. Zeiller. The centralizing tendencies in Fischer's designs reach their most extreme in the abbey church of Rott-am-Inn (1759–63), where the interior is dominated by the great central octagon with its fresco by M. Günther. The clarity of the architectural forms takes on a new strength through the reduced amount of Rococo stucco work.

## Fischer von Erlach J.B. 1656–1723

The first major architect active in central Europe since the Middle Ages, Johann Bernhard Fischer von Erlach was the son of a sculptor in Graz, Austria. He left his homeland in 1674 to study for 12 years in Italy. During this period, in Rome and Naples, he continued to work as a sculptor and two medals executed by him then are known. After his return to Austria he submitted designs for the decoration of the Mausoleum in Graz (c1687). These were unsuccessful; but by 1690 he was well established in Vienna, and designed two triumphal arches for the entry of Joseph I. These introduced the ideas of the Roman High Baroque into Vienna. In 1705 he was appointed Chief Imperial Inspector of all Buildings for Court and Festivities, a post he retained until his death.

Fischer von Erlach's sculptural work on the Pest Column in Vienna was done during the years 1687 to 1689. Much of his earliest work was more sculptural than architectural, though the first project for the palace of Schönbrunn (outside Vienna) can be dated to c1690. During the mid 1690s he began two important churches in Salzburg, while working on the central section of Prince Eugene's town palace in Vienna (1695–1700). The Dreifaltigkeitskirche (1694–1702) is remarkable for its sharply concave facade flanked by low towers, and the clearly articulated longi-

J.M. Fischer: the basilica of the Benedictine abbey of Ottobeuren; mid 18th century

tudinal oval which forms the nave. He developed these ideas further in the Karlskirche. In contrast, the much larger Kollegienkirche is a modified Greek cross in plan, with a strongly convex central section to the facade, held in check by the twin towers. The vitality of the designs is enhanced by the limited decoration; in the Kollegienkirche the dazzling white plasterwork of the later high altar by Diego Carlone provides a fitting climax.

The palace of Schönbrunn was modified during construction (1696–*post* 1711), and once again for the Empress Maria Theresa, so that today it bears little resemblance to Fischer von Erlach's intentions. However, the richly articulated facades of the Bohemian Chancellery in Vienna (*post* 1708–14) and the Clam Gallas Palace in Prague (begun 1713) reveal his dynamic mature style.

In 1715 Fischer von Erlach began his work on his masterpiece, the Karlskirche in Vienna. The structure was completed by his son Joseph Emmanuel with modifica-

tions in 1725. The relatively low central portico is flanked by two enormous columns, and the facade is completed by a pair of bell towers over archways. The tension between these elements, and the dome behind, provides both the basis for the dynamic balance of the facade, and a foretaste of the vigorous treatment of the oval nave. In the Kárlskirche Fischer von Erlach strove to create a specifically Imperial Baroque style; these ideas reached their climax in his Imperial Library in Vienna, begun the year before his death.

**Further reading.** Kunoth, G. *Die Historische Architektur Fischers von Erlach*, Düsseldorf (1956). Sedlmayr, H. *Johann Bernhard Fischer von Erlach*, Munich (1956).

## Flandrin J.-H. 1809–64

The French painter Jean-Hippolyte Flandrin was born in Lyons. He moved to Paris and entered the studio of J.-A.-D. Ingres in

1829. He became one of Ingres' most zealous followers, and won the Prix de Rome in 1832. After six years in Italy he returned to France. There he developed a style that combined early Renaissance formal austerity with a characteristic mid-19th-century sentimentality. The strength of Flandrin's style appears to be particularly well-suited to portraiture, in which he was extremely gifted. He was also to become one of the most important 19th-century religious artists, as his murals in the church of St-Germain-des-Près, Paris, demonstrate.

## Flavin Dan 1933–1996

Dan Flavin is an American sculptor in light. He uses columns of tubular light to create open-ended paintings in a darkened gallery area. Flavin's work is part of a trend towards systematic and optical art which began in the 1960s; it is related to the painting of Richard Anuszkiewicz, Frank Stella, and Kenneth Noland, and to

J.-H. Flandrin: Theseus Recognized by his Father; oil on canvas; 115×146cm (45×57in); 1832. École des Beaux-Arts, Paris

Dan Flavin: untitled, to the "innovator" of Wheeling Peachblow; pink, gold, and daylight fluorescent light; 244×244cm (96×96in); 1966–8. Museum of Modern Art, New York

the later sculptures of Richard Lippold. With its use of modern technology and lighting, Flavin's work is also a direct development of early "color-field" painting: in many ways his works are the electrified equivalent of paintings by Barnett Newman (1905–1970), such as Newman's earlier *Vir Heroicus Sublimus* (1950; Museum of Modern Art, New York).

## Flaxman John 1755–1826

The English Neoclassical artist John Flaxman was probably the most internationally famous British sculptor before the 20th century. Flaxman was trained at the Royal Academy in the early 1770s and began his career designing for Josiah Wedgwood's pottery factory. Flaxman was interested in all kinds of archaic and primitive art, including Gothic and early Renaissance, as well as having a conventional admiration for Antiquity. He managed to establish a reputation as a tomb sculptor in England and visited Italy in 1787, remaining in Rome until 1794. He studied as many different styles as possible, filling small notebooks with his researches, and the result of these studies appears in the works of his Italian period.

Flaxman was friendly with the Italian sculptor Canova whose influence secured a few important patrons for the British artist. His greatest Roman statue was *The Fury of Athamas* (1790–4; Ickworth House, Suffolk), a marble group of four figures, 7 ft (2.1 m) high, which depicts a subject from Ovid's *Metamorphoses*. Although the patron, Lord Bristol, admired the carefully researched "Antique" style of the work, he was not prepared to pay the sculptor adequately. Flaxman was forced to find new commissions and, in doing so, produced a series of graphic masterpieces—outline illustrations to Dante, Homer, and Aeschylus. These were engraved in black and white lines which recalled the flat, painted decorations on the sides of Archaic vases. The success of these outlines confirmed Flaxman's reputation abroad and they were copied by artists as diverse as Ingres, Goya, Géricault, and Seurat.

On his return to England Flaxman became a leading society sculptor, designing famous tombs which included those for Lord Mansfield (1795–1801; Westminster Abbey, London), Admiral Nelson (1808–18; St Paul's Cathedral, London), and Dr

Joseph Warton (1804; Winchester Cathedral). Flaxman's main talent appears in relief work, and his memorial plaques often convey a simple moral message. Like his outline illustrations, his achievement in relief was revolutionary in the placing of firm silhouettes or sinuous contours against a plain background. In this way his graphic work and the images he made in relief anticipate later styles, such as Art Nouveau. Flaxman also made very beautiful small models in terracotta or plaster, based on Classical designs, as in the *Sketch Model for a Monument to Barbara Lowther* (1807; University College, London). These models, however, were less successful when enlarged to the required size for a finished tomb.

Despite his eminence among foreign contemporaries, Flaxman's popularity in England declined in the two decades before his death. His market was taken by more successful artists like Chantrey, and Flaxman died bankrupt. It was not until the 1850s, when his studio models and drawings were acquired by University College in London, that his reputation in England revived. On the Continent, however, Flaxman never lost his popularity. During a visit to Paris in 1802 he was received as a celebrity by his French fellow artists. In 1865 Ingres included Flaxman's portrait among the elect in the second version of

*The Apotheosis of Homer* (Louvre, Paris); Goethe and A.W. von Schlegel in Germany also admired Flaxman's work and wrote the earliest critical accounts of his outline illustrations.

In 1817 Flaxman published a final set of illustrations, to the poems of Hesiod, and these were engraved by his friend William Blake. They were less popular than the previous designs, but they were collected abroad, especially in Germany where Flaxman's reputation as one of the greatest graphic artists of the 19th century has survived.

## Flinck G.T.  1615–60

Govert Teunisz. Flinck was a Dutch painter. Although he was born in Cleves, on the German side of the border, he studied at Leeuwarden and spent most of his working life in Amsterdam. His early works reveal the powerful influence of Rembrandt, with whom he studied in the 1630s. In the following decade he adopted a lighter, more Flemish style, which suggests a knowledge of works by van Dyck and van der Helst.

Although his fame has been obscured by that of his greater contemporaries, Flinck enjoyed a considerable reputation in his day. A prolific artist, he received several important state commissions. The contract for *The Conspiracy of Julius Civilis*, intended for Amsterdam town hall, was only given to Rembrandt to realize after Flinck's premature death.

## Floris brothers  16th century

Frans Floris (*c*1518–70) and his brother Cornelis (1514–75), were Flemish artists of Antwerp. Frans was a painter who traveled extensively in Italy in the 1540s. His most important work, *The Fall of the Rebel Angels* (1554; formerly Antwerp Cathedral, now Royal Museum of Fine Arts, Antwerp) shows evidence that he had studied Italian Mannerist painting and Michelangelo's *Last Judgment* in the Sistine Chapel. He was also a successful portraitist.

Cornelis was a sculptor who absorbed a number of influences—Italian, Classical, and French—and whose work was in demand in a number of north European centers (see his tomb of Christian III of Denmark, 1568; Roskilde Cathedral). The large Floris family workshop dominated Netherlandish design in the 1560s.

## Fontana Carlo  *c*1636–1714

Carlo Stefano Fontana was an Italian architect and engineer. After leaving his native north Italy, he served as assistant to Cortona, Rainaldi, and Bernini. After Bernini's death, he emerged as the most influential architect in the Holy City.

His facade of S. Marcello al Corso, Rome (1682–3), with its comparatively static and orderly articulation, reveals a dramatic contrast with the exuberant compositions of his predecessors. Other important commissions, such as the Jesuit church and college at Loyola in Spain, have been criticized for their cold eclecticism.

Despite such failings, Fontana's numerous smaller buildings, plans, drawings, and notes reveal his immense energy. Deeply respected by the following generation, his work was an important influence upon late Baroque classicism.

## Fontana Domenico  1543–1607

The architect Domenico Fontana was born in northern Italy but worked mainly in Rome and Naples. During his Roman period, his fortunes depended very much on those of his patron, Cardinal Felice Peretti, who became Pope Sixtus V in 1585, for whom he had built the Villa Montalto. After Peretti's death in 1590 Fontana found it difficult to obtain further work in Rome and went to Naples to work for the Viceroy.

Due to Peretti, Fontana was able to play a major role in no less than three papal palaces. He built a new wing at the Vatican (which houses the present papal apartments) and a new library in the Cortile del Belvedere; he worked at the Quirinale, and was responsible for the Lateran Palace (completed 1587) which was Sixtus' summer residence. In accordance with the Pope's program of urban renewal Fontana also designed new streets and waterworks.

Fontana was perhaps best known in his own day for the erection of two Egyptian obelisks, remarkable features of Rome's skyline, one in front of the choir of S. Maria Maggiore and the other in St Peter's Square. He describes this immense operation in *Della Transportatione dell'Obelisco Vaticano* (1590). In fact, he placed it a few degrees off the principal axis of Michelangelo's St Peter's. He served Sixtus literally until the end, building his mausoleum at S. Maria Maggiore.

In Naples his main work was the Palazzo Reale (1600–2), which helped to spread

G.T. Flinck: A Young Negro Archer; oil on panel; 68×52cm (27×20in); 1639–40. Wallace Collection, London

Roman classicism in the city. His style is often criticized as monotonous and severe, and in the case of the Lateran palace it is plainly derivitive (from Sangallo's Palazzo Farnese).

## Fontana Lucio 1899–1968

The Italian sculptor, painter, and ceramist Lucio Fontana was born in Rosario, Argentina. He spent his childhood in Milan, then in 1922 returned to Rosario where he opened a sculpture studio. From 1928 to 1930 he studied under Wildt at the Brera Academy, Milan. In 1935 he became a member of the *Abstraction-Création* group in Paris. Fontana lived in Argentina from 1939 to 1947. In 1946 he was a cofounder of the avant-garde Academia Altamira in Buenos Aires, which led to the publication of his *Manifesto Blanco*. In 1947 he returned to Milan, where he issued the *Manifesto Spaziale,* founding the "Spazialismo" movement. He died in Comabbio in 1968.

Fontana made his first Abstract sculptures in 1934. He returned to figurative art from 1939 to 1946 (and until 1960 as a subsidiary activity). From 1947 to 1949 he created ceramic sculptures. Fontana made his first pierced canvases in 1949, and in 1958 began to make cuts *(atesse).* These were made either in raw canvas, on monochrome grounds, or combined with informal painting, graffiti, drawing, glass, and stone collage. From the early 1950s onwards Fontana worked in pierced sheet metal, terracotta, and bronze. Beginning in 1948, his environmental and architectural projects incorporated neon, painting, holes, and suspended sculpture.

Vincenzo Foppa: Adoration of the Magi; poplar panel; 239×211cm (94×83in). National Gallery, London

## Foppa Vincenzo 1427/30–1515/16

Vincenzo Foppa was an Italian painter, from Brescia. His first signed work is a *Crucifixion* (Galleria dell'Academia Carrara, Bergamo) dated 1456. Resident in Pavia by 1458, he worked extensively there, in Milan, and in Genoa, primarily for the Sforza Dukes of Milan. He returned to Brescia c1489–90.

Foppa was the most important painter of the Milanese School before Leonardo da Vinci. Traces of late Gothic in his early style soon yielded to the influence of Giovanni Bellini and Mantegna. His paintings, often bathed in silvery-gray light, tend to have a rather coarse finish. An example is the *Virgin and Child with Saints* (1485; Pinacoteca di Brera, Milan).

## Forain Jean-Louis 1852–1931

The French painter and illustrator Jean-Louis Forain was born at Reims. He had little formal training, but by the late 1870s he was painting in a style derived from Edouard Manet and Edgar Degas. He exhibited with the Impressionists, mostly interior scenes, for instance of backstage at the Opera. His work displayed sharp observation of modern life in Paris. He is now remembered less for his painting than for his illustrations in the weekly press, where his incipient satirical bent found freer rein. His output of caricatures was considerable; but he continued to paint, and some of his courtroom scenes recall Daumier's caustic comments on the legal profession.

## Foster Norman 1935–

The British architect Norman Foster is one of the leading exponents of "hi-tech" architecture, an approach in which technology, instead of being hidden or disguised, is made explicit, often with structure and services being exposed. He studied at the universities of Manchester and Yale, and in the early 1960s formed a design partnership with Richard Rogers (and their wives) known as Team 4, which ended in 1967. One of his first outstanding buildings was the Sainsbury Centre for the Visual Arts, Norwich University (1976–78), a work uncompromising in its use of modern materials and engineering, and typical of Foster in its elegant detail and innovative use of space and light (for example, electronic shutters in the roof, subtly controlling the flow of daylight). His skillful use of technology in determining form can also be seen in his best-known building, the Hong Kong and Shanghai Bank, Hong Kong (1979–85), and in the Stansted Airport Terminal, Essex, England. Since 1988 Foster has been employed on the redevelopment of a site around Kings Cross railroad station in central London.

## Fouquet Jean c1420–c80

Jean Fouquet was born in Tours. Although he is the principal French painter of the 15th century, little is known of his initiation into the craft. By 1447 he was certainly in Rome, where he painted a portrait of Pope Eugenius IV with his nephews—a privilege that would only have been bestowed on a painter of some distinction. The portrait, now lost, attracted the praise of the theorist Filarete, whose opinion remains on record. Fouquet appears to have been familiar with Rome. He also knew Paris and may have studied there though much of his working life was spent in the provinces. In his miniatures, he has depicted monuments of both these cities.

On his return to Tours in 1447 he was taken under royal patronage by Charles VII—patronage that was extended after 1461 by Louis XI. Of more immediate importance was his acquaintance with Étienne Chevalier, diplomat, treasurer of France, and friend of both kings. For Chevalier, Fouquet painted the miniatures of the magnificent *Hours of Étienne Chevalier*; 13 of these illustrations and the text have been lost, but the remaining 47 miniatures constitute Fouquet's finest work. (Forty of the miniatures are in the Musée Condé, Chantilly, two are in the Louvre, Paris, one is in the British Library, London, and the other four are in private collections.) On the death of Chevalier's wife, Cathérine Budé, in 1452, Fouquet was commissioned to paint the diptych for her tomb in Notre-Dame de Melun; Chevalier himself appears as donor, together with St Stephen. Fouquet's *Portrait of Charles VII* (Louvre, Paris) and his decoration of the church of Notre-Dame-la-Riche in Tours date from the same very productive period, as do the miniatures for Boccaccio's *Les Cas des Nobles Hommes et Femmes Malheureuses* painted for Laurens Gyrard (1458; Staatsbibliothek, Munich).

Jean Fouquet (attrib.): Portrait of a Man; panel; 47×40cm (18×16in); 1456. Liechtenstein'sche Fürstliche Sammlungen, Vienna

Until 1458 Fouquet's style is consistent, and suggests some slight debt to Fra Angelico. Single figures or groups offer a point of focus, in architectural settings of the utmost solidity, sometimes with considerable fidelity to recognizable models. In the few paintings from the *Hours of Étienne Chevalier* where crowds are portrayed, there is always a figure that provides a center of attention.

After 1458 Fouquet's work shows evidence of a greater dispersion of subject matter, concern with altogether less intimate scenes, and an increasing regard for the landscapes of France. The *Chronicles of the Kings of France* (1458; Bibliothèque Nationale, Paris) abandoned a relatively static style for the dynamic possibilities of the battlefield. This new dynamism is also seen in the illustrations to the *Jewish Antiquities* of Josephus (1470–6; Bibliothèque Nationale, Paris) painted for Jacques d'Armagnac, Duke of Nemours.

Fouquet's versatility was considerable: his portraits *Charles VII* and *Guillaume Juvénal des Ursins* (Louvre, Paris), and his self-portrait, demonstrate his sensitivity to human features. His style as a miniature painter shows constant evolution, and his influence continued long after his death. The work at Notre-Dame-la-Riche and at Nouans suggests ability in a larger dimension. The overall effect of his achievement was to release French painting from the last ties of a persistent and belated Gothicism.

## Fragonard Jean-Honoré
### 1732–1806

Jean-Honoré Fragonard was the last of the French Rococo painters. He outlived the movement, and died poor and unnoticed during the heyday of Neoclassicism. He was born at Grasse in Provence, but his family moved to Paris before Fragonard was 10 years old. He trained at first under Chardin, leaving after only 6 months to work in Boucher's studio.

In 1751, Fragonard became the pupil of François Boucher, who was at the height of his career; Fragonard must have learned his fluent handling of paint, speed of execution, and pure professionalism from the elder painter. More important, he may have learned how to draw; for under Boucher, superb academic drawings formed the backbone of studio production. Fragonard's graphic style is unlike his master's, however, being more vivacious and independent. In many of his smaller oil paintings and sketches the paint is literally drawn on with a brush.

Fragonard was something of a prodigy. He won the highly coveted Prix de Rome at his first attempt in 1752, but instead of leaving France immediately he went to the École des Élèves Protégés to study under Carle van Loo. Fragonard had won the prize for his painting *Jeroboam Sacrificing to the Idols* (1752; École des Beaux-Arts, Paris), an Old Testament subject that gave the artist scope to work in the grand style. It is a skillful painting with tension created by two groups of dramatically opposed figures. This was not the sort of work that Boucher produced. Fragonard had based his work on the style of the contemporary Venetian history painter Giovanni Battista Pittoni, simplifying the Venetian's crowded compositions and gaining an increased intensity.

Fragonard made his mark with the *Jeroboam*, and to his peers and contemporaries he seemed destined for great things. He studied under van Loo for three years, then in 1756 left Paris for the French Academy in Rome. Whatever he learned and however much he studied in Rome, Fragonard was a disappointment to his teachers. Natoire, the Director of the French Academy, accused him of not being the painter of the *Jeroboam;* he criticized his pupil's carelessness and lack of fire.

Jean-Honoré Fragonard: The Swing; oil on canvas; 81×65cm (32×26in); 1767. Wallace Collection, London

Perhaps not surprisingly, very few paintings are known from his time in Rome. In Paris his drawings were more admired than his paintings.

Although Fragonard may not have been a model pupil at the Academy, his Italian sojourn was not wasted. His very individual response to Italian art may have raised eyebrows at the French Academy; for Fragonard admired not the works of Raphael and the Antique, but the modern artists Pietro da Cortona, Solimena, and Giambattista Tiepolo. Fragonard was to become the greatest of late French Rococo painters; he was sensible to study at first-hand works by the founders of the movement. Italy to Fragonard meant Italian landscape as well as art, in particular the gardens of the Villa d'Este at Tivoli.

Although landscape was never a major part of his output in the way that it was with his English contemporary Gainsborough, his response to it was highly unusual. Trees and clouds have a pulsating life of their own, far more intensely alive then the little manikin figures that inhabit their world. Landscape, especially in Fragonard's drawing, is a natural force, never a pretty back-cloth to a *fête galante*. This was Fragonard's own discovery, which he did not share even with his close friend and colleague Hubert Robert. It is a facet of his art that seems closer to Romantic painting of the 19th century than to the Rococo. At Tivoli, Fragonard worked with Robert under their patron the Abbé de Saint-Non. It was with Saint-Non that Fragonard visited Naples and Venice, and with whom he made his long leisurely journey back to Paris, visiting and revisiting the towns and cities of northern Italy.

Fragonard returned to Paris in 1761. He may then have worked for art dealers—producing landscapes in the style of Ruisdael and Castiglione, painting a series of character heads in the manner of Rembrandt and Tiepolo, and probably even producing fakes. In 1765 he exhibited *Coresus and Callirrhoé* (Louvre, Paris) at the Salon; the picture brought his name back into the public eye and established him as the master of contemporary history painting. This was a role Fragonard was unwilling to accept, for he very soon turned his back on the Salon, exhibiting there for the last time in 1767. He became a private painter, valuing his independence from the art establishment as much as many painters do today.

A work produced c1768 or 1769 has the type of subject matter that Fragonard was often to choose during the years that followed his break with the Salon. The commission for *The Swing* (*L'Escarpolette*, 1767; Wallace Collection, London) was originally given by the Baron de Saint-Julien to the religious painter Doyen. The patron asked Doyen to paint his mistress on a swing with a bishop pushing her; the painter was instructed to place him, Saint-Julien, in a good position to see her pretty legs. Doyen was scandalized and rejected the commission, but suggested Fragonard's name.

The delightful painting that resulted must have pleased the Baron, for he later owned a similar erotic painting by Fragonard. The surface of *The Swing* is very carefully worked, in Fragonard's finished rather than freely sketched manner. The same is true of the canvases he painted for Madame du Barry a few years later at the beginning of the 1770s. *The Progress of Love* (1771–2; Frick Collection, New York) a set of four amorous scenes, is Fragonard's masterpiece. Indeed these are among the greatest decorations of any age. Amusing and charming, they are not frivolous—though Madame du Barry may have believed them to be so when she rejected them for her Neoclassical pavilion at Louveciennes.

In *The Progress of Love* the lovers make their advances and form their alliances against an enchanted background where statues and landscape are alive, encouraging and protecting them. Whatever the reasons for Madame du Barry's action (and it was something that Fragonard refused to discuss), her rejection of the paintings was evidence of a break with Rococo taste well over a decade before the political revolution took over.

In 1789, the Revolution brought about an abrupt change of patronage. Until that year Fragonard still had plenty of patrons, indeed he was extremely active. After 1789 his fortunes declined, and it was only through the help of Jacques-Louis David that he managed to obtain the administrative posts that provided his inadequate income. His later works may have been adapted for the change in artistic climate; erotic girls and cherubs became contented mothers and children, and the settings of his paintings were more likely to be the hearth and the classroom than the bedroom.

Outliving his era, Fragonard left no successors; it was not until with Renoir that France produced an artist of similar vitality, decorativeness, and originality.

**Further reading.** Ashton, D. *Fragonard in the Universe of Painting*, Washington, D.C. (1988). Goncourt, E. and J. de *French Eighteenth-Century Painters*, Oxford (1981). Nolhac, P. de *J.-H. Fragonard, 1732–1806*, Paris (1906 and 1931). Wildenstein, G. *The Paintings of Fragonard*, London (1960).

## Francesco di Giorgio Martini
1439–1502

Francesco di Giorgio Martini was an Italian artist of the Sienese school. He was active chiefly as an architect, although his first documented work is a carved wooden figure of *St John the Baptist* paid for in 1464 (Pinacoteca Nazionale, Siena). In the 1470s he worked for Federico da Montefeltro at Urbino, where he was responsible for the completion of work in the Ducal Palace begun by Luciano Laurana (*ob.* 1479).

The most important of Francesco's surviving architectural projects is the church of S. Maria del Calcinaio outside Cortona (1484–5) which is a model of early Renaissance purity. His treatise on architecture (c1500) shows an indebtedness to Alberti but is more practical in approach. Francesco executed small-scale sculptural works throughout his life, particularly in bronze. There are authenticated paintings by him in Siena, showing a tender linearity akin to Botticelli.

## Francia Francesco c1450–1517

Francesco Francia was a Bolognese goldsmith and painter. He matriculated in the goldsmiths' guild in 1482. Save for some medals and coins nothing of this side of his activities remains. First recorded as a painter in 1486, he seems to have specialized in devotional Madonnas and altarpieces. An example is *The Adoration* (1499; Pinacoteca Nazionale, Bologna). About 30 of these altarpieces survive, many signed. Highly esteemed by his contemporaries, Francia avoided the Ferrarese style, which dominated the Bolognese art of his day, by adopting the softer, mellower forms of Perugino. Typical of his paintings are the gentle, rather wistful facial expressions of his figures, and the pleasing but simple landscape backgrounds.

Francesco di Giorgio Martini: The Nativity; detail; panel; c1486–94. S. Domenico, Siena

## Francis Sam 1923–1994

Sam Francis is a second generation Californian Abstract Expressionist who was based in Paris from 1950 to 1961. During the 1950s his work was better known in Europe than that of American painters like Pollock and Rothko; and Francis' association with Parisian *Art Informel* led to an erroneous conclusion that New York School painting was part of an international movement. Francis' own painting moved from a dense overall Abstract Expressionist technique as in *Blue Black* (oil; 1952; Albright-Knox Art Gallery, Buffalo), to the creation of a neutral center or large areas of dusty canvas enlivened by peripheral action as in *Abstraction* (oil; 1959; Whitney Museum of American Art, New York) which presages "color-field" painting.

## Francken family
16th and 17th centuries

The Francken were a family of 14 painters active mainly at Antwerp over five generations. In the second generation Hieronymus I (1540–1610), Frans I (1542–1616), and Ambrosius I (1544–1618) accepted the Venetianizing Mannerism of Maerten de Vos, turning in middle life to a harsh, classicizing formality (examples in the Royal Museum of Fine Arts, Antwerp).

Frans II (1581–1642), in the third generation, was the most widely known of the family. He combed mythology, history, and the Bible for subjects for small genre pictures, prolifically and repetitively produced, apparently for collectors of middle rank. Frans Francken made use of opulent and exotic accessories in a manner reminiscent of Lastman and Vignon. His figures have a pert, theatrical elegance; later they became rounder, and blander in color, under the influence of Rubens. Francken is represented in many of the older collections in northern and central Europe such as the Rijksmuseum, Amsterdam.

## Frankenthaler Helen 1928–

The American artist Helen Frankenthaler is one of the most original and consistent of the painters who matured in the 1950s after the main achievements of the Abstract Expressionists. Frankenthaler was

Sam Francis: Around the Blues; oil and acrylic on canvas; 43×76cm (108×192in); 1957 and 1962. Tate Gallery, London

Helen Frankenthaler: Mountains and Sea; detail; oil on canvas; full size 220×298cm (87×117in); 1952. Private collection, on loan to the National Gallery of Art, Washington, D.C.

helped by Meyer Shapiro, Clement Greenberg, and Hans Hoffman to an appreciation of recent events in American painting, in particular to the aims and techniques of Jackson Pollock and Arshile Gorky. Frankenthaler's own painting was from the outset more "open" than that of the Abstract Expressionists. As early as 1952 in *Mountains and Sea* (private collection) she developed a "soak-stain" technique, applying thin washes of paint in lyrical and carefully articulated areas on a relatively empty canvas. The technique was later used extensively by Kenneth Noland and Morris Louis.

**Further reading.** Baro, G. "The Achievement of Helen Frankenthaler", *Art International*, Zurich (September 1967). Rose, B. *Frankenthaler*, New York (1972).

## Freud Lucian 1922–

Born in Berlin, the British artist Lucian Freud, grandson of Sigmund Freud, came to England in the early 1930s, and in the 1940s studied briefly at the East Anglian School of Drawing and Painting. Freud's early works—he has concentrated largely on portraits of friends and relatives throughout his career—are in a taut, linear style, his sitters remote and ambiguous, their eyes and lips exaggerated: see *Girl with a Kitten* (1947; British Council). By the late 1950s, however, he had evolved a far more painterly style, his subjects, often nudes of a disturbing frankness and vulnerability, acquiring an intense physical presence that deepens their emotional remoteness. For Freud, this physicality is intimately linked with the act of painting: "As far as I am concerned the paint *is* the person. I want it to work for me just as flesh does." *Night Portrait* (1985–86; Smithsonian Institution, Washington, D.C.) is typical.

**Further reading.** Gowing, L. *Lucian Freud*, London (1982).

## Friedrich Caspar David
### 1774–1840

Caspar David Friedrich was the leading landscape painter in Germany during the Romantic era. His views of the desolate coastlands of his native Pomerania and of the mountainous regions of central Europe combine a careful observation of natural features with a deep sense of the spiritual.

Friedrich's pantheistic approach to landscape, shared by so many writers and painters of his generation, seems to have derived from his home background. The son of a prosperous soap-boiler and candlemaker in the Baltic harbor town of Greifswald, he was taught from 1790 to 1794 by J.G. Quistorp, the drawing master

at the local university. Through Quistorp he came into contact with the poet and pastor L.T. Kosegarten, a writer who combined the nature sentiment of J.-J. Rousseau and such English poets as Thomson and Gray with a traditional north German pietism.

In 1794 Friedrich went to study at the leading art academy of northern Europe, the Copenhagen Academy. From such teachers as Jens Juel and Christian Lorentzen he learned the current modes of picturesque local views and sublime stormy and mountainous scenes. A series of exquisite watercolors of the parklands around Copenhagen—notably the *Landscape with a Pavilion* (1795; Hamburger Kunsthalle, Hamburg)—show how fully he mastered his teachers' use of nature to convey sentimental moods. At the same time his study in the drawing classes of the Academy developed the habit of using a fine outline for describing the forms of his pictures. This practice, which remained with him throughout his life, enabled him to achieve great precision in the balancing of his compositions.

In 1798 Friedrich moved to Dresden. The town was then a leading art center, because of both its superb gallery and the local landscape school that had grown up in emulation of the Dutch 17th-century masters. He was to remain there for the rest of his life, apart from a number of return visits to Pomerania (the longest being for 18 months in 1801–2) and frequent tours of the Harz, the Riesengebirge, and other scenic areas in central Europe.

Friedrich first built a reputation as a painter of views of his Baltic homeland. These were executed for the most part in sepia, a monochrome technique that gave full scope for the Neoclassical emphasis on form. While specializing in this method, Friedrich developed a careful control of lighting effects, most effective for misty and nocturnal scenes, as in *View of Arkona with Rising Moon* (1806; Graphische Sammlung Albertina, Vienna).

At the same time Friedrich began to invest his landscapes with the religious and national themes made topical in Dresden by such Romantic writers and critics as Ludwig Tieck and the Schlegel brothers. This can be seen in the two sepias that were awarded a prize by Goethe at the Weimar exhibition of 1805, *Summer Landscape with a Dead Oak* and *Pilgrimage at Sunrise* (Schlossmuseum, Staatliche

Caspar David Friedrich: Stages of Life; oil on canvas; 73×94cm (29×37in); c1834. Museum der Bildenden Künste, Leipzig

Kunstsammlungen, Weimar). The latter is particularly explicit in its imagery, showing a procession bearing a monstrance towards a wayside cross and passing between two trees which lean together in the form of a Gothic arch. Despite this interweaving of religion and nature, the scene was sufficiently conventional in its presentation for Goethe, who was deeply suspicious of the new movement, to concentrate on praising its naturalism and technical expertise.

It was not possible, however, to ignore the spiritual nature of the work that caused a sensation three years later, *The Cross in the Mountains* (1808; Gemäldegalerie Alte Meister, Dresden). Intended as an altarpiece for a private chapel, it took the remarkable step of presenting the Christian faith in terms of pure landscape. Even more striking were the means by which the artist conveyed his message, for he discarded the conventions of landscape composition to concentrate upon the silhouette of the triangular top of a mountain against the setting sun. Such radicalism could also

be found in the two works he exhibited in Berlin in 1810, which were bought by the Prussian Crown Prince: *Abbey in the Oakwoods* and *Monk by the Sea* (Schloss Charlottenburg, Berlin). The latter conveyed the sense of isolation with unprecedented intensity.

It is a mark of Friedrich's increasing self-confidence and reputation that these large works, like the majority of his pictures after 1807, were painted in oil. The growing nationalist movement in Germany that followed on the Napoleonic invasions of 1806 also favored his art, with its emphasis on northern spirituality. Friedrich was in fact an ardent nationalist himself, and celebrated the defeat of the French in 1814 with a number of patriotic landscapes. One of these shows a French dragoon lost in a Germanic forest of firs (private collection).

After the Napoleonic Wars Friedrich's life became more settled. In 1816 he was elected to the Dresden Academy, and in 1818 he married a local girl, Caroline Bommer. At the same time he began to

abandon his repertoire of monks, ruins, and other theatrical motifs in favor of more contemporary themes. Under the influence of the Norwegian painter Dahl, who settled in Dresden in 1819, his painting manner became more spontaneous, and he adopted the fresh greens and blues associated with naturalism. While strongly opposed to the scientific analysis of natural phenomena (he refused to assist Goethe in his study of cloud formations), Friedrich followed Dahl in making *plein air* oil sketches at this time (for example, *Evening*, 1824; Städtisches Kunsthalle, Mannheim).

Despite these changes, Friedrich did not abandon the spiritual approach to landscape. Such topical themes as the *Arctic Shipwreck* (1824; Hamburger Kunsthalle, Hamburg), in which a ship is crushed to pieces beneath an ice-floe, were every bit as symbolic as his earlier more arcane images. A recurrent motif in his pictures during the 1820s was the inclusion of figures, viewed from behind, contemplating the landscape (for example, *Moonrise over the Sea*,

1822; Nationalgalerie, Berlin). Such works emphasized the importance of the individual response to nature. It was this attitude—so evident in a series of critical aphorisms that he wrote c1830—that made him increasingly unpopular with the younger generation.

Friedrich was an isolated, lonely figure whose fatalism has often been seen as the outcome of a personal melancholia. However, his art has a universal dimension, which made him a source of inspiration for later Symbolist painters.

**Further reading.** Börsche-Supan, H. *Caspar David Friedrich*, London and Munich (1974). Sumowski, W. *Caspar David Friedrich Studien*, Wiesbaden (1970).

## Froment Nicolas c1435–c86

Born in Uzès, the Provençal artist Nicolas Froment was the last great painter of the Avignon School. His work displayed a

Nicolas Froment: center panel of The Burning Bush triptych; height 410cm (161in); 1476. Cathedral of the Holy Savior, Aix-en-Provence

taste for distortion and the grotesque which was not typical of 15th-century Provençal painting. For this reason his style can be interpreted in two different ways. He may have been an eccentric individualist, but within the Provençal tradition, or he may have been a decadent artist subject to Flemish or German influence. His earliest known work, the triptych of *The Raising of Lazarus* (Uffizi, Florence), dates from 1461; his masterpiece is the highly complex and symbolic triptych of *The Burning Bush* (1476) in the Cathedral of the Holy Savior, Aix-en-Provence.

## Fry Roger 1866–1934

The English painter Roger Fry was also an important art critic and theorist. He read for a science degree at Cambridge between 1885 and 1888. During these years he began to paint and to study the history of Italian painting with J.H. Middleton. In 1888 he studied painting with Francis Bate, a member of the New English Art Club, and made his first trip to Italy in 1891. In 1894 he began giving University Extension lectures on the Italian Renaissance. From 1900 onwards he wrote articles and reviewed exhibitions for *Athenaeum*, *The Monthly Review*, and *The Burlington Magazine*.

Roger Fry was Curator of Painting at the Metropolitan Museum in New York from 1905 to 1910. In December 1910 he arranged the exhibition "Manet and the Post-Impressionists" at the Grafton Galleries, London, which established his reputation as an advocate of modern painting. In 1912 he organized the "Exposition de Quelques Indépendants Anglais" in Paris and the "Second Post-Impressionist Exhibition of English, French and Russian Artists" at the Grafton Galleries.

In 1913 Fry opened the Omega Workshops Ltd; it involved such artists as Duncan Grant, Vanessa Bell, and Wyndham Lewis—until its closure in 1919. Fry was given a retrospective exhibition at the London Artist's Association in 1931 and he gave three highly successful series of lectures in 1927, 1932, and 1934, at the Queen's Hall, London. These were sponsored by the National Art Collections Fund. Fry was made Slade Professor of Fine Art at Cambridge in 1933. He published numerous articles and books of art criticism and aesthetic theory, among them *Giovanni Bellini* (1899), *Vision and Design* (1920), *Transformations* (1926), *Cézanne: A Study of his Development* (1927), and *Henri Matisse* (1930).

Fry's own painting (for example *White Road with Farm*, c1912; Scottish National Gallery of Modern Art, Edinburgh) was very important to him; but it is overshadowed by his importance as an exhibition organizer, writer, and lecturer on aesthetics and the history of art. By 1904 Fry was recognized for his study of the Old Masters, particularly for his interest in the Italian Primitives. But by 1910 he had become known as an advocate of the modern movement.

Most important to Fry's theories was the role of plastic values. It was this that led him to the "discovery" of Cézanne in 1906 and the organization of the "Manet and the Post-Impressionists" exhibition in 1910. The first English critic to acknowledge Cézanne's importance, Fry was much criticized for his seeming abandonment of the Old Masters. However it was his ability to recognize the formal virtues of the new art, and to see the continuity of these same virtues down the ages, that led him to his own oversimplification, that the essence of the art lay in *disegno*, in its formal values.

After 1920 Fry was not closely concerned with avant-garde art, though he was still considered a spokesman for modern French painting. He will be best remembered for his involvement with the major artistic endeavors of the 1910s, for the critical recognition in England of the importance of French and British modern painting, and for his writings, which are rich in insight into individual works of art.

**Further reading.** Bell, Q. *Roger Fry*, Leeds (1964). Fry, R. *Vision and Design*, London (1957). Shone, R. *Bloomsbury Portraits*, Oxford (1975). Woolf, V. *Roger Fry*, London (1957).

## Fu Pao-shih 1904–65

Fu Pao-shih was born in Kiangsi and spent much of his life in east-central China. He went to Japan for a few years from 1935 onwards, to study in the Imperial Academy. An academically trained painter, he seems to have been a follower of Shih T'ao; like that 17th-century master, he wrote a great deal about the theory and philosophy of painting. Fu became professor of painting at the National Central

Roger Fry: The Barn; oil on canvas; 25×36cm (10×14in); c1916. Private collection

University, and at the time of his death was Principal of the Nanking Academy of Art.

Fu Pao-shih's own painting is in various styles, ranging from an archaistic figure-painting of beauties to a romantic painting of landscape. He built upon Shih T'ao's experiments with color and texture, following a Japanese interest in the actual surface of the paper. Using a coarse fiber paper, Fu used to scuff up the surface, achieving some very beautiful effects. He became one of the leading painters of the mid 20th century, and has had great influence over his contemporaries and students. He and Kuan San-yueh collaborated on some of the major paintings for the new Chinese State after Liberation (1949), notably the large wall painting in the Hall of the People, Peking, depicting the sun rising over the eastern hills.

## Fuseli John Henry 1741–1825

John Henry Fuseli (Johann Heinrich Fussli) was born into a family of distinguished Zurich intellectuals and artists. In 1761 he was ordained a Zwinglian minister after studying with the influential literary critics J.J. Breitinger and J.J. Bodmer. It was Bodmer who introduced him to the writings of Milton and Shakespeare and who supported his early interest in art. In 1764 he went to London where he worked as an illustrator and published an English translation of Winckelmann's *Gedanken* (*Reflections...*; 1765). Determined to become a history painter, he was encouraged by Reynolds to study in Italy,

and to this end he departed for Rome in 1769. His years in Rome, from 1770 to 1778, influenced him profoundly. He soon found himself at the center of a talented group of like-minded English and continental artists which included Alexander Runciman, Johan Tobias Sergel, and Nicolai Abildgaard. In addition to the Antique, Fuseli studied carefully the works of Michelangelo and certain Mannerists,

and from these diverse sources forged a distinctive personal style.

In 1779 Fuseli returned to London and began exhibiting history paintings regularly at the Royal Academy. His picture *The Nightmare* (1782; Tate Gallery, London) was an immediate success, and in 1786 he was commissioned to paint nine illustrations for Boydell's Shakespeare Gallery (opened 1789). In 1800 he exhibited 47 paintings of subjects from Milton which had occupied him during the 1790s. He became a member of the Royal Academy in 1799, Professor of Painting in 1800, and Keeper in 1804. His important contributions to the literature and theory of art included his series of lectures to the students of the Royal Academy and his additions to *Pilkington's Lives of the Artists* (1805).

The characteristics of Fuseli's mature style were well defined before his departure from Italy. They included dramatic foreshortening of figures, strong light–shade contrasts, extravagant gestures and distortions of scale, and a preference for new, often obscure, literary subjects which stressed the demonic side of human nature. In his works, the aesthetic of the Sublime was given its most extreme visual articulation.

John Henry Fuseli: The Nightmare; canvas; 101×127cm (40×50in); 1782. Detroit Institute of Arts

# G

## Gabo Naum 1890–1977

The Russian sculptor and painter Naum Gabo was born in Briansk. He spent the years 1910 to 1914 studying natural science in Munich; his only contact with the fine arts during this period came through attendance at Heinrich Wölfflin's lectures in art history. In 1913 and 1914 he made frequent trips to Paris where his brother Antoine Pevsner was working as a painter. When the First World War began he went to Scandinavia; in 1915 his brother joined him in Oslo.

There he made his first sculptures, a series of heads which rejected the use of solid volumes, building up forms instead from a series of curved planes. Archipenko's constructed figures certainly influenced him, but unlike Archipenko he did not use a painterly treatment to compensate for the lack of solid modeling. Gabo's monochrome works boldly postulated the possibility of sculpture in which space takes precedence over mass.

After the Revolution of 1917 both Gabo and Pevsner returned to Russia. In 1920 they published the *Realistic Manifesto*, actually written entirely by Gabo, to accompany an outdoor exhibition of their work in Moscow. It proclaimed the failure of Cubism and Futurism to create an art appropriate to the new civilization arising out of the Revolution. Rejecting applied color as being an "idealizing agent", it advocated "freeing the volume of mass", justifying this by reference to the principles of engineering. The works that followed this manifesto were totally Abstract and used thin planes of plastic, wood and glass to define space, while employing transparent materials to render the structure clear to the spectator.

While sharing the Constructivists' concerns, Gabo disagreed with Tatlin and Rodchenko's view that in a Socialist state pure art was a redundant luxury, and that the artist should devote himself to tasks of direct practical value. He believed that to be of the greatest value to society the artist should keep his independence. In 1922, aware that the more narrowly utilitarian view of art prevailed, he left Russia for Berlin. Moving to Paris in 1932, he joined the international *Abstraction-Création* group. In 1935 he visited England, where

Naum Gabo: Linear Construction no. 2; plexiglass and nylon thread; 114×84×84cm (45×33×33in); 1968–9. Tate Gallery, London

his presence was to stimulate the growing interest in Abstract art whose adherents included Ben Nicholson and Barbara Hepworth. In 1937 he co-edited *Circle*, a publication in which advanced architects and Abstract artists sought to explain their ideas to a wider public.

At that time a new element entered his work, and space was defined by line as well as surface. This was achieved by incised lines across the surface of transparent perspex, and later by stretching taut steel or plastic threads across an overall framework. This defined space with the

minimum of volume, and built a three-dimensional void logically from an outline in space. In 1946 Gabo moved to New York. During the 1950s he was at last able to realize his ideas on a monumental scale, through commissions such as that for the sculpture outside the Bijenkorf building in Rotterdam in 1957.

**Further reading.** Pevsner, A. *A Biographical Sketch of my Brothers, Naum Gabo and Antione Pevsner*, Amsterdam (1964). Read, H. and Martin, L. *Naum Gabo*, Cambridge, Mass. and London (1964).

Jacques-Ange Gabriel: the Petit Trianon, Versailles; 1763–9.

# Gabriel Jacques-Ange 1698–1782

Jacques-Ange Gabriel was the greatest French architect of the 18th century and a talented decorative draftsman. He was the pupil and colleague of his father, Jacques Gabriel (1667–1742), also known as Gabriel Père, from whom he took over the reconstruction of the Royal Palace at Fontainebleau in 1742.

At the age of 30 he was made *Contrôleur-Général des Bâtiments du Roi* and a member of the Académie Royale. He trained in Paris, never went to Italy, and built almost exclusively for Louis XV and his mistress, Madame de Pompadour. At first this restricted his work to additions or alterations to Royal Palaces, but he was lucky in that the second half of the King's reign saw a great increase in public building.

From 1755 to 1775 he laid out the Place Louis XV in Paris (now the Place de la Concorde). His Hotel de Crillon (1757–75) and Gardemeuble (1758–66, now the Ministry of Marine) echo the Louvre Colonnade by Perrault (begun 1667), thus bypassing Rococo architecture in favor of the French classical tradition of François Mansart (1598–1666).

At the École Militaire (begun 1751) and the perfectly cubic Petit Trianon, Versailles (1763–9), he worked in a more mixed spirit, combining elements of Antiquity (which was increasingly popular in the 1760s) and Palladianism.

His blend of elegance and restraint determined the style of official architecture under Louis XV. The "style Gabriel" was widely imitated, influencing among others the Neoclassical architect Claude-Nicolas Ledoux (1736–1806) in his early designs.

# Gaddi family 14th century

The Gaddi were a family of Florentine painters, the greatest being Taddeo Gaddi (1300–66). Taddeo's father Gaddo Gaddi (*fl. c*1308–30) was a painter and mosaicist, and traditionally the author of some of the surviving work in the Cathedral and the Baptistry in Florence. None of his work is now known with certainty.

Taddeo Gaddi was Giotto's pupil and assistant for 24 years. His first independent work dates from the mid 1320s, a *Madonna and Child* in S. Francesco, Castelfiorentino. Not surprisingly it is a highly individual version of Giotto's *Ognissanti Madonna* (Uffizi, Florence). Taddeo's

Taddeo Gaddi: the Annunciation to the Shepherds; fresco; 1332–8. Baroncelli Chapel, S. Croce, Florence

Agnolo Gaddi: The Legend of the Holy Cross; fresco series; c1380. S. Croce, Florence

**Gaibano** Giovanni *fl.* 1253–93

Giovanni Gaibano was an Italian miniaturist who worked a great deal in Padua. First heard of in 1253 near Ferrara, he is known chiefly for his illuminated Epistolary in the Chapter Library of Padua Cathedral (*c*1260). One of the miniatures (f. 98v.) probably shows Giovanni himself at work on the book. He died in 1293.

The Padua Epistolary is illustrated with 16 full-page miniatures on a gold ground. These show scenes relating to the chief festivals of the Christian year, such as the Nativity and the Epiphany. As so often with miniatures of this date, they are surprisingly well-preserved; the bright blues, reds, and greens, with white detail, give life to a style of illumination which is of high quality, if unadventurous.

**Gainsborough** Thomas 1727–88

The English painter and landscape draftsman Thomas Gainsborough was born at Sudbury in Suffolk. About 1740 he went to London where he trained with Gravelot; later he assisted Francis Hayman with the painted decorations at Vauxhall Gardens. During his years in London he also studied the paintings of the 17th-century Dutch landscapists, in particular Wynants and Jacob Ruisdael. He contributed his most important early landscape, *The Charterhouse*, to the Foundling Hospital, London in 1748. He returned to Suffolk and by 1752 was settled in Ipswich, where he painted landscapes while supporting his family by portraiture. His early portraits, of which *Mr and Mrs Andrews* (1748/9; National Gallery, London) is the most remarkable example, feature small figures casually disposed in landscape settings and are close in style to the contemporary conversation pieces by Hayman. His approach to landscape during this period was an ornamental blend of French and Dutch influences enriched by sensitive observations of light effects and of naturalistic detail. This is seen in such pictures as the so-called *Gainsborough's Forest* (*Cornard Wood*; 1748; National Gallery, London) and *River Scene with Figures* (*c*1747; National Gallery of Scotland, Edinburgh).

Upon moving to Bath in 1759, Gainsborough rapidly established a fashionable portrait practice. He began painting on life scale, at first retaining the informal poses of his Ipswich style, but gradually introducing a more conventional elegance in emulation of van Dyck. Among the mas-

fresco decoration of the Baroncelli Chapel, S. Croce, Florence, with *The Life of the Virgin*, probably dates from 1328 to 1330. As the altarpiece of the chapel is signed by Giotto (a workshop product) it seems possible that Taddeo carried out the frescoes according to ideas Giotto left behind when he went to Naples in 1329. There are several major innovations in the chapel, including some *trompe-l'oeil* still-life cupboards, and a *nocturne* scene of the Annunciation to the Shepherds. A rare survival from this period is Taddeo's drawing on paper for *The Presentation of the Virgin* (Louvre, Paris).

All his work is most distinctive, and shows a deep understanding of Giotto together with a feeling for beautiful color,

as is clearly seen in the tiny, delicate Franciscan Scenes on 29 cupboard door panels (Galleria dell'Accademia, Florence). His *Last Supper* in the Refectory of S. Croce is extraordinarily realistic and foreshadows 15th-century frescoes of the same subject.

Taddeo was an influential artist and teacher; among his pupils were his three painter sons, Giovanni, Niccolò, and Agnolo, of whom Agnolo (*c*1350–96) is the most important. He developed even further his father's love of color. Some idea of his contemporary standing as an artist can be gained from his commission to decorate the main chapel behind the high altar in S. Croce, with *The Legend of the Holy Cross* (*c*1380).

Thomas Gainsborough: River Landscape with Figures in a Boat; oil on canvas; 119×168cm (47×66in); c1768–70. Philadelphia Museum of Art

terpieces of the Bath period are *Mary, Countess Howe* (c1765; Kenwood, The Iveagh Bequest, London); *Jonathan Buttall* (known as *The Blue Boy*, 1770; Huntington Library and Art Gallery, San Marino); and *Elizabeth and Mary Linley* (1772; Dulwich College Picture Gallery, London). He continued to paint landscapes in the picturesque vein, peopling his woodlands with an increasingly idealized peasantry. As lyrical evocations of an idyllic world, such paintings as *Return from Market* (1767–8; Toledo Museum of Art, Toledo, Ohio) and *The Harvest Wagon* (1767; Barber Institute of Fine Arts, Birmingham) are rivaled in the 18th century only by the landscape masterpieces of Boucher.

Gainsborough was a founder member of the Royal Academy in 1768. He moved to London in 1774, and became the favorite painter of the royal family soon afterwards. He had a series of quarrels with the Academy, and after 1784 exhibited only in his own studio. From the late 1770s, "fancy pictures" of beggar children in rustic settings began to figure more prominently in his work. He experimented with techniques of transparency painting, mixed media drawing, and printmaking, as well as new subject matter, including historical scenes and seascapes. His portrait style became increasingly impressionistic, while his late landscapes reveal great stylis-tic diversity and a new poetic force.

In the history of Western painting, Gainsborough ranks with the greatest technicians and colorists. His approach to art combined empiricism and imagination, and he generally shunned the intellectual-ism of contemporary academic theory. His influence on English portraiture was small in comparison to that of his rival, Reynolds; but his importance to subsequent genre and landscape painting in England was considerable.

**Further reading.** Hayes, J. *The Drawings of Thomas Gainsborough* (2 vols.), London and New Haven (1970). Waterhouse, E. *Gainsborough*, London (1958).

## Galilei Alessandro 1691–1737

Alessandro Galilei was an Italian architect. Leaving his native Florence in 1714, he spent five years in England, before returning home to become court architect to the Medici. The Florentine Pope Clement XII called Galilei to Rome in 1730.

He won the competition (1732) for the facade of S. Giovanni in Laterano, Rome (completed 1736). The acceptance of his severely classical design marks the beginning of late Baroque classicism in Rome. While it has been suggested that his design reveals a knowledge of nascent English Neo-Palladianism, it also derives from the Roman tradition of Carlo Maderno and Michelangelo. Other important Roman works of Galilei were the Corsini Chapel, also in S. Giovanni, and the facade of S. Giovanni dei Fiorentini.

Alessandro Galilei: the facade of S. Giovanni in Laterano, Rome; completed 1736

## Gallegos Fernando *fl. 1467–1507*

The Spanish painter Fernando Gallegos (or Gallego) was born in Salamanca, and was foremost among the few painters known to have been working in that province in the late 15th century. His first work was the six-paneled altarpiece of San Ildefonso in Zamora Cathedral (1467), commissioned by Cardinal Juan de Mella. He later painted in Valencia Cathedral, and in the University Chapel and the old cathedral of Salamanca (*c*1507). His facial types are unmistakably Spanish, but his spatial effects, dream-like clarity of background, sculptural notions of form, and heavily decorative textiles suggest affinities with Flemish painting, especially that of Dieric Bouts.

## Ganku Kishi *c*1749–1838

The Japanese painter Kishi Ganku (or Kishi Ku) was the founder of the *Kishi* School. Little is known of his life. He was evidently known in Kanazawa and achieved some sort of official rank in that part of Japan, though he worked mainly in Kyoto. He was greatly influenced by the Nagasaki Chinese-style artists, but developed his own unmistakable manner, combining powerful, chunky line with delicacy of wash and detail. He was especially renowned for his paintings of tigers—animals he had never seen, but which he reconstructed from skins. One of his best examples is in the British Museum, London. Ganku's school gradually adopted the *Shijo* style, though they retained his thick, angled outlines of rocks and trees.

## Garnier Charles 1825–98

Charles Garnier was a French architect of the Second Empire. His best-known building, the neo-Baroque Opéra in Paris, is generally thought to epitomize the Second Empire taste for splendor and almost vulgar luxury. After winning the Grand Prix of the Academy in 1848, Garnier visited Rome and Athens. In 1861 he won the competition for the new opera house, but the building was not finished until 1875. This ornate work—very elaborate both on paper and in reality—stands as a focal point at the end of one of Baron Haussman's wide new boulevards which revolutionized the look of Paris. Garnier's Casino at Monte Carlo (1878) is an equally grandiose building.

Charles Garnier: the Casino at Monte Carlo; 1878

## Garnier Tony 1869–1948

Born in Lyons, the French architect Tony Garnier won the Prix de Rome in 1899. He soon began work on the designs that have since assured him a place in the history of modern architecture: for a Cité Industrielle, Lyons (1901–4). This embodied a new conception of urban planning and was greatly admired by Le Corbusier. Garnier's chosen material, reinforced concrete, was then in its infancy, and the forms he created were ones only made possible by the new material. Consequently, many of his designs anticipate developments of 20 or more years later. In Lyons Garnier built the Abattoir (1909–13), the Olympic Stadium (1913–16), and other public works. His Town Hall of Boulogne-Billancourt (1931–4) served as a prototype for many later administrative buildings.

Garofalo: A Pagan Sacrifice; oil on canvas; 128×185cm (51×73in); 1526. National Gallery, London

## Garofalo 1481–1559

Benvenuto Tisi, known as Garofalo was a worthy if not markedly individual Italian painter in the Ferrarese tradition. His illusionistic ceiling decorations in Ferrara (Palazzo del Seminario, 1517–19; Palazzo di Ludovico il Moro) show him practicing the North Italian style which had been initiated by Andrea Mantegna (1431–1506). His religious paintings range from early Holy Families reminiscent of the work of Giorgione (1477–1510), to monumental late altarpieces. These may show the influence of two visits he probably made to Rome, where he is thought to have seen works by Raphael, Michelangelo, and Sebastiano del Piombo.

## Gaudí 1852–1926

The Catalan architect Antoni Gaudí y Cornet came from a family of coppersmiths and wrought-ironworkers. He studied in Barcelona, graduating in 1878, and became interested in a variety of subjects: aesthetics, philosophy, medieval art and craft, Viollet-le-Duc's interpretation of Gothic architecture, and the nostalgic and primitivist sentiments of Catalan nationalism. The latter led him to the study of nature as a source of decorative and structural forms.

Like other architects brought up in a craft tradition Gaudí possessed an innate feeling for the properties of his material, in this case metal. In his first commission, the Casa Vicens in Barcelona (1878–80), one interesting detail is the naturalistic wrought ironwork of the gates and railings. The building as a whole carries connotations of both Moorish and Gothic architecture; this was also to be a feature of Gaudí's *magnum opus*, the Sagrada Familia church in Barcelona (1884–1926). Gaudí was put in charge of this building in 1883 and continued to work on it until his death.

With the Sagrada Familia, the architect gradually transformed what had been a normal neo-Gothic design into a fantastic confection, highly idiosyncratic. "Grotesque" is perhaps the only word to describe this product of Gaudí's imagination. The transept towers, crowned by pinnacles that resemble crustacea, call to mind such bizarre phenomena as Hittite caves eroded by the wind, or stalagmites. Indeed, the whole church is a giant grotto whose skin is molded into a continuously curving, twisting construction, studded with stone

Gaudí: the Parque Güell; 1900–14

sculpture and fragments of glass, china, tile, and mosaic.

Even more sculptural are Gaudí's two major secular works, the blocks of flats in Barcelona, the Casa Batlló (1905–7), which he remodeled, and the Casa Milá (1905–10). Here Art Nouveau breaks away from surface ornament to dictate the shape of the entire building, inside and out. The result, in the case of the Casa Milá, is a rippling, bulging organism, embossed with spiky wrought iron balconies, pierced by windows that look like eyes, and topped with crazy twirls. The interior has no straight walls or level ceilings.

In the Parque Güell (1900–14; now the Municipal Park of Barcelona), glass and ceramic mosaic are again prominent means towards Gaudí's monstrous ends, along with broken plates, bottles, china dolls, and other relics. They are all part of an extremely colorful, almost Surrealist collage, which spreads itself all along the serpentine seat-parapet of this sunny Barcelona park. As an antidote to the puritanism and rationalism of the International style, the Parque Güell—or any other of Gaudí's creations—is without equal.

**Further reading.** Casanelles, E. *Antonio Gaudí: a Reappraisal*, Greenwich, Conn. and London (1968). Collins, G.R. *Antonio Gaudí*, London and New York (1960). Sert, J.L. and Sweeney, J.J. *Antonio Gaudí*, London and New York (1960).

## Gaudier-Brzeska Henri
### 1891–1915

The French-born sculptor Henri Gaudier-Brzeska was born Henri Gaudier, at St-Jean-de-Braye, Loiret, France. He met the Polish Sophie Brzeska in Paris. They lived together from 1910 and he added her name to his in 1911; the couple moved to London in the same year. Powerful portraits such as *Ezra Pound* (1914; Yale University Art Gallery, New Haven, Conn.) and *Horace Brodzky* (1913; Kettle's Yard, Cambridge) celebrate the new friendships he formed at this period. He was associated with the Omega Workshops, and then with the rival Vorticists. Gaudier made many drawings of animals, and in 1914 produced such vivid sculptures as the semi-Abstract *Stags* (alabaster; 1914; Art Institute of Chicago) and the stark, stylized *Bird Swallowing a Fish*

Henri Gaudier-Brzeska: Crouching Figure; marble; 22×30×10cm (9×12×4in); c1914. Walker Art Center, Minneapolis

(1914; alabaster in Kettle's Yard, Cambridge). He joined the French army in 1914 at the outbreak of the First World War. An artist of incalculable potential, he was killed at Neuville-Saint-Vaast at the age of 24.

**Further reading.** Brodzky, H. *Henri Gaudier-Brzeska, 1891–1915*, London (1933). Cole, R. *Burning to Speak*, Oxford (1978). Ede, H.S. *Savage Messiah: a Life of Gaudier-Brzeska*, London (1931).

## Gauguin Paul 1848–1903

The French painter Paul Gauguin was also a sculptor, ceramist, and printmaker. He was born in Paris; his mother was Aline-Marie Chagal the daughter of the political activist Flora Tristan (1803–44) and the engraver André Chagal. Gauguin's parents decided to emigrate from the France of Louis Napoleon to Peru in 1851: his father Clovis Gauguin, a liberal journalist, died on the voyage. In Peru, his mother's relatives, rich and politically powerful, provided a tropical paradise the infant Paul was to remember all his life. He was six years old when his mother returned with him to France.

Gauguin left school at 17; he was a merchant seaman from 1865 to 1867, and served in the French navy from 1868 to 1871. When his mother died (aged only 41) in 1868, a wealthy banker, Gustave Arosa, became his legal guardian. It was through his guardian that Gauguin entered a stockbroker's office in Paris in 1871. Two years later he married Mette Sophie Gad, a Danish governess whom he had met through Arosa; in 1874, the first of their five children was born. Early in his married life Gauguin became a Sunday painter, introduced to this too by Arosa, and attended evening classes. He exhibited at the Salon in 1876 and about this time met Pissarro. In 1879 he exhibited with the Impressionists and became a regular contributor to their last four group shows between 1880 and 1886.

Enjoying moderate financial success, he started collecting paintings by Manet, Monet, Renoir, and Degas, buying one or two by each of them. Above all he collected works by Cézanne and Pissarro. His own early paintings were strongly influenced by these two painters and by Degas. In 1883, he gave up his job to become a full-time painter. The following year he went to Rouen, and then to Copenhagen; but he was unable to find patrons in either place and, humiliated by his Danish relatives, he returned to Paris in 1885. Estranged from his family, beset by poverty and debt, prone to illness, longing for a tropical paradise, Gauguin existed from 1886 onwards in repeating phases of hope and despair.

His odyssey took him to Brittany, Provence, the West Indies, and, finally, Oceania. Between 1886 and 1891, he spent most of his time in Brittany at Pont Aven and Le Pouldu, broken by his visits to Panama and Martinique in 1887, his two months' stay with Van Gogh in Arles (from October to December 1888), and his sojourns in Paris. His Breton works began as continuations of the lessons he had learned from Pissarro and Cézanne. But his restless, experimental nature—not least, the excitement of producing pottery—drove him to search for a new means of pictorial expression. During these years he was sustained by the Japanese prints and Javanese and Indonesian art he saw at the Paris World Fair of 1889. He found refreshment in contact with the Symbolist poets Mallarmé, Morice, and Moréas, and he picked up religious and Symbolist impulses from two younger friends, Bernard and Aurier. Two Dutchmen gave him financial help at this time, the art dealer Theo van Gogh, and the artist Meyer de Haan.

Gauguin was never a prolific artist—his total oeuvre amounts only to some 600 paintings and pastels. Nor did his development proceed in a straightforward way: he would push far ahead into unexplored stylistic territory, and then withdraw. His landscapes, still lifes, and even portraits were produced without deliberate Symbolist overtones. His use of color was often arbitrary, his line simplified and abrupt. Words like "Synthetism" and "Cloissonism" were used to describe the characteristics of his art at that time: Post-Impressionism is the later, all-embracing term.

Gauguin once wrote of his Breton pictures: "I love Brittany. I find a wildness and a primitiveness there. When my wooden shoes ring out on its granite soil, I hear the muffled, dull, and powerful note I am looking for in my painting." Important pictures from this period include the *Vision after the Sermon* or *Jacob Wrestling with the Angel* (1888; National Gallery of Scotland, Edinburgh), the *Yellow Christ* (1889; Albright-Knox Art Gallery, Buffalo), *Christ in the Garden of Olives* (1889; Norton Gallery, West Palm Beach) and *Loss of Virginity* (1891; Collection of Walter P. Chrysler Jr, New York). Gauguin and his friend Meyer de Haan collaborated in decorating the dining-room of a Breton inn, which they carried out in a fully liberated, nonnaturalistic style. Gauguin's ceramics and his sculpture, especially the painted wood relief *Be in Love and You Will be Happy* (1889; Museum of Fine Arts, Boston) proclaim his Symbolist tendencies. He often theorized about his art, in letters to his friends, in articles, and in illustrated manuscripts.

Gauguin's yearning for a tropical paradise led him to organize a sale of his work in Paris in 1891. By June of that year he was in Tahiti, where he remained until August 1893. He did not find a primitive paradise or a primitive art, nor did he discover a primitive religion being practiced. He had therefore to create his own myths, his own series of allegorical works, which were interspersed with "straight" landscapes, still lifes, and portraits. He took with him photographs of Greek, Roman, and Egyptian art, of the works of French 19th-century painters (Delacroix, Degas, Puvis de Chavannes), and of the Buddhist reliefs at the Javanese temple of Borobudur. An account of Tahitian society published in 1837 provided the basis for his illustrated manuscript, *Ancien Culte Mahorie*. From this source he composed his semiautobiographical, semi-imaginary account of his first Tahitian visit, *Noa Noa (Fragrance)*. As illustrations, Gauguin prepared a set of colored woodcuts, which were themselves a landmark in the history of printmaking. In Paris in November 1893, a one-man show of his Tahitian paintings revealed their bright, flat colors, exotic subject matter, esoteric titles (often in misunderstood Tahitian), and their Symbolist intent.

Gauguin revisited Brittany in 1894; unhappily he broke an ankle in a brawl, and eventually—after another sale of his work in Paris—left France for good in June 1895. He returned to Tahiti. He worked at a slower rate during this second stay—producing only 100 paintings between 1895 and 1903, as against 90 between 1891 and 1893. The paintings became direct and bold in spatial organization, although often more grave and somber in both color and mood than his earlier works. Many of them suggest a mural scale and style. Privation and illness continued to haunt the artist's life. Eighteen ninety-seven was a disastrous year for him, culminating in the news of the death of his favorite daughter, Aline, and the final rupture with Mette. In utter despair, he planned his largest and most philosophically ambitious picture, *Where Do We Come From? What Are We? Where Are We Going?* (1897; Museum of Fine Arts, Boston). He wrote of it: "My dream is intangible, it implies no allegory. To quote Mallarmé: 'a musical poem, it needs no libretto'". After completing it, he made an unsuccessful suicide attempt.

Paul Gauguin: Ea Haere Ia Oe (Where are you going?); oil on canvas; 91×72cm (36×28in); 1892/3. Hermitage Museum, Leningrad

Paul Gauguin: Where Do We Come From? What Are We? Where Are We Going?; oil on canvas; 139×375cm (55×148in); 1897. Museum of Fine Arts, Boston

He painted little during his last years in Tahiti. But after moving to the Marquesas Islands in 1901, his enthusiasm revived and several important canvases date from the last two years of his life. He continued to sculpt, and in January 1903 he completed a rambling piece of autobiography, Avant et Après. After his death a large retrospective exhibition at the Salon d'Automne of 1906, guaranteed his continuing influence on 20th-century art.

Further reading. Brettell, R. et al. The Art of Paul Gauguin, Washington, D.C. (1988). Gray, C. Sculpture and Ceramics of Paul Gauguin, Baltimore (1980). Wildenstein, G. and Cogniat, R. Gauguin, Paris (1964).

## Gaulli Il 1639–1709

The Italian painter Giovanni Battista Baciccia was known as Il Gaulli. Born in Genoa, he left his native city in 1657 to follow a career in Rome. There he painted large illusionistic frescoes, among which is the Triumph of the Name of Jesus (1676–9) in the nave vault of the Gesù. In Genoa he was influenced by the colorism of the work of van Dyck and Rubens. This, combined with the impact of the sculpture of Bernini (whose circle he joined in Rome), led to his developing one of the most exuberant painting styles of the High Baroque.

## Geertgen tot Sint Jans
### 1455/65–85/95

Very little is known about the career of the Netherlandish painter Geertgen. He was probably born in Leiden, but he seems to have worked mainly in Haarlem, where he apparently died at the age of 28. His name

Il Gaulli: St John the Baptist; oil on canvas; 184×119cm (72×47in); c1676. City of Manchester Art Gallery

("Little Gerard of the Order of St John") indicates that he was a lay brother of the Confraternity of St John the Baptist, for whose church he painted his most important work: an altarpiece showing on one side the Passion of Christ and on the other episodes from the Life of John the Baptist. Only two fragments from the altarpiece still exist, the Lamentation over the Body of Christ and the Burning of the Bones of the Baptist (both in the Kunsthistorisches Museum, Vienna). These panels show the influence of Flemish artists such as Dieric Bouts and Rogier van der Weyden, and above all of Hugo van der Goes: one figure is a direct quotation from the latter's Monforte Altarpiece (Staatliche Museen, Berlin).

It is possible that Geertgen learned about the work of these painters in Bruges, where he may have served an apprenticeship in the guild of goldsmiths and illuminators in 1475–6; but his use of Flemish art was wholly personal and idiosyncratic. The most characteristic feature of his style is the reduction of figures to simple geometric forms, with spherical, almost doll-like heads and very little indication of facial details. At the same time his work reveals a delight in genre elements and a humorous approach. These qualities can to a certain extent be paralleled in manuscript illumination in Holland at this period, as well as in the masterpieces of 17th-century Dutch painting. Geertgen's simple and unpretentious style seems to reflect the influence of his teacher Albert van Ouwater, who also worked in Haarlem. Ouwater's only securely identified work, The Raising of Lazarus (Staatliche Museen, Berlin) was certainly the major source for Geertgen's early Holy Family in a Church (Rijksmuseum, Amsterdam).

Geertgen's masterpiece is probably St John the Baptist in the Wilderness (Staatliche Museen, Berlin). The Baptist is shown in a state of bemused contemplation in a rich and poetic landscape, which is painted with a marvelous luminosity and remarkably sure sense of recession. The preoccupation with light is perhaps this painter's most outstanding quality—reflected in his extraordinary Nativity of Christ (National Gallery, London). This is the earliest known true night scene in European painting, in that it uses nonsolar light sources within the picture itself. Together with the Berlin panel, Geertgen's Nativity reveals him as one of the most innovative artists of his generation.

## Gehry Frank O. 1929–

The American architect and designer Frank O. Gehry was born in Toronto, Ontario, Canada. In 1947 he emigrated to Los Angeles; he later became a naturalized U.S. citizen. He studied architecture at the University of Southern California (1949–51, 54) and urban planning at the Harvard Graduate School of Design (1956–7). After training in several architectural firms, including Victor Gruen and Associates, he established his own practice in Santa Monica, California, in 1962.

Gehry first gained mass attention for his industrial designs, not his architecture, with the "Easy Edges" series of furniture in the late 1960s and early '70s. He used corrugated cardboard and metal rods to create affordable, well-designed items.

Gehry continued to explore unexpected, humble materials in the redesign of his own house (1978, 1991) in Santa Monica. Originally a conservative two-story bungalow, Gehry transformed the structure by encasing it in a layer of chain link and corrugated steel and slashing out spaces for new windows and skylights. The raw quality of the final structure led many to classify him as a Deconstructivist.

The project received widespread attention, and Gehry received commissions across the world, including the Vitra Design Museum (1987–9) in Weil-am-Rhein, Germany. In contrast to the ragged quality of his home, in this and other commissions Gehry showed a more refined interest in shapes. The building's white cubic forms recall the modernism of Le Corbusier. However, in contrast to the pristine logic of modernism, the shapes seem almost to have been crashed together into one biomorphic sculpture; this reworking of tradition caused some to classify Gehry as a Post-Modernist.

Gehry also continued to explore issues of context, first raised in the redesign of his own home, in commissions such as the Nationale-Nederlanden Building (1992–6) in Prague. On its west facade, the building seems to fit into the historic neighborhood. However, as it turns a corner, it explodes into two diverging towers, one matching the style of the neighborhood, the other made of dramatically curved glass. The towers suggest movement and interplay with each other; to many, they resemble two dancers, hence the building's nickname, "Fred and Ginger."

By the 1990s computer technology had advanced dramatically. With the aid of the new technology, Gehry was able to work with engineers to make the extreme angles and curves of his sketches become a reality. He achieved the apotheosis of this new direction in the Guggenheim Museum in Bilbao, Spain (1991–7). Sheathed in lightweight titanium that undulates and curves, the gleaming, organic exterior represents an entirely new vocabulary for architecture that dispenses with models from the past. The building's audacity received international media attention, and it generated an uncommon level of excitement among the general public. In the early 21st century, Gehry has continued to explore new forms and new technology in numerous new commissions. Among many awards, in 1989 he received the prestigious Pritzker Architecture Prize.

## Gentile da Fabriano c1370–1427

Gentile da Fabriano was an influential, itinerant painter from the Italian Marches, who disseminated the International Gothic style through northern and central Italy. The high reputation he enjoyed in his lifetime must be partially taken on trust, since many of his works have disappeared or survive only in a fragmentary state.

He was born to a prominent family in Fabriano, but little is known of his training and early career. Though influenced by the art of his fellow-townsmen Allegretto Nuzi and Francesco di Cecco Ghissi, he seems to have assimilated the International Gothic style mainly from the miniaturists and painters of Lombardy. Signs of this are evident in what is perhaps his earliest surviving panel, the signed *Madonna and Child with St Nicholas, St Catherine, and Donor* (c1395; Staatliche Museen, Berlin), painted for the church of S. Niccolò in Fabriano.

Between 1395 and 1400 Gentile painted the Coronation Altarpiece for the Franciscan convent in Fabriano (now divided between two private collections) and the more advanced Valle Romita Polyptych for the hermits' church of S. Maria di Valdisasso, near Fabriano (now in the Pinacoteca di Brera, Milan). In this signed polyptych—long dismantled, but now re-

Gentile da Fabriano: The Presentation in the Temple; tempera on panel; 26×61cm (10×24in); 1423. Louvre, Paris

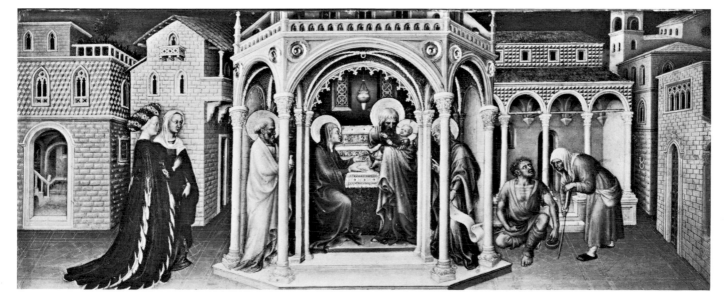

assembled in a modern frame—the Lombard International style is tempered by a new softness, as in the features of the Madonna and the undulation of her silk gown.

Gentile must have traveled to Venice *c*1406 or 1407; there is a record of his presence there in 1408. A 1581 guide to Venice mentions an altarpiece by Gentile in S. Felice, and murals by him in the Grand Hall of the Ducal Palace: none of these survive—all of Gentile's Venetian works are now lost. But the fact that he—an immigrant artist—was commissioned to paint the main hall of the Ducal Palace is proof of his reputation.

From 1414 to 1419 Gentile worked at the cosmopolitan court of Brescia in Lombardy, where he painted a chapel for Pandolfo Malatesta (destroyed at the beginning of the 19th century). On its completion, he accepted an invitation to work for Pope Martin V, who was making his way south to Rome. But owing to the Pope's delay, it was another seven years before Gentile entered his service. He might have returned to a career of provincial obscurity in Fabriano, has not his arrival in Florence, in the Pope's footsteps, occurred at an opportune moment: at a time, that is, when the rich Florentine burghers were beginning to ape the tastes of the courts of northern Italy and France.

Gentile catered to this taste. His versions of *The Madonna of Humility* (examples in the Museo Nazionale, di S. Matteo, Pisa, and Fitzwilliam Museum, Cambridge; both *c*1420/22) are refined and aristocratic. Fashion predominates over saintliness, as in his Washington *Madonna* (*c*1422; National Gallery of Art, Washington D.C.), her tunic sleeve, under a mulberry-red robe, embroidered in gold with a pomegranate pattern.

The fashionable International Gothic style Gentile brought to Florence was already known there, but in a diluted, Sienese version. Gentile expressed its full force in the signed and dated altarpiece he painted for the wealthy Florentine businessman Palla Strozzi (1423; Uffizi, Florence). It consists of a single main panel of the *Adoration of the Magi*; there are lunettes above the three arches at the top of the panel, and a three-panel *predella* below. An inseparable component is the Gothic frame, of which the polygonal corner posts are painted with miniature panels of Mediterranean flowers. In the main panel, Gentile depicts the Epiphany as a courtly cavalcade. Sumptuously at-

Artemisia Lami (Gentileschi): Judith Beheading Holofernes; oil on canvas; 199×162cm (78×64in); c1620. Uffizi, Florence

tired in gold-encrusted brocades, the three Kings have dismounted before the Madonna. A veritable menagerie (which may have been painted by Gentile's friend Pisanello) accompanies the entourage that crowds the foreground. In the background, passing through cities and castles on their way, the Magi journey towards Bethlehem: a seemingly endless procession meandering flamboyantly from one side of the panel to the other. The *predella* panels show an attempt—new in Italian painting—to represent real sky instead of a gold background: the Nativity by night, the Flight into Egypt by day.

Soon after finishing the Strozzi Altarpiece, Gentile began work on another Florentine private commission: the polyptych painted for the Chapel of the Quaratesi family in S. Niccolò sopr'Arno. Vasari called this "indubitably the best of all the works of this artist which I have seen". Consisting of five gabled panels and a *predella*, the Quaratesi Polyptych was

unfortunately dismantled in the early 19th century, its frame (with the date 1425) destroyed, and the panels dispersed throughout various collections. The central panel of the *Madonna and Child with Angels* is now in London (Hampton Court Palace) and the side panels of saints are in Florence (Uffizi). Once again, the emphasis is on sumptuous accoutrements, as in the Magdalen's ermine-lined mantle and the embroidered stole of St Nicholas.

After May 1425 Gentile went to Siena, where he painted a now-lost *Madonna and Saints*. At the end of the same year, traveling south, he frescoed a *Madonna and Child* in Orvieto Cathedral; although damaged, this gives some impression of his more monumental late style.

Arriving in Rome in 1426, Gentile finally entered the service of Pope Martin V, for whom he executed frescoes of *St John the Baptist* in the Lateran Basilica (1427). These were later destroyed to make way for Borromini's Baroque interior. Gentile's last work in Rome seems to have been a *Madonna and Saints* in S. Maria Novella described by Vasari but now lost. It was in the adjoining convent that he died in the autumn of 1427. The Lateran frescoes were completed by Pisanello, who has left one or two drawings that relate to them, and who inherited Gentile's belongings. Though nothing appears to have survived of Gentile's work in Rome (apart from a ruined *Madonna and Child* in Velletri), its importance cannot be minimized. The first great Quattrocento artist to work in the city after the return of the Papacy, he laid the foundations of Renaissance painting there, as to some extent he had already done in Venice and Florence.

**Further reading.** Christiansen, K. *Gentile da Fabriano*, New York (1982). Colnaghi, D.E. *A Dictionary of Florentine Painters*, London (1928). Degenhart, B. and Schmitt, A. "Gentile da Fabriano in Rom und die Anfänge des Antikenstudiums", *Münchner Jahrbuch der Bildenden Kunst* vol. 11, Munich (1960). Grassi, L. *Tutta la Pittura di Gentile da Fabriano*, Milan (1953). Molajoli, B. *Gentile da Fabriano*, Fabriano (1934).

## Gentileschi family
16th and 17th centuries

Born in Pisa, Orazio Lomi Gentileschi (1562–c1639) worked from 1576 until 1621 in Rome, where he was influenced by Caravaggio. Later he reverted to the elegance and light colors of Florentine art. He spent periods in Genoa, Turin, and Paris. Then in 1626 he became painter to the English monarch Charles I. He held this post till the end of his life, painting nine canvases for the hall of the Queen's House at Greenwich.

In 1638 he was visited by his painter daughter, Artemisia Lomi (1597–1651). Besides working in England, she was also active in Rome, Florence, and Naples. Artemisia's work shows the influence of the brutality of Neapolitan Caravaggism; she liked violent subject matter and dramatic contrasts of light and shade.

Orazio Gentileschi: Danaë; detail; oil on canvas; full size 162×229cm (64×90in); 1621–2. Cleveland Museum of Art

Baron Gérard: Corinne at Cape Misène; oil on canvas; 256×277cm (101×109in); c1819–22. Musée des Beaux-Arts, Lyons

## Gérard Baron 1770–1837

The French painter Baron François-Pascal-Simon Gérard was born in Rome, but moved to Paris when he was 10 years old. He studied in the studios of the sculptor Augustin Pajou and the painter Brenet, before working under J.-L. David in 1786. In 1789, he won the second Prix de Rome, and spent the years 1791 and 1793 there. On his return he was allotted a studio in the Louvre. His great popularity stemmed from his *Cupid and Psyche* (Salon, 1798; now Louvre, Paris), which is similar in its slightly erotic and porcelain Neoclassicism to the contemporary sculpture of Canova (marble also in the Louvre, Paris). At the time, it was praised for its "primitive" appearance—a feature that appears again in his several versions of the popular Ossian theme.

In spite of some work as a battle painter, his main claim to fame is for his career as a portraitist which lasted through several regimes from Napoleon to Louis XVIII. He was loaded with honors, and created "Baron" in 1819. His *Mme Récamier* (1805; Musée Carnavalet, Paris), preferred by the lady to David's version, displays an atmosphere of subdued and graceful grandeur. In his basically Baroque portrait manner, and in the types of commissions he accepted, he bears comparison with Sir Thomas Lawrence in England.

## Gérard Jean 1803–47

The French illustrator and caricaturist Jean-Ignace-Isidore Gérard was also known as Jean Grandville. He was born in Nancy in 1803, and was taught by his father, a miniaturist, until he left for Paris in 1820. He created two early series of lithographs, *Chaque Âge à ses Plaisirs* (1827) and *Les Dimanches d'un Bourgeois de Paris* (1828). These were followed by *Les Métamorphoses du Jour* (1829), an album of 72 colored lithographs consisting of scurrilous caricatures which ascribed appropriate animal guises to the human subjects. Analogies of facial types with animals have been commonplace since Antiquity, but Gérard developed the metamorphosis to a point at which satire took on a dream-like existence of its own.

A fierce anti-Royalist, Gérard was among the artists who collaborated on the journals published by Charles Philipon. From

Jean Gérard: Madame Moon paints a Self-portrait; 1844

LA LUNE PEINTE PAR ELLE-MÊME.

1835, after these had been suppressed, he concentrated on illustrating books, notably *Fables de La Fontaine* (1838), *Gulliver's Travels* (1839), and *Robinson Crusoe* (1840). A later series of lithographs, *Scènes de la Vie Privée et Publique des Animaux* (1842), made his direction clear; the only theme of his masterpiece, *Un Autre Monde* (1844) was his determination to follow his fantasy wherever it led. ("I myself claim to act as guide to myself." Standing on his head he added, "Vive la liberté".) Thus were Philipon's republican aspirations transposed into the realm of graphic imagination. Many of the obsessions that haunted his time appeared undisguised in this remarkable book, introduced by an invocation to Heaven to protect an innocent pencil setting out on its journey alone. Nothing protected its creator; he died insane in 1847.

## Gerhaert van Leyden Nikolaus c1430–73

The Dutch sculptor Nikolaus Gerhaert van Leyden was presumably born in Leiden. He was probably trained in the Low Countries, and is first documented in 1462 as the carver of the tomb of Archbishop von Sierck in Trier (its lid and effigy survive in the Bischöfliches Museum, Trier). The walnut *Crucifixion* in the high altar of the church of St George, Nördlingen, generally attributed to him, was made the same year. It therefore seems likely that Gerhaert was based in Strasbourg for some time before 1463, when he is first recorded in the city, and that these early works were executed on excursions from there. From 1463 to 1467 he lived in Strasbourg, although he also worked in Constance. After two invitations from Emperor Frederick III, he moved to Wiener Neustadt, where he remained until his death.

The destruction of Gerhaert's early work in Holland and the loss of his most substantial wooden retable, the high altarpiece in Constance Cathedral, renders proper assessment of his stylistic development extremely difficult. His Trier tomb effigy is very deeply and vigorously carved, with a tremendous sense of volume, while the complexly undercut drapery of the Nördlingen figures imbues them with tense and dynamic movement. About 1464 Gerhaert carved a sandstone portal for the New Chancellery in Strasbourg, of which three fragments survive in Strasbourg (Musée de l'Oeuvre Notre-Dame) and Frankfurt am

Main (Städtische Galerie Liebighaus, Museum Alter Plastik). These heads have astonishing realism and it seems likely that one of them, of a man deep in thought (Musée de l'Oeuvre Notre-Dame, Strasbourg), is actually a self-portrait. The 1464 monument of Canon Conrad von Busnang in Strasbourg Cathedral depicts Gerhaert's patron bust-length before the Virgin and Child within an illusionistic niche: a novel sculptural theme which has points of contact with Netherlandish art.

Gerhaert executed his altarpiece of the Virgin and Child in Constance Cathedral during the years 1465–7. Its loss has repercussions which extend far beyond his own oeuvre, as the influence of this major work upon South German sculpture was extensive. In 1467 he carved the sandstone Crucifix which stands in the Old Cemetery at Baden-Baden. Although it may be broadly associated with Claus Sluter's Dijon *Crucifixion*, and Christ's fluttering loincloth could derive from Rogier van der Weyden's representations of the theme, the stunning naturalism of this figure remains entirely personal.

After his move to Wiener Neustadt, Gerhaert's last years were devoted to the red marble tomb effigy of Frederick III in St Stephen's Cathedral, Vienna. The Emperor's effigy, within the shadows of a cavernous Flamboyant Gothic niche, is surrounded by heraldic symbols. Gerhaert's relief is so remarkably pictorial that it quite belies its function as a horizontal effigy and would function more appropriately as a vertical composition. Other works frequently attributed to him include a walnut Virgin and Child in Berlin (Staatliche Museen) and a sandstone representation of the same subject in Hamburg.

Compared with the work of earlier sculptors, Gerhaert's figures have an entirely new dynamism and expansiveness combined with profound characterization. The widespread diffusion of his style was stimulated not only by his own travels across the breadth of the Empire, but also by the prints of the Master ES and Martin Schongauer, which incorporate many features of Gerhaert's art. More than any other individual, he prepared the way for the great period of German sculpture which spanned the late 15th and the early 16th centuries.

Géricault: study for The Wounded Cuirassier; oil on canvas; 55×46cm (22×18in); c1814. Brooklyn Museum, New York.

# Géricault 1791–1824

One of France's first Romantic painters, Jean-Louis-André-Théodore Géricault lived as well as painted with all the verve of the Romantic style. Independently wealthy, he could indulge his twin passions, for painting and horses, as and when he wished. He had less formal training than most artists of his day, and only applied himself seriously to his art when inspired—as with his masterpiece, *The Raft of the Medusa* (1819; Louvre, Paris). His untimely death came after many months of suffering following a fall from a horse.

Born the son of a wealthy bourgeois in Rouen, Géricault moved to Paris as a boy. During his youth, he was fascinated by all aspects of equestrianism, such as races, circuses, and riding schools. When in 1808 he joined his first studio, it was that of Carle Vernet, who was primarily a horse painter. In 1810 he transferred to the studio of Pierre Guérin for more serious academic training; but his real artistic education was derived from the three years he spent copying in the Louvre (1811–14). His first Salon exhibit, *Officers of the Imperial Guard* (1812; Louvre, Paris) is a blaze of color and movement, quite natural in the context of Imperial France; it is strongly reminiscent of the work of A.-J. Gros, who was much admired by Géricault. Until his departure for Rome in 1816, most of Géricault's work was in this vein, and he was sufficiently inspired by the military life actually to enlist for a few months in 1814.

Géricault spent a year in Italy, where he fell under the spell of Michelangelo. The monumentality of the latter is instantly visible in the series of sketches of the famous *Race of the Riderless Horses*; the series is also strongly affected by Géricault's study of the Parthenon frieze. Some sketches are basically realistic, and concentrate on capturing the life and color of 19th-century Rome with crowds cheering these brave men who struggle to restrain the bucking, prancing horses. Perhaps the most impressive, however, is *The Riderless Horse Race in Rome* (1816–17; Louvre, Paris). It transposes the event to a timeless era, uniting the heavily muscled figures from Michelangelo (particularly those on the extreme right) with the flat relief-like depiction of the horse in the center, so like the friezes of Greek art.

On his return to Paris in the autumn of 1817, Géricault was in a quandary. His work had gained power through his study of the Renaissance, but he was dissatisfied with works like the *Race of the Riderless Horses* which did not depict specific happenings. A child of France's most heroic age, he could not ignore the dynamic representation of contemporary reality as practiced by artists like Gros, nor the influence of the increasingly popular British Romantic writers, notably Byron and Walter Scott. He wanted to paint a subject from modern life in monumental terms. Having experimented rather unsuccessfully with various themes, he came across a pamphlet describing the privations of those who had survived the raft of the "Medusa". Left to their fate on the raft by a mutinous crew, the survivors returned to France to tell a horrifying tale of exposure and near starvation, avoided only by cannibalism. Burning with enthusiasm, Géricault interviewed the authors of the pamphlet, and determined to paint a vast canvas. He toyed with sketches of many different scenes before he settled on the final version, but once decided he worked with complete dedication. To force himself to remain in his studio, he shaved his head; and to ensure the correct representation of dead bodies, he worked in the company of corpses. *The Raft of the Medusa* (1819; Louvre, Paris) is a truly innovative painting, not only in raising a subject from modern life to the proportions once reserved for paintings of the Antique, but also in its construction. Géricault was extremely daring in organizing his painting around a pyramid, which culminates in the figure of the Negro waving a rag in the direction of the rescue ship, faintly visible on the horizon. However, this composition gives such power to the expression of hope among the shipwrecked survivors that it succeeds admirably.

Despite its qualities, the *Medusa* was not well received by the critics, nor was it bought by the government as Géricault had hoped it would be. Disillusioned by his relative failure after so much intense work, he took the painting to England early in 1820; he made a considerable amount of money by showing it there in a traveling exhibition. In England, Géricault's style again underwent a radical change. He had been, in 1817, one of the first artists to take up the newly invented process of lithography; he now put this expertise to good use, producing a series of 13 plates illustrating the life of the English poor. These engravings are inspired in part by the work of English genre painters, although they have nothing of the maudlin sentimentality of the latter. The most important work he produced in England is undoubtedly *The Epsom Derby* (1821; Louvre, Paris). Returning to his first love, horses, Géricault here conceives the movement of that most gracious of animals in entirely new terms. The whole impression given is one of movement, with the horses shown galloping flat out to increase the feeling of speed. Minor English sporting painters may have suggested this style to Géricault, but it is essentially new, and no echo of it is found in French art until the advent of Degas, almost 50 years later.

Géricault's entire history is one of change and innovation, and nothing is more novel than his portraits of the insane. Painted for a Dr Georget, one of the pioneers of psychiatry, each of these paintings illustrates a different psychotic condition such as kleptomania, delusions of grandeur, and so forth. It is not certain whether these works were painted by Géricault as a favor to Dr Georget, or whether they were in fact a kind of occupational therapy prescribed by Georget for one of Géricault's frequent bouts of depression. Géricault painted ten of these canvases in all; only five are extant, a fine example being *The Mad Assassin* (1822/3; Museum of Fine Arts, Ghent). The uniqueness of the works lies in the fact that they were among the first to depict an abnormal mental state as an illness, rather than as a subject for laughter.

Between his return to France in 1822, and his death two years later, Géricault painted very little, the only really significant work being *The Lime Kiln* (1822–3; Louvre, Paris). Successive equestrian accidents weakened him, and as he was unwilling to take good care of himself, he eventually died. Near death, he exclaimed in typical Romantic but essentially untrue fashion: "If only I had painted five pictures: but I have done nothing, absolutely nothing."

**Further reading.** Berger, K. *Géricault and his Work*, Lawrence, Kan. (1955). Eitner, L. *Géricault's Raft of the Medusa*, London (1972). Friedländer, W. trans. Goldwater, R. *David to Delacroix*, Cambridge, Mass. (1952).

# Gerthner Madern c1391–c1430

A group of works is closely connected with the name of the German sculptor and architect Madern Gerthner, who was

Marcus Gheeraerts the Younger: Portrait of Elizabeth I; oil on canvas; 241×152cm (95×60in); 1592. National Portrait Gallery, London

## Gheeraerts family
### 16th and 17th centuries

The Gheeraerts family are held responsible for a series of full length costume-portraits which were produced in England between *c*1590 and *c*1625. The work of individual hands is difficult to disentangle, but their style originates in the Flemish studio work of the Jacobean period. Marcus Gheeraerts the Elder (1516/21–1604) came from Bruges. He worked in England between 1568 and 1577, and married a sister of John de Critz, another Anglo-Flemish painter who also came from Bruges. Marcus Gheeraerts the Younger (1561–1635) also intermarried with the de Critz family, and his daughter became the second wife of the miniature painter Isaac Oliver. The Gheeraerts' highly decorative portraits can be found in English country houses such as Woburn Abbey, Bedfordshire, Penshurst Place, Kent, and Welbeck Abbey, Nottinghamshire.

## Ghiberti Lorenzo 1378–1455

Lorenzo Ghiberti was the major Florentine sculptor of the early Renaissance. His autobiography (the first to be left by a Western artist) begins with his professional debut in 1400, when he left Florence for Pesaro to paint murals for Pandolfo Malatesta. He had been trained as a goldsmith in the workshop of Bartoli di Michele, known as Bartoluccio.

Ghiberti was recalled to Florence in 1401 by news of the competition announced by the Arte di Calimala (cloth guild) for the commission of a new bronze door to the Baptistery, to match the one completed by Andrea Pisano in 1338. The competition involved casting a specimen panel in relief on the subject of the Sacrifice of Isaac. Brunelleschi, Jacopo della Quercia, and Ghiberti were among the seven finalists. Ghiberti, the youngest, won; a comparison between his competition relief and Brunelleschi's (the only two to survive: both in the Museo Nazionale, Florence) suggests he deserved to do so. Artistically more mature than his rival's and technically more advanced, it already establishes his taste for figures *all'antica* (the nude kneeling figure of Isaac derives from an antique torso). In fact, the relief combines a mixture of Classical and Gothic influence which was, in varying measures, to persist in his art to the end.

When the contract for the new Baptistery door was eventually signed in 1403, a New

active in the lodge of Frankfurt am Main Cathedral. These display an extremely painterly treatment of sculptural style. Gerthner sculpted monuments to Werner Weiss von Limpurg (Karmelitenkirche, Frankfurt am Main) and Siegfried zum Paradies (Nikolaikirche, Frankfurt am Main). They point the way to the *Adoration of the Magi* on the south portal of the Liebfrauenkirche in Frankfurt (*c*1420) and the lyrical figures on the Memorienpforte of Mainz Cathedral (*c*1424–5). The climax of Gerthner's achievement is reached, however, in the effigy of Archbishop Konrad von Daun (*ob*. 1434) in Mainz Cathedral.

Testament program of 28 quatrefoil panels, arranged four in a row, was stipulated. The work, which was interrupted by other commissions, spanned two decades. Ghiberti's workshop increased in size during this period. In 1407 he was employing 11 assistants, and later he added more—Donatello, Uccello, Michelozzo, and Benozzo Gozzoli among them. It was the largest and most influential sculptor's workshop in Florence during the first half of the 15th century. By c1415 most of the quatrefoil reliefs had been cast. The frame surrounding them was cast afterwards. There were 48 heads of prophets at its corners (many derived from Roman sculpture), and the bronze jambs and lintel were foliated with wild roses, daisies, crocuses, violets, forget-me-nots, pine cones, and hazel nuts. It was not until April 1424 that the Baptistery north door was finally installed. Ghiberti, who had begun it as a young man, was now in his mid forties.

He had concurrently undertaken other commissions: designs for stained glass (for Florence Cathedral), papal miters, and jewelry. Three Florentine guilds had commissioned from him three bronze statues for the exterior niches of the guild church of Orsanmichele: *John the Baptist* (1413–14); *St Matthew* (1419–22); and *St Stephen* (1425–29). The first of these was predominantly International Gothic in style; the second was Classical (influenced by Donatello and Nanni di Banco); and the third synthesized the two. Technically, all three show Ghiberti's unrivaled mastery of large-scale casting in bronze.

Several shallow bronze reliefs belong to the same years: the two reliefs for the Baptismal Font of Siena (1420–7), the tomb plaque of Leonardo Dati (1425–7; S. Maria Novella, Florence), and the shrine of Saints Protus, Hyacinth, and Nemesius (Museo Nazionale, Florence). Their growing pictorial accomplishment culminates in the four superb reliefs of the shrine of St Zenobius (1432–42; Florence Cathedral); the Classical nature of these reflects Ghiberti's visit to Rome (c1425–30). The visit profoundly influenced the new style he developed during the 1430s, notably in the new Florence Baptistery door commissioned by the Arte di Calimala in 1425 (eight months after the north door had been installed).

Ghiberti claimed he had been given *carte blanche* over the design of the new door, but it is possible that the Old Testament program was drawn up by Florentine humanists. In any case, the new door abandons the quatrefoil pattern of its predecessor. The doors measure 8 ft 6 in by 3 ft 7 in (2.35 m by 1.1 m). They consist of ten 31 in by 31 in (79.5 cm by 79.5 cm) relief panels; each wing, consisting of five panels, is surrounded by a frame ornamented with 24 heads of prophets in roundels, alternating with 24 statuettes in niches, with four reclining figures above and below. Michelangelo is said to have dubbed the new door "The Gates of Paradise", though the story is probably apocryphal.

Apart from their size, it is their pictorial quality and narrative complexity that differentiate the new panels from those of the north door. They display both linear and aerial perspective, reinforced by a gradation from high relief in the foreground to shallow relief in the background, corresponding to the diminution in the size of the figures. Ghiberti described the perspective

Lorenzo Ghiberti: the north doors of the Baptistery, Florence; cast bronze; 457×251cm (180×99in); 1403–24

system in his autobiography. He also emphasized that his narratives were "abounding with figures"—an International Gothic preoccupation. What he omitted to say is that many of these figures, in contrast to his previous *all'antica* repertoire, were derived from Roman sarcophagus reliefs visible in Rome. Ghiberti must certainly have made drawings of them. Yet it is paradoxical that his style, in spite of prolific antique borrowings, never achieves the Classicism of Donatello, who assimilated the Antique without quoting it so directly.

The ten panels of the Gates of Paradise took a decade to cast (c1428–37), but work on the chasing and the frames continued into the 1440s. It was not until 1452, after the final process of gilding, that the Gates of Paradise—Ghiberti's finest achievement—were installed at the east entrance to the Baptistery. Three years later Ghiberti was dead.

On his death, he left a flourishing workshop (which Vittorio, his younger son, took over), a distinguished collection of antiquities, and, in manuscript, an incomplete vernacular history and theory of the figurative arts, his three-part *Commentarii*. The first book treats of ancient art, the second of modern, while the fragmentary third is devoted to theoretical problems. Book two represents a pioneer attempt by an artist to describe his predecessors' achievements and thus articulate the epoch we now designate as Early Renaissance.

Ghiberti's status in Quattrocento Renaissance art remains contentious: to some he is one of its fathers; to others he is a late Gothic sculptor, outstripped in his lifetime by the relentlessly progressive Donatello. Undoubtedly Donatello did eventually erode Ghiberti's early unassailable lead in Florentine sculpture. Yet Ghiberti's career exemplifies the artist's new role in postfeudal society, so that to regard him merely as a reactionary champion of International Gothic (the style which had so powerfully influenced his youth) is absurd. The *Commentarii* show to what an extent he grappled with the fundamental pictorial problems underlying a true Renaissance style, and the Gates of Paradise what pains he took to resolve them.

**Further reading.** Goldscheider, L. *Ghiberti*, London (1949). Krautheimer, R. *Lorenzo Ghiberti* (2 vols.), Princeton, N.J. (1970). Schlosser, J. von *Leben und Meinungen des Florentinischen Bildners Lorenzo Ghiberti*, Basel (1941).

Domenico Ghirlandaio: Head of an Old Woman; black and white chalk on paper; 37×22cm (14×9in); c1486–90. Collection of the Duke of Devonshire, Chatsworth, Derbyshire

## Ghirlandaio Domenico 1449–94

The Italian painter Domenico Ghirlandaio was born in Florence in 1449. It is said that he once demanded, "Let me work ... now that I've begun to know how to do it, I only regret that I haven't been commissioned to paint narrative pictures on all the walls of Florence." Though never granted the commission in question, Ghirlandaio did receive many others for portraits, altarpieces, and frescoes. For a decade, between 1480 and 1490, he was the city's most popular and prolific artist.

Ghirlandaio's fresco cycles are evocative pageants of Florentine life. Whatever the ostensible subjects, they contain numerous portraits of his patrons, their families and friends. The tastes and values of his patrons—usually wealthy bankers—are reflected in the impeccable craftsmanship and restrained grandeur of his paintings. While responsive to his immediate surroundings, he also looked to the past for inspiration. In his last and most important works, he established an influential revival of the monumental tradition of Tuscan painting.

Little is known about Ghirlandaio's early training. According to Vasari, he began his career as a goldsmith but learned to paint from Alesso Baldovinetti. There is no strong evidence of training with Baldovinetti in Ghirlandaio's work. He always painted rather in the manner of a goldsmith. His paintings, early and late, are richly ornamented and metallic. Ruskin cruelly but perceptively summed him up as "a goldsmith selling plated goods". Ghirlandaio was not unique, for a similar goldsmith's style of painting dominated Florence during the late Quattrocento. Two goldsmith painters, Verrocchio and Antonio Pollaiuolo, deeply influenced not only Ghirlandaio but all the important artists who came to maturity during the 1470s, including Leonardo da Vinci, Botticelli, and Perugino.

Much like those artists, during the 1470s and early 1480s Ghirlandaio turned from the static style of mid-century Florentine painting to nurture a striking if stilted vitality. In early works—such as the frescoes of the S. Fina Chapel (1475; Collegiata, San Gimignano), *The Last Supper* in the refectory of the Ognissanti (1480; Florence), and the *St Jerome in his Study* (1480; Ognissanti, Florence)—Ghirlandaio adopted a linear style in which sharp highlights and shadows fragment hard, shiny forms into small, clear facets. Such angular, gleaming forms give tense energy to his early paintings.

Ghirlandaio's most famous works are those he painted during the 1480s. They include the frescoes of the Sala dei Gigli (1482; Palazzo Vecchio, Florence), the frescoes and altarpiece of the Sassetti Chapel (1482–85; S. Trinità, Florence), *The Last Supper* in S. Marco (c1485; Florence), and *The Visitation* (1491; Louvre, Paris). During this decade he constantly augmented the monumentality of his paintings, though he never fully embraced the austere nobility of his early Renaissance models. His late paintings are grand, but they are also garrulous. He always retained something of the vivacity of his early style, partly because he enlivened all his paintings with an abundance of naturalistic or Classical details.

The symbolic isolation of naturalistic elements in Flemish painting attracted Ghirlandaio. For example, he borrowed the bundle of wheat in *The Adoration of the Shepherds* (1485; S. Trinità, Florence) from the rich array of such naturalistic symbols in Hugo van der Goes' *Adoration of the Shepherds* (c1478; Uffizi, Florence), a painting that had only recently arrived in the city.

Similarly, Ghirlandaio shared his contemporaries' enthusiasm for antique art. He amassed an influential vocabulary of antique ornament and pictorial motifs which he used to enrich his paintings. In the *Adoration of the Shepherds* of 1485, for example, he placed the Christ Child before an antique marble sarcophagus with a Latin inscription prophesying His birth. In the Sala dei Gigli Ghirlandaio depicted six Roman heroes within painted architecture reminiscent of Roman triumphal arches, but imitative of no single antique model.

The culmination of Ghirlandaio's career was his decoration of the Tornabuoni Chapel, the presbytery chapel of S. Maria Novella in Florence. The ensemble is vast; there are 19 scenes from the lives of the Virgin, the Baptist, and Dominican saints. Ghirlandaio also designed, though he did not execute, the stained glass windows of the Chapel, and the altarpiece of the *Madonna in Glory* (now in the Alte Pinakothek, Munich).

In those paintings Ghirlandaio actively pursued a sweeping grandeur which helped to shape the artistic goals of younger artists such as Raphael and Michelangelo. He spread vast landscape panoramas across the low horizons to fling open the scenes. He gave the figures an impressive dignity and monumentality. And, perhaps with the help of the Florentine architect Giuliano di San Gallo, he constructed immense Classical architectural settings which ennoble the narrative scenes.

The Tornabuoni frescoes are at once religious narratives and magnificent pageants of Renaissance life. The architectural settings are idealized but also unabashedly contemporary. For instance, Ghirlandaio depicted *The Birth of the Virgin* in the richly decorated room of an opulent Florentine palace. His figures, too, depict the personages of his own era. He portrayed Ludovica Tornabuoni, one of the daughters of the family who were donors of the chapel; she is seen at the head of a group of solemn women in 15th-century costume who visit the Virgin's mother, St Anne.

Ghirlandaio had always used an anachronistic approach, placing portraits of contemporaries alongside religious figures. His settings are pastiches of classicizing fictions

Domenico Ghirlandaio: Portrait of a Lady, called Giovanna Tornabuoni; panel; 76×50cm (30×20in); 1488. Thyssen-Bornemisza Collection, Lugano

and real places. In the Sassetti Chapel, for instance, he showed *The Granting of the Rule to St Francis* in a lofty portico located in Florence's Piazza della Signoria.

Besides being invaluable records of Florentine culture, Ghirlandaio's paintings are also significant artistic achievements. He forged a distinctive, eclectic style from widely disparate elements in Florentine, Flemish and Classical art. His style commands special attention both because of the range of his borrowings and because of his effort to weave those borrowings together. His attempt to achieve a synthesis reflects an unprecedented self-consciousness about the personal and cultural implications of artistic style. The marked range and rapidity of change in Ghirlandaio's manner of painting, and in that of his great heirs Raphael and Michelangelo, sprang partly from this new approach to artistic style.

**Further reading.** Davies, G.S. *Ghirlandaio*, London (1908). Lauts, J. *Domenico Ghirlandaio*, Vienna (1943). Vasari, G. *Lives of the Great Painters* (4 vols.), London (1969).

## Giacometti Alberto 1901–66

The Swiss painter and sculptor, Alberto Giacometti was born in Stampa, the son of a successful post-Impressionist painter. After a year as an art student in Geneva, Giacometti traveled in Italy. He settled in Paris in 1922 and for the next three years studied under the sculptor Antoine Bourdelle.

Influenced by Cubism and by African and Cycladic art, his sculpture of the years 1925–9 became semiabstract, consisting either of simple, compact, tablet-like forms, or else of complex, openwork, cage-like structures. Between 1930 and 1935, he was active in the Surrealist group. Often his Surrealist constructions imply movement; some are actually kinetic. Some of his works, like *The Palace at 4 a.m.* (1932–3; Museum of Modern Art, New York), suggest complete environments and dramatic situations; most are nightmarish, evocative of violent torture, mutilation, and physical confinement.

In 1935, Giacometti's decision to work from nature led to his exclusion from the Surrealist group. Henceforward, his subject matter was taken only from the "real" world—the single human figure and full-length or portrait bust predominating.

Periods of working from the model or from memory alternated.

Throughout his career, Giacometti was obsessed by the desire to render exactly his sensation of the living reality of his subject. In 1940, he felt a compulsion to create miniature statuettes; but in 1945, he found that only exceptionally tall and thin figures came close to reality as he experienced it. From this time on, the surfaces of all his sculptures became deeply pitted, while, in his paintings and drawings, the forms were built up slowly by means of multiple lines and contours. Invariably the figures are frontal; occasionally they are given an environmental setting. Their gouged surfaces and attenuated silhouettes suggest physical decay; while the concentration on the single figure—even in the groups there is no communication between individuals —suggests man's tragic isolation.

**Further reading.** Genet, J. *L'Atelier d'Alberto Giacometti*, Paris (1958). Giacometti, A. "Ma Realité" in *XXᵉ Siecle*, new series no. nine, Paris (June 1957). Matter, H. *Alberto Giacometti*, London (1988).

## Giaquinto Corrado 1699–c1765

Corrado Giaquinto, a Neapolitan Painter, was one of the most important Italian Rococo artists in the first half of the 18th century. A pupil of Francesco Solimena, he moved to Rome in 1723. He worked both

Alberto Giacometti: Seated Nude; lithograph; 57×76cm (22×30in); 1961. **National Museum of Wales, Cardiff**

in Rome, where he decorated many churches (of which the most important is S. Lorenzo in Damaso; 1734), and in Turin, where he acquired something of the extreme sophistication and light and lovely colors of the French Rococo. His most important works are six voluptuous and magical scenes from *The History of Aeneas* (Palazzo Quirinale, Rome). From 1753 to 1762 he was court painter in Madrid, where his decorations at the Royal Palace form the climax of his career; he then returned to Naples.

## Gibbons Grinling 1648–1721

The fame of the Rotterdam-born sculptor Grinling Gibbons rests upon the skillful

Grinling Gibbons: **detail of the reredos in the chapel of Trinity College, Oxford**

woodcarvings he made in England as Master Carver in Wood to the Crown. In England, where he lived from c1672, Gibbons decorated the choir stalls of St Paul's Cathedral, London, for Sir Christopher Wren. His virtuoso carvings of fruit, flowers, and animals can also be seen at Windsor Castle and Hampton Court, where he worked under the patronage of Charles II. He maintained a flourishing practice, and also worked in marble and bronze.

## Gibbs James 1682–1754

The Scottish architect James Gibbs was born in Aberdeen. About 1703 he traveled to Rome where, after briefly contemplating a career as a painter, he entered the studio of Carlo Fontana. Fontana's influence is discernible in the bold, sculptural treatment of Gibbs' first London commission, the church of St Mary-le-Strand (1714–17). Thereafter the influence of Roman Baroque architecture was eliminated in favor of a more restrained, but still recognizably Baroque style. His manner was derived from Christopher Wren rather than Vanbrugh, and established him as the only mid-18th-century British architect to resist seriously the Neo-Palladianism of Campbell, Burlington, and Kent.

St Martin-in-the-Fields (1722–6), the largest of his London churches, was by far his most influential work. The interior repeated the formula of Wren's St James, Piccadilly (1682–4). But the exterior, with its steeple rising immediately behind the apex of the boldly projecting entrance portico, was entirely new; it was imitated by church builders throughout the 18th and 19th centuries. His country houses—for instance Ditchley, Oxfordshire (1720–5)—were less original. They are frequently distinguishable from their Palladian counterparts only by their elaborate, Italianate interiors, invariably ornamented by the stuccoists Artari and Bugatti.

As a Catholic and a Tory (possibly with Jacobite sympathies) Gibbs necessarily worked independently of the Whig establishment. His *Book of Architecture* (1728) exerted a considerable influence on British architecture, but he inspired no direct heir.

James Gibbs: the Radcliffe Camera, Oxford; 1737–49

His late masterpiece, the circular Radcliffe Camera, Oxford (1737–49) has strong Mannerist and Baroque features despite contemporary trends, and is considered one of the last fully Baroque buildings to be constructed in Britain.

## Gilabertus of Toulouse
*fl. c1120–30*
Gilabertus of Toulouse was a Romanesque sculptor active between c1120 and 1130. His works are now in the Musée des Augustins, Toulouse, and include almost life-size figures of Apostles from the chapter house of the Cathedral of St Étienne, and a series of capitals from the cloister. The Apostles are carved as four pairs and four single figures. It was at one time assumed that these figures formed part of a doorway; but it has recently been claimed that they were used inside the chapter house as *atlantes*, supporting the vaulting. However, this view is not universally accepted. Not all of the figures are by Gilabertus: some are in a different angular style which is related to that of the portal of Moissac. Two of the single figures originally had the signature of Gilabertus on them, but these are now obliterated.

The style of this sculptor has no precedents in Languedoc. It is soft and flowing, with gentle facial expressions, and shows a delight in ornamental details such as the jewel-studded hems of the robes. His method of carving is also new. Previously, a figure in a niche was carved from the front surface of a block of stone into its depth. Gilabertus attacked the block from two adjoining sides, so that the figure emerged from the diagonal axis of the block and not frontally. This method was universally adopted in carving Gothic column-figures.

## Gilbert Alfred 1854–1934

The British sculptor Sir Alfred Gilbert was born in London. His work reflected both the Art Nouveau style and the growing interest in mixed-media sculpture. Trained at the Royal Academy and in Paris, he then spent six years in Rome, before his debut at the Royal Academy in 1882. Lord Leighton encouraged him to return to live in England, where success came quickly. He received commissions from private bodies (for the Caldecott memorial, 1890; Westminster Abbey, London), from the State (for the memorial to Lord Shaftes-

Alfred Gilbert: Eros; aluminum; 1892. Piccadilly Circus, London

bury, the Eros fountain, 1892; Piccadilly Circus, London), and from the Crown. He was elected to the Royal Academy in 1892. But success vied with overcommitment and financial mismanagement, and Gilbert was declared bankrupt in 1901. He fled to Bruges in Belgium and did not return to England until 1922.

## Gilbert and George
1943– and 1942–
The English multimedia artists Gilbert and George—Gilbert Proesch and George Passmore—met at St Martin's School of Art, London, in the 1960s. Calling themselves "living sculptures", they soon established a reputation for their performance art: in *Living Statues* (late 1960s), for example, they painted their hands and faces with bronze paint, and, dressed in the ill-fitting suits that became their trademark, stood motionless for hours. Their preoccupation has been the creation of a single persona—they call their works "one-man shows"—in which a parody of middle-class Englishness, formal and old fashioned, contrasts ironically with their provocative, avantgarde strategies. Later works include large photoworks (a single image being made up of separately taken photographs) whose ambiguous political significance and increasingly explicit homoeroticism have helped to make them controversial figures.

## Gill Eric 1882–1940

The English sculptor and typographer Eric Gill was born Arthur Eric Rowton Gill in Brighton. He studied at Chichester and Central Schools of Art, and from 1903 worked as a letter-cutter and lecturer. From 1907 to 1924 he lived at Ditchling, Sussex, where, following his conversion to Roman Catholicism, he established a community of craftsmen.

In 1918 he completed *The Stations of the Cross* in Westminster Cathedral, London. In the 1920s he became involved with book design and illustration and designed the "Perpetua" and "Gill Sans" typefaces. Three carvings commissioned from Gill in 1929 for St James' underground station led to his receiving the commissions for *Prospero and Ariel* for the facade of Broadcasting House, London. He died at Harefield, Middlesex.

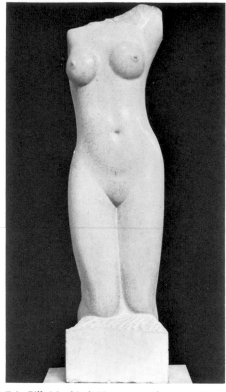

Eric Gill: Mankind; Hoptonwood stone; 242×61×48cm (95×24×18in); 1927–8. Tate Gallery, London

## Gillot Claude 1673–1722

The French painter Claude Gillot was born in Langres, near Dijon and trained by his father, Jean, and then in Paris by Jean-Baptiste Corneille (1649–95). He became an associate of the Académie in 1710 and Director of Costumes and Decoration at the Opéra from 1715. His importance in French art is due not so much to his qualities as a painter, which are not very high, but to his subject matter and influence. It was Gillot who introduced theatrical scenes, in particular those from the *commedia dell'arte*, into French painting, as in *The Tomb of Maître André* (c1707; Louvre, Paris). His pupils, Watteau and Lancret, adapted those scenes to advantage. Gillot's own paintings are crude, but his drawings have more vivacity; with those of Claude III Audran, his drawings for ornaments formed a repertoire of Rococo designs.

Claude Gillot: A scene from "The Tomb of Maître André"; oil on canvas; 100×139cm (39×55in); c1707. Louvre, Paris

## Gillray James 1757–1815

The English caricaturist and engraver James Gillray was born in Chelsea, London. At an early age he was apprenticed to the metal engraver Henry Ashby (1744–1818), and he produced his first caricatures in 1775. He was a contemporary of Rowlandson, and like Rowlandson was greatly influenced by Mortimer's pen-and-ink satires. He attempted some serious engravings in the 1780s, including a series of illustrations to Henry Fielding's *Tom Jones*. After 1790 he worked almost exclusively as a freelance satirist, disseminating his extravagant designs through etchings tinted with watercolors. In an age that relished the wit of vituperative social and political commentary, Gillray stands out as the supreme master of this art.

## Giordano Luca 1632–1705

The Neapolitan artist Luca "Fapresto" Giordano opened a new era in grand decorative painting. His early style was influenced by Jusepe de Ribera (1591–1652). Later he traveled widely, studied deeply the works of Pietro da Cortona (1596–1669) and Veronese (1528–88), and imitated many other styles. Based in Naples, he was much in demand. Between 1680 and 1682 he painted frescoes in the Palazzo Medici-Riccardi in Florence; for ten years, from 1692 to 1702, he was court painter in Spain. His output was immense and his speed of execution proverbial (hence his nickname, *fa presto*). He excelled in covering vast spaces with brilliantly improvised compositions; his touch is light and airy and the spirit of his work anticipates the Rococo.

## Giorgione 1477/8?–1510

Giorgio Barbarelli, called Giorgione, was an Italian painter born in Castelfranco on the Venetian mainland; in the space of a short career he brought about many of the changes that were of crucial importance for the development of Venetian art in the High Renaissance.

SHAKESPEARE - SACRIFICED; - or - The Offering to AVARICE.

Above: James Gillray: Shakespeare Sacrificed or the Offering to Avarice; engraving; 47×37cm (19×15in); 1789. British Museum, London

Below: Luca Giordano: Commerce and Navigation from the series of allegories of Medici rule; fresco; c1680–2. Palazzo Medici-Riccardi, Florence

There are very few documents concerning Giorgione's career, and only one signed and dated work, *Laura* (Kunsthistorisches Museum, Vienna) although a group of others has by tradition been attributed to him. His date of birth is unknown but Vasari suggests 1477 or 1478. The first certain dates do not occur until the first decade of the 16th century. The panel of *Laura* has the date 1 June 1506 inscribed on the reverse; in 1507 and 1508 there are payments for work (destroyed later in the century) in the Doge's Palace, and records of the frescoes on the facade of the Fondaco dei Tedeschi (now the Venetian Post Office). Late in 1510 Giorgione died of the plague in Venice; he left behind him a fine reputation and a small number of exquisite works, many of which were seen and recorded in the private homes of Venetian collectors by 16th-century connoisseurs, especially Marcantonio Michiel and Vasari.

The difficulty of placing Giorgione in a historical context is partially helped by our knowledge of his collaboration with other artists. Early commentators, including Vasari, record Giovanni Bellini as his master. The inscription on the back of *Laura* records his collaboration with Vincenzo Catena in this small work. Michiel relates that Sebastiano del Piombo completed the *Three Philosophers* (Kunsthistorisches Museum, Vienna) and that Titian completed and altered the *Dresden Venus* (Gemäldegalerie Alte Meister, Dresden), while we know from a variety of evidence that Titian as well as Giorgione worked on the Fondaco frescoes.

From this slender documentation generations of art historians have attempted to piece together some notion of his artistic development. There are, however, other important factors to be taken into consideration. Firstly, Leonardo's visits to Venice in 1500 and 1503: Vasari noted their importance for Giorgione; a Leonardesque *sfumato* and softness of outline is one of the characteristics of Giorgione's style. Secondly, in the absence of fuller documentation we cannot afford to ignore remarks such as that made by Vasari that "by about 1507 Giorgione had begun to show a greater softness and depth in his work".

*Laura* is perhaps the best documented of Giorgione's works. It is dated 1506, but there are complications—principally in size—for using it to provide a touchstone for dating other works. It is generally

Giorgione: Tempesta; canvas; 82×73cm (32×29in); c1506–10. Gallerie dell'Accademia, Venice

agreed that those paintings on which Titian and Sebastiano collaborated—the *Three Philosophers*, the *Dresden Venus*, and probably *Tempesta* (Gallerie dell'Accademia, Venice)—date from after 1506; while the *Allendale Nativity* (National Gallery of Art, Washington D.C.) and the Castelfranco Altarpiece (Castelfranco Cathedral) are earlier. They both suggest a prior knowledge of Leonardo's art. Vasari states that early in his career Giorgione painted a large number of panels representing the Madonna and Child: the *Madonna Reading* (Ashmolean Museum, Oxford) may be one of these, although the technique suggests that it is probably a mature work. There is, in fact, no painting among the generally accepted works of Giorgione which dates from before Leonardo's influential visits to Venice.

The Castelfranco Altarpiece has been connected with the date 1504; a young member of the family that commissioned the painting died in that year. This work

owes much (including the pose of St Francis) to Giovanni Bellini; but the setting is entirely external and the placing of the figures does not resemble Bellini's. The Virgin is enthroned high above the other figures to introduce us to a beautiful landscape background behind the foreground wall. Giorgione consistently preferred to set his compositions in landscape, where the relationship of one figure to another is consequently blurred. The figures are rarely involved in action or dialogue—they are usually resting, or engaged in contemplation.

That is certainly the case with the *Tempestà* (Gallerie dell'Accademia, Venice). The painting is probably the one described by Michiel in 1530 in the house of Gabriele Vendramin in Venice. This enigmatic work has been the subject of numerous studies arguing a variety of interpretations: whatever the answer, the preponderance of landscape and atmospheric conditions in the painting set it apart as a new type of picture. Other works by Giorgione seen by Michiel in private houses in Venice have similarly puzzling subject matter and novelty of purpose: such is the case with the *Three Philosophers*, the *Dresden Venus*, and to a lesser extent with *Laura* as well. It is significant that Vasari could not identify the subject of Giorgione's frescoes on the Fondaco dei Tedeschi, and suggested that perhaps no meaning was intended.

Apart from *Laura* these frescoes are the only documented works by Giorgione to survive even in part: the fragments of painted plaster in Venice (Gallerie dell'Accademia), plus Zanetti's engravings, combine to give us a rough idea of their original appearance. Giorgione's frescoes were on the side of the Fondaco facing the Grand Canal; they consisted of individual figures, nude or seminude, either standing in fictive niches or seated in quasi-Classical poses. They introduce us to a branch of Renaissance painting that has almost disappeared, and which is governed by different factors to those determining the appearance of panel paintings or canvases.

The innovatory elements of Giorgione's art were taken up and developed by his followers. Palma Vecchio continued to paint faithfully in the Giorgionesque vein, as did Sebastiano del Piombio until his move to Rome. For Titian, features such as Giorgione's technique and the importance given to landscape were of prime importance until the end of his days.

**Further reading.** Coletti, L. *Tutta la Pittura di Giorgione*, Milan (1955). Pignatti, T. *Giorgione*, London (1971). Richter, G.M. *Giorgio da Castelfranco, called Giorgione*, Chicago (1937). Venturi, L. *Giorgione e il Giorgionismo*, Milan (1913). Zampetti, P. (ed.) *Giorgione e i Giorgioneschi*, Venice (1955).

## Giotto di Bondone 1266–1337

A Florentine, born in Colle di Vespignano, Giotto was the supremely influential painter of the 14th century. His is the most remarkable individual achievement in the stylistic revolution that took place in Italy in the latter part of the 13th century and the first part of the 14th century. In this revolution towards greatly increased naturalism, Giotto's name is linked with those of Cavallini and Cimabue in painting, and the Pisani in sculpture.

While much of his life is obscure, it seems clear that Giotto was in Rome early in his career and he may have been a pupil of Cimabue; it was probably between 1295 and 1300 that he created the mosaic of *La Navicella* (St Peter's, Rome; much restored), and the Stephaneschi Altarpiece (Vatican Museums, Rome) which contains a considerable amount of assistants' work. During the same period he executed a series of frescoes in the apse of St Peter's, of which only a minute fragment has survived (private collection, Assisi). It is in Rome rather than in Florence that we now look for the development of the new naturalism of late-13th-century painting. For it was in Rome at this time that the richest and most active patronage was centered in the hands of the church. In Rome, too, there still survived a number of Early Christian fresco cycles; these were beginning to be restored and studied anew, creating a direct link with the Antique. The important position of Rome was maintained until the Pope's removal to Avignon in 1309; thereafter, Rome was excluded from any place in the history of 14th-century painting.

Not the least of the achievements of the Roman Church patronage before the papal exile was the fresh impetus given to the decoration of the new Basilica of St Francis at Assisi. The work was ordered by Pope Nicholas IV in a bull of 1288. Here we come to one of the main problems in the history of western art: was it in fact Giotto who painted the famous *Legend of St Francis* in the Upper Church of St Francis at Assisi? While for many centuries it was popularly supposed to be the work of Giotto, opinion in this century has tended steadily towards denying him the authorship of the *Legend*. The basic reason for this is the difficulty in reconciling the style of the *Legend*, both its execution and design, with that of the frescoes in the Capella dell'Arena in Padua. These are universally accepted as Giotto's, painted *c*1303–6. It is increasingly felt that the date of the Arena Chapel frescoes is far too close to that of the Assisi frescoes (probably late 1290s) for the difference in style to be explained by the changes wrought on Giotto's style by time. The *Legend* is certainly executed by a number of different masters, perhaps to the design of one of them, who is sometimes called "the Master of *The Legend of St Francis*". The idea that the work was probably done by a Roman school of painters is entirely in keeping with previous artistic activity in Assisi, and

its connections with the church of Rome.

In order to explain the popular connection of Giotto with Assisi, attempts have been made to identify his hand in other parts of the Basilica, particularly with the Master of the Isaac Frescoes who painted some frescoes higher up on the wall above *The Legend of St Francis*. The Basilica at Assisi is a double church; and in the Lower Church there are a number of works by painters close to Giotto, one of whom (the painter of the Magdalen Chapel, *c*1320) is perhaps identifiable with Giotto's chief assistant in Padua.

The Scrovegni Chapel, S. Maria Annunziata dell'Arena, Padua, is Giotto's greatest surviving work; the chapel itself may have been designed by him for his own frescoes. These are a series of paintings covering the walls and roof of the nave of a small chapel, which was built by Enrico Scrovegni in expiation of his father's usurious activities. They are designed to be read from the center of the chapel, descending clockwise from the top right near the chancel to bottom left at the same end. In three rows they tell *The Story of Joachim and Anna* and *The Early Life of the Virgin* (both top row) and *The Life and Passion of Christ* (lower two rows). On the chancel arch is *The Sending of Gabriel* by God the Father to the Virgin, and the *Annunciation* itself (the Chapel is dedicated to the Virgin Annunciate). Below, on either side of the chancel arch, are scenes from the stories mentioned above, together with two remarkable illusionistic chapels which are probably meant to represent tombs. The whole west (entrance) wall is covered by a *Last Judgment*. Along either side of the nave below the other frescoes are, on the left, seven *Vices*, and one the right, seven *Virtues*. These allegorical figures are in grisaille, set among illusionistic marbling. Indeed the light falls on the marbling in the frames of all the frescoes in every detail so as to be consistent with a point of view in the center of the Chapel.

The 39 narrative scenes are distinguished by their extraordinary dramatic intensity, in which the weight and three-dimensionality of Giotto's figures and the naturalism of the draperies play a decisive part—notably in the famous *Kiss of Judas* and *Lamentation*. Both these pictures demonstrate Giotto's compositional power and control in the creation of his essentially human drama.

Giotto's major surviving panel-painting is the huge *Ognissanti Madonna* (*c*1307;

Giotto di Bondone: The Lamentation from The Life and Passion of Christ; fresco; 200×185cm (79×73in); 1304–6. S. Maria Annunziata dell' Arena (Scrovegni Chapel), Padua

tempera on panel; Uffizi, Florence). This is the last of the great Tuscan panels of the Madonna and Child of the kind typified by Duccio's *Rucellai Madonna* (1285) and Cimabue's *S. Trinità Madonna* (*c*1285; both in the Uffizi, Florence). In Giotto's work the central group of the Madonna and Child retains a hierarchical difference in scale from the surrounding angels, saints, and prophets, but the careful arrangement of the architecture and figures

creates a realistic space. The naturalism of the drapery in the central group, and the feeling of real limbs and bodies beneath the clothes, helps to create the sensation of a far more human relationship between Mother and Child than had been usual. Yet the sense of grandeur is undiminished in this altogether monumental work.

The Bardi Chapel (*c*1312–*c*17) and the Peruzzi Chapel (*c*1320–*c*28), both in S. Croce in Florence, present problems of

dating, and to some scholars problems of authorship. Both chapels are typical Florentine commissions of the 14th century. The Bardi and the Peruzzi were great international banking families who like other wealthy Florentines bought and decorated private chapels in the new building of S. Croce. The condition of the frescoes is very bad owing to the maltreatment of centuries, not least that of the 19th century when they were rediscovered and then repainted. Both chapels have recently been restored. One reason for the poor condition of the Peruzzi Chapel (*Stories of St John the Baptist and St John the Evangelist*) is that Giotto, contrary to his usual custom, painted it not in *buon fresco* (on patches of wet plaster) but in *fresco secco* (on a complete area of dry plaster)—a far less durable method. There are certain advantages in using *fresco secco*, especially the way it enables the painter to see the whole scene taking place at once. In view of the extraordinary artistic advances Giotto was making in the Chapel, the decision to use this exceptional technique must have been a deliberate one.

It is only reasonable to suppose that the Peruzzi Chapel follows the Bardi Chapel in date, and that both represent stages of Giotto's response to a problem very different from that of the Arena Chapel. Both S. Croce chapels are tall and very narrow; not only are the scenes difficult to see, but the shape of the picture field is an awkward lunette or rectangle, unlike the regular squares of the Arena Chapel.

In the Bardi Chapel *Life of St Francis* Giotto seems to have concentrated on a mainly frontal viewpoint, and in the Peruzzi to have exploited instead a viewpoint from the entrance to the Chapel. In the Bardi, the architecture is everywhere confined by the picture frame, while in the Peruzzi the architecture often disappears behind the picture frame, much more as if the scene were a hole in space. The execution of the Bardi Chapel was largely left to assistants, which has further complicated the attitude of scholars to these two chapels. But even in its sad state of repair, the Peruzzi Chapel still shows us a shadow of the breadth and magnificence of the late achievement of Giotto. It explains why Michelangelo at the height of the Renaissance wished to learn from a study of the figures in *The Ascension of St John*, and why Masaccio learnt so much from Giotto in the early 15th century. In *The Raising of Drusiana*, for example, there is an entirely new naturalism in the relationship of figures to architecture, and a new richness in figure and drapery style.

The same richness, and great elegance, can be seen in the soft, repeated folds of the robe of the *Madonna and Child* in the Kress Collection (*c*1320; National Gallery of Art, Washington, D.C.). Here the Gothic influence of such sculptors as the Pisani has been taken to new heights. If we could imagine the Kress *Madonna* full-length, we would surely see a figure with a pronounced Gothic S-curve, the weight on one leg, the Child on one hip. It is not too difficult, allowing for the passage of 20 years, to see the identity of authorship between this panel and the Badia Altarpiece (*c*1295–1300; Uffizi, Florence). That was an early work painted for the high altar of the Badia in Florence where Giotto also painted some frescoes, only fragments of which survive. Unfortunately the Badia Altarpiece is in rather poor condition.

None of the works so far mentioned is signed. Curiously, it is signed altarpieces, such as *The Madonna and the Saints* from S. Maria degli Angeli, Bologna (*c*1328; Pinacoteca Nazionale, Bologna), and *The Coronation of the Virgin* in the Baroncelli Chapel (*c*1328; S. Croce, Florence), which are held to be the work of assistants and not of Giotto, as though they required some such guarantee of authenticity.

Towards the end of his life (*c*1328–32) Giotto was called to Naples; all works from this period have since been lost. In 1334 he was back in Florence, appointed chief of works at the cathedral. The most famous testimony to his skill as an architect is the Campanile of Florence Cathedral, which does seem to have been initially designed by him though altered later.

There are several works traditionally connected with Giotto, particularly *The Dormition of the Virgin* (Staatliche Museen, Berlin), which was painted for the same church of the Ognissanti as the *Madonna* in the Uffizi, the very fine *Crucifix* in S. Maria Novella, Florence, while the *Crucifix* in Rimini (Tempio Malatestiano) seems typically derivative from a Giottesque model. The Museo Civico at Padua contains Giotto's small *Crucifix* from the Arena Chapel. Workshop products include *The Stigmatization of St Francis* in the Louvre, Paris, probably dating from the early 1300s, and an interesting group of seven panels of *The Life of Christ*. These are separated between Museums in London, Munich, Boston, New York, and Florence.

Our view of Giotto must be based upon his small core of certain surviving works, especially the Arena Chapel, the *Ognissanti Madonna*, the Bardi and Peruzzi Chapels. It is a tribute to Giotto's stature that so many other outstanding works of the period should be associated with his name—not least, of course, *The Legend of St Francis* at Assisi.

**Further reading.** Barasch, M. *Giotto and the Language of Gesture*, Cambridge and New York (1987). Guillaud, J. and Guillaud, M. *Giotto: Architect of Color and Form*, New York (1988). Previtali, G. *Giotto e la sua Bottega*, Milan (1967). Schneider, L. *Giotto in Perspective*, Englewood Cliffs, NJ. (1974). Tintori, L. and Meiss, M. *The Painting of "The Life of St Francis" in Assisi, with Notes on the Arena Chapel*, New York (1962). White, J. *Art and Architecture in Italy: 1250–1400*, London (1966).

# Giovanni Bologna *c*1524–1608

Giovanni Bologna (or Giambologna) was a Flemish sculptor active in Italy. His original name was Jean Boulogne. He trained in his native Flanders under a major sculptor, Jacques Dubroeucq, mastering the techniques of modeling and carving, and learning the Italianate, classicizing style which Dubroeucq had evolved after a visit to Rome. Giambologna himself journeyed to Rome some time between 1553 and 1555 and made models of Greco-Roman and Renaissance sculpture.

When Giambologna met the elderly Michelangelo, the latter criticized one of Giambologna's models for displaying too high a finish, before the basic pose had been properly established. This was a fault characteristic of Northern Renaissance sculpture as a whole. The young sculptor never forgot this lesson, and became an assiduous maker of sketch-models in wax or clay while preparing his compositions. Several of these have survived (examples in the Victoria and Albert Museum, London). He was deeply impressed by the technical and anatomical virtuosity of Hellenistic sculpture, with its ambitious groups of figures in action—for example *The Farnese Bull*, excavated *c*1546 (Museo e Gallerie Nazionali di Capodimonte, Naples).

On his way homewards Giambologna visited Florence, to study the sculpture of the early Renaissance and of Michelangelo. Bernardo Vecchietti, a rich patron of the arts, offered him accomodation and financial support and soon introduced him to Francesco de' Medici (later Grand Duke). This encouraged the artist to settle in Florence: by 1561 he was being paid a monthly salary by the Medici. He produced ephemeral sculpture for public spectacles, made bronzes and marbles for Medicean gardens, and explored the medium of the small bronze statuette, destined for collectors' cabinets.

From the work of Michelangelo and his Florentine followers Tribolo and Pierino da Vinci, Giambologna evolved a style of composing figures using a contrapposto exaggerated far beyond the Classical norm, with a serpentine axis and a flame-like contour. This instilled new life into Florentine sculpture, which had become academic and stilted in the middle of the century, in the hands of Baccio Bandinelli and Benvenuto Cellini.

Giambologna's developing powers were catalyzed in 1563 by a commission for bronze sculptures to decorate a Fountain of Neptune in Bologna (Piazza del Nettuno). The fountain is pyramidal in design, with a host of lively and sensuous subsidiary figures below. These lead the eye up to the mighty Neptune, who has an energetic spiral pose, momentarily arrested by the gesture of the arm and sharp turn of the head. Hellenistic and Michelangelesque motifs are amalgamated into a brilliant, original composition. Possibly during his stay in Bologna, Giambologna produced the earliest of several versions of a "flying" figure of Mercury. This was to become his most celebrated composition: a statuette initialled "I B" (Kunsthistorisches Museum, Vienna) was sent as a diplomatic gift from the Medici to the Holy Roman Emperor in 1565; a larger bronze version in the Museo Nazionale, Florence was cast later. The vigorous but beautifully balanced pose owes much to earlier bronzes, such as Verrocchio's *Boy with a Dolphin* and Rustici's *Mercury*, both of which were in the Medici collections. The subject may have been inspired by the Mercury statuette on the base of Cellini's *Perseus with the Head of Medusa* (1554; Loggia dei Lanzi, Florence).

On Giambologna's return to Florence, Francesco de' Medici commissioned his first major sculpture in marble, a political allegory of *Florence Triumphant over Pisa* (Museo Nazionale, Florence). This was intended as a pendant to Michelangelo's *Victory*, which had been released from the studio after the master's death in 1564. The young Giambologna was forced to seek a means of uniting two figures into a satisfying action group. The problem had been first posed by Michelangelo in his designs for the tomb of Pope Julius II, and it was later attempted by most of the sculptors in Florence in the middle of the century. Giambologna resolved it with the help of preliminary models in wax and

Giovanni Bologna: Mercury; cast bronze; height 180cm (71in); 1580. Museo Nazionale, Florence

plaster; the final composition is an amalgamation of spiraling curves and zigzag lines, working within a conical volume. Next he carved a group showing *Samson slaying a Philistine* (Victoria and Albert Museum, London) as the centerpiece for a large fountain. Both subject and treatment recall a project of Michelangelo's from the 1520s, which is known only from a number of casts in bronze recording a lost original wax model (examples are in the Museo Nazionale, Florence, and the Louvre, Paris).

Giambologna's third great marble group was the *Rape of the Sabines* (1579–82; Loggia dei Lanzi, Florence). It represented the climax of his career as a figure sculptor, combining three figures into a cohesive group. This was an idea that had obsessed Michelangelo without his ever having brought himself to realize it in marble.

Giambologna's first thoughts are embodied in a bronze group with a standing man and a woman raised in his arms, which he produced in 1579 for Ottavio Farnese. The subject, he wrote to this patron, was chosen to give scope to the knowledge and study of art—it was a conceptual rather than a narrative composition. The sculptor's contemporaries subsequently compelled him to identify the particular episode shown in the full-scale marble version by adding a bronze relief below, showing the Romans and Sabines fighting over the Sabine women. The development from a group of two to one with three figures is plotted in preliminary wax models (Victoria and Albert Museum, London). The three figures are linked psychologically, by the directions of their glances, as well as formally, by the arrangement of their limbs and bodies. The spiral composition means that the group cannot be fully comprehended from any single viewpoint. In technical terms, the sculpture is a masterpiece of virtuosity, carrying to the furthest limits the technique of undercutting which Giambologna had observed in Hellenistic carving, and the use of which distinguishes his work so sharply from Michelangelo's.

In monumental sculpture, his other major achievement was the equestrian statue in bronze of *Cosimo I* (Piazza della Signoria, Florence), which set a precedent soon to be copied by virtually every monarch in Europe.

There are few points of reference in the enormous production of bronze statuettes by Giambologna and his principal assistant, Francesco Susini: most were original, small compositions rather than reductions from full-scale statuettes. Apart from the *Mercury* of 1565 mentioned above, the gilt-bronze female allegory of *Astronomy* (Kunsthistorisches Museum, Vienna), also signed, is probably an early masterpiece. The closed composition and spiral axis given to the figure is characteristic, appearing, for example, in the larger statuette of *Apollo* that he contributed to the Studiolo of Francesco de' Medici (Palazzo Vecchio, Florence). Apart from the human figure, his repertoire included animals, particularly horses, bulls, and groups showing animals attacked by lions. He also sculpted life-size bronzes of birds, which were used to decorate garden grottoes (examples include the *Turkey, Owl,* and *Peacock* in the Museo Nazionale, Florence). For his bird sculptures he invented an "impressionistic" rendering in wax of their plumage, which was faithfully translated by skillful casting into the final bronze versions. His animals pointed the way for the 19th century French school of "animaliers".

The Counter-Reformation created a demand for religious scenes with a clear exposition of narrative. For this purpose Giambologna developed a logical relief style that owed much to Donatello in its sense of perspective. Giambologna's immediate predecessors, Bandinelli and Cellini, had been fascinated by Mannerist surface patterns, which had resulted in a loss of clarity in their work.

Giambologna exerted great influence during his lifetime and for some years afterwards, both in Italy and in the North. His statuettes made handsome gifts and were rapidly distributed through the courts and studios of Europe, disseminating an enthusiasm for his elegant style far beyond Italy. Later, his many pupils, often Flemings or Germans, were in demand to serve these very courts, thus reinforcing his influence, though with personal variations on his basic style (for example the sculptors Adrian de Vries, Hubert Gerhard, and Hans Reichle). Giambologna occupies a crucial position in the history of sculpture in between the better known figures of Michelangelo and Bernini; his style was only superseded by the advent of the Baroque in Rome.

**Further reading.** Avery, C. *Florentine Renaissance Sculpture*, London and New York (1970). Avery, C. *Giambologna*, London (1987). Dhanens, E. *Jean Boulogne*, Brussels (1956). Holderbaum, J. "Giambologna" in *Maestri della Scultura* vol. 13, Milan (1966). Pope-Hennessy, J. *Italian High Renaissance and Baroque Sculpture*, London and New York (1970).

## Giovanni di Paolo 1403–83

Giovanni di Paolo di Grazia was a Sienese painter and miniaturist whose work in Siena is documented from 1426 to 1475. Although he experimented with Florentine innovations, he remained within the Sienese Gothic tradition.

Like his contemporaries Sassetta, Sano di Pietro, and Vecchietta he was inspired by the eloquent moral preaching of the reformer San Bernardino of Siena (1380–1444), which also encouraged Sienese families and institutions to commission altarpieces for their chapels. This provided

Giovanni di Paolo: detail of The Expulsion of Adam and Eve from Paradise and the Annunciation; tempera and gold on wood panel; full size 40×46cm (16×18in); c1445. National Gallery of Art, Washington, D.C.

the basis for Giovanni's work, and many of his altarpieces are still in Siena.

Few of his works are signed and dated, but his style is unmistakable. It shows his sympathy for the natural world, particularly for landscape, and it also displays a profound identification with the religious

stories and saints he portrays with such meticulous detail. The major figures of the polyptychs contrast with the small-boned participants of the lively *predella* narratives.

The male faces have peaked eyelids, a rim of white under the iris, sunken cheeks, and depressive mouths. Unlike Sassetta's serenely spaced features, Giovanni's are compressed, particularly in the female saints and the small figures of the *predellae*. His technique in handling drapery shows the exquisite skill of the miniaturist. Each hair is delineated against a darker ground. He sometimes paints or incises outlines on gold leaf.

In his landscapes he leaves the Byzantine conventions he used in the late 1420s (as in *Christ, Suffering and Triumphant*, Pinacoteca Nazionale, Siena; Pecci Altarpiece, 1426, 4 *predella* panels in the Walters Art Gallery, Baltimore); those of the 1430s become more specifically Sienese (*Flight into Egypt*, c1436?; Pinacoteca Nazionale, Siena). Of all the varieties of the Sienese countryside, he preferred the dream world of the *crete*, to the east of Siena: miniature deserts next to cultivated land, with crevassed clay hills (seen in *St John in the Desert*, c1454; Art Institute of Chicago).

Giovanni's altarpiece of 1463 for the church of the humanist Pope Pius II in Pienza had a Renaissance frame with a dead Christ based on a Classical relief in the lunette. But this experiment in Renaissance taste did not have a lasting effect on his style. In his last works, in Gothic frames, the major figures become massive and distorted. The *predellae*, however, continue to show his sense of wonder at the natural world, making use of topographical landscapes.

Paradoxically the most traditional and the most adventurous of Quattrocento Sienese painters, Giovanni di Paolo's vision was too personal to be developed by others.

## Girardon François 1628–1715

François Girardon was the favorite sculptor of Louis XIV during the period in which the classical ideal and the direction of Colbert were the controlling influences in French art.

Born at Troyes, he studied in Rome and at the Académie before being received as a member in 1657. The decoration of Versailles offered abundant opportunities, and the marble group *Apollo Served by the Nymphs* (1666–72, made for the grotto of Thetis at Versailles, but dismantled and rearranged in the late 18th century) shows the spirit in which he worked; it is almost the translation into stone of a pictorial composition. For his group, Girardon copied the Greek *Apollo Belvedere* (Vatican Museums, Rome), with Apollo's heroic pose only slightly adjusted; Apollo is now shown (rather incongruously) laved and pomaded by the nymphs of Thetis who surround him. The principles of the composition are Poussinesque but a certain dandified virility is Girardon's own.

Girardon's *Rape of Proserpina* (1677–9), also made for the gardens at Versailles, recalls Italian models. It is significant that statuettes attributed to the school of Giambologna (Giovanni da Bologna) and casts after Giambologna and Bernini, as well as from the Antique, formed part of Girardon's large private collection of sculptures.

The tomb of Richelieu (church of the Sorbonne) is considered Girardon's masterpiece. It originally stood in the choir on the main axis of the church. The three-figure freestanding group was begun in 1675. Careful consideration was given to its position in the church, which afforded two main views of the sculpture, one from the altar and one from the north. In the middle of the 18th century it was still regarded by authorities as the most perfect monument in France.

Other important works include *Le Bain des Nymphes* relief (1668–70) and the Pyramid fountain of 1668 for the gardens at Versailles. His bronze equestrian statue of Louis XIV (1683–99) was destroyed in the Revolution.

After Colbert's death in 1683 Girardon lost favor. He died in Paris in 1715, having completed his most important work before the end of the 17th century.

**François Girardon: Apollo Served by the Nymphs; marble; 1666–72. Grotto of Apollo, Versailles**

Girodet-Trioson: Joseph Recognized by his Brothers; oil on canvas; 120×155cm (47×61in); 1789. École des Beaux-Arts, Paris

## Girodet-Trioson 1767–1824

The French painter Anne-Louis Girodet de Roucy, known as Girodet-Trioson, was born at Montangis. He was later a pupil of J.-L. David, entering David's studio in 1786. After two attempts, he won the Prix de Rome in 1789 with *Joseph Recognized by his Brother* (École des Beaux-Arts, Paris). A *Deposition* (church of Montesquieu-Volvestre, Haut-Garonne) dates from the same year. The shadowy emotion of this work prefigures the fuller Romanticism of his *Funeral of Atala* (1808; Louvre, Paris), inspired by the popular novel by Chateaubriand.

Girodet's versatility in this period of great stylistic change—even confusion—meant that he could paint in a "straight" Neoclassical manner when required. He did this in his *Hippocrates Refusing the Presents of Artaxerxes* (painted in Rome, 1792; now Faculty of Medicine, Paris). He could also adopt a blatantly mannerist approach, as in *Mlle Lange as Danaë* (1799; Minneapolis Institute of Arts). He painted bright, brash battle scenes, like *The Riots in Cairo, 21 October 1798* (Versailles), again with mannerist elements. Perhaps the key to his work is a sense of poetry, as in his Ossianic *The Apotheosis of the French Heroes* (1801; Malmaison, Rueil).

## Girtin Thomas 1775–1802

The English watercolorist Thomas Girtin was born at Southwark, London. In 1789,

after training with a drawing-master, he was apprenticed to the topographer Edward Dayes. Girtin's earliest drawings date from around this time, and bear witness to the strong influence that Dayes exerted on his apprentice. Dayes' influence continued to predominate during the period that he and Girtin were employed by the antiquarian James Moore, from 1792 to 1794.

There is reason to believe that Girtin was well acquainted with his exact contemporary J.M.W. Turner, since for three years, from c1794, Girtin worked for the amateur and collector Dr Thomas Munro. Joseph Farington reports in his diary that Girtin was chiefly employed by Dr Munro in copying the outlines or unfinished drawings of J.R. Cozens, while Turner washed in the effects.

During the next few years, Girtin frequently toured north Wales, the west country, Yorkshire, and Northumberland. He embarked on the first of these many sketching excursions in 1796. At this point he began to develop a highly original style, perhaps partly as a result of his contact with the work of Cozens. Recording a subjective response to nature, Girtin began to interpret subjects in optical terms, using loose, broad color washes to reduce the detail of a landscape to its formal elements.

Girtin's chief source of inspiration appears to have been found in the north of England, and the works of the last two or three years of his life reflect a sensitive interpretation of atmospheric values that undoubtedly paved the way for the "poetic" landscape of English Romantic painting. Girtin's *Eidometropolis* was a vast panorama of London, almost 2,000 ft (609 m) square. It was exhibited in 1802 and is now lost, but studies for it remain in the British Museum, London, along with a good collection of watercolors. Subject to asthmatic illness, Girtin died in the November of 1802. He spent the last few months of his life preparing a set of soft etchings of Paris, after a visit there late in 1801 for health reasons.

Thomas Girtin: Kirkstall Abbey on the Banks of the River Aire; watercolor; 32×52cm (13×20in); c1800. Victoria and Albert Museum, London

## Gislebertus of Autun 12th century

The name of the French sculptor Gislebertus of Autun is known from an inscription on one of the masterpieces of Romanesque art, the tympanum of the Cathedral of St Lazarus at Autun. He is one of the very few sculptors of the Romanesque period whose career can be reconstructed with some accuracy, not with the help of documents, but exclusively from the study of his surviving works.

It is almost certain that young Gislebertus was employed on the decoration of the celebrated abbey of Cluny in Burgundy at the turn of the 11th and 12th centuries. He subsequently worked in the Abbey of St Mary Magdalene at Vézelay, where several of his reliefs on capitals can be seen. He left Vézelay in order to take charge of the sculptural decoration of the cathedral of St Lazarus at Autun. Working there from c1125 for at least ten years, he carved a large number of capitals for the interior, and two external portals. When the church was completed, Gislebertus was no doubt engaged on making the furnishings; but of these only one wooden statue of the Virgin survives, possibly intended for an altar (Metropolitan Museum, New York).

The capitals show Gislebertus as an artist with a great range of expressive moods, from the lyrical in *The Infancy of Christ* series, to the dramatic in the two *Temptations of Christ*. From the north portal comes the relief of Eve (now in the Musée Rolin, Autun): a frank, if not openly sensuous portrayal of the female nude, probably unique in Romanesque art. The west portal contains a huge tympanum, framed by carved ornamental molding. The subject is the *Last Judgment*, dominated by Christ in a mandorla: a severe, awe-inspiring creation. The composition includes scenes of the elect being led to heaven, a group of humble apostles worshiping Christ, and the horrifying details of the torments of the damned. It is a work of wonderful technical skill, great piety, and a supreme power of expression.

## Giulio Romano c1499–1546

The Italian painter Giulio Pippi, called Giulio Romano, is one of the outstanding artists of Mannerism in the range of his work, in the elegance and wit of his style, and in his inventive relationship with the Antique. Born in Rome, he trained in Raphael's workshop, executing his master's designs in the Villa Farnesina and in

Giulio Romano: the architect's house in Mantua; facade reconstructed probably c1540–4

the Stanza dell'Incendio in the Vatican Palace. At Raphael's death in 1520 Giulio, together with G.F. Penni, was appointed executor of his will and completed a number of commissions begun by Raphael. Notable among these was the *Transfiguration*, now in the Vatican Museums, Rome.

In the Sala di Costantino, Raphael had initiated a brilliant decorative scheme where the story of the life of Constantine is shown on frescoes painted to resemble tapestries; these are framed by Popes seated on complex thrones, flanked by allegorical figures. He had also left drawings for the major narrative fresco, *The Battle of the Milvian Bridge*. Giulio was responsible for both the design and the execution of the remaining frescoes of the series. *The Allocution of Constantine* is based on Classical reliefs of an *adlocutio* (in which a general exhorts his troops before battle). Giulio echoes Raphael's interest in 'antiquarian' details of costume and setting. These are combined with a close study of Michelangelo's figure-style in the second half of the Sistine Ceiling, from which Giulio develops the contrapposto of his figures.

Giulio helped to complete the decoration of the loggia of the Villa Madama, de-

signed by Raphael. His work there was combined with stucco decorations by another of the artists from Raphael's workshop, Giovanni da Udine. Giovanni's rediscovery of the ancient technique of stucco, and his elegant reinterpretation of Roman ceilings, are important as the inspiration for later designs by Giulio.

During the Renaissance, architecture was often designed by painters and sculptors, and Giulio conformed to this practice by designing the Villa Lante on the Janiculum in Rome. Its severe entrance facade, with its Doric and Ionic pilasters, contrasts with the Salone at the back where the rhythmic interplay of the windows opens out on to a view of the gardens.

In 1524 Giulio was invited to Mantua as court artist for the Gonzagas. His acceptance of the invitation had profound effects on painting, sculpture, and architecture in Venice, the Veneto, and northern Europe; it offered him the opportunity to develop to the full the talents he had established in Rome. He made many drawings for items such as decorative plates and jugs; prepared a set of tapestries of *The Triumph of Scipio* for the King of France; and designed the frescoes of the *Assumption of the Virgin* in Verona Cathedral, which were executed by his studio.

His outstanding achievement in Mantua was his architecture, whose wide range reveals both his response to differing commissions and his sense of decorum. The nave of Mantua Cathedral is a brilliant revival of the Early Christian basilican church carried through with a sense of harmony and of proportion, and a brilliant control over lighting; while his rebuilding of S. Benedetto Po reveals his skill in modernizing an older structure, much of which he had to retain. The villa of Marmirolo outside Mantua that he designed and decorated no longer survives, but the facade of his own house in Mantua shows his inventive approach to tradition.

The Palazzo del Tè is one of the crucial works of Mannerism in North Italy; its influence extended from the Veneto to Germany and Fontainebleau. The Palace was set on the island of the Tè, outside Mantua, where the Gonzagas had their stables; it was used for hunting and for entertainment after the hunt. Because it replaced older structures it was not built all at one time; the old foundations that remained forced upon Giulio many slight irregularities in the handling of the facades, which are most notable in the first block to have been built, the one to the north. These irregularities were corrected in the other later blocks, which completed the square design around the courtyard (which once had a maze), and also in his plan of the palace, which we know from a near-contemporary copy.

The palace is an extension of the earlier design of the Villa Lante. The severe and massive rustication of the three main facades, which are articulated by Doric pilasters and triple openings in the doorways, is contrasted with the open garden facade. Here the triple rhythm of the doorways was to have been combined with a massive Classical pediment derived from Roman triumphal arches. (The pediment was not executed but is recorded in drawings after the original project). The courtyard is lighter and more playful in character than the forbidding facades, and in his design for the fallen triglyphs of the pediment Giulio quotes the Antique with characteristic wit and invention.

Giulio directed a large workshop to execute the decoration. The combination of stucco and frescoes both in the Palace and in the small grotto continued the pattern of the work of Villa Madama. The horses in the Sala dei Cavalli reflect the interests of the patrons, and the illusion that they stand in front of the architecture in the spectator's space derives from Mantegna's frescoes in the Camera degli Sposi in the Ducal Palace at Mantua. This new interest in illusionism also influenced the daring foreshortening of the scenes from the story of Cupid and Psyche. It culminated in the Sala dei Giganti: here Jupiter and the Olympian gods throw down massive, Michelangelesque giants who seem to fall on to the spectator—in their struggles, they even appear to pull the building down on top of him. The effect was much enjoyed by Vasari, who visited the Palace with Giulio, and who gave an enthusiastic description of the room in his *Lives of the Artists*. The illusion was repeated by Zelotti in his frescoes at Villa Thiene, and by Battista Franco at Villa Malcontenta, both probably dating from the 1550s.

**Further reading.** Hartt, F. *Giulio Romano* (2 vols.), London and New Haven (1958). Jestaz, B. and Bacou, R. *Jules Romain: l'Histoire de Scipion*, Paris (1978). Shearman, J. "Giulio Romano, Tradigione, Licenze, Artifice", *Bollettino del Centro Internazionale di Studi di Archittetura "A. Palladio"* vol. IX, Rome (1967). Verheyen, E. "Bemerkungen zu einer Zeichnung aus Giulio Romanos Mantuaner Studio", *Mitteilungen des Kunsthistorischen Institutes in Florenz* vol. XIII, Florence (1968). Verheyen, E. *The Palazzo del Te in Mantua: Images of Love and Politics*, Baltimore and London (1977).

## Glackens William 1870–1938

William James Glackens was an American painter and illustrator, and a member of the group of artists known as The Eight. He was born in Philadelphia and studied at the Pennsylvania Academy of the Fine Arts, and later in Paris. His first employment was as a newspaper illustrator for the *Philadelphia Press*, but he moved to New York in 1896. With the encouragement of his fellow artist Robert Henri he turned increasingly to painting. Glackens' Manet-inspired café picture *Chez Mouquin* (1905; Art Institute of Chicago) was shown at The Eight's only group exhibition in 1908. He continued to work as a much admired illustrator for *Life* and other magazines, while producing paintings of everyday New York life in an increasingly bright colored palette. He died in Westport, Connecticut.

## Glarner Fritz 1899–1972

The Swiss-American painter Fritz Glarner was born in Zurich. He studied art in Naples and in Paris, and in 1933 became a member of the Abstract artists' group *Abstraction-Création*. He moved to New York in 1936 and subsequently became an American citizen, without ever relinquishing his close ties with Paris and Switzerland.

It was in New York during the years 1943 and 1944 that Glarner became closely associated with Mondrian. He introduced a new style which he called "Relational Painting". This involved the use of the slanted line, and frequently, of the tondo format.

Fritz Glarner: Relational Painting no. 70; oil on canvas; 71×41cm (28×16in); 1954. Galerie Louis Carré et Cie, Paris

## Godefroid de Claire 12th century

Godefroid de Claire, also known as Godefroid de Huy, is often described as one of the outstanding goldsmiths of the 12th century. He worked in the valley of the River Meuse in Belgium, the "Mosan region". A large number of reliquaries and enamels have been attributed to him, but he remains a difficult figure to establish historically. His death is recorded in the late-12th-century register of the monastery of Neufmoûtier near Huy. A mid-13th-century addition in the margin says that Canon Godefroid, citizen of Huy, had "no equal as a goldsmith and he made many shrines in many places and objects for Kings".

We only know of two reliquaries certainly made by him, the house-shrines of St Mangold and St Domitian, made at the order of Bishop Raoul of Zähringen in 1173 for the church of Notre Dame of Huy. (These were recorded in an inventory of 1274.)

On the basis of this information Godefroid has been identified as the goldsmith to whom some letters were addressed as "My dear son G." by Abbot Wibald of Stavelot (born 1098, Abbot 1130, *ob.* 1158). "Master G." was responsible for making the Head Reliquary of Pope Alexander in 1145 (now in the Musées Royaux des Beaux-Arts de Belgique, Brussels) and the Remaclus Retable (known only from a 17th-century drawing) mentioned as being under construction in 1148.

It seems likely that Master G. engraved some Imperial seals for the Emperor Frederik Barbarossa, through the mediation of Abbot Wibald. It is still not proven that Master G. is identical with Godefroid de Claire. An analysis of the two Huy shrines, although these are poorly preserved, makes it seem distinctly possible. The rather indiscriminate attribution to Godefroid of a very large number of enamels and other goldsmith's work produced in this area between 1145 and 1173 has not helped our understanding of the development of Romanesque metalwork.

Hugo van der Goes: The Fall of Man; panel: 36×23cm (14×9in); c1467–77. Kunsthistorisches Museum, Vienna

## Goeritz Matthias 1915–1990

The architect, sculptor, and painter Matthias Goeritz was born at Danzig, Germany. Goeritz studied in Berlin where he obtained a doctorate in art history; he was greatly affected by the 1920s international avant-garde. He left Germany for Morocco in 1940 and moved to Spain at the end of the Second World War. In 1949 he left Spain to take up a teaching post at a new school of architecture in Guadalajara, Mexico.

In Mexico, where Goeritz has lived ever since, his output in all branches of art and design has been prolific. His visionary, "emotional" architecture has taken shape in a series of remarkable projects, notably

the El Eco Museum of Experimental Art (1952–3) and the Five Towers outside Mexico City (1957). Goeritz has also held major teaching posts in architecture and visual education.

## Goes Hugo van der c1436–82

Hugo van der Goes was the most remarkable Flemish painter of the second half of the 15th century. He became a master in the Painter's Guild in Ghent in 1467, and was Dean of the Guild from 1473 to 1475. More than any other Flemish painter of his time, van der Goes felt at home working on a large scale, as he shows in his

Portinari Altarpiece (c1475; Uffizi, Florence). By a quirk of history, the fame of the great Flemish artist largely rests upon this altarpiece in Italy. His most important work, the altarpiece exerted a considerable influence on Italian painters of the 15th century, while it must have remained all but unknown in the Netherlands. The story of the altarpiece helps to explain this.

Tommaso Portinari was the agent of the Medici bank in Bruges, where van der Goes' presence is documented in 1468. When Portinari commissioned a painting from a famous artist of the country he was living in, he must have wanted it to suit its surroundings back in his own city of

Florence. As the altarpiece was for the family chapel in the church of S. Egidio, Portinari no doubt specified that the work should be the size of the usual Florentine altarpiece. There were certainly Netherlandish paintings (and even painters) in Italy by the time the Portinari Altarpiece arrived there; a similar realism of portraiture and heightened naturalism of observed detail was known from other works. But the Portinari Altarpiece is distinguished not only by its exceptional quality, but by its size, which is unusual for a Flemish picture of this period. The altarpiece is in the form of a triptych, with the Nativity in the center panel and portraits of the donor and his wife on either wing. When closed, the shutters show an Annunciation in grisaille.

The work had both iconographical and technical significance for the Florentine painters who saw it c1475. The Child lies on the ground surrounded by adoring figures—a particularly Northern iconography of the Nativity which became popular in Italy. An influential group is that of the three shepherds, who are shown in a markedly unidealized study of three peasants. Apart from its iconographical importance, the altarpiece serves as a superb demonstration—in such details as the glass of water—of the Northern technique of oil painting. The technique was known in Italy by this time, but there was no oil painting in Florence on this scale, and no work that could give such a consummate demonstration of the advantages of oil painting over tempera. There is a rich luminosity about the rather cool colors which is very attractive.

The composition of the Portinari Altarpiece has a certain looseness about it which contrasts with another large work by van der Goes, The Adoration of the Kings (the Monforte Altarpiece, c1463–75; Staatliche Museen, Berlin). This is a much more compact picture, earlier in date, and closer in spirit to the work of van der Goes' great predecessors: artists such as Rogier van der Weyden. A painting later than the Portinari Altarpiece is the Death of the Virgin (State Museum, Bruges), a work which displays the rather unsettled grandeur characteristic of van der Goes.

It is easy to project into all these paintings our knowledge of van der Goes' final insanity. There is a remoteness in his work, which is especially evident in the rather haunting Death of the Virgin. His working life must have been fairly short as he went into semiretirement in a monastery near Brussels in 1478. From this time he became increasingly subject to fits of madness. The rather self-satisfied account of van der Goes' suffering left by a fellow monk suggests that these fits took the form of religious mania, with a conviction of his own eternal damnation. While in the monastery, van der Goes continued to receive visits from his rich and powerful admirers; but he succumbed to a distressing attack on a visit to Cologne c1481, and died in the following year.

**Further reading.** Friedländer, M.J. *Early Netherlandish Painting* vol. IV, Leiden (1967). Winkler, F. *Das Werk des Hugo van der Goes*, Berlin (1964).

## Gogh Vincent van 1853–90

The Dutch artist Vincent van Gogh is one of the most popular artists in the world today, but much of his fame may be due to his sensational life history and the drama and pathos of his short creative span. His work, his personality, and his intellectual interests, so articulately expressed in over 600 surviving letters, claim a more profound consideration. He was a man of great intelligence, sensitivity, and determination. He read widely in contemporary literature, philosophy, and history, and responded to the many exciting currents in 19th-century art and society. He is a touchstone for our understanding of many of these ideas and experiences, and his appeal for us today may be that he seems to epitomize modern man.

Before Van Gogh died at the age of 37, his short life had centered around three focal points: religion, art, and literature. He was born at Zundert in Holland. His father was an evangelical pastor, and he had uncles who were art dealers, admirals, and booksellers. It was natural that he should start work at 16, in 1869, in the family art-dealing firm in The Hague; this had been merged with a French company and was known as Goupil and Cie. He loved his work in the gallery and was absorbed in art. He visited museums and exhibitions wherever he went—his list of admired artists was almost endless—and he read widely the current literature, in magazines such as *Gazette des Beaux-Arts*.

His first acquaintance with art was from the standpoint of dealer and amateur critic, and his judgment was shrewd and sure. He loved the 17th-century Dutch artists, Rembrandt, Hals, and Jacob Ruisdael, and the French 19th-century landscape painters of the Barbizon School, Millet, Rousseau, and Dupré. He also promoted and supported the newly formed Hague School, the work of a group of Dutch artists, many of whom he got to know personally during his stay in the Hague from 1869 to 1873. He carried these tastes with him throughout his life. In 1888 he wrote to his friend and fellow artist Émile Bernard, "As for me, when I'm in the Louvre, I still go, with a great love in my heart, to the Dutch, Rembrandt first of all".

Van Gogh worked for Goupil and Cie in London (1873–5) and in Paris (1875–6), but he became depressed after an unhappy experience with the daughter of his London landlady, and was finally dismissed from the firm in April 1876. He turned more and more to religion, and to the Bible. He spent a few months working for a bookseller in Dordrecht in 1877. His love of literature expressed itself in wide reading and varied tastes. Among the authors he admired were the French historian Michelet, English authors like George Eliot, Dickens, and Carlyle, and French novelists such as Zola, the de Goncourt brothers, and de Maupassant. He later included his favorite books in paintings. In the late portrait of *Dr Gachet* (1890; private collection) the doctor leans his elbow on novels by the de Goncourt brothers, *Germinie Lacertueux* and *Manette Salomon*. Books also inspired his paintings directly. The important painting in the Kröller-Müller Museum, Otterlo, Holland, of Madame Roulin, wife of the Arles postman is entitled *La Berceuse*, the cradle-rocker: Vincent had been reading Pierre Loti's *Pêcheurs d'Islande* ("Fishermen of Iceland") and felt that sailors would need to take to sea just such an image of maternal comfort.

Van Gogh became more and more religious in the late 1870s. He spent nine months in England helping Methodist ministers, and even composed and delivered a lengthy sermon. By the middle of 1877 he had decided to follow in his father's footsteps and train for the church. With this intention he studied in Amsterdam and then in Brussels, and was able in November to go as a probationary evangelist to the poverty-stricken mining district of Belgium, the Borinage. This was a crucial period, for here Van Gogh lived out the practice of the Gospel, dedicating himself to the miners, giving away his clothes and food, and nursing the injured after fire-damp explosions in the mines. But his zeal and his willingness to carry out the commands of the Gospel in a literal manner found no support among the respectable churchmen. His behavior contradicted the accepted conventions of his class and profession, and he was dismissed.

Van Gogh became deeply suspicious of the hypocrisy of the established church and of so-called respectable people. Time and again he found himself rejected for conducting his life too closely in accord with his religious theory. In The Hague, for example, he took in a destitute and abandoned woman, and was dropped by many of the artists in the town. In Nuenen, in 1884, his friendship with Margot Begemann was the subject of such slander that the woman attempted to kill herself. To his brother, Theo, Van Gogh exploded:

But for heaven's sake, what is the meaning and standing of that absurd religion which respectable people maintain?—oh they are perfectly absurd, making society a kind of lunatic asylum, a perfectly topsy-turvy world ...

At the age of 26 Van Gogh had tried many professions and had failed in each of them. He wandered around the Borinage in bitter desperation, which he described most movingly to Theo in a letter written in July 1880. All his interests began to be synthesized into one activity: art. He turned to the art he knew, Rembrandt, Delacroix, Millet; and to the books of Dickens, Hugo, and Michelet; he wrote:

There is something of Rembrandt in Shakespeare, ... of Delacroix in Victor Hugo; and then there is something of Rembrandt in the Gospel, or something of the Gospel in Rembrandt.

In his footsore wanderings in the Borinage, Van Gogh had made an abortive journey to Courrières to meet an artist he admired, Jules Breton. There he made a decision:

Well, even in that deep misery I felt my energy revive, and I said to myself—In spite of everything I shall rise again: I will take up my pencil, which I have forsaken in my great discouragement and I will go on with my drawing. From that moment everything had seemed transformed for me.

Van Gogh had drawn before 1880. He had drawn skillfully in his youth, producing fine copies of engravings and prints. He drew tiny sketches and caricatures for a small girl in The Hague in 1872 and 1873. He has left us images of most of the houses he lived in. Now he took up his pencil with a clearer idea of what he wanted to produce. He would make strong drawings of working people, in a rugged style matched to his subject matter, in order to express his feeling about "the people": first the miners, then the weavers, and then the peasants of Brabant and Provence.

His subsequent career falls easily into periods marked by the places in which he lived: Etten in 1880, The Hague from 1881 to 1883, Drenthe in 1883, Nuenen from 1883 to 1885, Antwerp from 1885 to 1886, Paris from 1886 to 1888, Arles in 1888, St Remy from 1889 to 1890, Auvers in 1890. He spent the first half of his active life as an artist in Holland, studying and finally bringing his own individual touch to the current style of the Hague school. It would be a mistake to dismiss the earlier works of his short career as a beginner's studies. The somber colors, the richly applied paint, the loving depiction of peasants in their cottages or at work in the fields echo the work of Josef Israels (1824–1911) and Anton Mauve (1838–88).

Van Gogh was related to Mauve by marriage and had become a personal friend. He turned to him for advice and encouragement when he undertook to become an artist. Mauve was his only real teacher in the conventional sense; Van Gogh remained devoted to him. When he heard of his death in 1888, Vincent inscribed on one of his best paintings of a tree in blossom, "Souvenir de Mauve" and sent it to his widow.

Van Gogh was drawn to figure-painting in these years and felt the highest form of modern art was the depiction of the peasant figure in action. Some of his best drawings are inspired by the men and women of Nuenen engaged in agricultural tasks. His most important figure-subject is of these peasants at rest, *The Potato Eaters* (1885; Rijksmuseum Vincent van Gogh, Amsterdam), which shows a family of five around the table in the dim light of their old oil lamp, eating the potatoes they have sown and dug. This subject was depicted many times by other Dutch artists of the period and entitled "The Frugal Meal" or "Potato Eaters"; Josef Israels particularly loved the theme. Van Gogh's painting, however, is stripped of all sentimentality, anecdote, or obvious social comment. The handling is more vigorous, the color more resonant, and the painting is alive with the powerful feeling Van Gogh had for these peasants. He saw how their way of life was being gradually undermined by the encroachments of industrialization on to the simple existence in which man lived by the soil.

Van Gogh felt isolated in the country far from other artists and left for Antwerp, where he enrolled in an Academy in order to draw from the model. Suddenly, however, he decided to leave for Paris and sent Theo this note: "Dear Theo, Do not be cross with me for having come all at once like this ... Shall be at the Louvre from midday or sooner, if you like."

Paris was alive with new ideas, and movements to stimulate the imagination of a young artist. Van Gogh could see the Impressionist exhibition, the annual Salon, the new Salon Nationale exhibition, a retrospective of his favorite artist, Millet, a show of Monet and Renoir at Petit's gallery, Symbolist works by Gustave Moreau and Odilon Redon. He went to study at the studio of an established artist Ferdinand Cormon, where he met Henri de Toulouse-Lautrec. The work of the Impressionists, particularly that of Claude Monet, affected his work enormously; it produced new, brighter colors, a gayer, freer choice of subject, and an interest in landscapes and views of Paris. But he soon began to experiment with the ideas of the Neo-Impressionists through Paul Signac. Dots of broken color begin to run across his canvas, and urgent trails of hurried dashes.

Van Gogh arrived in Paris when a new growth of ideas among younger artists was developing beyond Impressionism, and when the older men, Monet and Renoir, were themselves exploring fresh ideas. Van Gogh digested all this, but began to find his own direction under the powerful influence of the Japanese colored woodcuts that were then the rage in Paris. Their use of bold areas of pure, bright color, and their popular subject matter made them for Vincent more than lively decorations. They represented a golden paradise of color and light.

The tensions of Paris and the battles waged between artists of differing persuasions proved too much for Van Gogh, so he decided to go south to find his own Japan, in the sun and color of southern France. He hoped to found there a cooperative community of artists, similar

Vincent van Gogh: Self-portrait with Bandaged Ear; oil on canvas; 60×49cm (24×19in); 1889.
Courtauld Institute Galleries, London

part of his left ear with a razor.

This first fit of insanity led to Van Gogh's incarceration and release, then a reincarceration requested by the people of Arles, and finally his voluntary entry into the mental asylum of St Paul at St Rémy. Van Gogh's illness was characterized by numerous attacks, followed by periods of lethargy and inability to work, followed in turn by complete lucidity and amazingly concentrated activity. It has been variously explained as schizophrenia, as epilepsy, or as an inherited family weakness. The inadequacy of medical records and the crudity of diagnosis in mental illness make it difficult to be certain, but it seems likely that Van Goth suffered from a form of temporal lobe epilepsy whose symptoms often mirror the features of schizophrenia. It is possible that his "madness" did not directly affect his art; but the experience and fear of attacks, and the ensuing depression would inevitably have had a disturbing and distressing effect on his equilibrium.

Van Gogh was able to paint in St Rémy but there is a change in his style: the tone of the color is more somber and the forms seem convulsed by their own energy, which seems now beyond Van Gogh's control. Clouds twist and swirl through a disturbed sky, cypresses lick the skies like flames. Significantly, Van Gogh turned back to the inspirations of his early years: to Millet, to Rembrandt, and to Delacroix, whose work he translated into his own color. He asked Theo to send him earlier drawings, and he produced a series of peasants, cottages, and landscapes which are called "Memories of the North". He even drew a version of *The Potato Eaters* from memory.

One of the most important works of this period is his rendering of Rembrandt's etching *The Raising of Lazarus* (1890; Rijksmuseum Vincent van Gogh, Amsterdam). In black and white etching, Rembrandt used the fall of light to symbolize the emanating power of Christ. Van Gogh eliminates the figure of Christ and replaces it with a huge yellow sun whose light, embodied in the pervasive gold of the paint, represents the force of life itself. Rembrandt is transformed by the sun; north and south are joined; religion, art, and nature are combined in one single statement.

Van Gogh went north again in May 1890. He passed through Paris, saw a few exhibitions, and met his sister-in-law and

to groups of the Barbizon School, The Hague School, and the workshops of the Japanese printmakers.

Van Gogh was charmed by the South, and felt he had found his Japan; but it also brought back strong memories of his native Holland. He wrote to his sister that what he had learned in Paris was leaving him; and in his letters to Theo he wrote how the Provençal countryside reminded him of the works of Ruisdael and Hobbema. The landscapes he painted there recall the wide flat plains of 17th-century Dutch landscapes, and he repeated the Dutch motif of drawbridges, which had actually been built by Dutch engineers in Provence. In 1888 Paul Gauguin had been persuaded to join Van Gogh in Arles as the beginning of their planned artists' society, "Studio of the Tropics". The two painters differed dramatically in their views about art, and this led to tremendous arguments

which Van Gogh described as "electric". Gauguin wanted to free art from a dependence on nature, while Van Gogh was dedicated to the reality of the natural world. He had written to Émile Bernard: "We can—and this was done by the old Dutchmen ... we can paint an atom of chaos, a horse, a portrait, your grandmother, apples and a landscape ..." Such subjects could, he believed, be transformed with color and feeling into powerful symbols. For instance, the simplest bowl of flowers that Van Gogh painted, *The Sunflowers* (1888; National Gallery, London), is as potent an evocation of the sun—its light, its power, its energy—as anything in the history of art. Yet it remains an "atom of chaos" observed with humility and love. The tension with Gauguin culminated in Van Gogh's violent attack on his friend followed by a horrific self-mutilation when Van Gogh cut off

Vincent van Gogh: Group of Houses seen against a Hill (View at Auvers); oil on canvas; 50×100cm (20×40in); 1890. Tate Gallery, London

infant nephew for the first time before going to Auvers. At this village near Paris he was able to stay under the sympathetic eye of Dr Gachet, physician, painter, and friend of the Impressionists. Van Gogh worked incredibly hard, producing drawings and paintings often at the rate of two or more a day. In the light of the knowledge of his suicide in July of that year, one is tempted to read this period backwards and endow the often sunny and powerful paintings of these months with a meaning and menace born of further knowledge. Vincent was worried about his brother Theo, who had provided his only financial support for the past ten years. The strain of dependence, his lack of success, fear for the future, failure of his cooperative schemes, and anxiety about recurring breakdowns and possible inability to work weighed understandably heavily on him. In one of his last letters, Van Gogh is acutely concerned about the vulnerability of artists to the commercial art world. Undoubtedly some of his paintings are desolate and harrowingly empty.

On 27th July 1890 Vincent tried to kill himself with a revolver; he died from his wounds two days later, in Theo's arms, at the age of 37. The tragedy of his death has overshadowed his life, and his work often seems accompanied by an invisible label,

"This was painted by a man who was 'mad' and who committed suicide."

Van Gogh was both a brilliant colorist and an equally consummate draftsman. He began his career as an artist by drawing for almost two years, and some of his most satisfying work is to be found in the drawings of the peasants of Nuenen at their labors, and in the panoramic landscapes of Provence. At first, he worked in a vigorous style emphasizing the outline, but he gradually broadened his range when he came to draw landscapes. For these he developed a wonderfully varied and energetic technique made up of a myriad of different types of graphic marks—dots, dashes, and swirls. Everything combined to create a sense of energetic movement and heat-filled vibration. The best-known period of Van Gogh's work, in terms of paintings, is the creative time he spent in Arles, during 1888 and 1889. Here he combined his technical knowledge of new color theories, his love of strongly colored Japanese prints, his understanding of the work of Eugène Delacroix, and the effect of the southern sunflowers, sowers, harvesters and seascapes. He was acutely sensitive to color itself, but he wanted to use it to express something more than appearance. He wrote to Theo: "... instead of trying to reproduce exactly what I

have before my eyes, I use color more arbitrarily, in order to express myself forcibly."

To this end he used almost symbolic combinations of color, as in the portrait of a friend where he placed an exaggeratedly blond head against a deep blue ground in order to create the "mysterious brightness of a pale star in the infinite". He wanted to incorporate into his paintings the energy he was able to create in his drawings. So he applied his brilliant gemlike colors with graphic brush strokes, which curled around forms, ran in radiating haloes round bright stars and suns, and licked the flamelike branches of the cypresses. He used the direction of the strokes in painting and drawing alike to help to create space and perspective and to fill the whole canvas of paper with pulsating light. Sometimes, towards the end of his life, this energy seems beyond his control; forms break out and spread, or the figures bulge and buckle at the joints. In his greatest works, however, Van Gogh was able to express form, energy, and light by the marriage of line and color through which he recreated his intense perceptions of the natural world.

Van Gogh is rare among artists for he has left such a fascinating and revealing picture of his interests, and his acute responses to art, literature, music, and politics in his letters. But he searched above all for visual expressiveness. He brought into a new synthesis streams from all aspects of culture and of the history of art, and expressed them in a way accessible to anyone who cares to look or read. He is, paradoxically, one of the most comprehensible of modern artists and also one of the most profound.

**Further reading.** Castri, F. *Van Gogh*, New York (2003). Faille, J.B. de la *Vincent van Gogh, The Complete Works on Paper, Catalogue Raisonné* (2 vols.), San Francisco (1992). Fell, D. *Van Gogh's Gardens*, New York (2001). *The Complete Letters of Vincent van Gogh*, 3rd ed. (3 vols.), Boston (2000). Sweetman, D. *Van Gogh: His Life and His Art*, New York (1990). Walther, I. F. *Van Gogh: the Complete Paintings*, Cologne (2001).

# Goltzius Hendrick 1558–1617

The Dutch engraver and painter Hendrick Goltzius was born in Mulbrecht. He was at first the pupil of his father, Jan Goltz. In 1577 he followed his second master, Dirck Volckertsz. Coornhert, to Haarlem where he was influenced by the Flemish Mannerist Bartholomaeus Spranger. The slender and agitated forms of his chiaroscuro woodcut of *Proserpine* is typical of his style at this time. A consummate master of the engraver's art, his skill with the burin is well exemplified in *The Standard Bearer*.

In 1590, a visit to Rome caused him to abandon this extravagant style, in favor of a more classical approach. His panoramic landscapes and forceful portraits indicate both versatility and acute powers of observation. However, it was Goltzius' technical virtuosity that most impressed his contemporaries.

Goltzius also produced brilliant drawings, some on a life-size scale. His *Venus, Ceres, and Bacchus with a Self Portrait* in the Hermitage Museum, St Petersburg, was the most prodigious of these. He also produced some paintings in a Mannerist style, but these lack the verve and immediacy of his graphic work.

A complex artist, Goltzius' wit and audacity reflect contemporary Mannerism, and his technical mastery typifies the Northern tradition.

# Golub Leon 1922–

After military service during World War Two, the American painter Leon Golub studied at the Art Institute of Chicago. He moved to Paris in 1959 and returned to the United States in 1964. An overtly political artist, Golub is concerned to make painting relevant and disturbing at a time when the endless flow of mass media images of brutality has made people insensitive to the moral and political complexities of events. His large, imposing works typically show scenes of torture or interrogation, the explicit violence balanced by an ambiguity, and even a grace, that encourages an unsettling identification with both the victims and the perpetrators of violence. *Interrogation II* (1983; Art Institute of Chicago) is typical, both in its subject and its technique, the canvas painted, scraped and repainted many times to create a tense, skinlike surface.

# Gonçalves Nuno fl. 1450–71

The history of Portuguese painting in the 15th century is dominated by one man, Nuno Gonçalves. His reputation rests on the splendid altarpiece of *The Veneration of St Vincent* (National Museum of Art, Lisbon), from the monastery of São Vicente de Fora in Lisbon. Relatively little Portuguese painting from before the middle of the 15th century has survived; much of it shows strong Italian influence and none of the frescoes or portraits can be regarded as a convincing native source for Gonçalves' style.

The life of Nuno Gonçalves is thinly documented. As painter to Alfonso V he was active between 1450 and 1472. In 1471 he replaced the decorative artist João Anes as official painter to the city of Lisbon. Franciso de Olanda, friend of Michelangelo, reckoned Gonçalves among the "eagles"—the foremost painters of his age. According to Olanda, Gonçalves was the painter "who painted the altar of St Vincent in the Cathedral of Lisbon".

The polyptych of *The Veneration of St Vincent* (c1460) has six panels; the figure of the Saint appears twice, suggesting that the work stood in two sections on either side of a statue. In front of St Vincent—patron saint of the Portuguese Royal Family and the Army—are Alfonso V, Henry the Navigator, and a retinue including nobles, knights, clerics, and fishermen.

Gonçalves' style has often been compared with that of the early Florentine fresco painters, and also with that of Jan van Eyck, who worked in Portugal in 1428. Yet this altarpiece has its individual character: it is essentially a composition of human figures, from which Italianate or Flemish notions of decorative detail have been eliminated. There is neither architectural perspective nor landscape to distract the eye; it is even doubtful whether the setting is interior or exterior. Gonçalves

Hendrick Goltzius: The Fat Kitchen; pen and ink with brown wash on paper; 20×33cm (8×13in); 1603. Print Room of the University of Leiden

used color with restraint; gold is largely replaced by yellow, while the strong reds and greens of the fabrics are the more effective for the somber tones of the background. The faces suggest carved wood—long, fine-boned, and brooding, they are characteristically Portuguese.

No other painting can be safely attributed to Gonçalves. Works depicting St Theotonius and St Francis, and a portrait of a young man, indicate a vigorous following among his contemporaries and successors: he began a flourishing tradition, which lasted well into the 16th century.

## Gontcharova Natalia 1881–1962

The Russian painter and stage designer Natalia Gontcharova was born at Ladyzhino near Tula, the daughter of an architect of noble family. She studied at the Moscow School of Painting, where she met her husband and lifelong associate, Michail Larionoff. Together they were active in the Moscow avant-garde until 1913, participating in such exhibitions as "The Golden Fleece", "The Knave of Diamonds", "Donkey's Tail", and "The Target", and inventing the new Abstract style of Rayonnism. In 1913 Gontcharova met Diaghilev, and designed the opera *Coq d'Or* for his 1914 Paris production. She settled in Paris in 1915, and lived there until her death. Her later work was almost exclusively devoted to ballet and opera designs, and her reputation rests mainly on the Cubist-Primitivist and Rayonnist paintings she produced between 1908 and 1918.

**Further reading.** Chamot, M. *Natalia Gontcharova*, Paris (1972). Gontcharova, N. *Les Ballets Russes de Serge Diaghilev et la Decoration Theatricale*, Belves (1930). Gray, C. *The Russian Experiment in Art 1863–1922*, London (1971).

## González Julio 1876–1942

The Spanish sculptor Julio González was born in Barcelona in 1876. Both his father and grandfather were goldsmiths and metalworkers, and it was in the craftsman's tradition that Julio and his elder brother, Joan, grew up. They attended painting classes at the School of Fine Arts in Barcelona; among the young artists they met at this time was Pablo Picasso, who became Julio's lifelong friend.

In 1900 the González family moved to

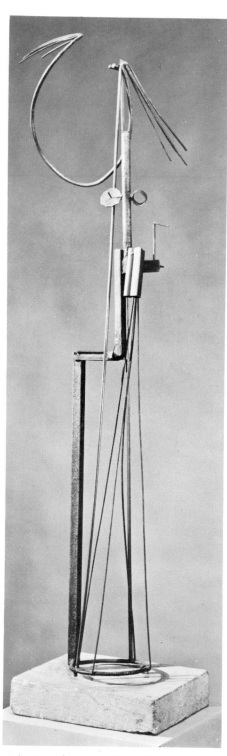

Julio González: Large Maternity; metal; 130×41×23cm (51×16×9in); 1934. Tate Gallery, London

Paris, producing decorative metal work that was shown at international exhibitions there and in Chicago. Julio was active in the family workshop; at the same time, with little success, he attempted to establish himself as a painter. He was at this period in the shadow of his brother, Joan, whose premature death in 1908 was a very serious blow that extinguished Julio's creative gifts for many years. He retired from the art world altogether; during the First World War he worked at the Renault car factory where he learned the technique of oxyacetylene welding.

Slowly Julio González returned to art, concentrating now on sculpture rather than painting; he worked in relief, coloring some of his metal sculptures. He gave much technical advice in metal sculpture to his friend Picasso (1930–1), and his renewed contact liberated his own imagination. From 1930 until his death 12 years later González produced a succession of iron sculptures that showed the formal possibilities of this intractable but powerfully eloquent material. Some, like *Montserrat* (1936–7; Stedelijk Museum, Amsterdam), were directly realist in style and subject; but others made use of metaphor, for example *The Kiss* (1930) and several *Cactus Men* (1939–40). These works displayed a new attitude to sculptural space that has made González one of the most influential of 20th-century sculptors.

**Further reading.** Descargues, P. *Julio González*, Paris (1971). *Julio González: Les Matériaux de son Expression*, Zurich (1969). Tucker, W. "The Sculpture of González", *Studio International*, London (December 1970).

## Gorky Arshile 1904–48

Gorky was an American painter who played a key role in the merging of abstraction and Surrealism to prepare for the new style of Abstract Expressionism.

He was born Vosdanik Manook Adoian in Khorkom, a village near Lake Van in Turkish Armenia, the son of a wheat farmer and trader. Victims of the Turkish persecution of Armenians, the family emigrated to the United States in 1920; they lived first in Boston then in Providence, Rhode Island, where Gorky began his art studies. About 1925 he moved to New York, and adopted the name Arshile Gorky. Befriended by the painter Stuart Davis in 1929, his first important paintings were Cubist still lifes; but the most charac-

Arshile Gorky: Waterfall; oil on canvas; 155×114cm (61×45in); 1943. Tate Gallery, London

teristic early works are the portraits, especially *The Artist and his Mother* which was based on a photograph taken in 1912 (1926–35; Whitney Museum of American Art, New York).

In 1933 Gorky got to know another young emigrant painter, Willem de Kooning, and his work changed under the influence of the Surrealist Picasso and the abstraction of Arp and Miró. He drew and painted certain subjects repeatedly: for example *Garden in Sochi* (1940–2; one version of 1941 in the Museum of Modern Art, New York). Such paintings used Gorky's memories of childhood to create a composition of suggestive forms.

By 1944 Gorky had met André Breton, Matta, and other Surrealist refugees in New York, and the final phase of his art began. His paintings now displayed the open fluid qualities of 1914 Kandinsky; and they became more Abstract. As Gorky faced such private disasters as the destruction by fire of his studio and an operation for cancer in 1946, his paintings became increasingly anguished and tragic in form and color. Such paintings as *Agony* (1947; Museum of Modern Art, New York) and *Betrothal II* (1947; Whitney Museum of American Art, New York) stand out among his hundreds of drawings. The period ended with Gorky's tragic suicide, after he had suffered an incapacitating motor accident in July 1948.

Further reading. Herrera, H. *Arshile Gorky: His Life and Work*, New York (2003). Jordan, J. *The Paintings of Arshile Gorky*, New York (1982).

## Goshun Matsumura 1752–1811

Matsumura Goshun was the founder of the *Shijo* School of Japanese painting. The *Shijo* was based on a mixture of the realistic *Maruyama* School with the neo-Chinese *Nanga* School; its name derived from the location of Goshun's studio on Fourth Street in Kyoto. It became a major style of painting and printed book illustration in the 19th century.

Goshun was born in Kyoto in 1752. He was not the son of a professional painter, and at first he worked as a letter writer in Shimbara. He studied painting under Onishi Suigetsu; and, even more important to his subsequent career, learned to write *haiku* under the great painter and *haiku* poet, Yosa Buson. He became a monk in 1782, when he took the name of Goshun

Jan Gossaert: Jean Carondelet, from the Carondelet Diptych; panel; 43×27cm (17×11in); 1517. Louvre, Paris

(of his many other names, the best known is Gekkei). Presumably he found the *Nanga* style unsuited to his taste, for in the early 1780s he asked Maruyama Okyo if he could become his pupil. Knowing of his skill as a painter, Okyo instead took him into his studio as an equal.

After he set up his own studio (some time after 1788) in Shijo-dori, Goshun's style, later to become the *Shijo* style, was formed. He had many famous pupils in-

cluding his younger brother Keibun, Okamoto Toyohiko, and Sato Suiseki.

Despite its *Nanga* ancestry, the style is essentially the least calligraphic of the later Japanese styles. Its abbreviation of realism is never so precise as to become formal, but in the hand of a lesser painter it can seem merely pretty. In the mid 19th century some members of the school veered back towards *Nanga* and away from realism, especially in figure-painting.

## Gossaert Jan c1478–1532

The Flemish painter Jan or Jennyn Gossaert is also known as Mabuse, this name deriving from Mauberge in Hainault, where he was born. From c1516 he usually signed his name in the Latin form of "Joannes Malbodius". He is recorded in the Antwerp guild records from 1503. By 1507 he had become court painter to Philip of Burgundy, an illegitimate son of the Burgundian ducal house who was Governor of Gelderland and Zutphen.

When Philip headed an embassy to Rome on behalf of the Emperor Maximilian in 1508, Mabuse traveled in his entourage. He stayed in Rome for some months after his patron had left; but he was back in the Netherlands, at Middelburg, by the end of 1509. He continued to serve Philip when the latter became Bishop of Utrecht in 1517, and he is also known to have worked at the court of Margaret of Austria, Regent of the Netherlands, at Malines.

The *Adoration of the Magi* (National Gallery, London) is the masterpiece of his early style. The work has the richly detailed quality of an elaborately carved altarpiece. There are debts to Hugo van der Goes in the angels, and to Dürer's prints in the careful perspective of crumbling walls and archways. The dog in the right foreground is a direct quotation from Dürer's *St Eustace* print of 1501. The complicated theme of the work matches its elaborate textural detail, for here the kings are joined in adoration by the shepherds, and the Trinity is also included.

On his visit to Italy Mabuse drew extensively after the Antique, showing more interest in this than in Renaissance art. His style became increasingly sculptural as a result. The *St Luke Painting the Virgin* (1515; Kunsthistorisches Museum, Vienna) is set in a Classical interior with applied antique ornament.

More unusual, however, is a series of small mythological paintings, many of them probably painted for Philip. Before this period the painting of nude figures had been almost exclusively confined to the subject of Adam and Eve. With paintings of *Neptune and Amphitrite* (1516; Staatliche Museen, Berlin), *Hercules and Deianeira* (Barber Institute of Fine Arts, Birmingham), and *Venus and Cupid* (1521; Musées Royaux des Beaux-Arts de Belgique, Brussels), Gossaert introduced a new range of subject matter. The nudes seem to be sculpture come alive. The figure-style shows the influence of the later works of Dürer and the engraved nude figures of Jacopo de' Barbari, with whom Mabuse collaborated on the decoration of Castle Souburg for Philip of Burgundy in 1516.

His portrait style is more conservative and he retains the traditional Flemish format of placing figures behind a ledge. His *Children of King Christian II of Denmark* (1526/7; Hampton Court Palace, London), is one of his more lively studies.

Gossaert's crucial role in the development of Netherlandish painting won early recognition. Guicciardini noted in his *Descrittione di tutti i Paesi Bassi* (1567) that "he was the first who brought from Italy to these lands the skill of painting histories and poetical subjects (*poesie*) with nude figures".

## Gottlieb Adolph 1903–73

The American painter Adolph Gottlieb was born in New York City. He had some lessons from John Sloan at the Art Students league, but he was essentially a self-taught artist. As a young man he worked on mural projects for the W.P.A. (Works Progress Administration), decorating the post office at Yerrington, Nevada, and the Millburn Synagogue, New Jersey. Later, his profound interest in ancient hieroglyphs and American Indian art led to a radical change in style.

He remained in New York for the rest of

Adolph Gottlieb: Counterpoise 1959; oil on canvas; 276×228cm (108×90in); 1959. Private collection

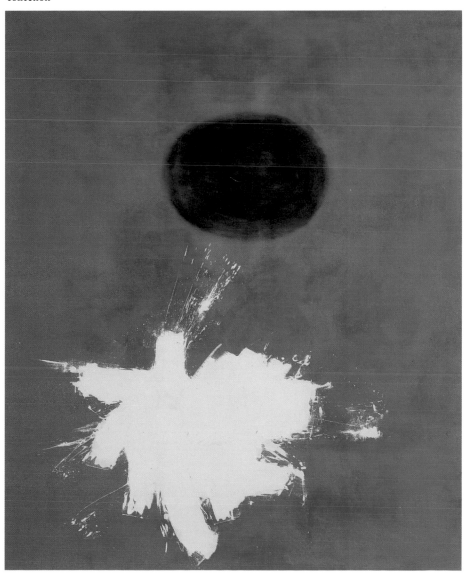

his life, and his close association with Rothko and Newman in the 1940s was an important element in the so-called New York School.

From 1941 Gottlieb called his paintings pictographs: he wanted to create visual images that would convey feeling without recourse to any kind of descriptive language. His work began with comparatively complicated structures such as *The Seer* of 1950 (The Phillips Collection, Washington, D.C.). A later development was the simplicity of the *Burst* series (begun 1957; for example, *Expanding*, 1962; Art Institute of Chicago).

Further reading. Frank, E. *Adolph Gottlieb: Vertical Moves*, New York (2002).

## Goujon Jean *c*1510–*c*65

Jean Goujon dominated French sculpture in the middle decades of the 16th century; he belonged to the group of native artists who emerged at the end of the period when France had owed both art and artists to Italy. His sculptural style owed much to the first generation of Italian artists working at Fontainebleau. Taking Mannerist characteristics from such artists as Rosso and Primaticcio, he added a delicate classicism that is typically French.

Information on his birth and early career

is sparse. The earliest works attributed to him in Rouen include the cathedral tomb of Louis de Brézé, husband of Diane de Poitiers. Certainly the caryatids of the tomb anticipate those he executed in 1550 as part of the interior decoration of the Louvre. He worked much of the time as a decorator of architecture in collaboration with the architect Pierre Lescot. In an appendix to the 1547 French edition of Vitruvius, Goujon is referred to as an architect and he discusses the optical problems involved in the positioning of sculptured reliefs in architectural frameworks.

His first commission in Paris, the decoration of the rood screen in St Germain-L'Auxerrois (and particularly the *Deposition* relief of 1544) is evidence of the influence of such Italian Mannerist artists as Rosso. Indeed much of his work was in the form of shallow-relief panels, with a stressing of the surface plane not unlike the strong emphasis on surface in many Mannerist paintings.

In his famous piece for the Rue aux Fers, the Fontaine des Innocents of 1550 (rebuilt in 1776 in the square that replaced the Cemetery of the Innocents), the typically French treatment of the combined classical and Mannerist features is obvious; this is especially true of the six tall narrow reliefs of nymphs bearing urns, who strike a variety of poses. In the middle of the 18th

century, the critic A.N. Dézallier d'Argenville wrote that they could not be admired too much, and in the 19th century they were still being copied by Renoir and Cézanne.

The most famous French sculpture of the middle of the 16th century, *Diana and the Stag* (Louvre, Paris), from the Château d'Anet, was traditionally attributed to Goujon. Its authorship is now uncertain.

Goujon worked at the Louvre from 1550 to 1562, producing work for both the exterior and the interior; but there is no further trace of his presence there after 1562. He died *c*1565.

## Govardhan 17th century

Govardhan was a Mughal court artist under the Emperors Jahangir (1605–27) and Shah Jahan (1628–58). His earliest surviving work is probably that in the *Akbar-nama* (1605–10; Chester Beatty Library, Dublin). Other early works are among the margin drawings of the Jahangir Album leaves in the Gulistan Palace Library, Teheran. On one of these is a painting of Govardhan by his fellow miniaturist Daulat. He later kept abreast of the times in his painting of genre scenes, especially those depicting fakirs and other religious figures (in the Minto Album, divided between the Chester Beatty Library, Dublin, and the Victoria and Albert Museum, London). There is also an album containing his work in the Hermitage Museum, Leningrad. In the Minto Album there is a pair of facing equestrian portraits of Timur and of Shah Jahan. He excelled in facial expression, as in the portraits of courtiers painted during the 1630s, now in the British Museum, London.

## Goya 1746–1828

The Spanish artist Francisco José de Goya y Lucientes, known as Goya, was born in Fuendetosdos, a small village outside Saragossa. His father was a master gilder. Goya's career as an artist was decided by the age of 14 when he was apprenticed to José Luzan, a busy church decorator. Spanish art had been for a long time in a state of decay, until Charles III remedied this by inducing Mengs and G.B. Tiepolo, the two finest artists working in Europe, to come to Madrid. It was under their shadow that Goya developed his own style. Some of Goya's earliest work survives, from a visit to Italy in 1771, and

Jean Goujon (attrib.): Diana and the Stag; marble; 211×258×135cm (83×102×53in); c1550–4. Louvre, Paris

these pictures show how far he was expected to bend to contemporary taste. The Goya we know from the late works does not emerge until after 1775.

Upon returning from Italy he won the first of a series of church commissions which began with the cathedral of El Pilar, in Saragossa, his home town. While working there he married Josepha Bayeu. She was the sister of Francisco Bayeu, who was Mengs' first assistant and the most respected native artist of his day.

Charles III had put Mengs in control of the Royal Tapestry Factory in Madrid; through the recommendation of Francisco Bayeu, Goya was employed to work on designs for the tapestries. These "cartoons", preserved in the Prado, Madrid, offer an illuminating account of Goya's rapid mastery of the medium, from the first oil sketch in 1774 to the last, in 1792. Apart from their painterly skills, Goya's designs outclass any decorative works done in Europe at this time. *The Parasol* (delivered in 1778; cartoons in the Prado, Madrid), strikes such a perfect balance between the ornate outlines of Tiepolo and the classical solidity of Mengs that it could be called one of the last great achievements of the Baroque school.

Goya's contact with the court led to the next important step in his development. In 1777–8 he made a series of etchings of Velazquez's paintings in the royal collection. This gave him his first experience of the technique of etching with aquatint, in which he soon emerged one of the world's masters. It also introduced him to Velazquez, who more than any contemporary influence helped Goya make a final step into complete maturity.

In 1779 Goya's application for the post of Court Painter was turned down; but his *Christ on the Cross* (1780; Prado, Madrid), a restrained diploma piece, gained him the title of Academician. During the next ten years Goya strove to be recognized as Spain's foremost artist. His winning of the royal commission to paint *San Francisco el Grande* in Madrid, his work for great Spanish families like the Osunas, the leading politicians such as the chief minister, Floridablanca, were all part of this steady uphill climb. That Goya was aware of his shifting position in society can be seen in the self-portraits included in the paintings that span these years, *Floridablanca*, 1783, *San Francisco el Grande*, 1781–3, and *The Family of Charles IV* 1800–1 (all in the Prado, Madrid).

Goya: Portrait of King Ferdinand VII of Spain in the Uniform of a General; detail; oil on canvas; full size 207×140cm (81×55in); 1814. Prado, Madrid

Goya was at last made Court Painter when the new King, Charles IV, succeeded to the throne in 1789. The new reign brought Goya an increasing burden of work. Besides continuing the tapestry designs and now-popular portrait commissions, he was expected to produce a whole new set of royal portraits. This period was also one of the darkest in Spanish history. Under the threat of the French Revolution, and dominated by the Queen (and her ally, the first minister, Godoy), Charles IV collapsed into a state of panic reaction. Two of Goya's pro-French liberal friends were banished and it was probably such anxieties, coupled with overwork, that brought on the illness Goya suffered during 1792 and 1793. Its exact nature remains a mystery, but we know it was a traumatic experience from which he emerged stone-deaf, and that it marks a change in his work. He became more isolated, and suddenly aware of the depths of his own mind. On a more practical level, the collection of paintings and prints of Sebastian Martinez (with whom he stayed during his illness) suggested a new range of imagery and subjects, and the period of convalescence allowed him a new freedom from the restraints of patronage.

A fascination with scenes of cruelty and affliction emerges in the small paintings on copper of 1794, but, at the same time, Goya's broad mastery as a painter remains intact, perhaps even augmented. Begun as the more idiosyncratic *Suenos* ("Dreams") *Los Caprichos* of 1797 became the first fruit of these new ideas. Many of the 80 captioned plates reflect the ideas of the liberal movement of the day, particularly of its leader, Jovillanos. The dome of S. Antonio de la Florida, Madrid, shows that this mastery was not confined to etching or oils but applied to fresco as well. Painted in 1798, when the artist had little sympathy for the rituals of the church, it makes its subject the common people of Madrid rather than the miracle they witness. All Goya's work of this period is marked with the same daring and intensity. *The Family of Charles IV* (1800–1; Prado, Madrid) with its delight in ornament and its disarming naturalism, is in part a celebration of his own position as First Painter to the Court. By the time the short-lived liberal

regime collapsed, by which time Goya had lost more friends through banishment and other intrigues, his own position was so well established that he could negotiate with both Godoy and the King. The two versions of the *Majas* (now Prado, Madrid), clothed and unclothed, were painted before 1805 and appear in an inventory of Godoy's estate in 1808.

From 1808 until the end of his life Goya was strongly affected, emotionally rather than physically, by political events. Napolean had become increasingly involved in Spanish affairs; in 1808 he not only forced the abdication of Charles IV but abducted his heir, Ferdinand, to imprisonment in France. In their place he appointed as King

his brother Joseph. For the next six years Spain suffered the "War of Independence", marked by Wellington's Peninsular Campaign and the first incidences of guerilla warfare. After violent civilian suffering and famine, this culminated in the reinstatement of Ferdinand VII in March 1814.

Apart from a brief visit to Saragossa in 1808, Goya spent the whole of this period in Madrid, in growing isolation. His portrait commissions from the Spanish nobility diminished; his wife died in 1812; and he concentrated largely on personal work. He did consent to paint such portraits of the conquerors as his splendid *General Nicolas Guye* (1810; Marshall Field Collection, New York) which demonstrates his continuing skill in portraiture in the grand manner: and official commissions such as the *Allegory of Madrid* (1810; Ayuntamiento (City Hall), Madrid), which originally included a portrait of the usurping king, Joseph Bonaparte. His personal reaction to the war is, however, recorded in his *Disasters of War*, a series of 80 plates in etching and aquatint designed to illustrate "the fatal consequences of the bloody war against Bonaparte in Spain" (1808–1814). The spectacular horror of these scenes, with their depiction (accompanied, like *Los Caprichos*, by ironic captions) of the inhumanity to which all classes in Spain had been reduced, contrasts with the self-confident sentimentality of official military art in Napoleonic France (for example, the works of Gros and Horace Vernet). In his scenes of murder, rape, and famine, executed with spectacular use of mass and grouping, Goya offers not a glimmer of hope. The *Disasters* were not published until 1863. At this period he also painted some small oils and, unusually, still lifes.

The Government that succeeded Joseph's disappointed liberal expectations. The new King initiated a series of purges of liberals and reintroduced the Inquisition; but Goya was not censured for his work for the previous regime, and remained Painter to the Chamber. He painted a series of portraits of the new King in which his disillusionment is rendered in the increasing repulsiveness of the monarch.

The end of the war was marked by some notable commissions. In England are the two portraits of Wellington, both painted in 1812 after the briefest of sittings (National Gallery, London, and Wellington Museum, London): the subject is

Goya: **Lady in a Black Mantilla**; oil on canvas; 54×43cm (21×17in); 1815–24. National Gallery of Ireland, Dublin

characteristic of Goya's flexible attitude to those in power. In 1814 he proposed to the Council of Regency a series of "the most notable and heroic events" of the war. *Madrid, the Second of May* (1808; Prado, Madrid), was painted to commemorate a revolt by the people of Madrid in favor of their Spanish king, which had been brutally suppressed by the French. The painting influenced Delacroix by its use of startling bright color and vigorous movement. His most revolutionary work at this period, however, is the *Third of May 1808* (1814; Prado, Madrid). Its stark composition is characteristic of Goya's increasing simplicity of style; so is its use of black priming and its violent coloring (compare with Manet's *Execution of the Emperor Maximilian*, 1867; Städtische Kunstalle, Mannheim).

Goya's unease is apparent in *The General Assembly of the Company of the Philippines* (1815; Staatliche Museen, Berlin), which shows his ability to introduce powerful emotion, in this case boredom and fear, into an apparently straightforward subject (a meeting chaired by the King). Goya conveys a sensation of space by his treatment of light. By this time, however, his work was not receiving such general acceptance. The blander academic manner of Vicente Lopez (1772–1850) was increasingly admired. Although in such works as *Seated Lady with a Fan* (1815; Louvre, Paris), Goya attempted to emulate this charming rectilinear style, he was never deeply in sympathy with the aspirations of Neoclassicism. His diminished official reputation is demonstrated by the inclusion in the Prado Gallery, on its opening in 1820, of only two of his works: the equestrian *Charles IV* and *Maria Luisa*.

During the last ten years of his life, Goya moved into retirement. In 1819 he bought a country house, the Quinta del Sordo ("House of the Deafman"), which in the next four years he decorated with the "Black Paintings", a series of 16 works on canvases of various dimensions, now in the Prado, Madrid. His program is now obscure: the works include literary, biblical, and genre subjects. The dark colors and the distortion of form and scale produce powerful and at times horrifying images, as in the *Saturn Devouring one of his Children*, demonstrating his increasing preoccupation with the darker side of human nature.

The liberal government which had forced Ferdinand to accept the Constitution of Cadiz in 1820 was overthrown three years later by a French army in conspiracy with the Spanish King. Goya, many of whose friends had already left the country, applied for permission to travel to France. In 1824, after a visit to Paris, he settled in Bordeaux, where he died. In his old age his activity did not diminish; he continued to paint portraits, with a new economy of brushwork and simplified composition, and the use of a narrow, dark palette. He experimented both with the recently evolved technique of lithography and with painting on ivory. These last years were marked by loneliness and despair.

The development of Goya's style can be seen in his treatment of figure-painting: in an early work such as his portrait of *José Moniño, Count of Floridablanca* (1783; Urquijo Bank, Madrid) the 18th-century French *grand style* is still dominant. The painting shows stiff treatment of a man in an official position, and it lacks the penetrating sense of character which becomes apparent later in works like *Manuel Godoy in the Field* (1801; Academy of San Fernando, Madrid). Here Goya suggests the worldliness and superficiality of Godoy's character through the arrogant pose and gaudy coloring, and the illusion of depth is created through color rather than perspective. Goya's portraiture is at its most powerful in paintings like *The Countess of Chinchon* (1800; Collection of the Duke de Sueca, Madrid). The lady was married against her will to Godoy. Her wistful isolation is conveyed not only by the delineation of her features and the nervous clutching of her fingers, but also by the startling juxtaposition of the flimsy gilt chair and the surrounding blackness.

Goya's style is characterized by his method of building up his coloring through several thin glazes. This is first apparent in *Francisco Bayeau* (1795; Prado, Madrid). After his work on the engravings (*Los Caprichos* and *The Disasters of War*) a more Rembrandtesque awareness of chiaroscuro emerges. His self-proclaimed masters were Nature, Velazquez, and Rembrandt.

Goya achieved an enormous reputation in 19th-century France. He was praised by Baudelaire, Hugo, and Gautier for his prefiguring of Romanticism and Impressionism, and he inspired artists like Delacroix, Guys, Daumier, and Manet. The English, on the whole, showed little interest in him until the end of the century, when in 1896 the National Gallery acquired three of his paintings. Today he has come to be recognized as the greatest artist of the period c1800, not only in Spain but probably in the whole of Europe.

The best view of his work can be obtained in the Prado, Madrid; he is also represented in most other European and American major collections.

**Further reading.** Gudiol, J. *Goya*, Barcelona (1971). Harris, T. *Goya's Graphic Work*, Oxford (1964). Hughes, R. *Goya*, New York (2003). Sanchez Canton, F.J. *Goya*, Paris (1930) and Madrid (1951).

## Goyen Jan van 1596–1656

Jan Josephsz. van Goyen was a prominent Dutch landscapist who was born at Leiden. Studying under six different teachers from 1606 onwards, he spent a year in Harlem with Esaias van de Velde, who was to have the most decisive influence. His earliest works date from 1620 and are often circular in shape. They are close in character to those of Esaias van de Velde in their use of *coulisse*-type compositions, strong colors, and richly illustrative detail, depicting small panoramic views of country roads and Dutch villages. At this stage atmospheric treatment remains insignificant, and the figures seem detached from the landscape.

Van Goyen settled in Leiden in 1618. In the late 1620s, he abandoned his early style in favor of a simpler subject-matter. Concentrating on a closely observed section of landscape, a few peasant cottages along a road or in the dunes, he developed a monochromatic palette. He used tonal treatment in browns, pale yellows, and greens to subdue local color and present atmospheric effect. At this stage he introduced such devices as the leading diagonal, or a dark strip of shadow along the foreground, lending unity and a sense of depth to the work.

In 1634, van Goyen moved to The Hague. During the 1630s, he introduced water into his scenes. In yellowish and gray-green tones, his fluid brush strokes depict settlements beside canals, or broad silhouettes of towns by rivers, dominated by vast skies that lend a transparent airiness to the horizon. In the 1640s winter landscapes predominate, with people skating or riding in sleds, as well as city views, river scenes, and seascapes.

Jan van Goyen: The Sea at Haarlem; oil on canvas; 39×54cm (15×21in); 1656. Städelsches Kunstinstitut, Frankfurt am Main

Van Goyen's late work is enlivened by a deepening tonality, warmer browns, stronger contrasts of luminous skies and water against dark foregrounds, with a thin and vibrant quality to the paint. Van Goyen visited France as a young man and later traveled frequently and extensively in the Netherlands and the regions of the Lower Rhine: he has left many sketchbooks filled with rapid black chalk drawings.

As in the case of his contemporaries, van Goyen's financial position was insecure. He supplemented his income through work as a picture dealer and valuer, as well as speculating in property and tulip bulbs. Despite these efforts, he died insolvent in 1656. A respected member of the Painters' Guild, he had a profound influence upon many artists, notably Salomon van Ruysdael, Nicolaes Berchem, and Aelbert Cuyp. A prolific worker, he left over 1,000 pictures which are well distributed among major galleries, such as the Rijksmuseum, Amsterdam; Smith College Museum of Art in Northampton, Mass; Royal Museum of Art (Mauritshuis), The Hague, and many private collections.

## Graf Urs c1485–1527

The Swiss draftsman, engraver, and goldsmith Urs Graf was born in Soleure in 1485. He frequently left his goldsmith's shop in Basel to fight as a mercenary soldier, making many sketches of camp life as well as drawing horrifying studies of battle and its aftermath. He is revealed by legal documents as a lusty bully and cutthroat, and his work, immensely popular in his day, reflected the same unbridled force.

Graf's characteristic subjects were coarse variations on themes of love and death. The late Gothic style took on a fierce vitality in his hands. His capricious exuberance led him naturally to etching, traditionally a part of the craft of the armorer. It had probably been used as a graphic medium in the armorer's shops at Augsburg soon after 1500; but the first dated etching, of a typically salacious subject, was made by Urs Graf in 1513. He disappeared from Basel in 1527; he may have died in the Italian campaigns of that year.

## Gran Daniel 1694–1757

Born in Vienna, Daniel Gran was one of the leading fresco painters employed in the decoration of the great Austrian Baroque buildings. He was taught by Gregor Werle, whose patron, Adam Schwarzenberg, enabled him to travel to Italy. He studied under Ricci in Venice and Solimena in Naples.

After his return to Vienna, he painted the ceiling frescoes of Schwarzenberg's palace (1724–5) and of the Imperial Library (1726–30). The latter work, an allegory of Charles VI as patron of the arts and sciences, established his reputation; it brought him numerous commissions for ceiling frescoes and altar paintings, mainly in Lower Austria.

Gran's style, though displaying the joyful splendor of the Austrian Baroque, departs from the exuberance and illusionism of the main Baroque tradition. His figures hover rather than soar, and express a feeling of serene composure and dignity. Like his compatriots, Fischer von Erlach and Raphael Donner, he thus achieved a synthesis of Baroque and Neoclassical values.

## Grant Duncan 1885–1979

The British painter Duncan Grant was born at Rothiemurchus in Invernesshire. He studied briefly at the Slade School of Fine Arts and with Jacques-Émile Blanche in Paris. In the years before 1914, Grant was a member of the Bloomsbury circle: a group of friends that included the economist John Maynard Keynes, the novelist Virginia Woolf, the critic Clive Bell, and the painter Vanessa Bell. Grant's association with the last two was an intimate one, and from 1916 the three lived together at Charleston in Sussex.

Grant's painting was adventurous in color and form in the years between 1910 and 1920, when the influence of Picasso and Matisse can be discerned. His later work consisted of landscape, still life, and portraiture, in a more conservative impressionistic idiom. His talents as a large-scale decorator never had the opportunities they seemed to demand.

**Further reading.** Shone, R. *Bloomsbury Portraits*, Oxford (1976).

## Grasser Erasmus c1450–1518

The German sculptor and architect Erasmus Grasser seems to have been trained in Munich. In 1480 he executed his first known work, 16 *Morris Dancers*, for the town hall in Munich. These exciting, free-standing figures are full of movement and character; even in their comic *grotesquerie* they express the tendency of contemporary German sculpture to evolve from the late Gothic style. Grasser's much more profound achievement, extremely characteristic of Renaissance sculpture in Germany, is his masterpiece, the sculptured St Peter Altarpiece for the church of St Peter's in Munich (1492). The life-sized figure of St Peter has a great air of solemnity and realism of characterization. Grasser is recorded as architect in 1484 in Kloster Mariaberg near Rorschach. Among his other works is the signed and dated Aresinger tomb in St Peter's, Munich (1482). (*See* overleaf.)

## Grassi Giovannino de' *fl.* 1389–98

Giovannino de' Grassi was an Italian illuminator, sculptor, and painter. He was a leading representative of the internationally influential Lombard school of miniaturists, which flourished under Visconti patronage. These artists were distinguished for their vivid representation of the natural world; Giovannino's achievement in this field can be seen in those pages he executed in a model-book in the Biblioteca Communale, Bergamo (MS. Delta VII. 14). His studies of birds in this volume are delightful not only for their scientific accuracy but also for their lovely coloring. Giovannino's was a courtly art, and with

Duncan Grant: Portrait of a Woman; oil on canvas; 72×58cm (28×23in); 1927. Tate Gallery, London

his son Salamone he made the highly decorated *Uffiziolo* (Book of Offices) for Gian Galeazzo Visconti (Visconti di Modrone Collection, Milan). He was involved in many aspects of work on Milan Cathedral. His single documented work as a sculptor is the relief of *Christ and the Samaritan Woman* (1391–6) in the northern sacristy of the building.

## Gravelot 1669–1773

The French designer and engraver Hubert François Bourguignon was commonly known as Gravelot. A native of Paris, he achieved distinction for his book illustrations and his *rocaille* designs for cabinet-makers, upholsterers, and metalworkers. From 1732 to 1745 he lived in London where his sophisticated illustrations of contemporary manners and costumes considerably influenced English artists. Thomas Gainsborough and Francis Hayman were his pupils, and the style of Joseph Highmore's literary illustrations is clearly related to that of his colleague Gravelot. Exacting in his standards, he revitalized illustrative engraving in England; an accomplished school of native engravers continued to work in his manner well after his return to Paris. The descriptive precision and elegance of his line and the inexhaustible variety of his inventions can be seen in the drawings for two of his more important commissions, the second volume of Gay's *Fables* (1738; 13 drawings in the British Museum, London) and the second edition of L. Theobald's *The Works of Shakespeare in Eight Volumes* (1740; 28 drawings in the Graphische Sammlung Albertina, Vienna, and the Huntington Library and Art Gallery, San Marino).

## Graves Morris 1910–2001

Morris Graves is one of the American West Coast painters whose work has been deeply affected by Oriental art and thought. He was born in Fox Valley, Oregon. He taught himself and traveled extensively in the East, though he settled in Seattle and in later years spent more and more time in Ireland.

In the late 1930s he met Mark Tobey,

Erasmus Grasser: the tomb of Dr Ulrich Aresinger; stone; 1482. Church of St Peter, Munich

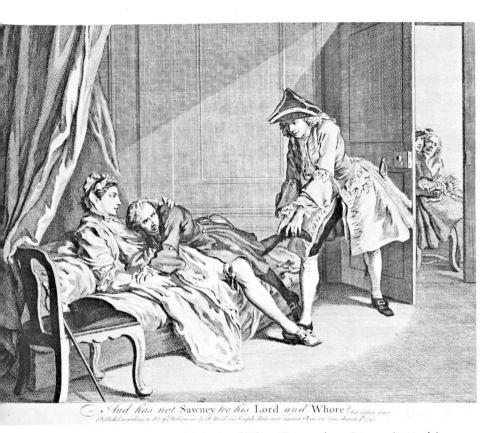

Gravelot: "And has not Sawney too his Lord and Whore?"; engraving; 28×33cm (11×13in); 1742. British Museum, London

whose so-called "white writings" Graves adapted to his own technique. Working mainly in gouache and watercolor, Graves paints strange landscapes and creatures that belong to dreams and visions rather than to the everyday world. *The Bird Singing in the Moonlight* (1938/9; Museum of Modern Art, New York) is a characteristic example of his work.

# Greco El 1541–1614

The Spanish painter Domenico Theotokopouli was commonly known as El Greco. He was born in Crete, which was then a Venetian possession, but little information exists about his early life. It is likely that he is to be identified with a master painter recorded in Crete in 1566. According to the contemporary miniaturist Giulio Clovio, he had been trained at Titian's workshop in Venice before traveling to Rome in 1570. A few years later he visited Madrid, possibly to obtain commissions from Philip II to paint pictures for the Escorial. In 1577 he went to Toledo to paint the altarpieces and design the architectural framework and sculptural decoration for the church of S. Domingo el

Antiguo. He remained in Toledo until his death.

El Greco's interest in literature, history, philosophy, and theology is reflected in the inventory of his library, and corroborated by the intellectuals whose company he frequented in Italy and Spain. During his stay in Rome he met Fulvio Orsini, antiquarian and librarian of the Farnese Palace, and Pedro Chacon, the Toledan employed to reform the Gregorian calendar. In Toledo he seems to have gained the favor of the sophisticated and cosmopolitan Mendoza family. He was also a close friend of the clerics Luis and Diego da Castilla, the antiquarian Antonio Covarrubias, and the historian Salazar de Mendoza. The celebrated poets Góngora and Paravicino sang his praises.

Contemporary philosophical and theological ideas in Spain had a profound influence on the art of El Greco. From the 1580s onwards his paintings appear to express Christian doctrine according to the concepts of Neoplatonism. He rejected the notion of seeing the manifestation of God in naturalistic forms and sought to create abstract forms as an aid to religious contemplation. The dazzling brightness of El

Greco's light and color is intended to be a reflection of divine light which will illuminate the mind of the beholder. The soaring movement from naturalistically described forms to heavenly beings of superhuman proportions will enable the viewer's soul to reascend to God. This combination of light metaphysics with the ascent from the material to the immaterial was derived from the *c* 6th-century *Celestial Hierarchy* of Pseudo-Dionysius the Areopagite, and was a concept shared by contemporary spiritual writers.

In his early work in Italy El Greco strove after naturalistic representation. For instance *The Purification of the Temple* (1560s; National Gallery of Art, Washington, D.C.) is a bold but abortive attempt to emulate the achievements of the great Venetian painters Titian, Jacopo Bassano, Tintoretto, and Veronese. The composition is loosely organized, the treatment of space confused, and the drawing imprecise. Yet his handling of iridescent colors and flickering highlights, together with the rhythmic outline of his forms, anticipate the style of his Toledan masterpieces. Under the impact of the works of Michelangelo and Raphael in Rome, his second version of *The Purification of the Temple* (Minneapolis Institute of Arts) achieves greater clarity in the treatment of space by the elimination of superfluous anecdote. It reveals a more accurate observation of the structure of forms, with a more carefully modulated tonal range.

This style reaches its climax in his earliest works in Toledo, the altarpieces for S. Domingo el Antiguo (1577–9) and the *Espolio* (1577–9) painted for the cathedral sacristy. In the former he adapted Vignola's design for the facade of the church of the Gesù in Rome to the architectural framework of the high altar, thereby imposing on the native Plateresque style a sense of classical harmony and restraint. This is echoed in the central canvas, the *Assumption of the Virgin* (Art Institute of Chicago), in which a knowledge of Roman draftsmanship and design is coupled with a Venetian sensibility to color, to express the glorification of the Virgin.

In the *Espolio* (the disrobing of Christ before the Crucifixion) he created, by means of precise drawing, convincing three-dimensional forms that suggest polychrome sculpture. The jostling crowd presses down on Christ while the executioner, unmoved by his plight, bores a hole in the Cross which seems to lie at our

El Greco: Lady in a Fur Wrap; oil on canvas; 62×50cm (24×20in); c1577–8. Pollok House, Glasgow

feet. But this claustrophobic space, with its grim foreboding of death, is pierced by the scarlet robe of Christ. Faceted like a jewel, its intensity reassures the beholder of the triumph of Christ. The Cathedral authorities objected to the inclusion of the three Marys, as well as to the placing of the heads of the crowd higher than that of Christ. However, the picture remained unaltered. El Greco probably defended his interpretation by referring to the *Meditations on the Life of Christ* by Pseudo-Bonaventura. This late-13th-century text, with its vivid description of the Passion of Christ, was in vogue during the Counter-Reformation.

El Greco's imaginative response to subject matter is best illustrated by *The Martyrdom of St Maurice* (1582; Escorial, near Madrid) commissioned by Philip II. The picture was rejected, and a substitute painted by a mediocre Italian artist, Romulo Cincinnato. The latter painted decapitated bodies almost spilling out of the picture, in true orthodox fashion, whereas El Greco had removed them to the background. He abandoned the carnage of Cincinnato's version and the blatant emotion of his own *Espolio* in favor of a polemic on the theme of martyrdom. St Maurice and his generals are presented as graceful, attenuated beings set against a backcloth of cool and restrained colors: lemon, pale gray, pale blue, and pale pink.

From now on El Greco virtually confined himself to patrons in Toledo, and during the 1580s he developed a style characterized by flatter, more elongated forms compressed into a shallow space and woven into a pattern of rhythmic curves. Colors are more expressive, less descriptive, and there are distinct tonal transitions from light to dark.

*The Burial of the Count of Orgaz* (1586) for the church of S. Tomé, Toledo, is his most dazzling essay in this style. The picture commemorates the burial in 1323 of the Lord of Orgaz, a benefactor of Santo Tomé. St Augustine and St Stephen were said to have miraculously appeared at the ceremony and to have placed him in his sepulcher. The reality of the miracle is expressed through such naturalistic details as the damascened armor of the Lord and the diaphanous surplice of the priest, and by the depiction of contemporary Toledans.

Among the other figures who have been identified with certainty are El Greco's young son, Jorge Manuel, and the humanist Antonio Covarrubias. The figure of the dead man may be a portrait of Alvar Perez de Guzman y Mendoza, the 10th Lord and the Count of Orgaz. As the body is being lowered into the tomb (depicted in a fresco beneath the canvas which has since disappeared), an angel holds the soul of the Lord—portrayed in insubstantial form as a child—and spirals upwards to "an open heaven in glory". The celestial vision is evoked by a pronounced elongation of form, by abstract clouds, and by the exceedingly bright light emanating from Christ. No longer the embodiment of physical beauty and power as in the *Espolio*, Christ is now conceived of as a radiance of light. This vision of the divine is enhanced by the real light flooding downwards from the window above the painting.

After this painting El Greco's style

El Greco: Portrait of Brother Hortensio Félix Paravicino; oil on canvas; 113×86cm (44×34in); 1609. Museum of Fine Arts, Boston

changes. He no longer observes the structure or appearance of material but creates abstract forms to convey ideas. Light is more intense and seems to emanate from these forms. There is a greater variety of colors and these are juxtaposed so that they vibrate. Contours are no longer so clearly defined, and seem to release light and color from their confines. Thus the flat surface design characteristic of the 1580s is disrupted by the vertical thrust of forms and the projection of incandescent light and brilliant color.

His supreme technical skill and the conceptual handling of color, light, and form is evident in his portraiture as well as in his religious compositions. His portrait of the Inquisitor General, Cardinal Fernando Niño de Guevara (c1600–1; Metropolitan Museum, New York), has all the ingredients of a splendid state portrait, with its dazzling light flashing across folds of sumptuous drapery. But the acid color, spatial tension, and taut, sharp-edged contours create an atmosphere of restlessness. Guevara seems to fidget in his chair, his feet askew. His expression is furtive and he grips one arm of the chair uneasily. El Greco's ability to transcend physiognomy and conjure up the idea of the man is beautifully recorded in the portrait of his friend *Brother Hortensio Félix Paravicino* (1609; Museum of Fine Arts, Boston). With consummate skill he conveys the sophistication and spiritual intensity of the poet by sweeping red, black, and white paint into a pattern of rhythmic shapes.

This total concern with the realm of the spirit is conveyed in his decorative schemes for the Augustinian Church of Doña María de Aragón, Madrid (1596–1600), S. José Chapel, Toledo (1597–9), the Hospital of La Caridad, Illescas (1603–5), Oballe Chapel in S. Vicente, Toledo (1607–13), and the Hospital of Tavera (begun in 1608 and completed after El Greco's death by his son Jorge Manuel).

*The Immaculate Conception* (Santa Cruz Museum, Toledo) from the Oballe Chapel in S. Vicente is possibly the most splendid example. The painting originally rested on the altar. At the bottom there is a cluster of roses and lilies (symbols of the Virgin) naturalistically rendered so as to mirror real flowers placed on the altar. Elsewhere in the painting El Greco has distorted light, color, and form: heavenly beings of immense proportions soar effortlessly heavenwards; garments of bright blue and red and yellow are juxtaposed to create a

dazzling effect. Although the light originates from above, it is reflected off these garments with such intensity that each seems to have its own source of light. A vision of heavenly beings flares upwards from the naturalistic flowers, illuminating the dark night. The inclusion of naturalistic details at the bottom of the painting thus provides the beholder with a stepping stone from the "sensible to the intelligible"; that is, to the realm of heavenly beings. He will continue his ascent with their aid until ultimately he will reattain union with God. The function of El Greco's religious paintings is "to raise the soul of man heavenwards with its movement of spirit".

El Greco's art reflects his response to the spiritual climate of Toledo at the time of the Counter-Reformation. Even his painting of *Laocoön* (c1610; National Gallery of Art, Washington, D.C.) is almost certainly allegorical. As in a dream, the wooden horse trots towards the Visagra Gate of Toledo, the sky is ominous, and Toledo seems doomed. In subject matter, El Greco's pictures run the gamut of Counter-Reformation themes, such as the purification of the Temple, the Passion of Christ, the Immaculate Conception, the martyrdom of saints, the contemplation of death, and acts of charity. But his stylistic interpretations, especially after the 1580s, conflict with those proposed in the decrees of the Council of Trent with their emphasis on clarity and verisimilitude. It is not surprising that at a time of strict religious orthodoxy his art should find no successors. As Paravicino aptly remarked, "future ages will admire his genius, but none will imitate it".

**Further reading.** Cossio, M.B. *El Greco* (2 vols.), Madrid (1972). Gudiol, J. *The Complete Paintings of El Greco 1541–1614*, New York (1988). Wethey, H.E. *El Greco and his School* (2 vols.), London and Princeton (1962).

# Greuze Jean-Baptiste 1725–1805

Jean-Baptiste Greuze was the most important French painter of the mid 18th century. His most appreciated works today are his portraits, such as the superbly commanding *J.G. Wille* (1763; Musée Jacquemart-André, Paris). His true significance, however, lies in the contemporary success of his genre paintings. These, although superficially related to the Dutch

tradition, are in fact history paintings; but they are not couched in the usual aristocratic milieu. His subjects are peasants, the working class, and the lower bourgeoisie. Unlike a straightforward genre painter, Greuze is not interested in quaintness of detail, prettiness of color, or whimsicality of emotion. He neither pokes fun at the lower classes nor adopts an attitude of condescension towards them. Rather, like a traditional history painter, he is concerned with mankind in general, and with representing the balance or imbalance between the passions and the intellect.

His works are therefore moralized and idealized, since they seek to provide an exemplar of virtue. Often his scenes provoked the spectator to tears. Sensibility was very much *à la mode* then, as it is not now, and this forms a barrier to our comprehension of the dividing line between true and touching sentiment, and chocolate-box sentimentality.

His first great success was *The Village Bride* (1761; Louvre, Paris), which, like *The Paralytic tended by his Children* (1763; Hermitage Museum, Leningrad), eulogized the virtues of family life and *pietàs*. Both works are classical in style: a restrained color scheme parallels the restrained gestures and expressions, and the simple frieze of players on the "stage" is backed by plain walls, any details of which help to tell the story. *The Paralytic* may be considered as a reinterpretation of the classical deathbed scene, as used by Poussin in his *Testament of Eudamidas* (c1660; State Art Museum, Copenhagen) which was soon to be popular with Neoclassical artists.

In fact Greuze's manner, which owes much to the example of Raphael and Poussin (whom he was the first to revive), lays the foundations for Neoclassicism. Diderot did not live to see David's *Oath of the Horatii* (1784; Louvre, Paris), but he helped form the Neoclassical *credo* by his constant encouragement of Greuze, whose bourgeois genre painting is the counterpart of Diderot's plays. Both tell a story, and tell it with feeling, and these elements of narrative and sentimentality are the essence of early Neoclassicism. Details like the weeping women in *Oath of the Horatii* may derive partly from Greuze's example, although they have antique sources as well.

Greuze once attempted the full Neoclassical manner himself, in his *Septimius Severus rebuking Caracalla* (1769; Louvre, Paris), which was his reception piece to the

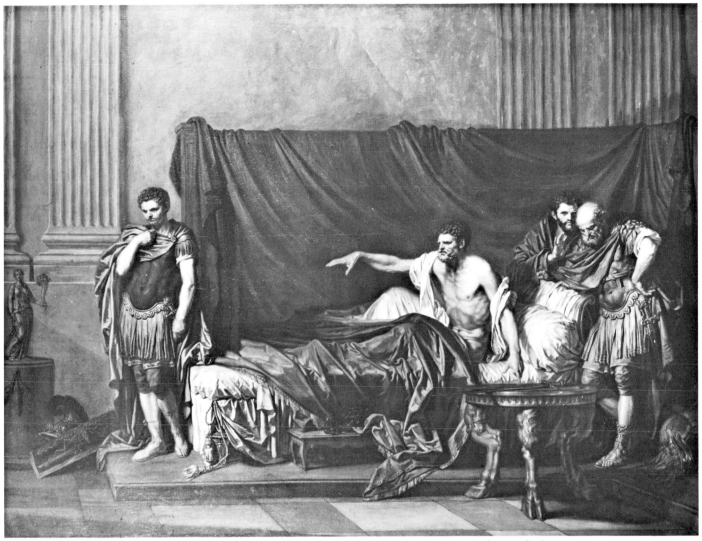

Jean-Baptiste Greuze: Septimius Severus rebuking Caracalla; oil on canvas; 124×160cm (49×63in); 1769. Louvre, Paris

Academy. Unfortunately, this was judged unacceptable as a history painting, and Greuze—to his chagrin—was received only as a genre painter. The work was quite rightly criticized for poor drawing, but it is indeed a history painting. It may have failed through a mixture of jealousy and an awareness of the applicant's immense vanity.

Although Greuze lived through the Revolution, his early Neoclassicism fell from favor during the 1780s when the sterner, antique manner of David came to the fore. He then made his money on the type of single-figure, mawkish, and broadly painted moralistic work represented by *The Broken Jug* (late 1770s; Louvre, Paris), in which the jug is a metaphor for the beginnings of the sexual experience of the sad-looking girl who carries it.

Greuze's quality as a painter is variable,

and his coloring is sometimes monotonous; so is his repetition of subject matter, often popularized through engravings. The fact that the Marquis de Marigny, Directeur des Bâtiments, bought *The Village Bride*, and that it subsequently went to Louis XVI, demonstrates the official policy of morality in painting—a program that was to nurture quite deliberately a Neoclassical style.

## Gris Juan 1887–1927

The Spanish painter José Victoriano Gonzalès was known as Juan Gris. He was born in Madrid, studied at the School of Industrial and Applied Arts, and worked as a draftsman for satirical magazines. In 1906 he moved to Paris, where he spent the rest of his life. In his early years in Paris, he continued to work as a freelance

illustrator. As a friend and neighbour of Picasso in Montmartre, he mixed in the avant-garde circle of painters and writers and by 1911 had turned seriously to painting. He rapidly became a central figure in Cubist painting.

He had not participated in the early experimental phases of Cubism, but with remarkable fluency he now accepted a highly sophisticated modern idiom as the normal vocabulary available to a painter. The fragmentation, dislocation, and near monochrome palette of Analytical Cubism feature in paintings like *Oil Lamp* (*Lampe à pétiole*, c1912; Kröller-Müller Museum, Otterlo). Characteristic qualities of his art are the dense immutable sense of surface, the almost austere clarity of the image, and the rhythmical structure in which lines and edges blend into a lyrical, disciplined architecture. There are no soft atmospheric

Juan Gris: Figure seated in a Café; oil and collage on canvas; 99×72cm (39×28in); 1914. Collection of Mr and Mrs Leigh B. Block, Chicago

edge with interlocked fragments of newspaper, wallpaper, and labels with fragments of painting and of drawing and of writing. In their choice of *collé* headlines and other materials (mirror, glass, reproductions, and so forth), they are packed with witty allusions to the reality and the artifice of art.

During the First World War Gris formed close friendships with Matisse, who supported him financially, and with Lipchitz.

He also worked as stage-designer (notably for Sergei Diaghilev) and book illustrator (for his friend Réverdy, for Jacob, Gertrude Stein, and Tzara).

His mature works were an extension of his own Cubist paintings: broader and softer in drawing, color, and mood. Subject matter is restrained. They are mainly still lifes such as *The Virgin* (1916; Öffentliche Kunstsammlung, Kunstmuseum Basel), and interiors, apart from a group of figure-paintings (*Pierrots and Harlequins*, c1919–22) and an impressive series of portrait drawings (such as his 1920 *Self-portrait*; Galerie Louise Leiris, Paris). The angularity of his linear Cubist constructions gave way in the 1920s to a broader, continuous curvilinear idiom linking muted color areas.

**Further reading.** Cooper, D. *Letters of Juan Gris 1913–1927*, London (1956). Gaya-Numo, J.A. *Juan Gris*, Barcelona and Paris (1974). Kahnweiler, D.-H. *Juan Gris: his Life and Work*, London and New York (1947).

# Gropius Walter 1883–1969

The German architect Walter Gropius was born in Berlin. His career as an architect and teacher was intimately associated with the development of modern architecture. Between 1903 and 1907 he studied architecture at university in Berlin and Munich. He then spent three years as assistant to Peter Behrens, who was employed as an industrial designer and architect by the German electrical company, A.E.G.

Gropius set up in practice in Berlin in 1910 and in 1911 was engaged with his partner Adolf Meyer (1881–1929) to design the Fagus shoe-last factory at Alfeld, the layout of which had already been determined. Gropius' design was free from historic ornament of any kind, and crisply cuboid; he exploited the building's steel frame in an imaginative way by treating the walls as a glass membrane,

allusions as in early Cubism. The two-dimensional integrity of the surface seems impregnable. Yet the painted objects have an extraordinarily physical reality and identity.

This first idiom closely anticipated the form and theory of Synthetic Cubism. Gris produced many outstanding works in the next few years, between 1912 and 1915; later he articulated some of the clearest statements of Synthetic Cubism's intent, stressing the authenticity of painting's new reality. "Cézanne turns a bottle into a cylinder, but I begin with a cylinder and create an individual of a special type: I make a bottle—a particular bottle—out of a cylinder" (1921).

His paintings of these years, mostly intimate still lifes, have a strong sense of the particular. They are tightly organized but sumptuous relationships of luminous color, texture, and pattern. The collages of 1913 and 1914 such as *Breakfast* (1914; Museum of Modern Art, New York) have a similar, meticulously organized precision. The surface is crowded from edge to apparently unsupported at the corners.

Dramatic use of glass also characterized the model factory and administrative building which Gropius and Meyer designed for the *Deutscher Werkbund's* 1914 exhibition in Cologne, although here the formal effect was somewhat indecisive. At this time Gropius also had the experience of designing a variety of furniture and industrial products, including a railway locomotive (1913) and a railway sleeping car (1914).

In 1918 Gropius was appointed head of the School of Arts and Crafts and the Fine Art Academy in Weimar, which he amalgamated as the Bauhaus. Here the skills of artist, craftsman, and architect were developed as specializations of a common approach to design, and the fine and applied arts were seen as "inseparable components of a new architecture". This approach, which derived from Arts and Crafts ideology, was strongly advocated by left-wing Expressionist architects. Gropius' sympathy for Expressionism at this time can be seen in the jagged outline of the memorial at Weimar that commemorated the victims of a 1920 uprising. It is also apparent in the angular forms of the Sommerfeld house, Dahlem, Berlin (designed in 1921 by Gropius and Meyer, with collaboration from Bauhaus students).

However, Gropius gradually turned from this very personal manner to a more rational and generally more cubic architecture. His *Internationale Architektur* (the first *Bauhausbuch*) was almost a guidebook to the emerging International style. Its publication in 1925 coincided with the removal of the Bauhaus from Weimar to Dessau, where new buildings were erected to Gropius' designs. Its clean white concrete forms, the large expanse of glass walling in the workshop wing, and the carefully balanced asymmetry of the whole made the new Bauhaus building a potent symbol of 20th-century rationalism.

This return to the regularity of industrial forms was perhaps partly motivated by the realization that individually commissioned houses and handmade goods could only be afforded by the rich. Gropius' desire to provide working people with well designed homes and furnishings led him to explore the possibilities of standardization. The housing he designed for the Törten estate in Dessau (1926) and for the Werkbund's Weissenhof exhibition in Stuttgart (1927) was prefabricated. The furniture he designed for the Feder stores (1927) was mass produced from standard components which could be combined in various ways. Other important designs of these years were Gropius' plan for a "Total Theater" for proletarian drama productions (1927), and the Dessau employment exchange (1927), on which a number of Bauhaus students assisted with furniture and fittings.

In 1928 Gropius resigned from the Bauhaus. During the next few years he continued to design prefabricated houses, mass-produced furniture, and industrial products (including car bodies and cast-iron stoves). He also planned a variety of schemes for multistory blocks of flats, since he believed that high building density was imperative in cities. The most ambitious of these schemes actually to be carried out was for four-story blocks of workers' flats at Berlin-Siemensstadt (1929). These were much lower than the 8 to 12 stories he advocated. The long white blocks were separated by generous expanses of lawn and trees which he saw as a major virtue of such developments.

With Hitler's assumption of power in Germany, political pressure on Gropius increased; in 1934 he emigrated to England, where he worked for three years with Maxwell Fry (1899–). The most important outcome of this association was Impington Village College (1936), a school community centre in rural Cambridgeshire. It was informally laid out and designed to make the most of fine weather: a predominantly single story building in brick, less purely geometric than much of Gropius' previous work.

Shortly after plans for the college were completed, Gropius was invited to be Professor of Architecture at Harvard University, and so left for America in 1937. In America he designed a number of private houses with a former Bauhaus colleague, Marcel Breuer (1902–70).

In 1941 the partnership planned a low-cost workers' housing scheme in New Kensington, Pittsburgh, devising a system of standardized timber frames for the 250 houses which were placed in short terraces about a hillside site. The possibilities of standardized wooden components were further exploited in the Packaged House System which Gropius developed with Konrad Wachsmann. This was the first of Gropius' schemes for prefabricated houses to go into large-scale mass-production (1943–5).

In 1941 Gropius' partnership with Breuer came to an end. Four years later Gropius joined forces with a group of younger men to create The Architects' Collaborative (T.A.C.), with which he worked until his death. Among the many products of this enterprise were the Harvard University Graduate Centre (1949), the United States Embassy in Athens (1956–61), and the Rosenthal china factory at Selb, Germany (1965).

Gropius wanted to design buildings that were as representative of the 20th century as the Gothic cathedral was of medieval Europe. He strove to reconcile technology with human needs, and gave sophisticated formal expression to this, most notably in the Fagus factory and the Bauhaus building. He believed that design involved the interplay of technical considerations and artistic creativity, and saw no reason why its advantages should be available only to the enlightened rich. Through his teaching in Germany and America, several generations of architects and designers were inspired by his ideals.

**Further reading.** Fitch, J.M. *Walter Gropius*, New York (1960). Giedion, S. *Walter Gropius, Work and Teamwork*, Zurich (1954). Gropius, W. *Apollo in the Democracy: the Cultural Obligation of the Architect*, New York (1968).

## Grosz George 1893–1959

Born in Berlin, Grosz studied art in Dresden and Berlin. His first works were caricatures in the style of *Die Jugend*; but in Berlin and in Paris, where he lived in 1913, his drawing matured under the influence of the French graphic tradition. He established a powerful style of drawing and painting, which incorporated the formal devices of Expressionism and Futurism (seen in *Metropolis*, 1917; Museum of Modern Art, New York). After settling in Berlin in 1918, he became a founder of the Berlin Dada movement and attacked the bourgeois supporters of the Weimar Republic with his bitingly satirical drawings (for example, *Couple*, 1930; Tate Gallery, London). He left Germany for New York in 1933 and focused his attention on urban America before returning to Berlin in 1958. (*See* overleaf.)

**Further reading.** Hess, H. *George Grosz*, New Haven (1985). Schneede, U. *George Grosz*, London (1979).

artist whose concern for painterly effects allows the brush to draw and describe in place of detailed preliminary preparation.

The Isenheim Altarpiece, dated 1515, was painted for the choir of the Antonite monastery at Isenheim, Alsace (the altarpiece, dismembered for display purposes, is now in the Musée d'Unterlinden, Colmar). Grünewald worked at the behest of Guido Guersi, the preceptor of the Order, whose coat of arms appears on the altarpiece. The Grünewald paintings were commissioned for the enlargement of a wooden altarpiece of 1505 which has carved figures of St Anthony, St Augustine, and St Jerome. His paintings turned the work into a polyptych in three stages. By means of three pairs of wings, two movable and one fixed, the altarpiece could be opened and reopened to show different sets of religious representations for weekday, Sunday, and Holy Day services.

The first stage shows the *Crucifixion*, flanked by fixed wings of St Anthony and St Sebastian, with a Lamentation on the *predella* below. The Christ of the Crucifixion dominates the scene, his body racked with pain, the flesh torn and turning green. His figure is larger than those of his mourners, fulfilling the prophecy of the pointing St John at the right as inscribed on the picture: "He will increase whilst I decrease". The dark setting throws the figures into relief and heightens the emotion of the scene. *Pentimenti*, or changes in brushwork, revealed by X rays, show how Grünewald accentuated the expressive content as he painted; the fingers of the Magdalene have been lengthened and the Virgin originally stood upright.

The second stage shows angels making music before the Virgin and Child and is perhaps best described symbolically as *The Incarnation of Christ and the Glorification of the Mother of God*. The angels show the artist at his most inventive coloristically, as they materialize before our eyes in pinks and yellows, sharp blues and greens. This visionary quality is matched by the building in which they appear, which seems itself to be in a state of metamorphosis with leaves and tendrils springing from the columns. This scene is flanked by the *Annunciation* and the *Resurrection of Christ*. In the latter scene the halo of Christ is the only source of light. The unearthly

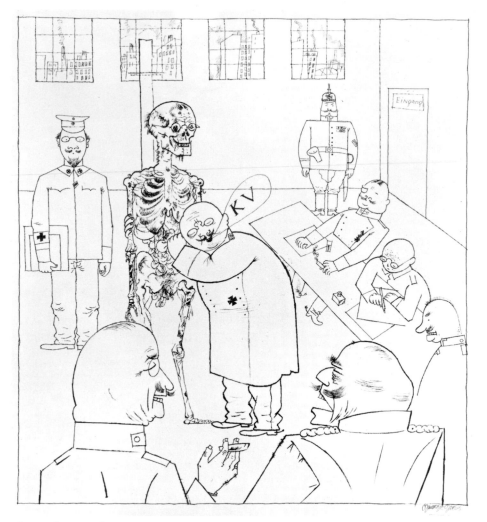

George Grosz: Fit for Active Service; india ink on paper; 51×36cm (20×14in); 1916–17. Museum of Modern Art, New York

# Grünewald 1470/80–1528

The German painter, Matthias Gothardt Neithardt (or Nithardt) has been generally known as Grünewald ever since that name was given him by the 17th-century historian, Joachim von Sandrart. His name appears in the rate books of the Town of Seligenstadt, near Würzburg, from 1501 to 1525. He became court painter to Uriel van Gemmingen and Albrecht of Brandenburg, successive Archbishops of Mainz; and he seems also to have advised on architectural and engineering schemes in the diocese. It is likely that he lost his place at court at the time of upheaval during the Peasants War of 1526; the 12 articles of faith found among his effects at his death suggest Protestant sympathies. He moved to Frankfurt and then to Halle, where he is recorded as in charge of the municipal waterworks and where he died in 1528.

Since much of Grünewald's work has been lost and there is a monogram signature on only three of his surviving paintings, chronology is problematical. His modern reputation has rested on one major work, the Isenheim Altarpiece, still in its complete state. There are also several smaller works, fragments of altarpieces, and about 40 drawings. Although so few of his works have survived, he emerges nevertheless as one of the most remarkable painters of his age, indeed of all time.

The small *Mocking of Christ* (1503; Alte Pinakothek, Munich), is probably his earliest surviving work and its features are characteristic of much that is to come. The religious drama is played out against a dark background, and the figures are highly expressive to accentuate the torment of the scene. There is a highly individualistic use of color, which suggests an

Grünewald: The Meeting of St Erasmus and Maurice; oil on pine panel; 226×176cm (89×69in); 1517–23. Alte Pinakothek, Munich

quality of this celestial light is especially evident in the trailing drapery where shades of white and blue turn to deep pinks and grays in the folds.

The third stage of the altarpiece consists of the original carved structure with Grünewald's painted wings of *The Hermit Saints Anthony and Paul in the Desert* to the left and *The Temptation of St Anthony* to the right. Here are the most overt references to the duties of the Antonite Order in caring for the sick, by the presence of the medicinal plants in the *Hermit Saints* and the diseased figure in the *Temptation*.

The chief iconographical source for the altarpiece as a whole has been identified as the mystical *Revelations of St Bridget of Sweden*, written in the 14th century and first published in Germany in 1492.

Grünewald painted three smaller versions of the *Crucifixion* (Öffentlich Kunstsammlung, Basel; National Gallery of Art, Washington, D.C.; and Staatliche Kunsthalle Karlsruhe). Fragments remain of two other major altarpiece commissions. *The Madonna in the Garden* (now in the parish church, Stuppach) and *The Miracle of the Snows* (Augustinermuseum, Freiburg) probably each formed a part of the altarpiece in the collegiate church at Aschaffenburg (1517–19). Grisaille panels of saints (Fürstenberg Collection, Donaueschingen, and Städelsches Kunstinstitut, Frankfurt am Main) are from the Heller Altarpiece at Frankfurt. Some of Grünewald's drawings can be connected with lost works, including three paintings for the cathedral at Mainz. Many of his drawings are taken from the life and are highly unusual for their period. He used black chalk, often with a watercolor wash, to obtain softened, painterly effects. He is interested in the palpability of forms rather than line and contour; studies for the arms of the St Sebastian of the Isenheim Altarpiece are concerned less with the construction of the human form than with light playing over the surface of the flesh.

Grünewald was almost the exact contemporary of Albrecht Dürer (1471–1528), against whom all German art of the period is inevitably judged. Dürer's surviving work bears witness to the fact that despite the range of his accomplishment he remains primarily a graphic artist; whereas the work of Grünewald shows an inspired quality of painterliness that Dürer never matched.

**Further reading.** Pevsner, N. and Meier, M. *Grünewald*, London (1958). Ruhmer, E. *Grünewald*, London (1958). Ruhmer, E. (ed.) *Grünewald Drawings*, London (1970). Zulch, W.K. *Der Historische Grünewald, Mathis Gothardt-Neithardt*, Munich (1938).

Guardi: View of the Grand Canal, Venice (the Church of the Salute and Customs House); oil on canvas; 71×94cm (28×37in); c1770–80. Wallace Collection, London

## Guardi brothers
### 17th and 18th centuries

Compared with Canaletto, Tiepolo, and Pittoni, the Guardi brothers were almost unheard of in 18th-century Venice. Their family came from the South Tyrol, and it was at first from there, and from other districts far from Venice, that the Guardi received commissions. Giovanni (Gian) Antonio (1698–1760) was the eldest of three painter brothers, and until his death it was he who ran the family workshop; it was under his name (if any were mentioned at all) that paintings were produced. This practice of coproduction has made it difficult to evaluate the individual merits of Gian Antonio and Francesco (1712–93) until c1750, when Francesco branched out on his own as a painter of views. The youngest brother, Niccolò (1715–85), is almost totally unknown as an artist.

The type of painting that the workshop produced is seen at its best in the altarpiece in Belvedere di Aquileia, Italy, where flimsy figures are painted in pretty pinks, pale greens, and light blues. In Venice their work may well have seemed bizarre; indeed, until Gian Antonio's death broke up the workshop, their art had more in common with Austrian Rococo painting than contemporary Venetian work.

Francesco Guardi seems to have taken up view painting 10 years or so before his elder brother's death. The early 1750s was an opportune time for a new specialist. Canaletto had left Venice for England in 1746, and except for a short break of a few months he remained there for a decade. Canaletto's rival Michele Marieschi had died in 1744. Not surprisingly, Francesco leaned heavily on both these artists; their influence, particularly that of Canaletto, is evident in the robust composition and feeling of space of his early works (for example, *Piazza San Marco*; National Gallery, London). Francesco may also have improved his technique by his study of Canaletto's works, for the latter was technically by far the better painter.

During his development as a view painter Francesco steadily freed himself from Canaletto's straightforward realism. His later views were not so much views of particular places as paintings of mood. Some of his most intimate works are scenes of the backwaters of Venice and the Lagoon; for instance the *Rio dei Medicanti* (Galleria dell'Accademia Carrara, Bergamo). This was one of the views etched by Luca Carlevaris at the beginning of the century; but unlike Carlevaris, Francesco Guardi was not interested in accurate topography—rather in the flickering sunlight on the gondoliers, and the passing shadows. His late views are nostalgic; his figures seem cocooned in a world of their own, oblivious of the decaying buildings that surround them.

Ironically it was the very qualities that caused Francesco Guardi's lack of success that were appreciated after his death. His wistful views of a city in decline, with their sketchiness and inaccuracies, have always appealed to a public that enjoys the idea of Venice as much as Venice itself.

## Guarini Guarino 1624–83

The Italian architect Guarino Guarini was born at Modena in 1624. He entered the order of the Theatines in 1639, studied architecture in Rome along with theology, philosophy, and mathematics. Ordained in 1647, he settled in Messina in 1660. His membership of the Theatine Order, and his position as the Theatine's Professor of Mathematics in Messina were the keys to his architectural career. Through his connection with the Order he built the facade of the Theatine Church of SS. Annunziata dei Catalani in Messina c1661, and in Paris he built the church of Ste Anne-la-Royale some time after 1662. Neither of these buildings survive and it is only in his works in Turin that his mature style can be fully appreciated.

His two notable Turinese churches, S. Lorenzo (1668–87) and the Capella della SS. Sindone (1677–90), perfectly express his concern for the inside rather than the exterior of his buildings, and his fanatical passion for vaulted construction. In his structural daring, and his undisguised preference for Gothic rather than classical solutions, he echoed the Roman work of Borromini. The Palazzo Carignano of 1679, in Turin, repeated in secular form these aspects of his religious architecture. His *Architettura Civile* was published posthumously by Vittone in 1737 and influenced much 18th-century Turinese architecture. (*See* overleaf.)

## Guas Juan *fl.* 1459–?97

The Spanish architect Juan Guas was born in France, at Lyons. He moved to Spain c1450 and by 1459 was working with his father on the Door of the Lions at Toledo Cathedral. He was master mason at Segovia Cathedral from 1473 to 1491 and at Toledo Cathedral c1483 to 1495. He was partly responsible for the richly carved screen surrounding the Toledo Cathedral sanctuary. In the years 1479 to 1480 he designed for Queen Isabella the church and monastery of S. Juan de los Reyes in Toledo. The church is his masterpiece, and combines elements from several architectural traditions. The wide single nave with recess-like lateral chapels is of southern French type; the star vaults and the decorative carving are Flemish, while underneath the capitals of the crossing hang miniature stalactites in Islamic fashion.

## Guercino 1591–1666

The Italian painter Giovanni Francesco Barbieri was known because of his squint as Guercino. He came from Cento, where he studied under Benedetto Gennari. More important to his early stylistic development were the painters Lodovico Carracci and Ippolito Scarsella. Between 1615 and 1617 he painted frescoes at the Casa Pannini, Bologna. In 1618 a visit to Venice encouraged his absorption of the painterly traditions and lyrical poetry of Venetian art. A dusky, flickering light, sweeping diagonals, and rich color and texture distinguished his early altarpieces; this phase culminates in *St William of Aquitaine Receiving the Cowl* (1620; Pinacoteca Nazionale, Bologna).

In 1621 the newly elected Bolognese Pope Gregory XV called Guercino to Rome. In that year he painted the huge *The Burial and Reception into Heaven of St Petronilla* (Palazzo dei Conservatori, Rome), and also, between 1621 and 1623, the ceiling fresco *Aurora* for the Casino Ludovisi. Above an illusionistic architectural framework Dawn in her chariot sweeps across the sky; on the end walls are figures representing Night and Day. This dramatic work, with its creation of a unified pictorial space, its sense of dynamic movement, and its boldness of handling, marks the beginnings of the High Baroque. Yet Guercino's own style, in response to the prevailing tendencies of Roman art, became more classical.

In 1623 he returned to Cento; he visited Piacenza in 1626 to fresco the cathedral dome, and went to Modena in 1633. On Guido Reni's death in 1642 Guercino moved to Bologna. He continued to paint many altarpieces and easel pictures. His late style conforms to the classical stan-

Guercino: Ermina and the Shepherd; oil on canvas; 149×178cm (59×70in); c1618–20. City of Birmingham Museums and Art Gallery

dards of Reni, and lacks his earlier powerful originality.

## Guglielmo of Pisa 12th century

Guglielmo of Pisa was the most prominent Romanesque sculptor in Tuscany. His pulpit for Pisa Cathedral (1157–62) provided a model for the more famous Tuscan pulpits by Nicola Pisano and his son Giovanni. It was, in fact, the pulpit by the latter that made Guglielmo's earlier version redundant; so it was shipped to Sardinia in 1311 and is now in the cathedral at Cagliari. Guglielmo was not trained in Provence, as has often been claimed; he evolved his classicizing style out of Italian Romanesque and, above all, Roman sculpture. He worked on the decoration of the facade of Pisa Cathedral, and his followers carried his style to many centers, not only in Tuscany but as far away as Roussillon in the Pyrenees.

Guarino Guarini: interior of the church of S. Lorenzo, Turin; 1668–87

## Guido da Siena 13th century

Guido da Siena was the almost legendary founder of the Sienese School of painting. Little of the legend has survived the probings of modern scholarship; but the nature of his true contribution to early Italian painting remains impressive.

For centuries, Guido's fame and reputation depended on a mystifying inscription on a painting of the *Madonna and Child* now in the Palazzo Pubblico at Siena. This not only identifies him as the artist responsible for the work, but goes on to state quite explicitly that it was painted in 1221. Since the painting exhibits characteristics that are not found in Tuscan art until the second half of the 13th century, the inscription, if taken at face value, would mean that Siena preceded Florence in the development of 13th-century painting. Not only Florentines have found this theory unacceptable. Modern criticism has demonstrated beyond all reasonable doubt that a painting with the particular stylistic features displayed by the *Madonna and Child* could not have been produced much before the 1260s and that it is probably a work of c1280.

Of the many ingenious theories that have

Guido da Siena: Madonna and Child; panel; 283×194cm (111×76in); c1280. Palazzo Pubblico, Siena

*Child*, first became established in the city.

The attribution of the *Madonna and Child* to the period *c*1280 makes possible a more convincing reconstruction of Guido's artistic personality. Modern criticism now accepts as Guido's work a number of other panels which appear to have come originally from the same altarpiece as this picture. Also accepted are a pair of reliquary shutters, a polyptych of the *Madonna and Child with Saints*, and a Lenten hanging painted on linen, all three of which are now in the Pinacoteca Nazionale, Siena. These appear to be earlier than the *Madonna and Child* and were perhaps painted in the 1260s and 1270s.

Guido's works reveal him as an artist whose great achievement was to transform Florentine spatial and formal innovations into a style now regarded as specifically Sienese. The delicacy and refinement which are so marked a feature of the great Sienese masterpieces of the next century make their first appearance in Guido's paintings.

**Further reading.** Stubblebine, J. *Guido da Siena*, Princeton (1964).

## Guimard Hector 1867–1942

The French architect Hector Guimard was born in Paris. He studied at the École des Beaux-Arts and the École des Arts Décoratifs, where he later taught. He was the most assured Art Nouveau architect working in France, and his early building was influenced by the Belgian Victor Horta. Guimard's achievements include several spectacular entrances to the Paris Métro with their serpentine forms in ironwork (1898–1901). Before this, he built the block of flats in Paris known as the Castel Béranger. Finished in 1897, the building uses metal in an extraordinarily imaginative way: the asymmetrical design on the gates seems like Rococo gone mad. He also made original use of glass and faience.

## Günther Ignaz 1725–75

The German sculptor Ignaz Günther was born at Altmannstein (Oberpfalz). He learned sculpture from his father, a cabinetmaker and wood-sculptor. In 1743 he went to Munich, where he entered the workshop of the court sculptor Johann Baptist Straub. From 1750 he moved around southern Germany and Austria, working in Salzburg, in Mannheim with the sculptor Paul Egell, and in Vienna,

been advanced to account for the appearance of the date 1221 on what is demonstrably a later painting, none is entirely satisfactory. Only two need be noted. It has been suggested that the *Madonna and Child* might be a copy of a painting executed in 1221, and that, for reasons of his own, Guido decided to incorporate the date of this older image into his own inscription. Other scholars have drawn attention to the fact that the *Madonna and Child* was substantially repainted by a Sienese follower of Duccio early in the 14th century, and have gone on to speculate that the inscription as a whole might have been added by the same hand. According to this theory, some allusion to the year 1221 would not have been out of place in the new inscription, because it was in that year that the Dominicans, for whose principal church in Siena Guido originally executed the *Madonna and*

Hector Guimard: an entrance to the Paris Métro: c1898–1901

where he came under the influence of Donner. Returning to Munich in 1754, he established himself there, eventually becoming the outstanding Bavarian Rococo sculptor.

Most of Günther's work is in the traditional South German form of altarpieces of painted wood. He was prolific, and his work is to be found in churches all over southern Germany. His sculptures stand out forcefully from their elaborate settings. Günther combined a graceful elongation in his figures, derived from a close study of late-16th-century Mannerist sculpture, with a hard realism recalling late Gothic. He produced powerfully religious images within the light and colorful convention of the Rococo.

Among Günther's early works the most impressive is the altar in the church at Kopřivná in Czechoslovakia (1752–3), in which his personal style is already quite recognizable. A characteristic work from his middle period is the great *Annunciation*

group in the church at Weyarn in Upper Bavaria. He can be seen at his most serious and expressive in his last known work, dated 1774, a superbly simple group of the *Virgin with the Dead Christ* in the cemetery chapel at Nenningen.

## Günther Matthäus 1705–88

Born in Upper Bavaria, the German painter Matthäus Günther received his formative training in the studio of C.D. Asam in Munich during the years 1723 to 1728. He became a master in Augsburg in 1731, and the remainder of his artistic career was based on that city. In 1740 he purchased the contents of the studio of J.E. Holzer and was influenced by him, on several occasions making use of his sketches. The leading Rococo fresco-painter of the Augsburg school, Günther worked all over southern Germany and the Tyrol; he succeeded J.G. Bergmüller as Catholic Director of the Augsburg Academy in 1762.

## Guston Philip 1913–80

Born in Montreal, Canada, the American painter Philip Guston moved with his family to Los Angeles in 1919. Until the mid 1940s, he worked in a figurative style, partly influenced by the Social Realist murals he had seen in Mexico in 1934, and partly by Surrealism. He worked on murals himself for the W.P.A. (Works Progress Adminstration) Federal Arts Project in New York from 1936 to 1940. After the Second World War, however, Guston was caught up in the Abstract Expressionist movement. By the early 1950s he was producing large canvases in which texture is as important as the shape of the forms. The pictures of the 1950s are often relatively light in tone and atmospheric in feeling (for example *The Return*, 1956–8; Tate Gallery, London). In the 1960s the forms became heavier, the coloring darker, and the mood often more somber. (*See* overleaf.)

Philip Guston: The Return; oil on canvas; 178×199cm (70×78in); 1956–8. Tate Gallery, London

## Guttuso Renato 1912–1987

The Italian painter Renato Guttuso was born in Palermo, the son of a land surveyor. He gave up his law studies and began to paint seriously in 1931. While living in Milan between 1935 and 1937 he met a number of artists and writers, among them Manzù, Fontana, Moravia, and Roberto Longhi. He was a member of the *Corrente* movement (1940–2) which opposed official Italian cultural policy. From 1943 to 1945 Guttuso was in the Italian Resistance movement. In 1947 he was a founder member of the *Fronte Nuovo delle Arti*.

A social realist, Guttuso has since the 1930s been influenced by the work of Goya and Picasso (particularly by Picasso's *Guernica*). This influence is evident stylistically, as well as in his choice of subject,

for example his polemics against war and social injustice. From the early 1960s his works have contained artistic quotations from paintings by Picasso and others (for example *Das Totenmahl*, 1973; Neue Galerie, Sammlung Ludwig, Aachen).

## Guys Constantin 1805–92

Born in Holland, but of French blood, Constantin Guys was essentially an illustrator. He worked for the *Illustrated London News* during the Revolution of 1848 and the Crimean War (1854–6). He traveled extensively in Italy, Spain, Germany, England, and the Orient. His work—in watercolor as well as drawing—was greatly admired by Manet, the Goncourt brothers, and, above all, by

Baudelaire. He himself thought little of it ("these sketches have no value"), but Baudelaire's essay "The Painter of Modern Life", published in 1863, produced a deserved recognition of his talents.

## Gyokudo Uragami 1745–1820

Admired in his circle as a man of general culture, and remembered after his death mainly as a master of the *koto* (zither), the painter Uragami Gyokudo has only in the mid 20th century been recognized as one of Japan's greatest artists. He now ranks among the Japanese as one of the four great *Nanga* masters; the others are Ike no Taiga (1723–76), Yosa Buson (1716–83) and Tanomura Chikuden (1777–1835). His *Frozen Clouds and Shifting Powdery*

Constantin Guys: The Promenade in the Woods; pen and ink and watercolor; 19×25cm (7½×10in). Private collection

*Snow* (hanging scroll, *c*1810; Collection Yasunari Kawabata, Kanagawa Prefecture) has the rare distinction of being listed as a Japanese National Treasure.

Although he undoubtedly belonged to the school called *Nanga*, which in the 18th and 19th centuries based its work on the ideals and theories of the *Bunjinga* "scholar-painters" of China, his painting was intensely eccentric. It was no doubt this quality that delayed his recognition until the 20th century, which has come to value individualism very highly.

The artist's life and circumstances explain much about his work. He was born Uragami Heiemon in 1745 of a samurai family in the house of his father's feudal lord, the head of the Okayama clan. Thus he was born into a class brought up to rigid self-discipline based on military virtues. This discipline accounts for his single-minded absorption in exploring in ink one aspect only of *Nanga* painting: landscape.

The religion of his class had for centuries been Zen Buddhism, which placed great importance on intuitive action and understanding. We must look to this for the immediate, white-hot intensity of his brushwork. At this period the totalitarian Tokugawa government had seen fit to promote Confucian doctrines, since their endorsement of a feudal order in society was politically convenient. Hence Confu-

cian studies, the doorway to the culture of China itself, became part of Gyokudo's education. Confucianism led him to the studies of a Chinese gentleman—music, literature, painting, and calligraphy—and so to the *Nanga* School.

As a young man he became an official Confucianist to his master Ikeda, received government appointments, and moved in intellectual circles in Kyoto and Edo (modern Tokyo). At this time he devoted himself to literature and the study of the *koto*. What paintings he did in his early and middle years must have been unexceptional, and they have not survived. His earliest dated paintings were done between 1787 and 1792; while pleasant, they show little of his later force. In 1779 he acquired his famous *koto* on which was the inscription *Gyokudo* ("Jade Hall"). Thereafter he called himself Gyokudo Kinshi (Gyokudo the *Koto* Master).

His life as an official came to an end for two main reasons. Firstly, in 1790 the Wang Yangming branch of Confucianism was found politically suspect by the government and suppressed. Gyokudo seems to have embraced its unorthodox doctrines and so to have been under a cloud. Wang Yangming's strong emphasis on intuition and on the unity of different ways of thought can be felt in Gyokudo's landscapes. There is no strain in them

between intent and expression. Every painting looks as though it came direct from his brain on to the paper, and as though the scenes he saw had all their disparate parts rendered into a whole by the strength of his vision.

Secondly, in 1792 his wife died. Adopting, perhaps consciously, the proper Confucian role, he resigned his post in 1793 and retired from the world of affairs. Taking his two sons Shunkin ("Spring *Koto*") and Shukin ("Autumn *Koto*"), his *koto*, and his artist's materials, he began a life of wandering around Japan, living simply, drinking heavily, playing on his instrument, and now more and more, painting. He returned occasionally to city exhibitions and literary gatherings, but he never settled down again. To these years belong the masterpieces of landscape painting for which he is remembered. He died in Kyoto in 1820.

The great majority of Gyokudo's paintings are done on paper. Silk had a more academic flavor which appealed to some painters of the *Nanga* School, but the material has the effect of slowing up the brush. It requires greater care from the painter and inhibits his freedom. Gyokudo's impetuous visions were clearly dashed down in a spirit of exaltation, or even drunkenness, and for them paper was the only suitable vehicle. The best Japanese paper is tough but alive, setting up its own relationship with the brush. It absorbs wet ink deeply, but allows the almost dry brush to skate lightly over its surface. These opportunities for exciting texture were fully grasped by Gyokudo, as in the intensely vibrant and bewilderingly complex welter of strokes and washes that make up the foreground trees in *Twin Peaks Embracing the Clouds* (*c*1805; Idemitsu Art Museum, Tokyo).

The medium of his art, as in nearly all Far Eastern painting, was the brush loaded with Chinese ink. Loaded in different ways, with wash or thick ink, or with one side wetter than the other, it was perhaps the most comprehensive vehicle for painting ever devised. Gyokudo found black ink alone almost enough for his purposes. Many of his most impressive landscapes have no color in them at all. He appears to have found that the adding of color obstructed the directness of his painting.

When he does use color it is brilliantly effective, although often arbitrary. In *Frozen Clouds and Shifting Snow*, for example, a majestic and bleak vision of a frozen gray mountain world is enlivened by a few apparently random spatters of blood-red ink on the trees and rocks. They represent nothing, yet they pull the eye into themselves and make the looker feel the inherent force of life in the dead terrain. Gyokudo's use of color, indeed, is almost limited to red inks in a few paintings. But so subtle is his use of them that in the famous page from the *Album of Mists* (1811) called *Green Mountains and Red Woods* (c1811; Umegawa Memorial Hall, Tokyo) the whole scene seems to glow with the varied colors of a Japanese autumn, although only red and black are used. (See also *Mountains Stained by Red Leaves*, a hanging scroll, c1815–20; Teizo Kimura Collection, Aichi prefecture.)

There were five main formats available to the Japanese artist: screens, handscrolls, hanging scrolls, albums, and fan-leaves. Gyokudo did not paint screens, nor did he do more than a very few handscrolls. The reasons are practical. Both these formats need careful organization; in the case of screens it would scarcely be possible with so large a form to paint direct from nature. The often inebriated Gyokudo needed to paint directly. The handscroll was designed to unfold slowly, a few feet at a time, in the hands of the connoisseur. It was a leisurely journey through changing scenes and even changing styles. It was therefore popular among the more scholarly *Nanga* painters; but for Gyokudo it would not do. The handscroll *Old Age in the Southern Mountains* (an approximate translation of a typically cryptic title; private collection) in the style of the Chinese master Mi Fu is one of his tamest works. It is also one of his earliest (1787).

Gyokudo preferred the simple unity of the hanging scroll, the fan-leaf, and the album-leaf. It was in the field of the large hanging scroll that his greatest triumphs were won. Because of his ability to transcend the scholarly restraints of his school, he became the grandest of its masters. He is unequaled in it for his ability to expand his technique and his vision into a really large surface. Such a work as *Idle in the Mountains* (c1807; Kyoto National Museum) has the exceptional length of painted area of 5 ft 9⅜ in by 3 ft 1⅝ in (1.76 by 0.95 m) yet it never collapses into its component sections as do the works of even such a master as Taiga.

Most of Gyokudo's works are landscapes painted in the last 20 years of his life, during which he was traveling almost constantly round the mountainous areas of Japan. There can be no doubt that his pictures—nearly all of which consist of round-topped mountains, covered nearly to their peaks by vegetation and rising out of thickly wooded valleys—are at heart portraits of his own land, however distorted the artist's vision may have been. This has to be emphasized, because the *Nanga* painters of Japan very often adapted or copied the landscapes of the Chinese scholar-painters, who themselves usually painted a highly idealized scene.

The Confucian idea laid down by the great Chinese theorist of painting Tung Ch'i-ch'ang (1555–1636) was that pure landscape, devoid of any but tiny human figures, was the proper practice of the scholar-painter. It was in reality a form of self-portrait. Gyokudo must have subscribed to this, for his works conform to the idea very closely; but to it he added the dimension of his passionate love of his own countryside. In many of his works we find the repeated idea of a tiny traveler on a bridge, among trees, looking up at the mountains which are majestic and yet close-by, not remote as in the Chinese masters. It is a scene he himself must have acted out many times.

In this sense, Gyokudo's landscapes are uncontrived. The mountains usually form a center to the picture, and are not artificially placed to one side, while below them the woods spread out naturally. The artifice added by Gyokudo is the wildly irrational welter of brush strokes imposed over the basic shapes. Sometimes a whole painting will be covered in apparently meaningless horizontal strokes, as in *Mountains Wrapped in Rain* (hanging scroll, c1805; Ohara Art Museum, Okayama prefecture), giving an intense feeling of nature in movement, in perpetual change.

This impression of flux is something that goes deeper than official Confucianism, for it is one of the basic doctrines of the Buddhism that had so affected the Japanese character since the 6th century AD. The intuitive nature of Zen Buddhist perception was something Gyokudo grew up with, and which must have attracted him to the Wang Yangming branch of Confucianism, the suppression of which led to his departure from official life. Wang Yangming had taught intuition and the unity of things and ways of thought.

As he grew older, Gyokudo's vision became more and more distorted. Strange circular shapes appear on his mountainsides, dominating the eye with peculiar force, as in *Quiet View in the Cloudy Mountains* (private collection). The mountains themselves become more and more fluid until in *High Wind, Slanting Geese* (1817; private collection) they resemble an explosion. At the same time, his mountain-tops tend to shapes so overtly phallic (as in *Retreat in Winter Woods* or *Leisured Spot in the Frozen Woods* (private collection) that one realizes there are more primitive forces behind his violent brushwork than mere philosophies.

Gyokudo's strength ultimately lies in his individual view of nature and the sheer visual excitement of the brushwork that expressed it. It is the achievement as much of a Zen painter as of a *Nanga* painter. His ability to suggest the violent energy of nature and of his own mind has appealed strongly to 20th-century man, particularly in the West.

His sons Shunkin and Shukin were conventional *Nanga* painters, the former admired more than his father in his day. They handed down nothing of his spirit, and he left no school. Only the last *Nanga* master, Tomioka Tessai (1836–1924), approaches his extraordinary insight into nature and his visual tensions. Uragami Gyokudo should not be confused with Kawai Gyokudo (1873–1957), an excellent lyrical nature-painter of the present century who belonged to an entirely different school.

**Further reading.** Akiyama, T. *Japanese Painting*, Cleveland (1961). Cahill, J. *Scholar Painters of Japan: The Nanga School*, New York (1972). Yonezawa, Y. and Yoshizawa, C. *Japanese Painting in the Literati Style*, New York (1974).

# Gyosai Kawanabe 1831–89

Kawanabe Gyosai was a Japanese painter, often called Kyosai. Of precocious gifts, he trained with *Ukiyoe* and *Kano* artists as well as studying more ancient Japanese styles. He emerged as perhaps the most accomplished copier of other artists, in a country where copying traditionally formed the basic artistic training. His personal genius was for *giga* (cartoon-like comic sketches) and for *diablerie* of a joyous vitality; these were often inspired by indulgence in drink, like the splendid series of hell scenes in the British Museum, London. He was also a serious painter and print artist of nationalist themes in the Revival-*Yamatoe* style. The British architect Josiah Conder became his pupil.

# H

## Hakuin Ekaku 1685–1768

The Japanese Zen painter, calligrapher, and mystic Ekaku Hakuin was born in Hara (Shizuoku Prefecture). He became a Zen monk at an early age and spent most of his life traveling in Japan and trying to popularize the sect. His writings on Zen experience are vivid, and he also developed a very powerful and heavy style of calligraphy which broke all the classical rules. His work was deliberately clumsy in appearance, often painted against an inked-in background. Its aim was to convey Buddhist truths to the common people through simple, effective images of figures like Boddhidarma and Kannon. Hakuin's semi-popular style has nonetheless great spiritual strength and confidence.

## Hals Frans c1581/5–1666

The Dutch painter Frans Hals was second only to Rembrandt in portraiture. He was born in Antwerp, the son of a Flemish clothmaker. His parents emigrated to the Northern Provinces in 1585 (the year Antwerp fell to the Spanish) and settled in Haarlem. Apart from one or two visits to Flanders, Hals remained in Haarlem (an important center of early-17th-century Dutch art) for the rest of his life.

Almost nothing is known of Hals' youthful years. There are no dated paintings earlier than a portrait from 1611, when the artist was between 25 and 30 years old. In this and other extant paintings from c1611 to 1615, the tendency is towards relatively detailed execution, with bright colors set off against dark backgrounds. Hals' professional success dates from 1616, the year of the first of his large group portraits: *The Banquet of the Officers of the Militia Company of St George* (Frans Hals Museum, Haarlem, where the artist's work can best be studied).

The Company of St George was one of Haarlem's two civic guards: bodies of men whose defensive role during the war against Spain had been reduced by 1616 to a purely social one. Following their three-year term, officers frequently commissioned portraits of themselves to hang in their company's headquarters. The costs of these portraits were borne equally by all the sitters—who therefore expected equal prominence, a consideration also demanded by the need to present adequate individual likenesses. Hals' innovation was to break up the customary monotonous rows of expressionless faces into differentiated groups of men whose varied facial expressions, gestures, and postures reveal his gift for individual characterization and desire for greater informality.

The immediacy Hals achieved in this first ceremonial scene was enhanced in the dazzling *Officers of the Militia Company of St Hadrian* (c1627; Frans Hals Museum, Haarlem), where varied directional movements in the figures are emphasized by the bold diagonals of sashes and banners. The lack of a clear focus of attention that would arrest this picture's excessive animation is corrected in a later version, the daringly assymmetrical *Officers of the Militia Company of St Hadrian* of c1633 (Frans Hals Museum, Haarlem). Here the diagonals are replaced by more architectonic vertical and horizontal elements. Certain figures are now subordinated to background positions, but although this contributed to greater formal unity, convincing psychological unity in such paintings was not achieved until Rembrandt's *Night Watch* of 1642

Frans Hals: Portrait of Isabella Coymans; detail; oil on canvas; full size 116×86cm (46×34in); 1648–50. Rothschild Collection, Paris

(Rijksmuseum, Amsterdam).

The majority of Hals' portraits are half- or three-quarter-length single-figure paintings, usually of professional men, merchants, and their wives. The celebrated *Laughing Cavalier* (1624; Wallace Collection, London) is typical of commissions from the 1620s, with their casual informality and brilliant but increasingly cool color. These portraits invariably suggest incipient changes of posture and expression, and rarely look posed.

Hals can be criticized for not penetrating his sitters' inner characters, but his intention was to extend the scope of a portrait from a visual likeness to something approaching a "speaking" likeness, particularly through the animation of the face by a smile, a laugh, or intimations of conversation. Hals heightened the sense of presence he sought by establishing emotional links between sitter and spectator. This is achieved by glances towards us, and also by such illusionistic devices as movements and gestures made in our direction: the raising of a glass is a favorite technique.

Genre pictures are frequent during the first half of Hals' career. The earliest examples are richly detailed, brightly colored, and boisterous. Typical of this period is *Merry Company* (c1615–17; Metropolitan Museum, New York), a theatrical scene in which Shrove Tuesday is being celebrated. The iconography and light tonality of several exuberant life-size musicians, drinkers, and harlots from the 1620s and early 1630s reveal the influence of the Utrecht School, with the difference that Hals' genre pieces invariably have a distinctly portrait-like character (for example, *Yonker Ramp and his Sweetheart*, c1623; Metropolitan Museum, New York; *The Merry Drinker*, c1628–30; Rijksmuseum, Amsterdam).

Hals was much in demand as a portraitist in the 1620s and 1630s, and had to rely on the help of assistants. But he received fewer commissions in the 1640s, perhaps because the informality of his work was unsuited to the more sober mood of the now well-established republic. His later portraits show a marked tendency towards monochromatic colors and darker tones: a development only partially explained by the move towards greater sobriety in Dutch costume after c1635. But his palette, although limited to blacks, whites, grays, yellowish browns, and flesh tints, was still rich in variety; Van Gogh remarked that Hals had no less than 27 different blacks.

Panache and movement disappear in Hals' later paintings; plain, frontal poses are common and the mood is quiet. His handling of paint, on the other hand, becomes increasingly broad and free; angular, vigorously applied brush strokes are capable of summarizing forms with the greatest economy. This direct approach made preliminary studies superfluous (no drawings survive). In his final paintings Hals even dispensed with underpainting, applying his oils straight on to the bare canvas. This spontaneous handling of paint gave vitality and animation to Hals' figures, heightened the sense of the momentary, and conveyed an impression of sparkling light effects. But it was incapable of distinguishing between different textures, and although suited to the dashing, extrovert character of young male sitters, was less appropriate to women and older models.

Hals' culminating works are the two great group portraits of the *Regents* and *Regentesses of the Haarlem Old Men's Alms House* (both c1664; Frans Hals Museum, Haarlem). These, painted when Hals was 80 years old and himself destitute, convey a sense of austere, solemn dignity with utmost simplicity of means. Their pathos is unprecedented in the artist's work.

Hals had little influence during his lifetime, nor was he properly appreciated after his death (only about 250 paintings have been preserved). The sketchiness of his virtuoso technique contributed to Hals' neglect by later generations. His rediscovery dates from the mid 19th century—when the Impressionists, Manet in particular, emulated his brilliant brushwork.

**Further reading.** Slive, S. *Frans Hals* (3 vols.), London (1970–4). Trivas, N.S. *The Paintings of Frans Hals*, London (1941). Valentiner, W.R. (ed.) *Frans Hals*, Stuttgart (1923).

## Hamilton Gavin 1723–98

Gavin Hamilton was a Scottish history and portrait painter. An associate of Stuart and Revett, Winckelmann and Mengs, and an early supporter of Canova, he has been regarded as a seminal figure in the development of international Neoclassicism.

Born in Lanarkshire, he went to study painting in Rome in 1748 and for a short time was a pupil of Agostino Masucci.

Gavin Hamilton: detail of Hector's Farewell to Andromache; oil on canvas; 315×399cm (124×157i 1788. Hunterian Museum and Art Gallery, Glasgow

Duane Hanson: Bowery Bums; fiberglass, polyester, found materials; 1969–70. Museum Ludwig, Cologne

Except for two brief visits to London, he remained in Rome for the rest of his life. His earliest recorded history painting, *Dawkins and Wood Discovering Palmyra* (1758; on loan to the Hunterian Museum and University Art Collections, Glasgow), anticipates in theme his own archaeological efforts. These resulted in the discovery of several pieces of antique sculpture. His two series of compositions based on Homer (1760s and 1782/4) received wide circulation in the form of engravings.

Hamilton's most important single painting, *The Oath of Brutus*, exists in several versions (one c1763; Paul Mellon Center for British Art, New Haven). This novel and grand conception of an incident recorded in Livy was a direct source for a number of Neoclassical pictures, the best known of which is David's *Oath of the Horatii* (1784; Louvre, Paris). In general, Hamilton's style reflects the eclectic tastes of the early Neoclassicists, combining as it often does elements from diverse antique and Baroque sources.

## Hamilton Richard 1922–

The British painter Richard Hamilton was born in London. He studied at the Royal Academy (1938–40; 1946–7) and at the Slade School of Fine Art (1948–51), and in 1952 was a founder member of the Independent Group. Hamilton was a pioneer figure in the development of Pop art in Britain in the 1950s. A friend of Marcel Duchamp, by whom he has been much influenced, Hamilton works in collage. He uses fragments of popular culture—such as magazine photographs—to create new

images that are both a tribute to their sources and successful as partially abstract works of fine art.

## Hanson Duane 1925–96

The American Super-Realist sculptor was born in Alexandria, Minnesota. He finished his studies with a year at the Cranbrook Academy of Art, Michigan, where he had his first solo exhibition in 1951. By the time he came to prominence in the late 1960s he had developed a technique of casting figures in fiberglass and dressing them in real clothes. He used this process to create tableaux from contemporary life, usually of a violent emotive subject such as *Vietnam Scene* (1969; Wilhelm-Lehmbruck-Museum, Duisberg). He then abandoned these so-called "Expressionist" groups for mostly single figures representing American types, such as *Supermarket Lady* (1970; Neue Galerie, Sammlung Ludwig, Aachen).

Richard Hamilton: Swingeing London 67II; screenprint, oil on canvas; 67×85cm (26×33in); 1967, Museum Ludwig, Cologne

## Harnett William 1848–92

The American painter William Michael Harnett was born at Clonakilty, County Cork, Ireland. Taken to Philadelphia as a child, he was apprenticed to an engraver. He studied at the Pennsylvania Academy, and at the National Academy, New York, then visited Germany between 1871 and 1881. His still lifes are noted for their extraordinarily convincing *trompe-l'oeil* effects. They show groups of objects, pinned on to, and hung from, walls and doors. They are similar to those of John F. Peter; between them these two artists established a style which forms an important part of the American tradition. Harnett's are superior to Peter's in that they use a wider variety of objects and textured surfaces.

## Hartley Marsden 1877–1943

Marsden Hartley was an American painter whose artistic ancestry stemmed from American Romantics such as Albert P. Ryder. Hartley was associated with the earliest modern art in New York, inspired by Alfred Stieglitz. Stieglitz helped him to visit Berlin, where he exhibited with the *Blaue Reiter* group. Works such as *Portrait of a German Officer* (1914; Metropolitan Museum, New York) are in a European Expressionist manner; but already Hartley's passionate identification with his native Maine had appeared in claustrophobic and menacing paintings such as *The Dark Mountain* (1909; Art Institute of Chicago). Hartley's mature style was a mixture of European Expressionism and a personal interpretation of the life and landscape of the northeastern American seaboard.

## Hartung Hans 1904–89

Hans Hartung was a German-French painter and graphic artist. He went to the Gymnasium in Dresden (1915–24) and the University and Academy of Fine Arts in Leipzig (1924–5), where he studied philosophy and art history. He was advised to go to the Bauhaus but chose instead the academies of Fine Arts in Dresden and Munich, studying with Feldbauer, Dorsche, Wehlte, and Dörner. By this time he had received inspiration from Rembrandt and Goya and discovered the German Expressionists, particularly Oskar Kokoschka and Emil Nolde. He spent the years 1927 to 1935 traveling and living in Minorca and Paris. Returning to Berlin in 1935 to sort out his finances, Hartung was forced to flee Nazi Germany. He went to Paris, with help from Will Grohmann and Christian Zervos. In Paris in 1936 he exhibited at the Galerie Pierre with Kandinsky, Arp, and Hélion; in 1937 he met Julio Gonzàlez, whose work he admired. Between 1939 and 1945 Hartung was in the French Foreign Legion. In 1945 he was made a French citizen, and thereafter lived and worked in Paris, exhibiting widely.

By the mid 1930s Hartung's work was developing the characteristics for which it came to be known in the 1950s: a rhythmic calligraphic style and automatism preceded by a period of meditation on the canvas (*Painting T 54–16*, oil on canvas; 1954; Musée National d'Art Moderne, Paris). By the early 1960s the brisk brush strokes had given way to scoring the paint while wet, and by the end of the decade dark stains on the canvas had gained over the graphic element.

**Further reading.** Apollonis, U. *Hans Hartung*, Paris (1967). Rousseau, M. *Hans Hartung*, Stuttgart (1949).

## Harunobu Suzuki 1725–70

The Japanese print artist Suzuki Harunobu worked in Edo (Tokyo); but stylistically he seems to have been a follower of the Kyoto *Ukiyoe* artists, and particularly of the book illustrator Nishikawa Sukenobu

Suzuki Harunobu: Interior with a Girl and her Maid; woodblock print; 27×20cm (11×8in); c1750–70. British Museum, London

(1682–1752). He came to prominence in 1764, when groups of connoisseurs first commissioned multicolored woodblock prints, the so-called "brocade prints" of which Harunobu was the first master.

He established a style of varied but delicate color, sensitive line, and mock-innocent romanticism, putting his women and their lovers in convincing domestic or outdoor settings which give unity to the compositions. He also introduced classical allusions and subjects into these basically bourgeois works, thus linking them more strongly with older artistic traditions.

## Hassam Childe 1859–1935

The painter and printmaker (Frederick) Childe Hassam was one of the leading American Impressionists. He began as a wood engraver in Boston, and spent the years 1886–89 in France, where he acquired a thorough knowledge of Impressionism. On his return to the United States he settled in New York, and in 1898 became a member of a group of American Impressionists known as "The Ten". His pictures, often of the streets of Boston and New York under snow, display a sensitive use of color and light, though their Impressionism is tempered by a strain of American realism. Among his best-known works are *Boston Common at Dusk* (1885–86; Museum of Fine Arts, Boston) and *Flag Day* (1919; County Museum of Art, Los Angeles).

Further reading. Adelson, W. et al. *Childe Hassam, Impressionist*, New York (1999).

## Haussmann Baron 1809–91

Baron Georges-Eugène Haussmann was born in Paris, although his family came from Alsace. In 1853 he was appointed by Napoleon III as Prefect of the Department of the Seine. It is to Haussmann, who held this post for nearly 20 years, that we owe the transformation of Paris from an essentially medieval city to the modern metropolis of today. Long, straight, and wide boulevards were cut through and around the city. At major intersections, or *rond-points*, important monuments and public buildings were erected (for example, the Opéra), thus opening out superb vistas. Haussmann was influenced in his choice of layout by military and political considerations, as well as by the requirements of hygiene and circulation.

Nicholas Hawksmoor: the Codrington Library (left) and the towers in the north quadrangle of All Souls College, Oxford; built 1716–35

# Hawksmoor Nicholas c1661–1736

Nicholas Hawksmoor was an English architect. His precise contribution to English Baroque architecture is surrounded by mystery and may never be completely understood. Introspective, with a marked lack of faith in his own talents, Hawksmoor spent much of his career as an assistant to his two most illustrious contemporaries, Sir Christopher Wren and Sir John Vanbrugh.

The extent to which these architects relied on Hawksmoor's genius is not fully known. The masterly assurance of his first completely independent commission (and only country house) Easton Neston, Northamptonshire (1696–1702), strongly suggests that his cooperation with Wren at Greenwich hospital (1696–1702) extended to more than merely supervising the Surveyor General's designs. It was undoubtedly Hawksmoor who transmitted Wren's late style to Vanbrugh at Castle Howard and Blenheim Palace.

His six London churches—St Alphege, Greenwich (1712–14), St Anne, Limehouse (1714–30), St George, Wapping (1715–23), St Mary, Woolnoth (1716–27), St George, Bloomsbury (1716–31), and Christchurch, Spittalfields (1714–29)—reveal the full extent of his inventive brilliance. Medieval in silhouette, Imperial Roman in detail, they form the culmination of the tradition of Wren's city churches. Their adventurous compositional massing—anticipated by the bold spatial contrasts of Hawksmoor's (planned but never completed) forecourt of Easton Neston—clearly relates to Vanbrugh's experiments in the field of country house architecture.

Outside London his work is best represented in Oxford, where he was responsible for the Clarendon Building (1712–15), Queen's College front quadrangle (1709–38), and the north quadrangle and towers of All Souls College (1715–40). The latter is in an austere Gothic style that anticipated his west towers of Westminster Abbey (1734), and found a classical counterpart in the gaunt silhouette of the mausoleum at Castle Howard (1729–36).

Francis Hayman: The Artist at his Easel; oil on canvas; 69×59cm (27×23in); c1745-50. Royal Albert Memorial Museum, Exeter

## Hayman Francis 1708–76

The English painter Francis Hayman was first employed in London as a scene-painter at Drury Lane. In the 1740s he collaborated with Gravelot in the designs and engravings for a number of literary illustrations, and in the ornamental decorations at London's Vauxhall Gardens. His depiction of the Wrestling Scene from *As You Like It* in *The Works of Shakespeare* edited by Sir T. Hanmer (*c*1744) is one of the most original early illustrations to Shakespeare. He offered his most ambitious history painting, *The Finding of Moses* (1746), to the Foundling Hospital in London. Conversations and theatrical portraits also figure prominently in his work at this time. Hayman's blend of realism with elements of French Rococo style was an important influence on Gainsborough. He played a key role in the founding of both the Society of Artists and the Royal Academy.

## Heartfield John 1891–1968

John Heartfield was a German graphic designer. In protest against German nationalistic fervor, he anglicized his name from Helmut Herzefelde during the First World War. He joined the Communist Party in 1918 and remained a committed political artist for the rest of his life. Prominent in the Berlin Dada group, he was one of the inventors—perhaps the greatest exponent—of the photomontage technique. This became in his hands a supremely effective satirical method. He was scenic director of the Max Reinhardt theaters in Berlin from 1921 to 1923, edited the satirical magazine *Der Knüppel* from 1923 to 1927, and produced some of his finest photomontages for the German Communist press in the early 1930s. Harassed by the Hitler regime, he lived as a refugee in London between 1938 and 1950. He died in East Berlin.

## Heckel Erich 1883–1970

Born in Döbeln (Saxony), Erich Heckel studied architecture at Dresden. Together with Fritz Bleyl, Ernst Ludwig Kirchner, and Karl Schmidt-Rottluff, he founded the *Brücke* artists association in 1905. Self-taught, his admiration for medieval German woodcuts and African sculpture is shown in his own powerful woodcuts. These were in advance of his painting style until *c*1907, when the influence of Van Gogh begins to appear in his work. After his move to Berlin in 1911, the wilder Post-Impressionist colors yield to an angular crystalline structure, reflecting Cubist influences. In Berlin he became a founder of the New Secession. His work was proscribed by the Nazis in 1937. After the Second World War he was a member of the Karlsruhe Academy from 1949 to 1955.

## Heemskerck Maerten van 1498–1574

Maerten van Heemskerck was a Dutch artist who trained in Haarlem and Delft. He was a pupil of Jan van Scorel whose influence is evident in the *Virgin and St Luke* (1532; Frans Hals Museum, Haarlem). On a journey to Rome during the years 1532 to 1535 he produced a series of drawings of the city which show a keen archaeological interest, acknowledged in the background of his *Self-portrait* of 1553 (Fitzwilliam Museum, Cambridge). His re-

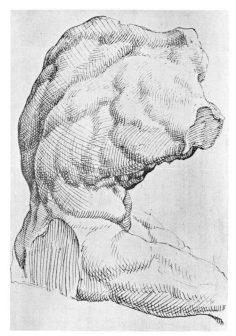

Maerten van Heemskerck: Torso, the Apollo Belvedere; ink on paper; c1532–6. Staatliche Museen, Berlin

sponse to Michelangelo was also profound, even as late as the *Erythræan Sybil* (1564; Rijksmuseum, Amsterdam), whose costume, turning position, and crossed legs are indebted to the figures on the Sistine Chapel ceiling.

## Hemessen Jan van c1500–?66

The Flemish painter Jan Sanders van Hemessen trained at Antwerp but moved north to Haarlem after 1550, probably for religious reasons. It is likely that he traveled to Italy. A knowledge of Italian Mannerist painting is evident in his *Judith* (c1540–5; Art Institute of Chicago), where the powerful nude form is accommodated within the picture space only by the turn of her body and the foreshortened arm. His biblical and genre paintings usually show figures close to the foreground plane with landscape purely as a backdrop to the action, as in the *Tobias Healing his Blind Father* (1555; Louvre, Paris).

## Henri Robert 1865–1929

The American painter and teacher Robert Henri was born in Cincinnati, Ohio. He studied at the Pennsylvania Academy of Fine Arts, and in Paris at the Académie Julian and at the École des Beaux-Arts. He returned to Philadelphia in 1891 and became friendly with Glackens, Shinn, Luks, and Sloan. He continued to travel, and he taught in New York, first at the Chase School and later, after becoming disenchanted with Academic methods, in his own establishment. Henri remains an important figure. This is not so much for his own art, which is an adroit but not original blend of Impressionism and older influences such as Hals and Courbet (seen, for example, in *Woman in White*, 1904; Joseph Hirshhorn Museum, Washington, D.C.), but for his influence as a teacher. In particular he encouraged the development of new aesthetic ideas. For example, after a rejection by the New York Academy he was involved in the independent exhibition of The Eight at the Macbeth Gallery in 1908. He was also involved in the Armory Show.

## Henriques Francisco *fl.* 1500–19

Francisco Henriques was a Portuguese painter, probably of Flemish origin, originally named Frans Hendricks. His only attributed work is a number of panels in the National Museum of Art, Lisbon, and in the Solar dos Patudos, Alpiarça, surviving from retables executed during the years 1509–11 for São Francisco, Evora. Here his Flemish heritage is evident in the folds of the robes, the tiled floors, interior views, and detailed backgrounds of town and landscape. The monumentality of the figures recalls Nuno Gonçalves. The expressions on the faces are, however, softer and the gestures more awkward. In the *Passion* series, some compositions are reminiscent of Schongauer's engravings.

## Henry of Reyns *fl.* 1243–53

The English master mason Henry of Reyns is first documented in 1243 working for Henry III at Windsor Castle. Here a wall arcade in the King's Chapel has stylistic affiliations with his greatest achievement, Westminster Abbey, begun in 1245.

As Master of the King's Works at the time, it is likely that Henry designed the Abbey. Controversy exists over whether he was from England or from Reims in France, as his name suggests. Westminster Abbey incorporates architectural features from both countries. The obvious similarities to Reims Cathedral, begun in 1211, are the plan and proportions of the polygonal apse with radiating chapels, the ambulatory wall passage, bar tracery, the pier forms, and the use of naturalistic foliage carving for the first time in England. Additional French influence, from the more recently built Amiens Cathedral (begun in 1218) and from the Sainte Chapelle (begun in 1243) is revealed in the window tracery, particularly in those windows shaped like spherical triangles. It has also been suggested that the plan and elevation of Westminster derive from the now ruined Royaumont Abbey, dedicated in 1236.

English features, however, include the gallery instead of triforium, the vault ridge rib, and especially the polygonal plan of the chapter house on the Lincoln Cathedral model of the 1240s. It is possible that Henry of Reyns was English, but visited France where he studied the latest architectural developments, or else that he was French but had English masons working with him in the traditional English style.

A masonry break can be detected at Westminster, one bay west of the crossing, so it is assumed that at this stage John of Gloucester, first mentioned in the documents in 1253, took control as master mason, due no doubt to his predecessor's death.

Henry of Reyns is also documented as having worked on Clifford's Tower in York in 1244 and the Tower of London in 1250, and he may have designed Hayles Abbey in Gloucestershire.

## Hepworth Barbara 1903–75

The English sculptor Barbara Hepworth was born in Wakefield, Yorkshire. As a child the beauty of the Yorkshire dales made a deep impression on her, and memories of this unspoiled countryside remained with her throughout her life. The importance of man in the landscape, and the unity of man and nature, were to become the basic impulses of her sculpture.

In 1920 Hepworth won a scholarship to the Leeds School of Art. There she met Henry Moore, with whom she was closely associated for the next 20 years. The following year she entered the Royal College of Art in London. Like Moore she was interested in direct carving, respecting the characteristics of stone or wood, letting the material dictate the forms of the sculpture. Although from the mid 1950s she also worked in bronze and other materials, Hepworth remained primarily a carver.

After she was awarded the Diploma of the Royal College of Art in 1924, she went

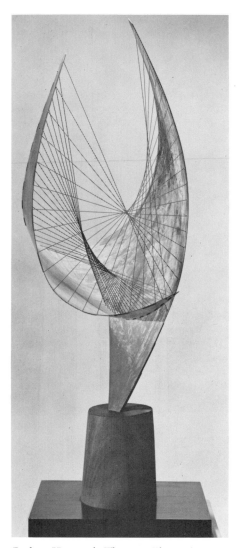

Barbara Hepworth: Theme on Electronics (Orpheus); second maquette; brass with strings on wooden base; 115×43×41cm (45×17×16in); 1956. Tate Gallery, London

to Italy, where she studied Romanesque and early Renaissance sculpture and architecture. The following year she married the sculptor John Skeaping, and moved from Florence to Rome. They returned to London in 1926.

Hepworth's interest in the art of the past centered on Egyptian, Cycladic, and Archaic Greek sculpture. Several naturalistic carvings of the late 1920s are stylistically related to the life drawings of the period. Four sculptures of birds, shown at her first one-woman exhibition at the Beaux-Arts Gallery, London, in 1928, reflect the influence of Epstein and Gaudier-Brzeska. In 1928 she moved to Parkhill Road, Hampstead, where she lived until 1939.

In *Pierced Form* of 1931 (destroyed in the Second World War) a hole was carved through the alabaster, an innovation

which was to have far-reaching effects in the development of her work. She has written of "the most intense pleasure in piercing the stone in order to make an abstract form and space".

In that same year Hepworth met the painter Ben Nicholson, who was to become her second husband. In 1932 Hepworth and Nicholson visited the Paris studios of Picasso, Braque, Brancusi, and Arp, and of Mondrian in 1933. Contact with these artists, particularly with the formal purity of the work of Brancusi and Mondrian, revealed the possibilities of Abstract art. Although Hepworth's sculpture of 1931 to 1934 was becoming more Abstract, it still retained tenuous references to the human figure. By 1935 her sculpture had become completely Abstract. She became a member of the *Abstraction-Création* group in 1933 and of Unit One in 1934, and contributed to *Circle: International Survey of Constructive Art*, published in 1937. She began using color and strings in her sculpture in 1939, and these were to remain lasting features of her work. Color in the concavities suggests water and caves; the strings express the tension between herself, and the sea, wind, or hills.

A week before the outbreak of the Second World War, Hepworth and Nicholson moved to St Ives, Cornwall, with their three children (triplets, born 1934). She grew to love the Cornish landscape (reminiscent of her native Yorkshire), with its rugged coastlines and cliffs, brilliant light, the blues, greens, and grays of the sea, the movement of tides and waves. A number of her sculptures reflect the influence of this landscape: *Figure in Landscape* (*Zennor*) (1952; private collection), *Hollow Form* (*Penwith*) (1955; Museum of Modern Art, New York), *Pelagos*, of 1946 (Tate Gallery, London) were inspired by the curve of St Ives Bay and the waves of the sea.

In 1949 Hepworth bought Trewyn Studios in St Ives. She lived there from 1951, when her marriage to Nicholson was dissolved, until her death. During the 1950s her work was exhibited at the 25th Venice Biennale (1950) and at the 5th Sao Paulo Bienale (1959) where she won the Grand Prix. In 1954 she visited Greece. A subsequent series of wood carvings attest to the tremendous impact the Greek landscape had made on her (they include *Curved Form* (*Delphi*), 1955; Ulster Museum, Belfast). As worldwide recogni-

tion grew she received important commissions: these produced, among others, *Meridian* (bronze; 1958–9; State House, London), *Winged Figure* (aluminum; 1962; John Lewis Building, London), and *Single Form* (bronze; 1962–3; for the United Nations Building, New York, as a memorial to her friend Dag Hammarskjöld). Major exhibitions were held at the Kröller-Müller Museum, Otterlo (1956), and at the Tate Gallery, London (1968). In June 1965 Hepworth was created Dame of the British Empire.

Hepworth died in a fire in her St Ives studio in May 1975. In April 1976 Trewyn Studios and garden, now the Barbara Hepworth Museum, were opened to the public. Carvings, bronzes, and drawings—embodying geometric purity, classical calm, grace and tenderness—are displayed in the town where Barbara lived and worked for 36 years.

**Further reading.** Hepworth, B. *Barbara Hepworth: a Pictorial Autobiography*, London (1970). Hepworth, B. "The Sculptor Carves because he Must", *The Studio*, London (December 1932). Hodin, J.P. *Barbara Hepworth: Life and Work*, London (1961).

## Herbin Auguste 1882–1960

The French painter Auguste Herbin was born at Quiévy. He studied at the École des Beaux-Arts and at the Atelier Winter, Lille, from 1898 to 1901. He moved to Paris, and in 1909 took a studio at the Bateau-Lavoir. In 1931 he was one of the cofounders of the *Abstraction-Création* group. He died in Paris in 1960.

From 1903 to 1907 his work consisted of Fauvist still lifes, landscapes, and figures. In 1909 contact with Picasso, Braque, and Gris caused him to turn to Cubism. He produced his first Abstract paintings in 1917, and between 1919 and 1921 produced symmetrical paintings and reliefs. In the period from 1922 to 1926 he returned to rigorously architectonic paintings from nature. In 1926 he began to create Abstract structured compositions of flat colored forms implying movement with arabesques and eccentric hard-edged shapes. During the 1940s he developed a system of Abstract painting, published in his book *L'Art Non-Figuratif Non-Objectif* in 1949 in which pure geometric shapes and colors were disposed against monochrome grounds and allied to musical notes.

Francisco Herrera the Younger: detail of The Triumph of St Hermengeld; c1654. Prado, Madrid

## Heron Patrick 1920–99

The British painter Patrick Heron was born in Leeds, and spent a part of his childhood in Cornwall (where he was to return later in life). He studied at the Slade School of Fine Art (1937–9) and between 1945 and 1958 published art criticism (in *The New Statesman* and other journals). He exhibited widely after 1947 and was awarded the Grand Prize at the second John Moores Liverpool exhibition (1959) and the Silver Medal at the 1965 Sao Paulo Bienal. Heron's earlier work was Abstract, but with a strong landscape association. He later developed a large-scale, wholly Abstract idiom, partly as a result of the influence of the New York School, and particularly of painters such as Rothko. In the paintings of the 1970s, large cut-out shapes—sometimes resembling pieces of a jigsaw, and strongly colored—are contrasted and combined. The jagged edges contribute a note of tension to the otherwise lyrical effects produced by the bold poster coloring (examples include a series of canvases painted between 1971 and 1975 and shown at the Waddington Galleries II, London, in May 1975).

## Herrera family
### 16th and 17th centuries

The Spanish painter Francisco Herrera the Elder (*c*1589/91–*c*1657) was active in Seville, working in a vigorous naturalistic style with occasional traces of Mannerism, before moving to Madrid *c*1640. His best works include the series of scenes from the life of Saint Bonaventura (1626) painted for various religious communities in Seville (*Healing* and *Communion* are now in the Louvre, Paris), *The Vision of St Basil* (1639; Provincial Museum of Fine Arts, Seville), and *Miracle of the Loaves and Fishes* (1647; Archbishop's Palace, Madrid).

His son Francisco Herrera the Younger (1622–85) studied in Italy and worked in Seville and Madrid, painting in a dynamic and colorful Baroque style. His masterpieces are the *St Francis* (1660; Seville Cathedral), and *The Triumph of St Hermengeld* (*c*1654; Prado, Madrid); but none of the still-life compositions that gained him contemporary fame are identifiable today.

## Herrera Juan de *c*1530–97

Juan de Herrera was a Spanish architect

who worked for Philip II in a heavy, monotonous, and unimaginative classical style which was named Herreran after him. After study in Italy he at first assisted, and then in 1572 succeeded, Juan Bautista de Toledo as architect of the monastery-palace at El Escorial. From Herrera's modified design, its church was executed from 1574 to 1582 as a centrally-planned aisled building, with a large entrance vestibule, and a mausoleum below a sacramental chapel behind the main altar. The granite facade is cold and austere.

At Valladolid Cathedral, Aranjuez, and Seville, Herrera later adapted the same style and proportions to different needs.

## Hesse Eva 1936–70

Although she had a very short career, the American sculptor Eva Hesse was one of the leading Conceptual artists of the 1960s. She was born in Germany, her parents emigrating to the U.S.A. in 1939. She studied at the Pratt Institute, at the Art Students League, and at Yale under Joseph Albers. In 1964 she turned from painting to sculpture, exploring the potential of a wide range of materials such as rubber, fiberglass, cloth and string. Essentially a "process artist", she was more concerned with her spontaneous response to materials, allowing their characteristics to suggest forms, than with a finished product. Works formed from latex or rubber, for example, often suggest fleshy, organic forms (reminiscent of the sculptures of Louise Bourgeois), while others have the austerity of Minimalist sculpture: *Addendum* (1967; Tate Gallery, London) consists of 17 cords hanging from a row of small, breast-like domes, while *Contingent* (1969; Australian National Gallery, Canberra) features hanging sheets of cheesecloth treated with latex and fiberglass. Her innovative use of materials influenced many later artists.

## Heyden Jan van der 1637–1712

Jan van der Heyden was the first and most important townscape painter of Amsterdam. His town views (mostly from the 1660s) are characterized by precise rendering of details such as brickwork, but this is combined with simplicity in the disposition of light and shade, atmospheric unity, and structural balance and clarity. Some of the townscapes are *capriccios* or imaginary views (for example, *An Architectural Fantasy*, c1667–9; National Gallery, London), and even the paintings purporting to be of particular places are not always topographically correct. Van der Heyden also painted a few *vanitas* still lifes: pictures containing symbols of life's transience.

Jan van der Heyden: The Huis ten Bosch at The Hague; oil on oak panel; 22×29cm (9×11in). National Gallery, London

## Hicks Edward 1780–1849

The landscape, religious, and historical painter Edward Hicks was the best known of those 19th-century American artists who worked in a "primitive" style. He was born in Bucks County, Pennsylvania, and spent most of his life there. He began to practice art as a trade, decorating coaches and signs. An active Quaker, he led his community and gave much of his time to depicting religious scenes. His *Peaceable Kingdom* (of which there are over 100 versions) is the most successful of these.

## Highmore Joseph 1692–1780

The English painter Joseph Highmore was born in London. Although a nephew of Thomas Highmore, Sergeant-Painter to the Crown, he was essentially self-taught. By 1730 he had gained a reputation in London as a painter of single-figure portraits and conversation pieces. The success of Hogarth's serial pictures probably persuaded Highmore to paint 12 illustrations for the novel *Pamela* by Samuel Richardson in the 1740s (now in the Tate Gallery, London). His painting with its nonchalant attitudes of pose, natural coloring, and slightly precious refinement, epitomizes the French influence on English artists towards the middle of the 18th century. Like Francis Hayman, Hogarth, and others, he contributed a history painting to the Foundling Hospital, London, in 1746. Dating from the end of this decade are some of his finest portraits, such as *Mr Oldham and his Friends* (c1750; Tate Gallery, London). This is an inventive, life-size composition, which represents an inspired digression from the dainty urbanity of his earlier works.

## Hildebrandt Johann von 1668–1745

The son of a German captain in the Genoese army, the architect Johann Lucas von Hildebrandt was born in Genoa and was educated there until c1690, when he went to study in Rome under Carlo Fontana. Trained initially as a town planner

Above: Edward Hicks: Peaceable Kingdom; oil on canvas; 83×105cm (33×41in); 1826. Philadelphia Museum of Art

Below: Joseph Highmore: Mr Oldham and his Friends; oil on canvas; 105×130cm (42×51in); c1750. Tate Gallery, London

and military engineer, Hildebrandt served under Prince Eugene in his Piedmontese campaigns (1695–6) and by 1698 was firmly established in Vienna when he was appointed an Imperial Councillor. In 1700 he became Architect to the Court, and eventually succeeded Fischer von Erlach as Surveyor General after the latter's death in 1723. Unlike Fischer von Erlach, however, von Hildebrandt received little direct Imperial patronage and his style is in considerable contrast to Fischer von Erlach's Imperial Baroque. Northern Italy left a deep impression on him, and he inherited from Italian Mannerist architecture his predilection for richly decorated surfaces, and his lack of interest in structure.

The important church of sv. Vavřinec at Jablonné v Podještědí in Northern Bohemia, begun by Hildebrandt in 1699, reveals in its ground plan his debt to Guarino Guarini. It is closely related to S. Lorenzo in Turin, but the church was completed by other hands and bears little resemblance to his later work. On the basis of comparisons with this ground plan the Piaristenkirche in Vienna (plan of 1698) is attributed to Hildebrandt; but again the church was substantially modified during construction. Shortly afterwards, Hildebrandt was himself responsible for modifying G. Montani's designs for the Peterskirche in Vienna (probably 1702/7), and he subsequently employed the longitudinal oval plan again for his Priesterseminarkirche in Linz (1717–25).

Hildebrandt's principal activity, however, was as a designer of palaces. His Schwarzenberg Palace in Vienna (begun 1697), with its restrained low relief treatment before Fischer von Erlach modified it *c*1720, illustrates his early secular style. His mature style is well revealed by the brilliant facade of the Daun Kinsky Palace in Vienna (1713–16). Here plain pilasters give way to elegant tapered forms for the three central bays, and the bizarre Borrominesque pediments add a rich counterpoint.

The decorated surface of the palace and the painterly qualities sought after by Hildebrandt reach a triumphant climax in the Upper Belvedere, built for Prince Eugene just outside the center of Vienna in 1721–2. The gardens rise up steeply to it and the richly orchestrated pattern of roofs crowning the separate units of the long narrow summer palace are always seen silhouetted against the sky.

In Germany Hildebrandt was called in by Lothar Franz von Schönborn to solve the problems of the staircase hall of Schloss Pommersfelden (1711). For the Elector's nephew, Friedrich Carl, Hildebrandt collaborated with Balthasar Neumann until 1744 in the design of the Würzburg Residenz. His rebuildings of the abbeys of Göttweig and Louka were never fully finished, but plans attest to his magnificent conceptions.

## Hill Anthony 1930–

The English constructivist, sculptor, and painter Anthony Hill was born in London. He studied at St Martin's School of Art and at the Central School of Art between 1948 and 1951. During 1951 and 1952 he visited Paris, meeting Picabia, Kupka, and Vantongerloo. He taught at Chelsea School of Art from 1957. He was Leverhulme Research Fellow in Mathematics at University College London from 1970 to 1972, and Research Associate thereafter.

By 1954 Hill had abandoned Surrealism. He began to make geometric paintings of straight black lines on white grounds, tentatively exploring kinetic effects. About this date he made his first relief constructions in perspex and aluminum. From 1960 he became increasingly concerned with symmetry and the physical and optical properties of light, reflection, space, and movement. From the late 1960s his freestanding aluminum sculptures and his two-dimensional paintings on perspex exploit the same mathematical structures, in which he explores the boundaries between aesthetic and mathematical concepts.

## Hilliard Nicholas *c*1547–1619

The miniaturist and goldsmith Nicholas Hilliard is the first English painter of whose career we possess a certain amount of knowledge. He was born in Exeter, the son of a goldsmith, and by the age of 13 had taken up miniature painting. At an early date he became goldsmith and limner to Queen Elizabeth I, and by the 1580s was well established in Court circles. In 1583/4 he was granted the right to make portraits of the Queen, and in 1584 designed and executed her second Great Seal. He may have visited France about 1577, and was certainly familiar with the work of French painters such as the Clouets, although he stated that he modeled himself on Holbein.

Nicholas Hilliard: Portrait of a Young Man; watercolor on card; 13.5×7cm (5½×2¾in); *c*1588. Victoria and Albert Museum, London

By 1572 Hilliard had completed a series of works, including his first dated portrait of the Queen (National Portrait Gallery, London), which showed his full mastery of miniature painting. His style is characterized by a craftsman's knowledge of line in defining form, but details such as hair and costume are expressed in a broad, flowing calligraphic manner. His most striking works are portraits of young men—painted in the period when Shakespeare was composing his sonnets—which reflect the virtues of the Elizabethan age.

By the turn of the century his style had become tighter, but his last years marked a return to mastery with his portraits of young ladies. In his *Treatise Concerning the Arte of Limning*, composed *c*1600, Hilliard shows himself very much the Renaissance man, true to the precepts of the humanists. His greatest pupil was Isaac Oliver who, by the mid 1590s, was working in a similar style.

Roger Hilton: Nude (Nude on All Fours); charcoal on paper; 27×21cm (10½×8in); 1962. Private collection

which was settled in 443 BC and where he is known to have lived for a while. There is clearer evidence that he laid out Piraeus, the harbor town of Athens, in the middle of the 5th century. Examples of the application of his principles can be seen in the excavated plans of cities such as Olynthus, founded in north Greece towards the end of the 5th century, and Priene, near Miletus, founded after his death, in the mid 4th century. He acquired a reputation as an eccentric, and also as a political thinker. This may have dictated his plans for the physical accommodation of new city states in the Greek world.

## Hiroshige Ando 1797–1858

The Japanese artist Ando Hiroshige is well known in the West for his landscape prints. He studied with the *Ukiyoe* artist Utagawa Toyohiro, but was also influenced by the *Shijo* School. This became clear after his master's death in 1828, when he began to produce his great series of woodblock landscapes, notably *Fifty-three Stations of the Tokaido Road*, which are full of *Shijo*-inspired poetry and brought him recognition. (See, for example, *Downpour at Shono*, 1833, from the series *Fifty-three Stations*, a copy of

Ando Hiroshige: The Iris Garden at Horikiri, from "One Hundred Views of Yedo"; woodblock print; height 27cm (10½in); 1857. British Museum, London

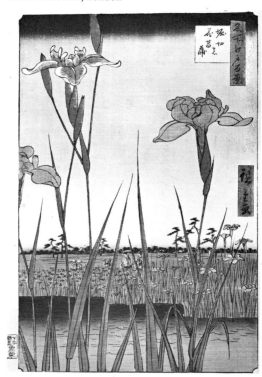

## Hilton Roger 1911–75

The English painter Roger Hilton was born in Northwood. He studied at the Slade School of Fine Art from 1929 to 1931, and at the Académie Ranson, Paris, with Roger Bissière. He taught at the Central School of Art from 1954 to 1956 and began to visit Cornwall, where he lived at St Just from 1965. By 1950 Hilton had painted his first Abstracts. In 1953, influenced by Mondrian, his paintings were of flat, rough-edged shapes in a few pure colors, black and white. He soon turned again to using figurative allusions, in works where nude or landscape are implied in sensuously painted earthy smudged color masses and loose drawing. In the early 1960s he produced some frankly figurative works in bright colors. He drew—particularly the nude—throughout his life, but especially after 1972, when he ceased oil painting because of illness.

## Hippodamus 5th century BC

The Greek town-planner Hippodamus came from Miletus. He was reported to have invented the grid plan for towns, with roads intersecting at right angles, laid out without regard to the contour of the site. The general idea of a grid for a new city had been known earlier in Greece, but he probably codified the practice and had several opportunities to impose it on new or ruined sites. Much probably depended on his layout of the relative positions of important areas of assembly, entertainment, marketing, and worship in relation to walls and gates, and the allocation of blocks or groups of blocks to larger complexes. His home town, sacked by the Persians in 494 BC, may have been instructive, and the final plan may be his work.

Hippodamus acted as traveling consultant to other states, probably including the Athenian town at Thurii in south Italy which is in the Museum of Fine Arts, Boston.) Before his retirement in 1858, Hiroshige had designed about 5,000 prints. No popular artist had ever before depicted the Japanese landscape with such realism and sensitivity. He is at his best in scenes of snow, rain, and mist.

## Hitchens Ivon 1893–1979

The English painter Ivon Hitchens studied at the Royal Academy Schools, London, intermittently during the years 1911 to 1919. He came away from his studies with a profound respect for the classical tradition, which helped to predispose him towards Cézanne, Matisse, and Cubism. The latter enabled him to break away from naturalism, and briefly—in the mid 1930s—Hitchen painted in a nonfigurative style. In 1940 he moved to Sussex where he lived and painted until his death. Here in relative isolation Hitchens developed his characteristic form of abstracted landscape, which was rich in color, broadly applied yet carefully structured. While a part of the English landscape tradition, these paintings possess much of the ordered clarity of French *belle peinture*.

Ivon Hitchens: Poppies in a Jug; oil on canvas; 103×69cm (41×27in); 1943. Sheffield City Art Galleries

## Hobbema Meyndert 1638–1709

Meyndert Lubbertsz. Hobbema was a Dutch painter from Amsterdam whose importance in the sphere of realist landscape is exceeded only by that of his teacher, Jacob Ruisdael. Hobbema studied under Ruisdael in the late 1650s. The two artists remained friends; they appear to have sketched together, and sometimes painted the same views. Hobbema's earliest dated pictures are from the late 1650s: small, lightly-colored river scenes in which his fondness for trees is already evident. During these early years Hobbema imitated Ruisdael's paintings, occasionally even using his teacher's drawings as studies.

Hobbema's greatest paintings were produced in the 1660s; these are larger, have fresher and more varied colors, and convey effects of sparkling sunlight in clear, luminous air. It is sometimes difficult to distinguish Hobbema's work from Ruisdael's. Hobbema's landscapes are more sunny and open than Ruisdael's brooding, melancholy scenes, and there is less sense of solitude. They give little hint of the power and majesty of nature suggested by the massive trees and dramatic style of his teacher. His range of motifs, too, is more limited, being largely confined to forest and river scenes.

At the age of 30 Hobbema married and found employment as a wine gauger with the Amsterdam Excise. Thereafter he painted less, and his increasingly schematic work lost much of its vividness, the major exception being *The Avenue, Middelharnis* (1689; National Gallery, London). Hobbema's genius was only properly recognized in the 18th and 19th centuries, especially in England—where he had a significant influence on the development of landscape painting.

## Hockney David 1937–

The British painter David Hockney is also an etcher, draftsman, and designer. Born in Bradford, Yorkshire, Hockney studied at the Bradford School of Art (1953–7) and at the Royal College of Art (1959–62), and soon gained critical attention with a series of Pop art paintings. These were extremely well designed, and light—almost jokey—in mood. Towards the end of the 1960s, however, Hockney became interested in a relatively straightforward kind of naturalism (seen in *Mr and Mrs Clark and Percy*, 1970–1; Tate Gallery, London), and this

Meyndert Hobbema: A Woody Landscape with a Cottage; oil on canvas; 99×130cm (39×51in). National Gallery, London

has been the basis of his art since then. Hockney is also a brilliant draftsman, and among his best works are the etched illustrations to Cavafy's *Poems* (1966) and Grimm's *Fairy Tales* (1969). He has also emerged as a successful designer for the theater (his work here includes sets and costumes for *The Rake's Progress*, Glyndebourne Opera, 1975). A strong flair for public relations has made Hockney by far the best-known of younger British painters. (*See* overleaf.)

David Hockney: Man taking Shower in Beverley Hills; acrylic on canvas; 167×167cm (66×66in); 1964. Tate Gallery, London

Further reading. Clothier, P. *David Hockney* (Modern Masters Series, Vol. 17), New York (1995). Evans, G. *Hockney's Pictures: the Definitive Retrospective*, New York (2004). Luckhardt, U. *David Hockney: Paintings*, London (2000).

## Hodler Ferdinand 1853–1918

The Swiss painter Ferdinand Hodler was born in Bern. After serving as an apprentice to a minor painter in Thun in 1872 he moved to Geneva, which became his lifelong home. He studied under Bar- thelemy Menn at the École des Beaux-Arts for five years. In the late 1870s and early 1880s Hodler's financial situation was desperate due to poor critical reception of his work in Geneva. In addition he went through a religious crisis in 1880, and was greatly affected by the deaths of his parents, brothers, and sisters between 1860 and 1885. Hodler painted over 30 self-portraits in the early and late periods of his life. *The Angry Man* (1881; Berner Kunstmuseum, Bern) boldly shows his emotions at the time. It was the first painting he exhibited in the Paris Salon, and was also the first of his works to be bought for a public institution, in 1887.

In 1886 Hodler undertook his first commission for a cycle of historical scenes in Geneva, and had his first solo exhibition in Bern. Competition entries and commissions for decorative historical paintings, mostly of national and patriotic subjects, formed a large part of his work throughout his career. They include the fresco *The Retreat from Marignano* (1890; Schweizerisches Landesmuseum, Zurich) and *The Rising of the Jena Students* (1908; Schiller University, Jena).

Hodler's style developed with little contact with the modern art movement in

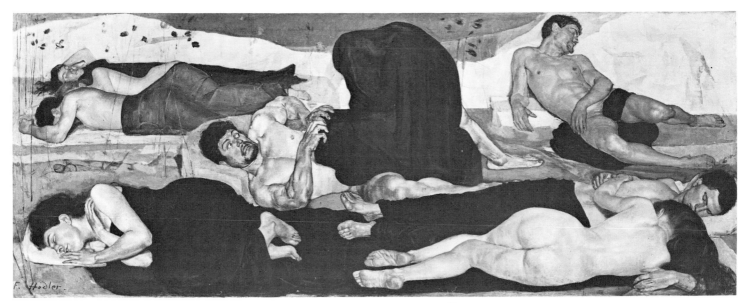

Ferdinand Hodler: Night; oil on canvas; 116×299cm (46×118in); 1890. Berner Kunstmuseum, Bern

Paris. His early landscapes reflected the influence of Corot. An example is *On the Shore of the Manzanares River* (1879; Musée d'Art et d'Histoire, Geneva) painted on a visit to Spain in 1878–9. His portraits and figures revealed knowledge of the works of Manet and Degas.

In the mid 1880s Hodler began to express his theory of Parallelism in landscapes like *Beech Forest* (1885; Museum der Stadt Solothurn) which illustrate a formal structure and the unity rather than diversity that Hodler found in nature. In 1890 Parallelism found expression in his great figure-painting *Night* (Berner Kunstmuseum, Bern) which marked the beginning of his international recognition.

Autobiographical, symbolic, *Night* combined themes of eros, sleep, death, and dream, and evokes feelings rather than depicts events. Paradoxically his first new work looks back to Raphael and Michelangelo. In 1891 the painting was enthusiastically received in Paris at the Salon du Champ-de-Mars where Hodler began to exhibit regularly. These large figure-paintings eventually went beyond the allegorical decoration of *Jugendstil* after the turn of the century when Hodler introduced a new realism combined with forceful color.

In 1892 *The Disillusioned* (Berner Kunstmuseum, Bern) was shown at the Salon de la Rose et Croix-Esthétique of which he became a member. In 1904 an exhibition of 31 paintings at the Vienna Secession, which he had joined a year earlier, established his European reputation, and he was

acclaimed by Klimt with whom he exhibited. Hodler taught at the Fribourg Museum of Decorative Arts (1896–9), and was awarded an honorary doctorate by Basel University in 1910. In 1913 he was featured at the Salon d'Automne and made an officer of the Légion d'Honneur. In 1916 he was given an honorary professorship at the Geneva École des Beaux-Arts where he taught drawing for a year.

Ferdinand Hodler: A Poor Soul; 72×94cm (28×37in); oil on canvas; 1890/1. Öffentliche Kunstsammlung, Kunstmuseum Basel

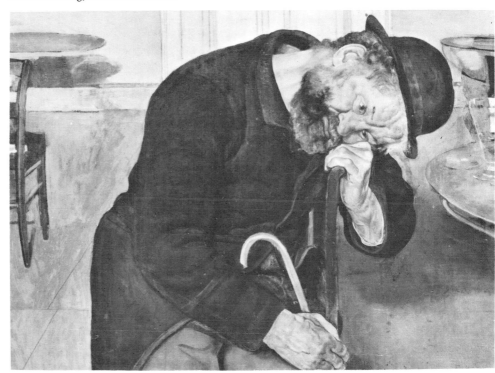

However, without doubt Hodler's modern reputation is based on his landscapes and portraits from after the turn of the century. The landscape views of Lake Thun and Lake Geneva and the mountains became increasingly symmetrical from the late 1890s. Possibly the greatest among them is *Eiger, Mönch, and Jungfrau in Moonlight* (1908; Museum der Stadt Solothurn), visionary, mysterious, and pan-

theistic, painted almost entirely in blues.

From 1908, when they first met, Valentine Godé-Darel was the subject of numerous drawings, studies, and paintings. From 1914 until her death in 1915, Hodler recorded her in her sickbed in a unique and moving cycle, and he painted her even after death, as in *The Dead Valentine Godé-Darel* (1915; Museum der Stadt Solothurn)—as he had also painted his first mistress, Augustine Dupin, in 1909.

In the last years of his life Hodler continued his landscapes, especially sunrises and sunsets painted in vivid, loosely brushed colors. *Landscape near Caux with Rising Clouds* (1917; Kunsthaus, Zurich) no longer displays clear contours; instead Hodler has allowed the features to dissolve. In 1917 he had a large retrospective exhibition in Zurich.

**Further reading.** Hirsh, S. *Ferdinand Hodler*, London (1982).

## Hoffmann Josef 1870–1956

The Austrian architect and designer Josef Hoffmann was a pupil of Otto Wagner and one of the founders of the Vienna Secession. Hoffmann's work is noted for its elegance and attention to detail. Except for the Sanatorium at Purkersdorf (1904–5), his buildings are not so "modern" looking as those of his more radical contemporary Adolf Loos, who scorned Hoffmann's indulgence in expensive and exquisite design. Luxuriousness dominates his most famous work, the Palais Stoclet in Brussels (1905–11), a collaborative effort with the painter Klimt and the Wiener Werkstätte. The latter was a workshop for applied art, based on English craft ideals and encouraged by Charles Rennie Mackintosh, which Hoffmann and others started in 1903.

## Hofmann Hans 1880–1966

The painter Hans Hofmann was a Bavarian who worked in Paris and Munich, and moved to America in 1932. He became the most influential teacher of modern art in the United States where he founded his own school in New York and Providence; his structured yet tolerant teaching was

William Hogarth: The Artist with the Pug; oil on canvas; 90×70cm (35×28in); 1745. Tate Gallery, London

Hans Hofmann: Effervescence; oil, india ink, casein, and enamel on plywood panel; 138×91cm (54×36in); 1944. University Art Museum, Berkeley

one of the prime factors in the emergence of the New York School. Hofmann's paintings in 1940 such as *Spring* (oil; private collection) presage the automatism and the technique of Jackson Pollock. His later works such as *Blue Rhythm* (oil; 1950; Art Institute of Chicago) are major works of the New York School.

**Further reading.** Hunter, S. *Hans Hofmann*, New York (1963).

## Hogarth William 1697–1764

The English painter, engraver, and satirist William Hogarth was born in London, where he lived and worked all his life. When he was 10 his family was put in a debtors prison, and this experience provided William with a chance to develop the keen observation of human foibles that he was later to use in his art. At 16 he was apprenticed to a silversmith, and learned to engrave armorial designs on gold and silver work. But his frustrated artistic ambition led him to take up unorthodox methods of self-instruction, which ultimately contributed much to his originality as an artist. He set up in business as an engraver in 1720 and in the following year he produced his first dated engraving, a satire on the government's "South Sea Company" investment crisis.

In his "conversation pieces" Hogarth developed tentatively as a painter; but after joining the Free Academy of Sir James Thornhill (whose daughter Jane he mar-

ried in 1729) he began to evolve a type of subject painting entirely new to English art, which the novelist Henry Fielding described as "comic-history". These concerns are already apparent in Hogarth's first major work, a series of 12 plates based on Samuel Butler's *Hudibras*.

His first public success was the launching of a subscription for engravings of *The Harlot's Progress* paintings. Instead of issuing them through a printseller he published them himself, and reaped a handsome profit. In 1735 the engravings of *A Rake's Progress* (Sir John Soane's Museum, London) appeared; and in 1736 he painted two large religious scenes—inspired by his father-in-law's work—for St Bartholomew's Hospital.

At the time Hogarth was also illustrating Shakespeare, and deriving inspiration from the theater. In his portraits—such as that of his friend *Thomas Coram* (1740; Foundling Hospital, London), founder of the Foundling Hospital—Hogarth also attempted to compete with his Continental rivals. No further satirical prints were issued until 1745 when the *Marriage à la Mode* paintings (National Gallery, London) were engraved; the pictures themselves remained unsold until 1750/1.

In the later 1740s Hogarth's reputation began to wane, and he turned to producing prints from drawings rather than paintings. The subject matter of his prints became more popular (for example *Gin Lane, Stages of Cruelty*, 1751), and the organization of his paintings much simpler, as in *The Wedding Banquet* (c1745; County Museum and Art Gallery, Truro), possibly painted as part of a projected series concerning a "happy marriage", where incident is reduced to a minimum and the paint takes on a purely expressive function.

In 1753 Hogarth published *The Analysis of Beauty*, the first formalist English art treatise, in which he related his experiments in form to their expression and meaning. Hogarth had done much to further the cause of English art, opening an art academy and urging the passing of an act to protect engravers from piracy, but his essentially anti-academic attitude made him unpopular in later life. In the 1750s the feeling of disillusionment in English politics brought on by the Seven Years War was reflected by a falling off in Hogarth's productivity, and his last years were marked by ill health and political quarrels.

**Further reading.** Baldini, G. and Mandel, G. *L'opera Completa di Hogarth Pittore*, Milan (1967). Bindman, D. *Hogarth*, London (1981). Einberg, E. *Hogarth the Painter*, London (1997). Paulson, R. *Hogarth: His Life, Art and Times* (2 vols.), London and New Haven (1971). Paulson, R. *The Art of Hogarth*, London (1975).

## Hoitsu Sakai 1761–1828

Sakai Hoitsu was a Japanese painter of the *Rimpa* School. A son of the rich Lord of Himeji he learned painting in the *Kano* School, but finally turned to the decorative style of Ogata Korin. He made a big colllection of Korin's works and published illustrated works on him.

Hoitsu was a "feminine" painter, elegant and soft, but rarely forceful. His screens on gold and particularly on silver backgrounds, like those of a *Stream Amid Summer and Autumn Flowers* (Tokyo National Museum) are exquisitely delicate and harmonious. His long scroll *Birds and Flowers of the Four Seasons* (1808; Tokyo National Museum) is perhaps his masterpiece.

## Hokusai Katsushika 1760–1849

The painter and print designer Katsushika Hokusai is the most famous of all Japanese artists in the West, though not in his own country. He is best known for his woodblock print series *Thirty-Six Views of Fuji* (published *c*1823–31; it contains 46 plates—it was so popular he added 10 new scenes) in which he virtually invented the landscape print, and made the first recorded use of Prussian blue in Japan. He used color to convey mood and light as never before in Japan. He is also celebrated for his woodblock books called *Manga* (1814–19), a huge series of endlessly inventive sketches, and for the monochrome *One Hundred Views of Fuji* (1834–5) which had enormous influence on Western design.

Despite his great output of prints and books, Hokusai remained basically a painter. Nearly all of his own works were destroyed in a fire in 1839. Most extant paintings and drawings are therefore of his rather wild old age, and his reputation as a painter has suffered.

Born in Tokyo, he studied with Katsukawa Shunsho, and for 20 years produced *Ukiyoe* prints of actors and beauties. He gradually developed an eclectic, rather eccentric style using Chinese landscape elements and a characteristic broad, somewhat Chinese face. These characteristics can be seen in his painting *Tametomo and the Demons* of 1811 (British Museum, London). They also appear in the brilliantly bold series of landscape prints which made his reputation—the *Fuji* series, the *Waterfalls*, and the *Bridges*, all of them depending on a powerful central subject.

Yet he was always capable of delicacy, especially in his deluxe *surimono* prints and his brush studies of birds. There are a great many ink sketches dating from his late years. Some of these are very successful, but many are by his large studio of followers.

**Further reading.** Hillier, J. *Hokusai*, Oxford (1978). Lane, R. *Hokusai and Hiroshige*, Tokyo (1976). Yasuda, G. *Gwakyo Hokusai*, Tokyo (1971).

## Holbein family
### 15th and 16th centuries

The Holbein family workshop dominated painting in Augsburg at the beginning of the 16th century and produced, in Hans the Younger, an artist of major European importance. Hans the Elder (1460/5–1524) seems to have traveled widely during his formative years as an artist. That he was familiar with the work of Martin Schongauer on the upper Rhine, and with paintings by leading Flemish artists, is shown by his earliest works. *The Death of the Virgin* (*c*1490–5; Öffentliche Kunstsammlung, Kunstmuseum Basel) is indebted to Rogier van der Weyden, though the linearity of Rogier is here softened both in contour and color.

Apart from his work at Augsburg, Holbein the Elder is recorded at Ulm, Frankfurt, and Isenheim, where he probably painted *The Martyrdom of St Sebastian* altar (*c*1515–17; Alte Pinakothek, Munich). This shows the increasing Italian influence upon him both in the pose of the archers on the main panel, and in the decorative panels of classical ornament which frame the monumentalized forms of Saints Elizabeth and Barbara on the wings.

The style of Hans Holbein the Younger (1497/8–1543) was at first close to that of his father, though at an early age he moved out of the Augsburg workshop. In 1514 he went to Basel with his brother Ambrosius, also a painter, and entered the shop of Hans Herbster as a journeyman-apprentice. For more than a decade he found employment at Basel on a variety of commissions: he painted frescoes for the Town Hall, illustrated books (including a woodcut series of *The Dance of Death* in 1523–6) and painted many altarpieces.

Katsushika Hokusai: Fuji in Clear Weather, from the series "Thirty-Six Views of Fuji"; woodblock print; 26×38cm (10×15in); c1823–9. British Museum, London

Hans Holbein the Younger: Portrait of Desiderius Erasmus; oil on panel; 43×33cm (17×13in); 1523. Louvre, Paris

An extended visit to Lucerne in 1517 and 1518 may have included a trip to Italy. The shutters of an altarpiece showing scenes from the *Passion of Christ* (*c*1520; Öffentliche Kunstsammlung, Kunstmuseum Basel) have quotations from the work of Mantegna, and a hard, enamel-like finish that seems influenced by Lombard painting. His virtuosity as a master of the decorative arts found scope on the facade of the *Haus zum Tanz* ("House of the Dance") in Basel, now known only through surviving designs; here he revived the antique style of house decoration with illusionistic reliefs and figures.

The stark realism of the *Dead Christ* (1521; Öffentliche Kunstsammlung, Kunstmuseum Basel), where the figure is stretched out in a long, narrow panel, displays the sharpness of observation and detachment from subject matter that made Holbein the Younger one of the most successful portrait-painters of the 16th century. The pendant portraits of the first identifiable patrons, the Basel Burgomaster *Jacob Meyer and his Wife* (1516; Öffentliche Kunstsammlung, Kunstmuseum Basel) typify the finely drawn quality of all his portraiture. A certain animation in the *Jacob Meyer* portrait was suppressed in later court portraits.

For the same patrons, Holbein painted *The Meyer family in Adoration of the Virgin and Child* (begun 1526, finished

Hans Holbein the Younger: Portrait of Sir John Godsalve; detail; black and red chalk, india ink, body color and watercolor on paper; full size 36×30cm (15×12in); c1532. Collection of H.M. Queen Elizabeth II

1528–30; Hessisches Landesmuseum, Darmstadt). Here a Northern concern for detail in the carpet and costumes is offset by Italian influences in the firm modeling of form and the shell niche that encloses the Madonna. It is one of Holbein's last religious pictures, for by this date the market for religious pictures in post-Reformation Basel had contracted sharply.

The European fame of Holbein the Younger came as a result of his contact with humanist, literary circles. While Erasmus was living in Basel Holbein painted his portrait several times, the most famous examples being those in the Louvre, Paris, and in Longford Castle, near Salisbury, England. The latter was probably presented to Sir Thomas More, and thus gained Holbein an entry into More's circle on his first visit to England from 1526 to 1528. He painted a large group portrait of the More family, now known only from a preparatory drawing (Öffentliche Kunstsammlung, Kunstmuseum Basel) and from copies. The depiction of a family group in domestic surroundings on this scale was unprecedented in Northern art.

Holbein's careful preparatory work for portraits is apparent from the many single-figure drawings in colored chalks that survive both for this work and later single portraits. The attention to surface texture and the high degree of finish in his work at this time can be seen in the single *Portrait of More* (Frick Collection, New York) where the tactile qualities of the curtain, the velvet sleeves, the fur of the cloak, and the sitter's beard are carefully rendered.

On his second visit to London in 1532 Holbein's success with portraits of foreign merchants and diplomats brought him to the notice of the Court. *The Ambassadors* (1533; National Gallery, London) represents the young Frenchmen Jean de Dinteville and Georges de Selve and demonstrates Holbein's ability—crucial to the success of any Court portraitist—to place his sitters in a context that flatters their social and intellectual pretensions. The figures are accompanied by symbols of the arts of learning and music in which they were accomplished. Even so, the reminders of death are also here, notably in the distorted skull of the foreground.

Holbein became Court Painter to Henry VIII in 1536, at a time when the King sought to establish his image as religious and temporal head of the new commonwealth, separated from the Church of Rome. Holbein first produced his standard

form for the King's portrait in an allegorical mural painting of the monarch, his parents, and his third wife, painted for the Palace of Whitehall. The mural is lost, but a fragment of the original cartoon survives (National Portrait Gallery, London) showing the formalized, hieratic image of the King. Holbein was also prolific as a designer of pageants, ceremonial dress, bookbindings, and jewelry for the Court.

Other portraits of his last years in England have the common characteristics of a half-length figure against a neutral ground, and care for detailed physiognomy at the expense of lively character description. The attention to details of dress, the placing of the hands, and sometimes an inscription identifying the sitter and his status, emphasize the rather withdrawn character of the image (for example, *Anne of Cleves*, 1539–40; Louvre, Paris). If the technical quality of his work was never matched, this formula for the portrait was to have a profound impact on English portraiture for more than half a century after Holbein's death from the Plague in 1543.

**Further reading.** Ganz, P. *The Paintings of Hans Holbein*, London (1956). *Holbein and the Court of Henry VIII*, London (1978). Parker, M.T. *The Drawings of Hans Holbein at Windsor Castle*, Oxford (1945). Strong, R. *Holbein and Henry VIII*, London (1967). Von der Osten, G. and Vey, H. *Painting and Sculpture in Germany and the Netherlands: 1500–1600*, Harmondsworth (1969). Waterhouse, E.K. *Painting in Britain: 1550–1790*, Harmondsworth (1978).

# Hollar Wenzel 1607–77

Wenzel Hollar, a widely traveled watercolorist, book-illustrator, and printmaker, was the most important topographical artist working in England during the 17th century. He was born in Prague, and trained in the Frankfurt studio of the famous engraver of biblical illustrations and publisher of topographical prints Mathäus Merian (1593–1650). While working in Cologne in 1636 he met the Earl of Arundel, a connoisseur with whom he traveled around Europe making views and studies of works of art. Hollar then traveled to England, where, after an interval in Antwerp between 1645 and 1652, he eventually settled in London. Following the Restoration, Charles II appointed him "His Majesty's Scenographer and Designer

Wenzel Hollar: The Realm of Venus; etching after a painting by Adam Elsheimer; 9×15cm (4×6in); 1646. National Gallery of Scotland, Edinburgh

of Prospects". In England he produced many etchings and engravings depicting contemporary events, maps, costumes, views of London before the Great Fire of 1666, and works of art.

# Homer Winslow 1836–1910

The American painter and illustrator Winslow Homer was born in Boston in 1836. He was apprenticed to a lithographer for three years and in 1857 began a career as a freelance illustrator. In 1859 he moved to New York and studied painting part-time. His first oil paintings were of the Civil War which he covered for *Harper's Weekly* (1862–5). In 1866 he spent ten months in France. His paintings in oil during the 1860s and 1870s and in watercolor after 1873 resembled early Impressionism in their concern for light and the direct rendering of motifs. He depicted mostly rural scenes and figures in outdoor settings, such as *Croquet Scene* (1866; Art Institute of Chicago). During 1881 and 1882 Homer visited Tynemouth, England, where he became attracted to the sea. On his return to America in 1883 he settled in Prout's Neck on the lonely Maine coast where he lived until his death. His main theme was the ocean—its grandeur, beauty, and power, and its dangers to those who sailed on it and lived by it, especially the fishermen. The late oils of sea rescues, such as *The Life Line* (1894; Philadelphia Museum of Art), and many other sea pictures, for example *Eight Bells* (1886; Addison Gallery of American Art, Andover, Mass.), became famous during his lifetime. They are painted in a bold

Winslow Homer: Snap the Whip; oil on canvas; 56×91cm (22×36in); 1872. Butler Institute of American Art, Youngstown, Ohio

naturalistic style, with strong formal qualities and color harmonies.

His watercolors make him one of the leading naturalistic painters in 19th-century America. His many views include scenes of his hunting and fishing trips in the Adirondacks and Quebec, for example *Adirondack Guide* (1894; Museum of Fine Arts, Boston), as well as the Maine coast. In the last ten years of his life he produced paintings of the Bahamas, Cuba, and Florida, where he spent his winter months. His style was original, fresh and strong in design, with brilliant colors.

**Further reading.** Hendricks, G. *The Life and Work of Winslow Homer*, New York (1979). Scott Atkinson, D. and Wierich, J. *Winslow Homer in Gloucester*, New York (1991).

## Honoré Master *fl.* 1280–1310

The French illuminator Master Honoré was possibly born in Amiens, but lived in Paris during the late 13th century. He is one of the first Gothic illuminators to emerge as a distinct personality, and his innovations provide a basis for subsequent developments in 14th-century Paris.

Honoré lived in the quarter of Paris favored by scribes and illuminators and close to the University. He owned his own house in the Rue Erembourc-de-Brie (now Rue Boutebrie) and worked there with his son-in-law, Richard of Verdun, and a valet. He must have been the most successful artist of his time; the Poll Tax register in 1292 informs us that he paid more tax than any other miniaturist in the Paris guild. From the royal accounts for 1296 he is known to have worked for Philip the Fair, King of France, and a royal Breviary of the same year is generally regarded as one of his key works (Bibliothèque Nationale, Paris; MS. Lat. 1023).

Honoré's personal style is best seen in the frontispiece of the Breviary of Philip the Fair and in a sumptuous copy of a moral treatise in French known as *La Somme le Roy* (British Library, London; Add. MS. 54180). In illustrating scenes from the life of David in the Breviary, or of Moses in the moral treatise, he aims at a dramatic presentation not intended simply to illustrate the text but to have pictorial value in its own right. His subtly modeled figures have a sturdy volume that contrasts sharply with the flat decorative treatment found in other court manuscripts of the

Gerrit van Honthorst: Christ before the High Priest; oil on canvas; 269×183cm (106×72in); c1617. National Gallery, London

mid 13th century. Their emergence from the picture-plane draws attention to the need for an independently created illusion of space; this must have encouraged later experiments in perspective such as those of Jean Pucelle in the 1320s.

Honoré is recorded only in Paris and his style must have developed there; but connections with northern France and with England have also been noted. He appears in some documents as "Maître Honoré d'Amiens". A Psalter and Book of Hours (Pierpont Morgan Library, New York, MS. 729) made for Yolande of Soissons, probably in Amiens, has some miniatures in a related style which may precede the

Paris works. On the other hand, there is a Book of Hours (Stadtbibliothek, Nuremberg; No. 4), where calendar and litany suggest an English owner. The style is that of Master Honoré's workshop, and it introduces an international element for which no complete explanation has been forthcoming.

A number of manuscripts have been attributed to Honoré on stylistic grounds and his probable lifespan is of relevance here. By 1318 his son-in-law, Richard of Verdun, had inherited the workshop. The absence of any mention of Honoré or the house he had inhabited when an extraordinary tax was levied on the citizens of Paris in 1313, suggests that he was then already dead. It seems probable that Richard, who was associated with him for many years, carried on the same workshop tradition, and that in the early 14th century products of the original workshop and its continuation become inextricably interwoven.

## Honthorst Gerrit van 1590–1656

A leading member of the Utrecht school, Gerrit (or Gerard) van Honthorst was one of the few Dutch painters of his day to acquire an international reputation. His historical importance lies mainly in his popularization of the chiaroscuro effects of Caravaggio and his followers, and his involvement in the development of early-17th-century Dutch genre painting. Honthorst began his career as a pupil of Abraham Bloemaert. This was followed by a period in Italy from c1610 to c1620, where he painted religious pictures for churches in Rome, and acquired several wealthy patrons and considerable celebrity.

The influence of Caravaggio's work in Rome (which he copied) was crucial during these years, and can be seen in the abrupt conjunctions of extreme lights and darks and the dramatically illuminated facial expressions in the *Christ before the High Priest* (1617; National Gallery, London). Honthorst (nicknamed "Gherardo della Notte") continued to exploit nocturnal effects, particularly candle light, long after his return to Utrecht. This can be seen in several of his large genre pictures of light-hearted, dissolute revelry—a central theme in the development of Dutch genre painting. These pictures may have been known to the young Rembrandt, who adopted their darkly silhouetted figures and concealed light sources in his *Money-Changer* painting (1627; Staatliche Museen, Berlin). Honthorst's later years were occupied with conventional portraits, and also with historical and allegorical pictures for the courts of northern Europe—paintings completed with the help of many assistants and pupils.

## Hooch Pieter de 1629–c85

The Dutch genre painter Pieter Hendricksz. de Hooch is second only to Vermeer in the complex spatial organization and feeling for light of his small-scale interiors. Born in Rotterdam, he began his career with paintings of stable scenes and guardrooms. In 1654 he moved to Delft (where Carel

Pieter de Hooch: Figures Drinking in a Courtyard with an Arbor; 67×57cm (26×22in); 1658. On loan to the National Gallery of Scotland, Edinburgh

Fabritius and Vermeer were working) in the service of a rich clothmaker to whom he was "Painter and Manservant". There he concentrated on domestic pictures of courtyards, gardens, and interiors: scenes in which orderly middle-class homes are the settings for women and maidservants going about their household tasks, burghers sampling a bottle of wine, and occasionally a family portrait.

These intimate pictures with their multiplicity of domestic details are much less intellectual than Vermeer's austere paintings, but their underlying formal organization is almost as complex. A typical preoccupation is with the walls and pictures that surround, and often frame his figures. (De Hooch usually began his pictures by painting the architectural framework, placing his figures within it afterwards.) The spatial organization very often involves a continuous series of cubic spaces. These provide vistas through open doors, in which depth is underlined by alternations of light and shade and the perspective of receding flagstones.

There is a less perfect balance between de Hooch's somewhat slight figures and their surroundings than is found in Vermeer's work. This is compensated for by the stillness, tranquillity, and sense of suspended movement in his interiors. De

Hooch shared Vermeer's interest in light as it streamed through a window or fell in a sunny courtyard, but he differentiated more between the textures of the objects on which the light fell, whether fabrics, furniture, brickwork, plaster or tiles. The quality of de Hooch's light is itself also different from Vermeer's: like his colors, in which reds and golden browns prevail, it is much warmer. The pictures painted during de Hooch's Delft period are generally considered his best; after settling in Amsterdam c1666/7 there is a decline, perhaps accounted for by his removal from the inspiration of Vermeer.

**Further reading.** Sutton, P.C. *Pieter de Hooch*, Oxford (1980).

## Hopper Edward 1882–1967

The painter and graphic artist Edward Hopper was one of the most important American realists of the 20th century. Born in Nyack, New York, he trained as an illustrator before studying with Robert Henri at the New York School of Art. He made four brief trips to Europe between 1906 and 1910, and though some influences are discernible (such as Manet and Degas) he remained unaffected by avant-garde developments, preferring to develop the potential of American realism. He exhibited at the Armory Show 1913, and between 1915 and 1923 concentrated on graphic works in which he quickly discovered his characteristic subjects and techniques. His vision of everyday American life—typically of empty streets, isolated buildings and solitary, remote figures—is dominated by a profound sense of loneliness and boredom. Major works include *Early Sunday Morning* (1930; Whitney Museum of American Art, New York) and *Night Hawks* (1942; Art Institute of Chicago). Hopper's concern with structure is emphasized by his skillful use of strong verticals, horizontals and diagonals, a simplification of forms and the use of oblique sunlight. At times—as in *Rooms by the Sea* (1951; Yale University Art Gallery), which is dominated by a blank wall and an open door framing a view of the sea—Hopper's work acquires a Surrealistic tone.

**Further reading.** Levin, G. *Hopper's Places*, 2nd edn., Los Angeles (1998). Wagstaff, S., Anfam, D. and O'Doherty, B. *Edward Hopper*, London (2004).

## Horta Victor 1861–1947

Victor Horta was the original architect of European Art Nouveau. Born at Ghent, he studied in Brussels under the Neoclassical architect Alphonse Balat (1818–95). His first work of importance was the Hotel Tassel (1892–3) in Brussels, whose interior was revolutionary in almost every respect: spaces flow into one another organically off an octagonal hall and a staircase, thus abandoning the conventional division into stories. In its use of iron, both structurally and decoratively (in the staircase for example), the Tassel house was the first of its kind. In his use of curvilinear forms derived from nature—the "whiplash" line which entwines itself round and over every surface—Horta initiated a style that gripped European architects for the next 10 years.

Exactly how he arrived at this style is something of a mystery. Familiarity with English design, with Continental Post-Impressionist and Symbolist painting, and with the theories of Viollet-le-Duc (1814–79) and Owen Jones (1809–74) all probably contributed to Horta's invention of a new architectural means of expression.

Next in Horta's domestic oeuvre came the Hotel Solvay (1895–1900), perhaps his most mature Art Nouveau building. A bold use of iron and glass characterizes his public commissions: for example, the Maison du Peuple (1896–9) and the Innovation store (1901) in Brussels.

**Further reading.** Borsi, F. and Portoghesi, P. *Horta*, New York (1991).

## Houdon Jean-Antoine 1741–1828

The sculptor Jean-Antoine Houdon was born in Versailles and brought up in the Académie Royale de Peinture et de Sculpture where his father became doorkeeper. He studied there under Michel-Ange Slodtz, obtained one of its Rome scholarships in 1764, and exhibited there regularly from the year of his return in 1768.

Houdon's first commission had been for the *St Bruno* in S. Maria degli Angeli in Rome (1766), an image of withdrawn and silent meditation. He also began the companion *St John the Baptist*. The latter work was never completed and was destroyed in 1894, but from it derives the *Ecorché* casts, which are to be found in many art academies, and which Houdon regarded as his most outstanding contribution to art. His experience of the Classical and Baroque masterpieces of Italy inspired such works as *The Priest of the Lupercals* (1768; Schlossmuseum, Gotha), the *Vestal* (1767–8; Metropolitan Museum, New York) and the naked, running *Diana* balanced on one foot (1776; Schlossmuseum, Gotha). Many of his religious works were destroyed at the Revolution, but these mythological sculptures and the *Tourville* (1781; Versailles) prove his capacity to create imaginative historical statues. Works such as the *Baiser Donné* and the *Baiser Rendu* (c1774), or the *Frileuse* (or *Winter*, 1781; marble of 1783 in the Musée Fabre, Montpellier) shivering in her inadequate covering, show him in the lighter vein of Rococo eroticism.

However, it is as a portraitist that Houdon ranks as one of the world's greatest sculptors. No intellectual, he had a profound respect for reality, never losing an opportunity to take a cast from the face of a dead celebrity, and inventing a machine as an aid to accurate drawing from nature. The quality of his work came from the life he could instil into these images, from the virtuosity of his carving of flesh, hair, and costume, from the inventiveness of his treatment of the eyes (often contrasting the shadow of a deeply cut pupil with a cube of projecting marble or bronze which flashes like a highlight), and from the taste with which he disposed the draperies round that artificially dismembered form, the portrait bust. A good businessman, he ensured that his works were produced in many examples, often in variant forms.

One of his earliest successes was the bust of *Denis Diderot* (c1771; terracotta in the Louvre, Paris), an admirer who secured for him powerful patrons in Germany and Russia. Houdon portrayed the aristocrats of Europe, the statesmen of France, the intellectuals of the *Encyclopédie*, and the leaders of republican America. He was justly proud of his bronze foundry, but his ambition to cast an equestrian statue of George Washington remained unfulfilled. However, he carved a standing figure of Washington as the new Cincinnatus (1788; Capitol, Richmond, Va.). His portraits of Voltaire, above all the seated figures in the Hermitage, St Petersburg, and in the Comédie Française in Paris (both 1781), have proved the most enduring visual images of the writer's intellectual vigor and mordant wit. Besides his busts of eminent men and beautiful women, Houdon created a number of the most charming but totally unsentimental portraits of children and babies ever produced.

## Hoyland John 1934–

The English nonfigurative painter John Hoyland was born in Sheffield. During a long and thorough training at the Sheffield College of Art (1946–56) and the Royal Academy Schools, London (1956–60), Hoyland gradually developed his nonfigurative style, at first by abstracting from landscapes and still lifes. From *c*1957, under the impact of the work of Rothko and Turnbull, he experimented with pure forms and colors. In order to achieve a greater integrity of the picture-surface, Hoyland began in 1963 to stain his canvases with acrylic paint. However, concerned with the richness as well as the unity of visual experience, he continued to paint independent forms (usually squares) on top of this ground. Encouraged by the work of Hans Hofmann, Hoyland further developed this aspect of his art in the 1970s; the shapes increased in number until they filled the whole of the canvas with a rich profusion of impastoed colors.

## Hsia Kuei *fl.* 1180–1230

Born in Ch'ien T'ang, the Chinese artist Hsia Kuei was an Academy painter of the later Southern Sung Court. He was a follower of Fan K'uan and Li T'ang and with his contemporary Ma Yuan, developed a style influential in Chinese painting known as the Hsia-Ma School. He often used ink and paper and composed pictures with the elegance associated with the Sung Court Academy.

His virtuosity of brushwork allowed him many dramatic effects ranging from the marvelously simple evocation of distance by controlled tone washes to effects of texture achieved by a bravura use of the "axe cut" brush stroke. Hsia Kuei liked to use a worn brush which, used with thick ink and dragged across the surface of the paper, produces an expressive stroke when painting rocks and bare landscape. Figures and animals appear as inhabitants of Hsia Kuei's landscapes, often painted with humor and always in a lively manner.

Hsia's most famous surviving painting is the long handscroll in the National Palace Museum collection, Taipei, *Ten Thousand Li of the Yangste*. This is in ink on paper and is 34 ft (10.1 m) long. It takes the viewer through many aspects of the course of the great river—from the rapids of Szechwan, where the boatmen struggle, to the wide flood plain of the lower reaches, where it is not always easy to see the other bank of the river. This masterpiece epitomizes all Hsia's characteristics: his daring composition, and directness of the brushwork combined with great sophistication.

Jean-Antoine Houdon: Madame de Serilly; marble; height 62cm (24in); 1782. Wallace Collection, London

John Hoyland: 17.3.69; acrylic on canvas; 198×366cm (78×144in); 1969. Tate Gallery, London

## Huang Chun-pi 1899–1991

Huang Chun-pi is Cantonese and a leading member of the *Ling-nan* School. Between 1929 and 1935 he was Professor at the Canton City Art School, but moved north to Nanking as a professor at the National Central University, Nanking. He is a traditional painter who depicts mountain landscapes in a rich ink style. In common with his school he favors the use of slight color with the rich dark ink, and so produces a heavy decorative effect. The Canton School of painters have a distinctive style of which Huang Chun-pi's work is a good example.

## Huang Kung-wang 1269–1354

The Chinese painter Huang Kung-wang was born the son of the Lu family, his original name being Lu Chien. He was very early adopted into the Huang family, when he was given the name by which he is now known (and also the name Tzu-chiu, indicating that he was a child for their old age). He was very gifted and soon reached a high standard in his studies in history and philosophy. He was to become a revered scholar, poet, musician, and painter. He served for a while as a clerk in the office of the Provincial Judge of Chekiang but retired early to live as a Taoist recluse in the Hangchow area, where his friend Ts'ao Chih-p'o also lived in retirement.

Huang wandered all over the Wu district and spent the last seven or eight years of his life in the Fu Ch'un mountains. During this time he painted the famous *Fu Ch'un Mountain* handscroll of which two versions remain in the National Palace Museum, Taipei, Taiwan. One of these bears the date 1338, the other, regarded as genuine, is dated 1354. This latter, longer scroll bears an inscription:

In the 7th year of Chih-chang [1347] I went back to the Fu Ch'un mountains and stayed there with Master Wu Yung. In the days of leisure, while living in the South Pavilion, I played with the brush and painted this scroll whenever I felt inspired. I did not weary myself; [yet] the composition grew gradually. I work as if filling in documents. In this way three or four years passed but the picture was not finished because I left it in the mountains when I went rambling about like a floating cloud. Then I brought it back in my bag and whenever I could spare the time in the morning or in the evening I worked on it, though without anxiety.

This describes the tempo of such painting by a man regarded by Tung Ch'i-ch'ang as the first to use painting both as a means of expression and for his own pleasure. He is also recorded as having gone about with paper and brush in his sleeve making sketches when he came upon a beautiful scene. He noted the effects of time of day and the seasons, working from nature but clearly with a very scholarly brush. He is noted for his extremely subtle ink tone and texture.

**Huang Kung-wang: Dwelling in Fu Ch'un Mountains, a detail of the second Fu Ch'un Mountain handscroll; ink on paper; full size 33×637cm (13×251in); 1354. National Palace Museum, Taipei**

## Huber Wolfgang c1490–1553

The Swiss painter Wolfgang Huber was born at Feldkirch in the Vorarlberg district of Austria. For several years from c1505 he traveled through the Hapsburg lands, visiting Innsbruck and Salzburg. The Danube school of landscape painting and the graphic works of Albrecht Dürer, especially his *Life of the Virgin* series, were the major sources of his early work. *The Flight into Egypt* (Staatliche Museen, Berlin), from an altarpiece of the *Life of the Virgin*, is a good example of his combination of these influences. Huber settled at Passau some time between 1510 and 1515 and there established a large workshop. Between 1515 and 1521 he painted an altarpiece for the Stadtpfarkirche at Feldkirch in which the color and linear quality of his earliest work have given place to a less assertive style. In portraiture he at first adopted the style of the Augsburg school and of the Holbein workshop in particular, placing the sitter against a setting of Classical architecture. In later works he favors a sky background, as in the portrait of *Jakob Ziegler* (c1544–9; Kunsthistorisches Museum, Vienna).

Much of his painted work appears to be lost, however, and he now emerges at his most original through surviving landscape drawings. In the early drawing of the *Mondsee* (1510; Germanisches Nationalmuseum, Nuremberg) he already declares his independence of the Danube school in the economy of line and description. The foreground is left bare, the background suggested only by a thin, jagged line of mountains, and the effect of distance is created by the placing of the horizontals of the bridge against the line of receding pollarded trees. Later his conception of landscape becomes more subjective; the *View of Feldkirch* (1523; British Museum, London) concentrates less on the city than on the strange and fantastic tree in the foreground, which by the loosening and thinning of the pen-work appears to be growing in front of the spectator's eyes.

## Hughes Arthur 1832–1915

The English painter Arthur Hughes was influenced by the work of the Pre-Raphaelite Brotherhood. After training in London at the Government School of Design and the Royal Academy Schools, he came into the orbit of first D.G. Rossetti, then Millais. Sharing the Pre-Raphaelite desire to depict intensely emotional incidents in mi-

Arthur Hughes: Ophelia; oil on canvas; 105×52cm (41×20in); 1859. City of Birmingham Museums and Art Gallery

nutely observed natural settings, Hughes produced works of a distinctive luminous coloring and soft handling (*April Love*, 1855–6; Tate Gallery, London; *Home from Sea*, 1856–62; Ashmolean Museum, Oxford). Later his style became more diffuse; with a lightening of palette and change in landscape mood (seen in *The First Easter*, 1896; William Morris Gallery, London) his works lost their impact.

## Hugo of Bury St Edmunds
*fl.* early 12th century

Hugo of Bury St Edmunds was an illuminator whose birthplace is not known, but who worked in England. There are documentary references to four of his works for the Abbey of St Edmund at Bury. He carved a crucifix with statues of John the Baptist and Mary flanking it, he cast a bell, he made the bronze doors for the Abbey's main entrance (the only bronze doors recorded in medieval England), and he illuminated a Bible now identified as one in Corpus Christi College Library, Cambridge.

The Bible was probably commissioned *c*1135: the Sacrist, Herveus, who found the money to pay for it, was apparently out of office by 1138. Herveus became sacrist in the mid 1120s but so early a date is scarcely possible given the advanced nature of the work's early Gothic script. The main illuminations are on separate sheets of vellum pasted into the manuscript. This vellum had to be specially imported from Scotland, presumably because locally prepared skins were not of high enough quality for the perfect finish that Hugo gave to his paintings. The illuminations have a richness and originality of figure-style and foliage decoration that fully account for the praise lavished on the artist in contemporary records. Furthermore, they embody a style that was of paramount importance for the development of English art in the middle of the 12th century. This so-called "damp fold" style is characterized by areas of drapery that cling to the body, and are divided from each other by single pipe folds which both model and articulate the forms. By *c*1150 the style had spread to Winchester, Canterbury, and Durham and had been transmitted to the Abbey of Liessies in Hainault. Artists working in Winchester particularly felt the influence, not only of Hugo's figure-style, but also of his vocabulary of foliage forms.

Hugo's other remarkable contribution was technical. Not only are his figures wonderfully graceful in pose, but the pigments with which they are painted are almost unbelievably refined and the color is of marvelous intensity and purity. His work is one of the most important manifestations of the concern for craftsmanship which found contemporary expression in the often quoted "materiam superabat opus": "the workmanship surpassed the material" (Abbot Suger of St-Denis). Hugo's art owes a great deal to Middle Byzantine and Ottonian sources and also has certain affinities with contemporary art from the Meuse Valley. In addition, there are clear late Anglo-Saxon elements, for example the small swirls of drapery on the shoulders. Although his exact origins are obscure, his work has all the liveliness and grace of the best English art of the period. The only other work almost certainly from his hand is the seal matrix of St Edmund's Abbey, of which several impressions survive.

## Hugo Victor 1802–85

Victor Hugo was not only the leader of the Romantic movement in French literature but also an artist who produced an important body of drawings. His early drawings record his travels in France and Belgium and on the Rhine during the years 1834 to 1843. These at first show a meticulous style influenced by contemporary illustrated travel books (for example, *View of Lierre*, 1837; Bibliothèque Nationale, Paris), and later become more imaginative and Romantic in conception (for example, *Le Tour des Rats*, 1840; Maison Victor Hugo, Paris). His work was visionary, using remembered or imaginary subjects floating in an empty space (seen in *Hanged Man*, 1859; Louvre, Paris). He anticipates Surrealism in his exploitation of chance effects and "automatic" drawing.

**Further reading.** Barbon, A. *Victor Hugo and his Times*, New York (1976). Richardson, J. *Victor Hugo*, London (1977).

## Huguet Jaime *c1415–92*

The Spanish painter Jaime Huguet was born in Valls, Tarragona. He worked at first in Saragossa and Tarragona, but by 1448 he had established his own workshop in Barcelona; he was the last painter in a Catalan tradition that extended from Ferrer Bassa to Bernardo Martorell. One phase of his activity suggests the Flemish influence of Dalmau; but his master-pieces—the altarpiece of SS. Abdon and Sennen (1460), and the altarpiece of the Chapel Royal of Santa Águeda (1464)—show a naturalistic concern with move-ment, with light and shade, and with facial expression which exceeds the limits of Gothic formalism and owes more to Mar-torell. He had numerous collaborators.

## Hui Tsung and the Academy
early 12th century

Hui Tsung (reigned 1101–26) was the eighth and last Emperor of the Chinese Northern Sung dynasty. His court at Kaifeng is remembered as one of China's most cultured. Though ineffectual as a ruler, and officiating over the loss of over half of his kingdom, the Emperor was a man of sensitivity and culture and was himself a painter and calligrapher of distinction. The Imperial Academy, which had already reached a position of respect in the time of his predecessors, was raised to a status equal to that of the bureaucratic Boards, thus giving artists an unprecedented standing in court society. Hui Tsung gathered around him the most gifted painters of his time; from contemporary accounts it would seem that the Emperor took a keen interest in their work, and indeed participated in the competitive painting that played a part in the life of this unique Academy.

This elite group developed a school of painting, particularly of bird and flower subjects in a small format, for which they evolved a sophisticated system of composition (for example, *Five-colored Parakeet on Apricot Branch*; Museum of Fine Arts, Boston). The surface pattern becomes dominant and depends on a nice judgment of balance, and near imbalance, of space, form, and line. Their quite unashamedly decorative style of painting, with its exquisite drawing and jewel-like coloring, is diametrically opposed to the aesthetic of the scholar painter. However, the painters of the Academy were also scholars; they developed an allusive quality in their paint-

Holman Hunt: The Lady of Shalott; oil on canvas; 188×146cm (74×58in); 1886–1905. Wadsworth Atheneum, Hartford, Conn.

ing similar to the poetic reference so important in literature. A good example of this is the reported incident of a prize-winning painting of butterflies fluttering around a horse's hoof to illustrate the couplet "The scent of trampled flowers follows the hoofs of the returning horse". The allusive character and poetic content of their paintings and a concern with very carefully controlled surface composition almost to the exclusion of a composition in depth, were characteristics of the Northern Sung Academy of Hui Tsung. These qualities are retained to this day in various schools and styles of Chinese painting.

Although its chief products were decorative works, the main line of landscape painting was also influenced by the Academy. The major landscape painter was Li T'ang (1049–1130), a traditional artist who followed Li Ssu-hsun. He and Chao

Ta-nien led the way in adapting the old "master mountain" style to the smaller format requiring a simpler composition and encouraging a more self-conscious use of brush strokes. Thus the Academy was the bridge between the classical landscape painting of the 10th and 11th centuries and that of the stylized Southern Sung. This connection is personified in Li T'ang himself: he outlived the Northern Sung and was persuaded to move to Hangchow to lead the new Academy established for the court of the Southern Sung.

## Hundertwasser Fritz 1928–2000

The Austrian painter Fritz Hundertwasser was born and named Friedrich Stowasser in Vienna in 1928. Largely self-taught, he has always worked on a small scale, mainly in watercolor. He has been influenced by his many travels, especially by a journey to Tunisia in 1951. A wide range of art—including Oriental miniatures, the *Jugendstil* of Klimt and Schiele, and the imagery of Klee—has provided the basis for his unique, imaginative, and poetic style. Unashamedly decorative, and tending towards the abstract, he used many bright colors, often incorporating gold and silver leaf, in flat patterns that frequently dominate the ostensible subject. In 1981 he was appointed a Professor at the Vienna Academy. Hundertwasser has also produced many prints, including woodblocks—inspired by Japanese prints—of great technical complexity.

## Hunt Holman 1827–1910

The English painter William Holman Hunt was the son of a London warehouse manager. He left his job as a clerk for an artistic career in spite of strong parental objections, and was accepted into the Royal Academy Schools aged 17; but neither technical confidence nor financial security were to come easily. One of Hunt's fellow students was John Everett Millais. Hunt and Millais discussed the artificiality of contemporary art and, following the aesthetic of Ruskin, determined to "go back to Nature". In their enthusiasm for the naivety of art before the revered Raphael they were joined by another dissatisfied youth, D.G. Rossetti, and in 1848 the "Pre-Raphaelite Brotherhood" was formed.

The principles contributed particularly by Hunt to this short-lived association are embodied in *Rienzi* (1848–9; private collection). Each element of the painting was executed before the motif, "abjuring altogether brown foliage, smoky clouds, and dark corners, painting the whole out of doors, direct on the canvas itself, with every detail I can see, and with the sunlight brightness of the day itself". The subject is characteristically high-minded: an Italian patriot and revolutionary, modeled by Rossetti, swearing an oath over the dead body of his young brother.

Hunt's painting *A Converted British Family Sheltering a Christian Priest from the Persecution of the Druids* (1849–50; Ashmolean Museum, Oxford) received critical derision when shown at the Academy exhibition. Though rich in biblical symbols such as vines, corn, and fishing nets, it retains credibility on a factual level, thus exemplifying Hunt's aim in all his religious works. The frames of these works are often inscribed with scriptural quotations; here they refer to the theme of persecution. Hunt achieved an almost preternatural luminosity by painting over a wet, white ground in a laborious, piecemeal manner reminiscent of fresco. The overall sharpness of focus and his casual-looking disposition of figures offended prevalent canons of centralized composition, while the angularity of his poses seemed willfully unattractive.

When *Valentine Rescuing Sylvia from Proteus* (1850–1; City of Birmingham Museums and Art Gallery) was attacked in the Press, the greatly respected Ruskin came to its defence with heartening praise for its "truth" and "finish". *The Hireling Shepherd* (1851–2; City of Manchester Art Gallery) derives partly from the pastoral imagery of Ruskin's ecclesiastical *Notes on the Construction of Sheepfolds*, published in 1851. The landscape was painted in summer near Ewell, Surrey, where Millais worked simultaneously on *Ophelia* (Tate Gallery, London). Flirting with a shepherdess whom he teases with a death's-head moth, and neglecting his flock, the hireling is intended to symbolize clergymen preoccupied by esoteric theological issues. The picture can be interpreted more specifically in terms of the topical dispute between High Church and Low Church Anglicans. Its purchase by a naturalist testifies to the "scientific" precision of Hunt's observation.

Executed by moonlight, *The Light of the World* (1851–3; Keble College, Oxford) shows Christ knocking at the weed-choked door of the human soul. As usual, Hunt insisted on the painting of every detail from an actual object, having Christ's lantern, for instance, specially manufactured for the purpose. *The Awakening Conscience* (1853–4; Tate Gallery, London) is a modern life counterpart to the last-mentioned work. A kept woman remembers the innocence of her childhood and is stirred to repentance. Light—for "Enlightenment"—is again the central symbol; the "light of other days" in the lyric of a song on the piano is actualized in the sunny brilliance of the garden out into which the girl stares through a window. The hallucinatory clarity of Hunt's technique befits her state of heightened awareness, while her predicament is epitomized in the detail of a cat tormenting a trapped bird beneath the table of the gaudily furnished room. Such subject matter, tackled also by Millais and Rossetti about this time, parallels social concerns in contemporary literature, notably Dickens's novels.

His desire for historical accuracy in sacred subjects led Hunt to paint *The Scapegoat* (1854–5; Lady Lever Art Gallery, Port Sunlight) entirely beside the salt-encrusted shores of the Dead Sea. Bearing away in its death the burden of sin, the scarlet-filleted animal is a symbol of Christ. The violently dazzling colors of sunset on the distant mountains are rendered with an uncompromising fidelity that well demonstrates Hunt's moral integrity as an artist, his devotion to emotional expression rather than pleasing visual effect.

He scored the great popular success of his career with another work done in the Holy Land: *The Finding of the Saviour in the Temple* (1854–60; City of Birmingham Museums and Art Gallery). Thematically less abstruse than *The Scapegoat*, which was poorly received, it appealed to the public's sentimental attitude towards children as well as to its liking for fact and detail, for instance in the use of genuinely Jewish costumes and faces. It was bought by the dealer Gambart for an unprecedented £5,500 including copyright, became enormously well known as an engraving, and established Hunt as the foremost religious painter of the age.

*The Shadow of Death* (1869–73; City of Manchester Art Gallery) and *The Triumph of the Innocents* (one version 1876–87, Walker Art Gallery, Liverpool; another 1880–4, Tate Gallery, London) constitute the mainstay of his unprolific later career. In the first, Jesus is seen in an accurately reconstructed carpenter's shop. Stretching out his work-weary arms, he casts an ominous cruciform shadow on the wall. Less ingeniously, the second depicts an apparition to the fleeing Holy Family of the far-from-ethereal spirits of the children martyred at Bethlehem. Its overloaded iconography is explained by Hunt in a long pamphlet.

The principal painting of his old age was *The Lady of Shalott* (1886–1905; Wadsworth Atheneum, Hartford), an early design expanded to allegorize "the failure of a human Soul towards its accepted responsibility". He also produced a life-size replica of *The Light of the World* (c1900; St Paul's Cathedral, London).

His eyesight failing, Hunt was now turning to the written word to propagate the artistic creed he had followed unflinchingly and in increasing isolation since the first days of the Pre-Raphaelite Brotherhood— that is, the exposition of religious ideas in terms of the minutiae of Creation, and, as far as possible, without the intervention of style.

**Further reading.** Bennett, M. *William Holman Hunt*, Liverpool and London (1969). Fredeman, W.E. *Pre-Raphaelitism: A Biblio-Critical Survey*, Cambridge, Mass. (1965). Gaunt, W. *Painting in Britain 1800–1900: The Restless Century*, London (1972). Hunt, W.H. *Pre-Raphaelitism and the Pre-Raphaelite Brotherhood*, London (1905). Landow, G. *William Holman Hunt and Typological Symbolism*, London and New Haven (1979).

## Hurley William *fl.* 1320–54

The English carpenter William Hurley (or Horlee, Hurlee, or Hurlegh) was already well established by 1320 when he was employed at St Stephen's Chapel, Westminster Palace, where he later made the timber vault (1345–8). In 1336 he was appointed chief carpenter for the King's Works south of the Trent. With the exception of the Ely Cathedral choir-stalls his only surviving work is the timber vault (1328–40) of the octagon there, constructed to replace the crossing tower that collapsed in 1322. This immense structure, imitating a stone vault, shows Hurley to have been an outstanding engineer in timber, and indicates the virtuoso quality of his lost work for the court. He died in 1354.

## Hyakusen Sakaki 1697–1752

Sakaki Hyakusen was the pioneer Japanese painter of the *Bunjinga* School. He was a skilled *haiku* poet, but his artistic origins are unknown. Earlier artists like Gion Nankai (1676–1751) had genuinely tried to follow the life-style of the Chinese amateur gentleman-scholar painters; but the low born Hyakusen merely followed Chinese styles as a full professional. This became the usual Japanese attitude, as was Hyakusen's eclectic mixture of varied Chinese styles. He was the first to transfer Chinese literary painting to the screen format, as in *Visit to the Red Cliff* (private collection) and the boldly eccentric *Banana Plants and Taihu Rocks* (private collection).

# I

## Ictinus 5th century BC

Ictinus was a Greek architect of the 5th century BC who worked principally in Athens. A striking feature of all the works attributed to him, which were regarded as the masterpieces of the Classical period, is his originality of design and ornament in a craft that tended to stereotype design. With Callicrates, he was the leading architect of the Parthenon in Athens. The Parthenon is the prime example of the Doric Order, but incorporates novel features such as the Ionic frieze. He also collaborated in the planning of the Hall of the Mysteries (Telesterion) at Eleusis, being responsible for its remarkable span of roof. He was alleged to have been the architect of the Temple of Apollo at Bassae in Arcadia, a Doric building which includes an Ionic colonnade within and the earliest known examples of Corinthian column capitals. Ictinus also wrote a treatise on the Parthenon.

## Inayat *fl.* late 16th–early 17th century

The Mughal artist Inayat was born in the Imperial household and worked in the reigns of three Mughal emperors, Akbar (1556–1605), Jahangir (1605–1627), and Shah Jahan (1628–1658). His early works, which are to be found in the British Museum, London, include the *Babur-*

Robert Indiana: The American Dream; oil on canvas; 183×153cm (72×60in); 1961. Museum of Modern Art, New York

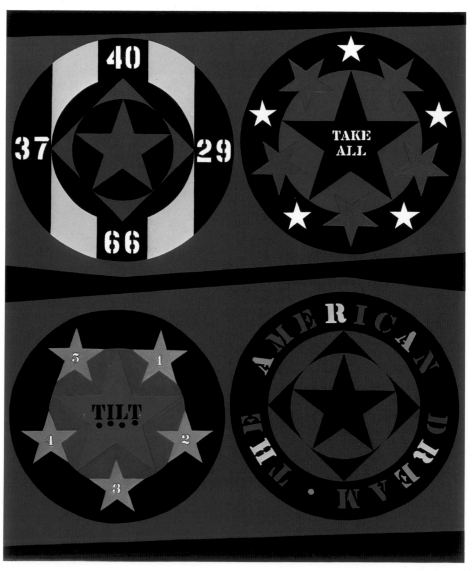

*nama* done in collaboration with Bishndas, and the *Akbar-nama*. Two other works, *Muzaffar Khan Taking Leave of Akbar* and *Sayyid Abd Allah Khan Brings News of Bengal Conquest* are both in the Chester Beatty Library Dublin. An animal drawing by Inayat (a wild goat or a *Markhor*, *c*1607) is in the Victoria and Albert Museum, London. He showed special skill in rendering night scenes and figures illuminated by firelight. Typical of these is *Ascetics Study by Firelight* in the British Museum, London (dated 1630).

## Indiana Robert 1928–

The American painter Robert Indiana was originally called Robert Clarke but changed his surname to that of his native state. Indiana uses road signs and other public signs and symbols with altered lettering to make a stark and challenging visual statement. *The Red Diamond Die* (1962; Walker Art Center, Minneapolis) and *The Black Yield Brother 3* (1963; private collection) demonstrate obsessions with motoring, sex, and food that the artist has turned into a powerful commentary on modern American life. Indiana moved to New York in 1956 and settled in lower Manhattan. His friendship with Elsworth Kelly, Jack Youngerman, and James Rosenquist placed him in a group of Hard Edge abstractionists at a time when Action Painting was the style of the majority in New York.

## Ingres J.-A.-D. 1780–1867

The French history, portrait, and genre painter Jean-Auguste-Dominique Ingres is conventionally seen as the upholder of Neoclassicism in France, in opposition to Delacroix and Romanticism. This view has been fostered by Ingres' own teachings on art, which assert a strict classical aesthetic, the supremacy of line over color. However, his painting in fact shows a variety of styles and a number of influential stylistic innovations. His subject matter includes the conventional classicist depictions of Greek and Roman scenes, and traditional Raphaelesque religious painting, but also genre scenes of French medieval history and exotic Near Eastern subjects. Today, Ingres is most appreciated for his portraiture which he saw as an inferior genre, rather than for the large works with which he fought his battle against the Romantics.

Born in Montauban, Ingres was guided towards the arts by his father (himself a minor artist), and entered the Academy of Toulouse in 1791. In 1797 he went to Paris to study in the studio of J.-L. David. He won the Grand Prix de Rome in 1801, but was unable to take it up until 1806. He remained in Italy until 1824, returning to Paris as an established artist. Though he received official recognition at this time, and had a flourishing teaching studio, his dogmatism and sensitivity to criticism led him into conflict with the critics. He withdrew to Rome again in 1835, this time as Director of the French Academy. He felt isolated from and misunderstood by his contemporaries, and abstained from showing his work in public for many years. On his return to Paris in 1841 he received a warm welcome; he remained there, holder of many high official honors, until his death in 1867.

His student years in Paris (1797–1806) exposed Ingres to a number of radical tendencies which later left their mark on works he saw as classical and orthodox. The archaic linear quality advocated in David's studio by the Primitifs led by Maurice Quay, and also seen in Flaxman's engravings, is vividly reflected in the early *Venus Wounded by Diomedes* (*c*1803; formerly, Collection of Baron Robert von Hirsch, Basel), and returns later in a subdued form as linear distortion for formal or expressive purposes. Archaic hyper-realism is seen in another early work, *Napoleon I on the Imperial Throne* (1806; Musée de l'Armée, Paris). Critics characterized it as "Gothic", referring to a van-Eyckian precision of detail. Thus Ingres before his first trip to Rome was in many senses an artistic revolutionary, in ways that affected his supposedly orthodox mature style.

Ingres remained in Rome after the end of his four-year term at the French Academy. He became acquainted with the French officials living in Rome under the Napoleonic occupation, who became the subject of a series of portraits. The early portraits are often set against a background of landscape, a device used in the portrait of *Mademoiselle Rivière* (1805; Louvre, Paris), where a fresh green landscape with a calm silvery river serves as the backdrop for a portrait of a 15-year-old girl. From the Italian period, the portraits of *Granet* (*c*1807; Musée Granet, Aix-en-Provence) and *M. Cordier* (1811; Louvre, Paris) are set against a background of a Roman hillside on a stormy evening and use the setting to bring out moods and personality characteristics in the sitter. Also from the Roman period date a group of exquisite pencil drawings of French officials and English tourists, commissions accepted by Ingres because of financial necessity (for example, *Sir John Hay and his Sister Mary*, 1816; British Museum, London).

Ingres' later portraits are usually set in interiors, and are characterized by the use of a rich material setting, in which luxurious fabrics and jewels are used to bring out the social position of the sitter. Painted with minute realism, they recreate for us the opulence of the Second Empire. An example is *Madame Moitessier Seated* (1856; National Gallery, London). This painting uses the device of reflection of the sitter in a mirror—one of Ingres' favorite techniques—to give a profile as well as a three-quarter view. The pose of Madame Moitessier is based on an antique model, a Roman fresco at Herculaneum. These portraits often have a compelling psychological presence, as in the *Portrait of Louis-François Bertin* (1832; Louvre, Paris).

The paintings that embody Ingres' doctrinaire views about art are less accessible to us today because their rigid conformity to classical rules seems formal and dogmatic. *The Apotheosis of Homer* (1827; Louvre, Paris) is based on Raphael's *School of Athens*, and uses a pyramidal composition placed frontally before a Greek temple. The carefully documented figures of artists and writers are arranged symmetrically around Homer, moving in a hierarchy from the ancients near the apex to the moderns at the base. In religious painting, a Raphaelesque prototype is often used, as in the *Virgin with the Host* (1854; Louvre, Paris). In many of these works, such as *The Martyrdom of St Symphorien* (1834; Autun Cathedral), the intellectual scheme is so heavily worked and apparent to the eye that the painting is a failure.

One of the richest themes of Ingres' genre painting was the exoticism of the harem, which he paints with voluptuous sensuality. *Odalisque with Slave* (William Hayes Fogg Art Museum, Cambridge, Mass.) contrasts the richly patterned setting with the fluid, linear contours of the body of the odalisque. Ingres does not attempt to render the precise anatomical line of the body, but to create an arabesque of abstract beauty which translates the grace

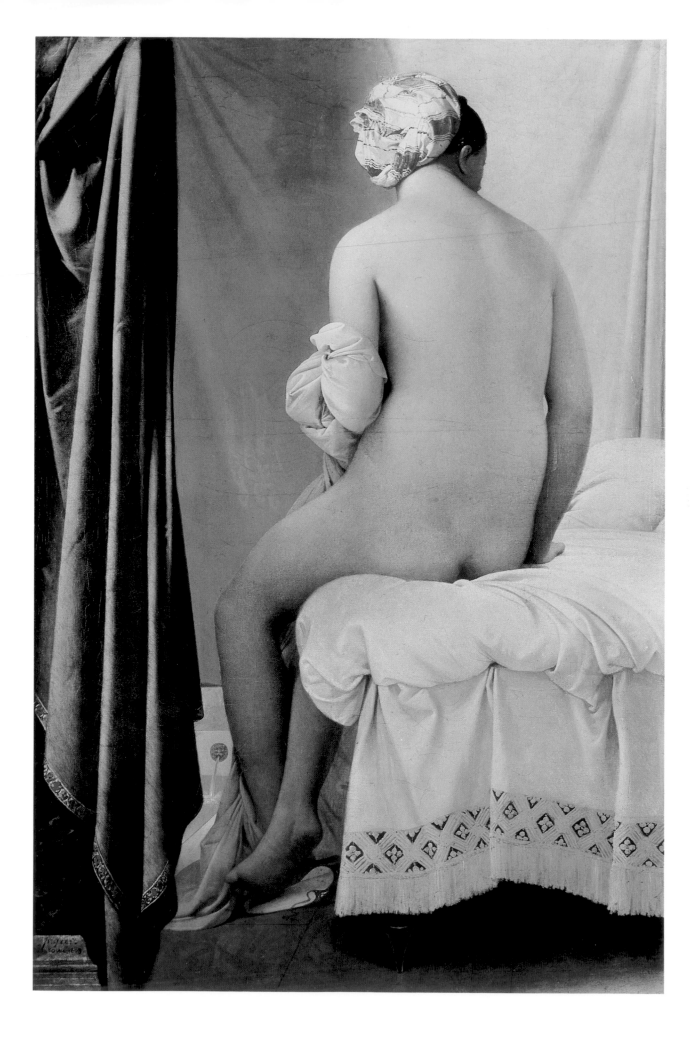

and abandon of the odalisque. He also painted genre scenes drawn from literature or from French history; these, like the larger works, are perfectly finished in every detail, and show the clear brilliant color that Ingres preferred to the chiaroscuro of Delacroix. He adapted his style to his subject, using an archaic, box-like space for a medieval subject, as in *Paolo and Francesca* (1819; Musée des Beaux-Arts, Angers).

Ingres' immediate influence among his pupils was strong, but, with some notable exceptions such as Théodore Chassériau, it led to insipid painting, since Ingres' official doctrines were not always successful when carried out by other hands. His stylized, schematic qualities influenced later artists such as Renoir, Degas, and Picasso.

**Further reading.** Friedländer, W. *David to Delacroix*, Cambridge (1952). Rosenblum, R. *J.A.D. Ingres*, London (1967). Vigne, G. *Ingres*, New York (1995). Wildenstein, G. *Ingres*, London (1954).

## Inness George 1825–94

The American landscape painter George Inness was born on a farm in New York State. He spent his youth in New York City, first exhibiting at the National Gallery when aged 19. He was made an Academician in 1853. His early works are broad, bright, and idealized landscapes in the manner of the Hudson River School (for example, *The Old Mill*, 1849; Art Institute of Chicago). Inness evolved his mature works through the influence of the Barbizon School during his visits to France and Italy between 1870 and 1874. His late works (for example, *Rainbow over Peigigia*, 1875; Museum of Fine Arts, Boston) reflect the soft forms of J.-F. Millet and Corot, as well as the pantheistic teachings of Emanuel Swedenborg. Innes eventually settled at Montclair, New Jersey, and died while in pursuit of the Picturesque at Bridge-of-Allan, Scotland.

## Ipoustéguy Jean 1920–

The French sculptor Jean Ipoustéguy was born in Dan-sur-Meuse. In 1938 he studied with Robert Lesbounit in Paris. He was commissioned to execute frescoes and

J.-A.-D. Ingres: The Valpincon Bather; oil on canvas; 146×98cm (57×39in); 1808. Louvre, Paris

stained glass windows for the church of St Jacques de Montrouge, Paris (1947–9). Ipoustéguy designed tapestries as well, but since 1949 has concentrated entirely on sculpture. His sculpture has been both Abstract and figurative, with bodies emerging from the mass of material (an example is *Man Pushing the Door*; bronze; 1966; Hirshhorn Museum and Sculpture Garden, Washington, D.C.). Frequently emphasizing sexual organs, Ipoustéguy's sculpture is brutal and aggressive with a strong element of the surreal.

## Israels Jozef 1824–1911

The Dutch painter, etcher, and watercolorist Jozef Israels was the leading figure painter of the Hague School. His humanitarian treatment of peasant subjects and his richly colored and painted style earned him comparison with Rembrandt. Born in Groningen, he was destined for the Rabbinate, but instead he studied art in Amsterdam and Paris, producing Romantic works in the style of Ary Scheffer (1795–1858). After 1855, his personal contact with the peasants at Zandvoort inspired him to change both style and subject and he slowly came to maturity in the 1870s. He settled permanently in The Hague in 1871 and produced series of works on themes of bereavement (such as *Alone in the World*, 1880; Hendrik Willem Mesdag Museum, The Hague) and peasants eating (such as *Frugal Meal*, 1876; Glasgow Art Gallery and Museum). He influenced a whole generation of Dutch painters, the most important of whom is Vincent van Gogh.

## Itcho Hanabusa 1652–1724

Hanabusa Itcho was a Japanese painter whose real family name was Taga. He used many pseudonyms until he adopted the invented name Hanabusa Itcho late in life. He studied with Kano Yasunobu (1613–85) from whom he learned both the firm *Kano* line, and Yasunobu's own skill in misty washes. He worked in Edo (Tokyo) in a personal genre style that is often compared with *Ukiyoe* but which is in fact much livelier in line and less idealistic in subject. An outspoken satirist, he was exiled in 1699 for political reasons to Miyake Island where he remained for many years. A notable stylistic feature of his work is the varied and eccentric series of viewpoints from which he paints his genre subjects.

George Inness: Short Cut, Watching Station, N.J.; oil on canvas; 96×74cm (38×29in); 1883. Philadelphia Museum of Art

Jean Ipoustéguy: The Death of the Father; marble; 600×310×125cm (236×122×49in); 1967–8. National Gallery of Victoria, Melbourne

# J

## Jacobsen Arne 1902–71

Born in Copenhagen, the architect Arne Jacobsen reacted strongly to certain aspects of the Danish Neoclassical tradition, which survived into the 20th century. He emerged in the early 1930s as an architect of the International style. An important influence upon him was the Swede Gunnar Asplund (1885–1940) who designed the Stockholm Exhibition of 1930, contributing a lightness and elegance that had not hitherto been special characteristics of modern architecture.

Jacobsen really came into his own after the Second World War with the Munkegard School at Gentofte (1952–6), a milestone in school architecture, and the Town Hall at Rodovre (1955–6), an architectural statement of extreme purity.

## Jacobsen Robert 1912–1993

The Danish sculptor Robert Jacobsen was born in Copenhagen. He lived in France from 1947, returning to Denmark in the late 1960s. Self-taught, he began to make wood carvings in 1931, influenced by German Expressionism. He joined the Danish "Host" group in 1940, and made his first Abstract pieces, a direction confirmed by meeting French sculptor Jean Arp, who advised him to carve in stone. He soon developed his mature style, working in metal from the late 1940s. He welded scrap iron to make small-scale open-form pieces, sometimes painted, in which space is carefully enclosed and defined. In the 1960s he also made larger sculptures and imaginative figures cut from sheet iron. He was a prizewinner in the 1966 Venice Biennale.

## Jakuchu Ito 1716–1800

The Japanese painter Ito Jakuchu was the son of a Kyoto greengrocer. He soon gave up the family business to become a Buddhist priest, and devoted the rest of his life to the study and practice of painting. His grounding was probably with the *Kano* School, but he studied the Sung and Yuan works in Kyoto temples, and also contemporary Chinese and possibly Korean works. He painted in two original but contrasting manners: dashing calligraphic ink studies mainly of cocks and hens, and extremely detailed flower and bird works in an expanded Nagasaki School manner. His masterpieces are the great series of paintings of the animal and vegetable kingdom (Imperial Collection, Tokyo).

## Janco Marcel 1895–1984

The Rumanian artist Marcel Janco was born in Bucharest. In 1915 he went to Zurich where he met Tzara and Arp. Both architect and painter, he was one of the original participants in the "Cabaret Voltaire" when it opened in 1916 as a center for the Dada movement; the savage masks he made for performances there were impressive in their provocative power. His work as an artist, though not aggressively iconoclastic, had a Dada inconsequentiality in its crude painting of plaster relief. These were sometimes Abstract, and sometimes based on Cubist still life. In 1922 he returned to Rumania; deprived of Dada stimulus, his work quickly declined into decorative slackness.

## Janssens Abraham c1573/4–1632

The Antwerp artist Abraham Janssens painted religious pictures, allegories, and portraits. The turning point in his career was a visit to Italy c1598–1601. Here, in Rome and possibly also in Bologna, his early predilection for a Mannerist idiom ultimately deriving from Bartholomaeus Spranger gave way to a more classicist style. His stylistic development can be traced from the elegant distortions of the early *Diana and Callisto* (1601; Museum of Fine Arts, Budapest) to the sculpturally conceived classicism of *Scaldis and Antwerpia* (1609; a commission for the States Chamber of Antwerp Town Hall, now in the Royal Museum of Fine Arts, Antwerp). Some writers see Caravaggio's influence in the latter, and suggest that Janssens may have made a second trip to Italy c1604.

## Jawlensky Alexei 1864–1941

The Russian painter Alexei von Jawlensky studied in St Petersburg with Ilya Repin, a member of the Realist "Wanderers" group. He moved in 1869 to Munich where he abandoned realism for Jugendstil. With Kandinsky he founded the *Neue Künstlervereinigung* in 1909 and was closely associated with the *Blaue Reiter* group. Influenced by Van Gogh and Gau-

Alexei Jawlensky: Portrait of Clothilde Sacharov; lithograph; 55×43cm (22×17in); c1909

guin, and by Matisse with whom he worked in 1907, he painted simplified forms rendered with flat areas of contrasting colors and heavy blue contours. In his series of *Heads* begun in 1910, Russian folk elements are combined with a mystical conception of painting. In 1924 he joined Kandinsky, Klee, and Feininger as "The Blue Four". His series of *Têtes Mystiques* of 1917 led him to abstraction.

Works can be seen in the Kunsthaus, Zurich, Nationalgalerie, Berlin, Art Institute of Chicago, the Solomon R. Guggenheim Museum, New York, and others.

## Jean de Liège fl. 1361–82

Described in 1361 as "faiseur de tombs demeurant à Paris", the sculptor Jean (Hennequin) de Liège had been a pupil and assistant of Jean de Huy in the Netherlands. The principal sculptor of Charles V of France, he carved an uncomplimentary effigy of Queen Philippa of Hainault (1367; Westminster Abbey, London). Later he executed the monument for the head of Charles V in Rouen Cathedral (1368). His simple, severe style and conventional draperies influenced English sculpture. The effigies of the Black Prince (Canterbury Cathedral) and Edward III

(Westminster Abbey, London), both c1377–80, are probably the products of his workmanship in Paris. He died in 1382.

## Jean d'Orbais 13th century

Jean d'Orbais was a French master mason. He was depicted in the now destroyed labyrinth of Reims Cathedral, which he designed after its Carolingian predecessor had burned down in 1210. The choir and transepts were unusually spacious in design, to cater for coronation ceremonies. He actually built these, and the first few nave bays, although he may not have completed the vaulting. At Reims he introduced bar tracery, a development from the slightly earlier plate tracery at Chartres. He also pioneered the use of *tas-de-charge*: bonding the lowest courses of the vaults into the wall, and also began linking clerestory mullions to the triforium. All these innovations are hallmarks of the mature Gothic style.

## Jenkins Paul 1923–

The American painter Paul Jenkins is, like Sam Francis, a second generation Abstract Expressionist who has become associated with art in Paris. His work has moved away from the claustrophobic density of Abstract Expressionism toward the considered open spaces of "color-field" painting. Born in Kansas City, Jenkins studied at the Art Students League in New York from 1948 to 1951. From 1953 he has lived in New York and Paris and developed an Abstract romantic style based loosely on the observation of nature. An example is *Phenomena in Heaven's Way* (acrylic; 1967; Martha Jackson Gallery, New York). His work has been widely exhibited and appreciated in Europe.

## Joan Pere *fl.* 1418–55

Pere Joan was the outstanding Gothic sculptor of Cataluña. Little is known about him, however. By 1418 he had completed the fine statue of St George on the facade of the Generalidad in Barcelona. In 1426 he carved, in alabaster, at least a part of the *Lives of St Tecla and the Virgin Mary* for the principal altarpiece of Tarragona Cathedral. His work in the church of the Espírito Santo in Saragossa has been lost, though the contract still exists. His confident and fluent style, possibly Burgundian in background, gives an im-

Augustus John: Portrait of W.B. Yeats; oil on canvas; 50×46cm (20×18in); 1907. Tate Gallery, London

pression of movement and depth which brings to life his essentially narrative subjects.

## Johannes von Valkenburg
*fl.* c1299

The German miniature and manuscript painter Johannes von Valkenburg was a Franciscan friar in Cologne. He illustrated two graduals (one is now in the Universitätsbibliothek, Bonn, the other in the Erzbischöflisches Diözesanmuseum, Cologne). Both include inscriptions naming Johannes, and the date 1299.

The graduals are important early examples of Rhenish Gothic work. The initial letters are usually composed within painted rectangles, and contain scenes with figures illustrating the text. The rectangles are filled with diaper pattern and sometimes contain a Gothic architectural framework. The borders of the text are also decorated with abstract or foliated patterns which sometimes tail off with stylized

flourishes. Both initials and borders are often enlivened by animals and birds that perch and leap about them.

The colors of the intial letters themselves are usually dark blue with the architectural decoration in gold. Other colors used were reds, green, and pale blue. The style of the painting is related to north French illumination but with characteristic Rhenish features in the bold, rather heavy rendering of the figures. Numerous later manuscripts have similarities to Johannes' work, particularly within the area of the Rhine and the Moselle.

## John Augustus 1878–1961

Augustus John was a British painter and printmaker. He trained at the Slade School of Fine Art, where he was thought to be the greatest draftsman since Rembrandt. However, his facility, spontaneity, and superficial brilliance were no substitute for the profounder virtues. John led a bohemian existence, painting gypsies and also his own rapidly growing family. He sought to emulate Puvis de Chavannes (1824–98) in his large decorative paintings. Some of his most successful early works are landscapes of his native Wales and of the south of France, where he produced his own version of Post-Impressionism. He painted many portraits of members of the official *nouveau riche* and literary establishment (for example, *Sir William Nicholson*, 1909, Fitzwilliam Museum, Cambridge; and *Lady Cynthia Asquith: Portrait of a Lady in Black*, 1917, Art Gallery of Ontario, Toronto). His portraits of *W.B. Yeats* (1907; Tate Gallery, London) and *Dylan Thomas* (1938; National Museum of Wales, Cardiff) are among his most successful, as are many studies of his family (for example, *Robin*, c1912; Tate Gallery, London).

**Further reading.** Easton, M. and Holroyd, M. *The Art of Augustus John*, London (1974). Lewis, W. *Blasting and Bombardiering*, London (1967). Shone, R. *Augustus John*, Oxford (1979).

# Johns Jasper 1930–

The American painter Jasper Johns was born in Augusta, Georgia. He studied at the University of South Carolina (1947–8) and moved to New York in 1949.

From the mid 1950s, working closely with artist Robert Rauschenberg, Johns painted commonplace subjects—flags, targets, and alphabets—in such a way that they acquired surprising overtones. He would use encaustic paint, applied very thickly, or introduce an unexpected element, such as the masks above the board in *Target with Four Faces* (1955; Museum of Modern Art, New York).

In the late 1950s and early '60s Johns took this idea further with a series of everyday objects such as beer cans, light bulbs, and flashlights that he cast in bronze and painted; such work suggests the influence of both Marcel Duchamp and Surrealism. In the 1960s he began to create large abstracts to which he affixed various objects—numbers, rulers, letters, even a cast of a human leg. The combination of painterly application and banal subject matter in these works marked a transition from Abstract Expressionism to Pop art.

From the early 1970s, Johns abandoned figuration for about a decade, focusing in-

Jasper Johns: Zero through Nine; oil on canvas; 137×104cm (54×41in); 1961. Tate Gallery, London

stead on "crosshatchings," abstract compositions in which he applied series of short, parallel lines across the picture plane. In the 1980s and '90s he began to use autobiographical imagery—for example, old family photographs. Johns's most famous work of this period, the "Seasons" series of 1985–6, comprises four paintings that allude to the different stages of his life and career. In the late 20th century, Johns was honored with several major retrospective exhibitions. His art repeatedly set records for the highest price paid for the work of a living American artist.

**Further reading.** Johns, J. *Jasper Johns: Writings, Sketchbook Notes, Interviews*, New York (2002). Varnedoe, K. *Jasper Johns: A Retrospective*, New York (1996).

# Johnson Cornelius 1593–1661

The Anglo-Netherlandish painter Cornelius Johnson was born in London of Flemish parents. His early work combines the influence of Dutch portrait painting with attention to detail derived from English miniature painting. By the 1620s his style had broadened and his painting became more vigorous and atmospheric. Although his work was never as bold and assured as that of his contemporary Daniel Mytens, his later work (for example, *The Family of Arthur, Lord Capel*, c1640; National Portrait Gallery, London) was on a grander scale and reveals the influence of van Dyck in composition and accessories. In 1643 he left for Holland, where his work was much in demand among Englishmen traveling in the Low Countries.

Cornelius Johnson: The Family of Arthur, Lord Capel; oil on canvas; 160×259cm (63×102in); c1640. National Portrait Gallery, London

copy in 19 handscrolls of the original work of the Heian period, *Events of the Year*; but with decorative features recalling the styles of Sotatsu (*fl. c*1600–30) and Shoi (1578–1651). In 1660 he was appointed official painter to the Sumiyoshi Shrine and adopted its name. He specialized in conventional illustrations to classical poetry and prose, but his style was more robust and colorful than that of the *Tosa* family.

## Jones Allen 1937–

The British painter Allen Jones was born in Southampton and studied at the Hornsey School of Art (1958–9) and the Royal College of Art (1959–60). In the early 1960s, he was involved in the development of Pop art, but in his case figurative imagery is often overlaid with a rich and

## Johnson Philip 1906–2005

The American architect, curator, and architectural historian Philip Cortelyou Johnson was born in Cleveland, Ohio. He graduated from Harvard in 1930 and became a curator at the Museum of Modern Art, New York. In 1932 Johnson and Henry-Russell Hitchcock organized a landmark exhibition and catalog of advanced European architecture since the First World War, coining the name "International Style" to describe their work. Returning to Harvard in 1940 to pursue a graduate degree in architecture, Johnson began as a convinced pupil of Mies van der Rohe, as can be seen in the "Glass House" (1949) he built for himself in New Canaan, Connecticut.

In the 1960s, Johnson moved toward a more personal brand of Neoclassicism (for example, the Sheldon Art Gallery, Lincoln, Nebraska, 1962). He collaborated with architect John Burgee on a number of luxurious commissions, many of them skyscrapers. Their design of the AT&T Building (1979–84) in New York served as the emblem of the burgeoning Post-Modern movement and placed Johnson at the forefront of modern architecture.

## Jokei Sumiyoshi 1599–1670

The Japanese painter Sumiyoshi Jokei, founder of the *Sumiyoshi* School, was also known as Hiromichi. The son of Tosa Mitsuyoshi, he learned the traditional *Yamatoe* techniques. In 1626 he began a

Allen Jones: Man Woman; oil on canvas; 215×189cm (85×74in); 1963. Tate Gallery, London

abstract use of color (as in *Sun Plane*, 1963; Sunderland Museum and Art Gallery). Since *c*1964, he has been concerned primarily with a type of erotic imagery based on "pin-ups", dressed in fetishistic shiny stockings and high heels (for example, *Wet Seal*, 1964; artist's collection). Details such as the shine on materials or the creases in cloth are often treated almost illusionistically, but the general effect of the pictures is wholly artificial.

## Jones Inigo 1573–1652

Inigo Jones was England's first Renaissance architect. He was born in Smithfield, London, the son of a clothmaker. Very little is known of his early career, but he certainly traveled to Italy *c*1600, and lived (perhaps for several years) in Venice. He had returned to England by 1603, when a payment recorded by the Duke of Rutland refers to him as "a picture maker". It was in this capacity—as a designer of elaborate masques—that he was first employed by the English court.

His earliest architectural drawings—executed with a precision and delicacy that immediately distinguish him from his Jacobean predecessors—date from 1608. The following year he was in France, examining the Château of Chambord, and in 1610 he received his first specifically architectural appointment, the post of Surveyor to Henry, Prince of Wales. No buildings survive from this period, but when, in 1613, Jones returned to Italy it was primarily to study architecture. He traveled widely, visiting Rome, Naples, and Florence. Most important of all, he went to Vicenza and Venice. Here in the Veneto he met Vincenzo Scamozzi, and made an exhaustive study of the palaces and villas of Palladio, whose architectural treatise, *I Quattro Libri dell'Architettura*, he had bought as early as 1601.

On his return to England in 1615 he was appointed Surveyor General. Soon afterwards, Jones produced his revolutionary designs for three buildings: the Queen's House, Greenwich (1616–18 and 1629–35), the first completely Renaissance building in England; The Prince's Lodging, Newmarket (1619–22, now destroyed); and the Banqueting House, Whitehall, London (1619–22).

"Solid, proporsionable according to the rules, masculine and unaffected", they broke decisively with England's lingering medieval traditions. They demonstrated his complete assimilation—and highly personal interpretation—of Palladian theory, and also his stubborn resistance to the proto-Baroque innovations of his Roman contemporaries Giacomo della Porta and Carlo Maderno.

Few of his late works have survived. The colossal Corinthian portico added (1634–42) to the west end of St Paul's Cathedral was demolished shortly after the Great Fire, while his plans (*c*1638) for a Royal Palace at Whitehall were never carried out. Of his solitary experiment in town planning, Covent Garden Square (1631–40), only St Paul's Church remains (1631; heavily restored 1795): a remarkable attempt to recreate Palladio's interpretation of the Vitruvian Tuscan Order.

Despite numerous optimistic attributions, Jones probably never designed a country house. However, he appears to have worked in an advisory capacity at Stoke Bruerne, Northamptonshire (*c*1629–35), at Chevening, Kent (*c*1630), and, especially at Wilton House, Wiltshire (*c*1632). The latter exemplifies his rich, but heavy style of interior decoration which had already, at the Banqueting House, provided a suitably grandiose setting for Rubens' *Apotheosis of James I* (1634–5).

**Further reading.** Allsopp, B. (ed.) *Inigo Jones on Palladio* (2 vols.), London (1977). Orgel, S. and Strong, R. *Inigo Jones: the Theatre of the Stuart Court* (2 vols.), Berkeley, Calif. (1973).

Inigo Jones: the Queen's House, Greenwich; built 1616–18 and 1629–35

## Jongkind Johan 1819–91

The Dutch painter and printmaker Johan Barthold Jongkind was born near Rotterdam, but from 1846 onwards he spent most of his time in France. His early landscapes tend to be dark in tone and deliberately composed. From the 1860s, however, his touch became lighter, his composition freer, and his exploitation of light and atmosphere more pronounced. He became friendly with Boudin and the young Claude Monet, who always acknowledged his debt to Jongkind. His views of Honfleur and of Notre-Dame of Paris certainly influenced Monet. He was also an accomplished watercolorist: his achievements were much praised by the Neo-Impressionist painter, Paul Signac. He contributed, too, to the revival of etching in the 1860s.

Johan Jongkind: The Harbour at Honfleur; etching; 25×33cm (10×13in); 1866. Rijksmuseum, Amsterdam

## Jordaens Jacob 1593–1678

The Flemish painter Jacob Jordaens was born in Antwerp and spent most of his working life there. He studied under Adam van Noort, whose daughter he married. At the time of his admission to the guild, in 1615, he was described as a "water scilder"—an artist who painted on tempera. As far as we know, Jordaens was primarily an oil painter, although he designed numerous tapestries, which entailed the preparation of large watercolor cartoons.

During the period when Jordaens began to work on his own account, Rubens was firmly established as the leading master in Antwerp, and the precocious van Dyck was just beginning to paint. Although Jordaens never studied directly under Rubens, he could not but be strongly influenced by the older man. Early studies suggest a certain amount of collaboration between Jordaens and van Dyck in the years before 1620, while the two were working as Rubens' assistants. All three seem to have had a hand in *Christ in the House of Simon the Pharisee* (c1618–20; Hermitage Museum, Leningrad).

The forms of an early Jordaens, such as the *Allegory of Fruitfulness* (or *Fertility*, c1617; Alte Pinakothek, Munich) indicate an obvious debt to Rubens. The sinuous interplay of line around which the composition has been constructed owes a debt to the Mannerist tradition, whereas the presence of certain realistic physical details suggests the work of Caravaggio. Several years later, the artist painted a second version of this theme, now in Brussels

(c1625; Musées Royaux des Beaux-Arts de Belgique). In composition this is a much tighter work, with the inevitable luxuriousness of the subject matter held in play by a system of dominant verticals. Later he returned to this subject again (one example c1645, now in the Wallace Collection, London).

This compositional tendency continued in other works of the 1620s, such as the Florida *Judgment of Paris* (c1620–5; Samuel H. Kress Collection, Lowe Gallery of the University of Miami, Coral Gables). Although the picture contains a large number of figures, dominant centralizing motifs impose a curiously restrained atmosphere. Jordaens worked once more beside van Dyck and Rubens in 1628, when each of the younger men provided an altarpiece to flank the older man's *Mystic Marriage of St Catherine* (1628) for the Augustijnenkerk in Antwerp. Jordaen's contribution, *The Martyrdom of St Apollonia* (1628), is a much more animated work than his earlier pictures, mentioned above. However, the abundance of varied forms is not lucidly organized, which has an extremely disruptive effect on the essential narrative of the composition. The slightly later altarpiece of *The Church Triumphant* (National Gallery of Ireland, Dublin) is rather more coherent, although it seems anecdotal by comparison with the grand religious pictures of Rubens.

Jordaens seems to have been happier when working within a narrower format. In his picture *The Fruit Seller* (c1625;

substantially reworked c1635; Glasgow Art Gallery and Museum), the main figure stands out in contrast to the artificially lit couple within the doorway, which provides a firm central accent to the composi-

Jacob Jordaens: Study of a Bearded Man with a Censer Descending a Step; ink, wash, and body color over chalk on paper; 52×29cm (20×11½in). Boymans-van Beuningen Museum, Rotterdam

tion. The florid Mannerist decoration of the door frame prevents the architecture from dominating the scene, enlivening the surface and amplifying the cheerful mood of the figures. This sort of picture reaches its high point of development in Jordaens' Flemish genre pieces, *The King Drinks* (c1638; Musées Royaux des Beaux-Arts de Belgique, Brussels) and *As the Old Sing, So the Young Twitter* (1636–40; Royal Museum of Fine Arts, Antwerp).

Both depict a festive gathering grouped around a table. Each composition is anchored by a frontal figure, placed slightly off-center, retaining the cohesion of the richly varied groups without mitigating the rumbustious and festive air of either.

Owing to Rubens' increasing infirmity, more and more work came Jordaens' way during the later 1630s. In 1635 he helped paint the triumphal arch of Philip IV, and in 1637 executed the *Apollo and Marsyas*, now in the Prado, Madrid. Both these works had been designed by Rubens. In 1639 Jordaens began a series of decorations for the Queen's House in Greenwich: another commission which had originally been given to Rubens. When the great man died the following year, it was apparent to the English agent at Antwerp that Jordaens was now the "prime painter here". He remained so for the next 30 years.

During the 1640s a vast number of commissions kept Jordaens and his assistants busy, often working on huge oil paintings and tapestry cartoons. Such pressure was not conducive to high quality. One of the most impressive of the monumental pictures executed during these years was *The Triumph of Frederick Henry* covering the walls of the Huis ten Bosch ("House in the Woods", a Royal country retreat near The Hague). Entirely the work of Jordaens himself, it was completed in 1652. The work is filled almost to bursting point with figures, swamping the architectural setting. In *Christ Among the Doctors* (1665; Mittelrheinisches Landesmuseum, Mainz), the rigidly symmetrical disposition of the numerous figures echoes that of the architecture. As a result, Jordaens' characters are powerless to animate the composition, despite their variety of dress and expression.

Jordaens also painted portraits. The painting of his younger daughter Anna Catherina (undated; Collection of the Marquess of Bute, Mt Stuart, Island of Bute, Scotland) reveals a remarkable lightness of touch when contrasted with the artist's more usual subject matter. Similarly, the *Portrait of a Girl and a Boy with a Dog and Sheep in a Landscape* of the late 1640s (formerly in the Hallsborough Gallery, London) is a radiant picture, which avoids potential sentimentality by a well-chosen balance of figures, landscape, and decorative motifs.

Jordaens apparently designed a set of tapestries as early as 1620, although these have not survived. In the 1620s he executed the suite of *The History of Alexander the Great* (for example, *Alexander Wounded at the Battle of Issus*, Holyrood House, Edinburgh) and the very popular *Scenes from Country Life* (for example, *Huntsman Resting with Hounds*, 2 versions; Kunsthistorisches Museum, Vienna). *The Story of Ulysses* series (for example, *Ulysses Threatening Circe*, Palazzo del Quirinale, Rome) dates from the 1630s. After Rubens' death, he contributed two designs to the *Achilles* series (for example, *Thetis Leading Achilles to the Oracle*, Museum of Fine Arts, Boston), begun by the older man and, in 1644, he began a suite of eight *Flemish Proverbs*. His last known essay in this field was *The History of Charlemagne* (Palazzo del Quirinale, Rome) which dates from the 1660s.

There are a great many surviving drawings by Jordaens, in a variety of techniques. In addition to ink and chalk, he used watercolor extensively in the preparation of preliminary sketches. As one might expect from his broad manner of execution, he was little interested in print-

Jacob Jordaens: The Four Evangelists; oil on canvas; 133×118cm (52×46in); c1620–5. Louvre, Paris

making. The seven etchings he made himself are not technically outstanding. During his lifetime, 31 engravings were made by other men after Jordaens' drawings.

It cannot be said that Jordaens' compositions compare with those of Rubens in their sense of mass and movement, nor with those of van Dyck in pathos. He was most successful with a less elevated subject matter, such as his festive genre scenes, which build creatively upon the Flemish tradition of the 16th century. For this reason, his productions are often criticized as vulgar, pedestrian, and anecdotal. However, he could certainly work effectively enough in the Grand Manner even though it was not his forte: to be rated second only to Rubens and van Dyck in this respect hardly betokens inferior status. While his more illustrious associates were frequently absent from the Netherlands, Jordaens never traveled far from Antwerp, throughout a long career, spanning 60 years. His art constitutes what is probably the single most important thread of continuity in the history of Flemish Baroque painting.

**Further reading.** Hulst, R.A. d' *Jordaens Drawings* (4 vols.), Ghent (1974). Gerson, H. and Ter Kuile, E.H. *Art and Architecture in Belgium: 1600–1800*, Harmondsworth (1960). Jaffe, M. *Jordaens*, Ottawa (1968). Puyvelde, L. van *Jordaens*, Paris (1953). Puyvelde, L. van (trans. Kendall, A.) *Flemish Painting in the Age of Rubens and van Dyck*, London (1971).

## Jorn Asger 1914–73

The Danish painter, sculptor, and ceramist Asger Jorn was born at Vejrum. He moved to Silkeborg in 1929, and from 1936 to 1937 studied at Léger's Académie Contemporaine, Paris. In 1937 he helped to decorate Le Corbusier's Pavilion des Temps Nouveaux, Paris. Throughout the period of the Nazi occupation of Denmark during the Second World War Jorn published a banned periodical. He founded CoBrA in 1948. From 1953, Jorn lived in Paris and Albisola. He was cofounder of the International Situationist movement in 1957. He died in Copenhagen.

The years 1937 to 1953 were marked by intense creativity and experiment, moving away from Purist influences and Surrealism. In 1940 he developed a calligraphic automatist technique, controlled by linear contours, creating an iconography of crea-

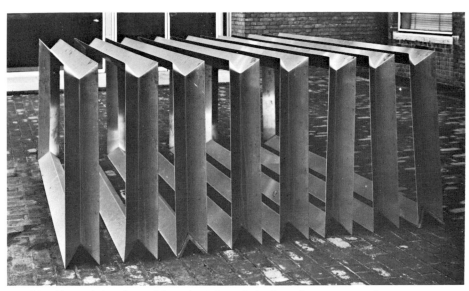

Donald Judd: untitled (eight-modular unit, V-channel piece); steel; 120×313×318cm (47×123×125in); 1966–8. Museum Ludwig, Cologne

tures and figures. From 1951 onwards, a greater luminosity, gestural freedom, and improvisation heralded his mature style. This showed an intense vision, embracing both figuration and abstraction. Jorn made a giant ceramic mural for Aarhus in 1959, tapestries in 1960, and several series of paintings in consciously contrived styles: examples are *The Sun Wearies Me*, 1961, and *Les Enfants*, 1962, both in Galerie Rive Gauche, Paris. He published many books and articles and a large number of graphic works.

## Jouvenet Jean-Baptiste 1644–1717

Born in Rouen, the French painter Jean-Baptiste Jouvenet joined the studio of Charles Lebrun after moving to Paris in 1661. In 1675 he became an Academician, and rose to be Director of the Académie. He was, after the deaths of Lebrun and Pierre Mignard, the premier painter of France.

An artist of great facility, he painted decorative cycles for the Salon de Mars, Versailles, the Parlements at Rennes and Rouen, and many altarpieces for Paris churches. *The Miraculous Draft of Fishes* (1706; Louvre, Paris), one of four altarpieces for St Martin-des-Champs, illustrates his debt to Lebrun and to the late work of Raphael. The painting displays the naturalism that set him apart from his contemporaries: the piles of fish given prominence in the foreground were sketched at Dieppe, where Jouvenet had gone to watch the catch being landed.

## Judd Donald 1928–94

The American Minimalist sculptor Donald Judd was born in Excelsior Springs, Missouri. Arguably his work was related to the sculpture of Anthony Caro, and to the painting of Barnett Newman on the one hand and Frank Stella on the other. But Judd himself denied any relation to previous or contemporary Minimal art, claiming his works were complete in themselves, excluding all outside references and even excluding the viewer. Made of galvanized iron or aluminum, Judd's sculptures are composed of series of mathematically related identical solids, which became increasingly subtle in their disposition throughout the 1960s.

**Further reading.** Judd, D. *Complete Writings 1959–1975*, New York (1975).

## Junge Johannes *fl. c1406–?c30*

The leading sculptor in Lübeck between 1406 and 1428, the Hanseatic artist Johannes Junge also worked for patrons in Denmark and Sweden. His delicate, serene figures from Niendorf (St Annenmuseum, Lübeck) are International Gothic in character, and the origins of his style are to be sought in the southern Netherlands. Johannes Junge also executed the alabaster carvings on the tomb of Queen Margaret of Denmark (completed 1423; Roskilde Cathedral) and the elegant alabaster *Pietà* for the church at Sønder-Alslev (National Museum, Copenhagen). It is uncertain whether he was responsible for the deeply impressive oak figures in the convent church at Vadstena, Sweden.

## Justus of Ghent *fl. 1460–c80*

Between 1473 and 1475 an artist named "Giusto da Guanto" (Justus of Ghent) is documented as the painter of the *Communion of the Apostles* altarpiece in Urbino. This man is clearly identical with a Flemish master named Joos van Wassenhove, active at Antwerp in 1460 and recorded at Ghent from 1464 to 1469. A Flemish document of 1475 states both that he was an associate of Hugo van der Goes and that he had gone to Rome some time previously.

A handful of pictures such as the *Adoration of the Magi* (*c* 1460–5; Metropolitan Museum, New York) have been attributed to Justus from the period before he left the Netherlands, by stylistic comparison with his only documented work, the *Communion* altarpiece. The most substantial of these is the *Mount Calvary* triptych in St-Bavon Cathedral, Ghent. Like the Urbino painting, it reveals points of contact with northern Netherlandish art, especially that of Dieric Bouts. The *Communion of the Apostles* (Galleria Nazionale delle Marche, Urbino) was produced for a confraternity (for the church of St Agatha in Urbino) under Montefeltro patronage (Federico da Montefeltro is actually portrayed in the painting). Joos is usually identified with

**Justus of Ghent: Communion of the Apostles; panel; 331×335cm (130×132in); 1473–5. Galleria Nazionale delle Marche, Urbino**

Filippo Juvarra: castle of Stupinigi, near Turin; begun 1729–33

the anonymous painter of a large group of pictures in a Netherlandish style executed for the Urbino court. These consist of 28 portraits of *Famous Men* (philosophers, writers, and poets) which were probably painted c1473–6 for the ducal study in Urbino. Four fragments from a series of *The Seven Liberal Arts*. These, together with a portrait of *Federico da Montefeltro Attending a Lecture*, were also painted c1476–80 for a similar study in Gubbio. The *Famous Men* group is divided between Paris (Louvre) and Urbino (Galleria Nazionale delle Marche) and the *Liberal Arts* between London (National Gallery and Hampton Court Palace), and (until their destruction in 1945) Berlin. It has often been suggested that Pedro Berruguete assisted Joos with both schemes. This seems probable, although it is clear that the Spaniard could only have played a very subordinate role in the work.

Joos is the only Flemish painter of the 15th century some of whose surviving works are actually known to have been produced in Italy. These paintings reveal his steadily increasing mastery both in the handling of illusionistic perspective and in the representation of Italianate subject matter. For these reasons he is a highly interesting forerunner of the rapprochement between Flemish and Italian art which took place during the early 16th century.

## Juvarra Filippo 1678–1736

The Italian architect Filippo Juvarra (or Juvara) was born in Messina. As a young man, he was trained in Rome under Carlo Fontana. The vast quantity of designs that survives from this early period in his career proves that he was already a prolific artist.

His great opportunity came in 1714, when King Vittorio Amadeo II of Savoy asked him to enter his service. He designed an immense number of buildings for this patron. Among the most important of these are the sanctuary of the Superga (1715–27), the Palazzo Madama (1718–20), and his masterpiece, the castle of Stupingi (begun 1718), all in or near Turin. Juvarra designed a number of projects for Rome, but few of these were carried out.

These works establish Juvarra as the most important Italian architect of the 18th century. They indicate the artist's knowledge of the Italian tradition stretching back to the Quattrocento, as well as the north European tradition exemplified in the great churches of Melk in Austria and Einsiedeln in Switzerland. Their characteristic scenic quality recalls his early experience as a stage-designer.

Other important works by Juvarra are the churches of S. Filippo Neri, Turin (1715), S. Croce, Rome (begun in 1718), and the Carmine, Turin (1732–6; restored after war damage, 1950–3), the Palazzo Birago della Valle, Turin (1716), the house built for Signor Rica di Convasolo, Turin (1730), the Palazzo d'Ormea, Turin (1730), the royal chapel and other works of the Veneria Reale palace complex in the Po Valley (1714–26), and the Castello in Rivoli (1718–21). He visited Portugal, London, and Paris, as well as Madrid, where he died while engaged on work for Philip V.

Juvarra was not so much an innovator as an extremely sophisticated composer of current ideas, with which he achieved novel and distinctive results. In this respect he is justly comparable with Tiepolo, his near-contemporary in the pictorial arts.

# K

## Kahlo Frida 1910-54

The Mexican painter Frida Kahlo was born in Coyoicoán, Mexico City; her mother was Mexican, her father German. She began painting at the age of 15 while recovering from a road accident that condemned her to a life of pain and increasing disability. Kahlo sent her works to the painter Diego Rivera, who encouraged her, and in 1928 they married.

Drawing in some degree on Surrealism, but more importantly on popular Mexican art (such as painted votive images), she created a series of highly original, often harrowing, self-portraits that are, in part, an ironic adaptation of traditional images of the Madonna. Though their immediate subject is her own physical and emotional suffering—her relationship with Rivera was stormy—they also explore political issues and the complex nature of Mexican identity. Well-known paintings include *The Broken Column* (1944; Delores Olmedo Collection, Mexico City) and *Self-portrait on the Borderline* (1932; Mr and Mrs Manuel Reyero, New York). One of her earliest supporters, the Surrealist André Breton, described her work as "a ribbon around a bomb".

**Further reading.** Herrera, H. *Frida*, New York (1983). Zamora, M. *Frida Kahlo: The Brush of Anguish*, London (1990).

## Kandinsky Wassily 1866-1944

The Russian painter Wassily Kandinsky was born in Moscow. In 1871 his family moved to Odessa. From 1886 to 1889 he studied law in Moscow. In 1896 he went to Munich to study art, and in 1901 he founded the Phalanx group, the main purpose of which was to introduce advanced French painting to the backward Munich art world.

His paintings of the early 1900s include landscapes executed in impasto with the palette knife, at first somber in color, later acquiring an almost Fauve intensity. At the same time he painted fantasies based both on old Russia and on an idealized view of the German Middle Ages. These works reflect a rejection of 19th-century materialism which at this point could only be

Frida Kahlo: Self-portrait; oil on canvas; 65×55cm (26×22in); 1930. Museum of Fine Arts, Boston

expressed in terms of picturesque evocations of a past age.

This period was also marked by technical experimentation. He used tempera against a dark paper, giving the impression of a transparent surface lit from behind. By painting in colored light against a consistent dark he united every part of the picture in an overall, flat pattern. At the same time he made a number of woodcuts in which the light areas form the positive of the image against a hard black. The very tonal consistency of both light and dark emphasizes pattern, undermining the distinction between the figures and their setting, and so bringing the composition closer to abstraction.

Towards the end of the decade Kandinsky's painting tended further towards flatness by giving each area of color equal intensity and creating a shimmering surface that destroyed all illusion of depth. In

the series of paintings of mounted riders in combat begun in 1909, the line of the horizon is gradually eradicated, together with other indications of space. In *Composition IV* (1911; Kunstsammlung Nordrhein-Westfalen, Düsseldorf) a residual relationship to this theme survives but the figures have become so simplified, the colors so arbitrary, and the space so confused that it is impossible to read the subject without reference to the earlier paintings.

Kandinsky's preference during these years was for violent apocalyptic themes, originating in the religious imagery of German and Russian folk art. Examples of Kandinsky's works were published in *Der Blaue Reiter*, the almanac he edited with Franz Marc in 1912, by which time his work had gone through many productive changes. These represented an alternative tradition to classical "High Art" and the materialistic view it stood for. Complex scenes involving many figures in violent action allowed him more scope for juggling with representational conventions. By 1913 when Kandinsky painted *Black Lines* (Solomon R. Guggenheim Museum, New York) one can no longer speak of abstraction from the subject. Color and line have taken on a life of their own, with a vitality and expressiveness that avoid mere pattern making. Works like this are among the earliest nonrepresentational paintings.

Kandinsky's development towards abstraction found a theoretical justification in the book *Abstraction and Empathy* by Wilhelm Worringer, published in 1908. It argued that the present hierarchy of artistic values, based on the High Renaissance, was invalid for art emanating from other cultures. Many artists created from an impulse to abstract from reality, as opposed to wanting to invoke within the spectator an empathy towards the subject.

At the same time Kandinsky was interested in the ideas of Theosophy, which sought a fundamental truth behind the externals of doctrine and ritual in all the world's religions. The belief in an essential reality underlying appearances provides an obvious rationale for Abstract art. Kandinsky was certainly influenced by Theosophy when in his book *On the Spiritual in Art*, published in 1912, he spoke of "a new epoch of great spirituality" and of the contribution of painting to this. The new art would be based on a language of color, and Kandinsky gave indications as to the emotional properties of each tint. Unlike previous color theorists such as Goethe, he was not concerned with the spectrum but only with the response of the soul.

At the outbreak of the First World War, Kandinsky returned to Russia. Such was the importance of the stimulus he had received from the avant-garde in Germany—not only from the painters Franz Marc and Paul Klee, who were also working towards abstraction, but also from the composer Arnold Schoenberg, whose struggle to liberate music from tonality mirrors Kandinsky's revolt against the subject—that there now followed a hiatus in his work: in 1915 Kandinsky painted nothing, although later in Russia he resumed his activity as an Abstract painter.

After the 1917 Bolshevik coup Kandinsky was kept busy by administrative work,

**Wassily Kandinsky: Panel III (Summer) of the four Campbell panels; oil on canvas; 162×92cm (64×36in); 1914. Museum of Modern Art, New York**

including the foundation of museums throughout Russia and attempts to reform the art school system. His plans for educational courses based on the theoretical analysis of color and form were opposed by the majority of artists: they were more concerned with the pressing problems of production, so Kandinsky's ideas were never put into practice. This convinced him that post-Revolutionary Russia would prove an unsympathetic environment for the development of pure painting, and in 1921 he returned to Germany.

In 1922 he began teaching at the Weimar Bauhaus. At this stage there were no painting classes. Kandinsky taught the foundation course, based on an investigation of the properties of form; this was the type of art education he had hoped to establish in Russia. The work of his Bauhaus years was more disciplined than that of the prewar period. While he was certainly influenced by the Russian avant-garde (there were strong parallels with works by Malevich and Lissitzky in the floating geometric shapes he painted in the early 1920s), Kandinsky's development had its own internal logic. He was concerned with building up his compositions from the tensions created by each form. This was a concept he tried to codify in his book *Point and Line to Plane*, published in 1926. He sought a theoretical basis for painting as strong as that existing for music. It was inevitable that he should now abandon the amorphous shapes he had used when his theoretical concerns were with color alone.

When the Bauhaus was closed by the Nazis in 1933, Kandinsky went to live in Neuilly near Paris. The biomorphism of Miró and Arp made a strong impact on him, and in the painting of his last years certain passages remind the spectator of living creatures, admittedly impossible to identify. This was no backsliding, for Kandinsky was still concerned with extracting the essential energy of the forms, rather than making an abstraction from natural appearances. At its best, his late work achieves an emotional force, through nonreferential means, truly analogous to music.

**Further reading.** Hahl-Koch, J. *Kandinsky*, New York (1993). Washton Long, R-C. *Kandinsky, the Development of an Abstract Style*, Oxford (1980).

# Kaprow Allan 1927–

The American painter Allan Kaprow is the founder of the modern "Happening". Happenings, as spontaneous, erratic, and

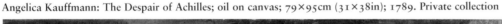
Angelica Kauffmann: The Despair of Achilles; oil on canvas; 79×95cm (31×38in); 1789. Private collection

mildly delinquent theatrical evenings, were first engineered by the Dada artists during the First World War. Kaprow recreated them as the theatrical and total environmental extensions of Pop art in the late 1950s in New York. He maintains that the idea first came to him in an exhibition of Jackson Pollock's painting which created a total and all-embracing environment. Kaprow's Happenings range from stage-managed, theatrically constructed environments to such events as *Household*, commissioned by Cornell University in 1964, in which students eat jam smeared all over the body work of an automobile.

**Further reading.** Higgins, H. *Fluxus Experience*, Los Angeles (2002). Kaprow, A. *Essays on the Blurring of Art and Life*, Los Angeles (2003). Kelley, J. *Childsplay: the Art of Allan Kaprow*, Los Angeles, (2004).

## Kauffmann Angelica 1741–1807

Maria Anne Angelica Catherina Kauffmann's portraits and Classical subjects were much sought after in her lifetime, and she worked in both England and Italy. She first trained under her father in Milan, and went to Rome in 1763 where she painted her *Portrait of Winckelmann* (1764; Kunsthaus, Zurich). In England from c1765 she became a society portrait-painter, exhibited regularly at the Royal Academy, and decorated the interiors of several Robert Adam houses. By the early 1780s she had returned to Italy with her second husband, the painter Antonio Zucchi. Kauffmann's portraits were painted in the Reynolds manner, and her highly decorative history paintings were widely known through engravings.

## Kazan Watanabe 1793–1841

The Japanese artist Watanabe Kazan painted in both the *Bunjinga* and "Western" styles. Born in Edo (Tokyo), he rose to become an adviser on coastal defence to the local lords of Tahara. He thereby came to study the forbidden Western science and learning, for which he was arrested in 1839; he killed himself in confinement.

Kazan inherited an eclectic attitude from his painting master Tani Buncho. In native styles he is at his best in his lively sketch-books, as in the *One Hundred Figures* (Tahara Local Museum). He is best known for his essays in Western realistic portrai-ture, done with native techniques but using light and shade, as in the *Portrait of Takami Senseki* (Tokyo National Museum).

## Keibun Matsumura 1779–1843

The Japanese painter Matsumura Keibun was born in Kyoto. He studied with his elder brother Goshun, founder of the *Shijo* branch of the *Maruyamal Shijo* School. Gentle in temperament, he took easily to the atmospheric and lyrical side of his brother's style, excelling in landscape and bird-and-flower studies, done in soft ink washes with light color. This side of his work represents the standard style of the *Shijo* school. He also developed a decorative manner using black outline with colors on gold background. This can be seen in the interiors of a princely palanquin in the Myohoin, Kyoto. Keibun was buried at the Kompukuji, Kyoto, where his brother and the painter Buson also lie.

## Kelly Ellsworth 1923–

The American painter Ellsworth Kelly was born in Newburgh, New York. He studied at the Pratt Institute in Brooklyn, New York (1941–2), Boston Museum of Fine Arts School (1946–7), and École des Beaux-Arts, Paris (1948–9). He stayed in Paris for six years and used simple images such as a chimney as a point of departure for abstract drawings and collages. In 1954 he returned to New York, where he developed his mature style: large, flatly painted canvases featuring masses of primary color. His work was a cross between the mathematical series of Josef Albers and the emotional "color-field" paintings of Mark Rothko; while cool and hard-edged, his works have an underlying sense of poetry and lyricism.

Kelly pursued these concerns in many forms, including prints, drawings, and flat sculptures that resembled his paintings. His paintings took on a sculptural quality, as he cut his canvases into unexpected shapes and created separate monochromatic panels that could be fitted together and mounted. In 1996 he was honored with a major retrospective at the Solomon R. Guggenheim Museum, New York.

## Kemeny Zoltan 1907–65

Zoltan Kemeny was a Hungarian/Swiss sculptor born in Banica, Transylvania. From 1921 to 1923 he was an apprentice joiner. In Budapest he studied architecture at the School of Decorative Arts (1924–7) and painting at the School of Fine Arts (1927–30). He went to Paris to work as a fashion designer (1939–40). From 1940 to 1942 he was in Marseilles, moving in 1942 to Zurich and working as fashion designer and editor of a Swiss magazine. Then he

Ellsworth Kelly: Green, Blue, and Red; oil on canvas; 185×254cm (78×100in); 1964. Whitney Museum of American Art, New York

started to paint again. By 1946, he was working on collages and reliefs, and by 1951 he was making translucent reliefs, designed to be set up in front of electric lights. The metal reliefs that Kemeny has come to be known for started to appear in 1954.

His reliefs give an impression of rhythmic movement through the interlinking of metal objects, either "ready-made" or "found" (for example, *Shadow of the Miracle*; copper T-sections mounted on wood; 1957; Museum of Modern Art, New York). Kemeny acquired Swiss nationality in 1957, and died in 1965 in Zurich.

## Kent Rockwell 1882–1971

The American painter and illustrator Rockwell Kent was born in 1882 in Tarrytown, New York. He first studied architecture at Cornell University and then painting under Robert Henri at the New York School of Art (1903–4). His paintings, mainly landscapes and marine subjects, were influenced by the Ash Can School; they were freely painted, expressing the vitality of contemporary rural American life and the grandeur of nature. His popular reputation was founded in the late 1920s and 1930s on his wood-engraved illustrations of the classics, including Shakespeare and the Decameron, and also on his illustrated travel journals. His left-wing political stance is apparent in much of his work from the late 1940s. He died in 1971 in New York.

## Kent William c1685–1748

William Kent was an English architect, painter, and landscape gardener. He is chiefly remembered as an architect, one of the major Palladian revivalists; but his early career was spent solely as a painter, working in the Baroque illusionistic style of Sir James Thornhill (1676–1734) and Louis Laguerre (1663–1721).

Born in Bridlington, Yorkshire, he trained in Italy for eight years, returning to England in 1719 in the company of his close friend and lifelong patron Richard Boyle, third Earl of Burlington. It was as a result of Burlington's influence that he turned his talents to architecture, although it was not until the mid 1730s and later that he designed his major works: Holkham Hall, Norfolk (begun 1734), the Treasury Building, Whitehall (1734–6),

William Kent: Rousham House, Oxfordshire; garden landscaped by Kent c1738–40

and the Horse Guards, Whitehall (1751–8), his last building.

As befitted an architect with little or no formal training, Kent interpreted Vitruvian canons with greater flexibility than the other major Palladians. If his exteriors exemplify the restraint, order, and discipline demanded by Burlington as the quintessence of English Palladianism, his interiors are less formal; they are characterized by a richness of ornament that found a historical precedent in the architecture of Inigo Jones, whose *Designs* Kent edited and published in 1727.

Kent's contribution to landscape gardening has long been recognized. According to Walpole, he was the first to have "leap'd the fence and seen that all nature is a garden". Many of his "innovations" had in fact been anticipated by Charles Bridgeman. But it was Kent who broke decisively with Baroque formality. At Rousham, Oxford (c1738–40), and Stowe, Buckinghamshire (c1740), he provided the inspiration for the apparently casual (but in fact carefully composed) landscapes popularized later in the century by Capability Brown.

## Kiefer Anselm 1945–

The German artist Anselm Kiefer came to prominence as one of the leading figures of the Neo-Expressionist movement of the 1970s and '80s. A student of Joseph Beuys, he shares the older artist's concern with broad political issues and also his belief that the artist has an almost shamenistic function in modern society. Kiefer's paintings, sculptures and books of photographs reveal a deep concern with Germany's recent past, in particular with Nazism; one of his aims has been to "bring to light things that are covered, that are forgotten". Early works showed somber images of architecture, scorched landscapes, and symbols of German history and myth. Typical works are the painting *Sulamith* (1983; Saatchi Collection, London) and the sculpture *Das Buch* (1985; Los Angeles County Museum), which comprises a huge pair of wings—a recurrent image—attached to a lectern.

## Kienholz Edward 1927–1994

The Californian artist Edward Kienholz is the most savage and powerful of the American Pop sculptors. His art is one of assemblage: the creation of works of sculpture from everyday "found" objects and three dimensional settings; these are peopled by plaster-cast characters to create environments of a ghostly and frequently hideous realism. Although the method derives from Dada, and in particular from Duchamp, the aim is a satirical environmental realism. This is sometimes almost surrealistic, as in the life-size recreation of a lunch counter, *The Beanery* (1965; Stedelijk Museum, Amsterdam), in which all the figures have the faces of clocks. Much more frequently the sculptor's satire is horribly pointed, as in *The State Hospital* (1964–6; Modern Museum, Stockholm) or *The Illegal Operation* (1966; Whitney Museum of American Art, New York).

## King Phillip 1934–

The British sculptor Phillip King was born in Tunis. He settled in England in 1945. After reading languages at Cambridge, he studied at London's St Martin's School of Art under Anthony Caro. He then became one of Henry Moore's assistants—and it is symptomatic of the conditions of 20th-century art that he was not influenced by the work of the great British sculptor. Instead, he became one of the first sculp-

tors in Britain to develop the possibilities of glass fiber and polyester, in a series of Abstract creations that are sometimes painted in bright colors.

## Kinkoku Yokoi 1761–1832

A Japanese painter of the *Bunjinga* School, Yokoi Kinkoku was born near Otsu on Lake Biwa. A man of many parts, he was Buddhist priest, sword-fighter, painter, poet, musician, and had many less reputable occupations. He made his living in early life by painting for temples and shrines in the *Yamatoe* style. Later he became a follower of Buson, though not his pupil. In his last years he painted in a more forceful, less poetic transformation of his earlier style, specializing in landscape. His works have great visual excitement, using one ink stroke over another, or spattered ink washes in the Chinese manner. His best landscapes have a monumental power rare in the *Bunjinga* School.

## Kirchner Ernst 1880–1938

Generally regarded as the leading spirit and most gifted member of the *Brücke* group, the German painter Ernst Ludwig Kirchner was born at Aschaffenburg. After living in Chemnitz he studied architecture in Dresden from 1901. By 1904 he had met Fritz Bleyl, Erich Heckel, and Karl Schmidt-Rottluff. From 1903 to 1904 he studied under Hermann Obrist in Munich, and assimilated the spirit of *Jugendstil* line. It was his sympathy for Post–Impressionism—particularly the work of Gauguin, Van Gogh, Toulouse-Lautrec, and Valloton, which he first saw in Munich—that influenced his early paintings and graphics.

If Kirchner's paintings before 1905 seem to reflect somewhat hesitantly different Post-Impressionist styles, his work in succeeding years became more forceful in color and form than that of his Fauvist contemporaries. His figurative paintings acquired the high-key color and brushwork of Van Gogh and the visionary aspect of Munch, whose influence is apparent in Kirchner's woodcuts of the period. By 1907 he was using line in his paintings to describe their form, in a manner he later described as his "hieroglyph" and which still relate his work to *Jugendstil*. In his *Self-portrait with Model* (1908; Hamburger Kunsthalle, Hamburg), violent, brash colors are combined in a flattened picture plane that recalls the distorted

perspective of Munch.

Kirchner's mature style and his liking for metropolitan subject matter reached fullfilment when, with the other members of the *Brücke*, he moved to Berlin. He became a cofounder of the New Secession in 1910. His woodcut style seems to have been responsible for an increased sensitivity to the expression of color and form in his paintings (as in *Nude with Hat*, 1911; Wallraf-Richartz-Museum, Cologne). Most of Kirchner's energies at this time were expended in formulating his reactions to city life, and in describing the rhythms and relationships of anonymous figures in urban streetscapes. In contrast to the curvilinear rhythms of his Dresden period, his Berlin paintings use jagged lines and angular forms set in uptilted perspectives to accentuate the tensions of his figures (for example, *The Street*, 1913; Museum of Modern Art, New York).

In Berlin, Kirchner's strong personality and his criticism of the work of his fellow *Brücke* artists was largely responsible for the break-up of the group when the *Brücke Chronik* was published in 1913, a personal statement by Kirchner which his friends objected to. He grew increasingly antagonistic towards his former associates, suf-

Ernst Kirchner: Self-portrait with Cat; oil on canvas; 120×85cm (47×33in); 1920. Busch-Reisinger Museum, Cambridge, Mass.

fered from a cycle of depressive illnesses, and retired to Switzerland in 1917 to recover from a nervous breakdown. His paintings became more peaceful in expression (for example, *Moonlit Winter Night*, 1918; Detroit Institute of Arts), but by 1922 he again displayed something of the strength and dynamism of the former period (seen in *The Amselfluh*, 1923; Öffentliche Kunstsammlung, Kunstmuseum Basel). In 1926 he depicted himself in the midst of his former *Brücke* colleagues in a group portrait (Wallraf-Richartz Museum, Cologne). The painting is outwardly calm but nonetheless suggests the tense dominance of his artistic personality. Kirchner committed suicide in 1938.

**Further reading.** Dube, W.-D. *The Expressionists*, London (1972). Gordon, D.E. *Ernst Ludwig Kirchner*, Cambridge, Mass. (1968). Selz, P. *German Expressionist Painting*, Berkeley (1972).

## Kitaj R.B. 1932–

The American painter R.B. Kitaj was born in Cleveland, Ohio. He studied at the Cooper Union Institute, New York (1950), in Vienna (1951), and, after a phase as a seaman and in the U.S. Army, at the Ruskin School of Drawing and Fine Art, Oxford (1958–9) and the Royal College of Art, London (1959–61). Between 1961 and 1967, Kitaj taught in London at the

Paul Klee: Fire in the Evening; oil on board; 34×33cm (13×13in); 1929. Museum of Modern Art, New York

Ealing School of Art, Camberwell School of Art, and at the Slade School of Fine Art. He became an important contributor to the development of Pop art in Britain, with a series of canvases that combine brilliant

draftsmanship, compositions with overtones of Cubism and Surrealism, and deliberately *recherché* subject matter (see *The Ohio Gang*, 1964, Museum of Modern Art, New York; *Walter Lippmann*, 1966, Albright-Knox Art Gallery, Buffalo). Retrospective exhibitions were held in Los Angeles, Hanover and Rotterdam.

**Further reading.** Lambirth, A. *Kitaj*, London (2004). Livingstone, M. *Kitaj*, London (1999). Ríos, J. *Kitaj: Pictures and Conversations*, London (1994). Rudolf, A. and Wiggins, C. *Kitaj: in the Aura of Cézanne and Other Masters*, London (2002).

## Klee Paul 1879–1940

In a massive output of paintings in oil and watercolor, drawings and etchings, the Swiss artist Paul Klee combined a multiplicity of Expressionist and other modern styles to convey, often in a humorous and satirical manner, a personalized vision of 20th-century man's inner imagination, fears, and fantasies. Klee was born at Münchenbuchsee near Bern into a middle-class cultured family. Both his parents were musicians. He soon became an ac-

R.B. Kitaj: From London (James Joll and John Golding); oil on canvas; 152×244cm (60×96in); 1975–6. Private collection

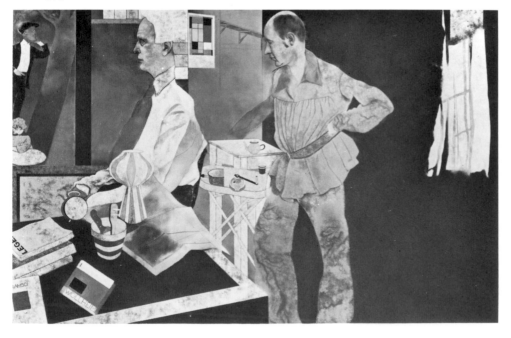

complished poet and musician and played the violin in the Bern municipal orchestra. He had a lifelong interest in the formal aspects of literature and music, both of which stimulated his art.

Although Klee was equally talented at an early age as a painter and draftsman, it was not until he was 35 that he came to fully regard himself as a painter. After his formal education had been completed he studied art in Munich from 1898 to 1900, first under Knirr and then under Franz von Stuck; he received a formal training in figure-drawing under the latter but devoted little attention to color. By this time he had decided to become a painter, and after traveling in Italy in 1901, where he became acquainted with the Western Renaissance tradition, he devoted himself on his return to Bern to a series of 17 grotesque satirical etchings. They reveal his admiration for the visionary symbolism of Blake and Goya, as well as for Ensor and Redon whose work he saw in Paris in 1905.

Klee's interests during this period included early Renaissance paintings and German woodcuts. The literary subject matter of his first etchings also reflects his wide reading, particularly Baudelaire and the French Symbolist writers. Ten of the etchings were exhibited at the Munich Secession in 1906; Klee moved to Munich that year and became familiar with Impressionist and Post-Impressionist painting, including the work of Van Gogh, Cézanne, and Matisse. Under the influence of French Impressionism he began to work from nature, and although his drawing now included color and reflected something of the flat planar distortions of Cézanne and Matisse, he did not abandon the intuitive approach to subject matter that characterized his early work.

Klee's first one-man exhibition in Munich in 1911 brought his work to the attention of the *Neue Künstlervereinigung*, and to Alfred Kubin, whose art Klee's superficially resembled at the time. Through Kubin, Klee was introduced to the circle of Kandinsky and Marc. Klee felt strong affinities with Kandinsky's theories of the spiritual essence of art, and he exhibited his work in the second *Blaue Reiter* exhibition of paintings and drawings in 1912. Franz Marc's interpretation of the rhythmic relationship of animal life also strongly appealed to him, and provided him with a basis for the exploration of the creative life-force which he was later to pursue.

In 1912 Klee visited Robert Delaunay in Paris. Delaunay's individual brand of Orphic Cubism, and his chromatic series of window pictures built up with overlapping color rectangles, further opened his eyes to the potential use of color. The following year he translated Delaunay's *Sur là Lumière* into German. However, it was not until 1914, when he journeyed to Tunisia with August Macke, that the strong light and intense color of North Africa prompted him to write in his diary: "Color has taken hold of me ... once and for all.... Color and I are one. I am a painter". In this, Macke, for long a strong colorist himself, proved a decisive influence.

Although Klee's art after 1914 is clearly indebted to Cubism, and particularly to Delaunay, it never became Abstract but was deeply rooted in nature. Between 1914 and 1920, in landscapes and cityscapes, Klee built up a tapestry of rectangles in prismatic colors resembling mosaics; they were strengthened by the grid-like structures of Cubism and painted with all the intensity of Expressionism. The theme of the city and tower in his work is imbued with the mystical qualities of a new Jerusalem, and as such still carries Symbolist and literary and mythological associations (seen in *City of Towers*, 1916; Philadelphia Museum of Art). In his immediate postwar work Klee was concerned with capturing not just the visual world as he perceived it, but with the processes of creation, genesis, and motion. It was these themes that he analyzed in pictorial terms in his teaching in the following decade.

In 1920 Walter Gropius invited Klee to join the staff of the Bauhaus at Weimar, where he taught at first in the departments of stained glass and weaving. Later he conducted his own course in the theory of forms. In 1925 his *Pedagogical Sketchbook*, which outlined his fundamental theories of points, lines, and planes, was published by the Bauhaus. He produced paintings during these years in a bewildering variety of different styles which he adapted to suit the requirements of content and subject matter. His subject matter included architecture, plant, animal, and human life, and incorporated reference to child art, primitive, medieval, and folk art. At times the strict geometry of his paintings is reminiscent of Constructivist form. In other instances he departed from the structural basis of Cubism to explore the inner world of the subconscious, although

his art in this decade is only tangentially connected to that of the Surrealists, who nevertheless admired his work (for example, *Fish Magic*, 1925; Philadelphia Museum of Art). In 1924 he exhibited with Kandinsky, Jawlensky, and Feininger as "The Blue Four".

It is possible to see in Klee's work during these years two distinct lines of enquiry. First there were his formal exercises in pictorial form, expressing growth and movement through line and plane. But there was also Klee's combination of mythological or philosophical truths expressed in more complex language, which are much indebted to concepts in poetry and literature as they are to visual art. Humor and fantasy are often used to explore deeper meanings, as are subjects depicting pain and grief, an approach Klee described as a "synthesis of outward sight and inner vision". In 1930 Klee left the Bauhaus for a teaching post at Düsseldorf, from which he was dismissed by the Nazis in 1933. His late works increased in size, and the symbolism became more graphic and prophetically doom-laden—yet humor and irony still often lie quite close to the surface (as in *Death and Fire*, 1940; Paul-Klee-Stiftung, Berner Kunstmuseum, Bern). Klee's art continued to bear out his belief that "art does not reproduce the visible, but makes visible".

**Further reading.** Grohmann, W. *Paul Klee*, London (1955). Klee, F. (ed.) *The Diaries of Paul Klee 1878–1918*, Berkeley (1964). Klee, P. *Notebooks* (2 vols.), London (1961 and 1973). Klee, P. *On Modern Art*, London (1966). Klee, P. *Pedagogical Sketchbooks*, London (1953). Lynton, N. *Klee*, London (1975). Pierce, J.S. *Paul Klee and Primitive Art*, New York (1976).

# Klein Yves 1928–62

The career of the French painter Yves Klein was short but fairly sensational. He was born in Nice and received very little academic training. He originally came into prominence with a series of paintings consisting of a single color, at first applied rather thickly but later put on more smoothly. Many of these pictures were blue, which he regarded as the most significant color. Klein was always antiacademic and soon extended his interests to gestural and performing arts. A show in Paris in 1958 (Galerie Iris Clert) simply consisted of the empty wall of the gallery,

Yves Klein: I.K.B. 79; paint on cotton scrim over plywood backing; 140×120cm (55×47in); c1959. Tate Gallery, London

while in the following years he concocted his *Anthropometries*, which had an audience and consisted of nude models, painted blue, rolling around on bare canvas and leaving chance imprints of form. It was a kind of Action Painting through body contact. Although his work was not always well received during his lifetime, Klein was commissioned to produce mural decorations for an opera house at Gelsenkirchen in Germany.

**Further reading.** Restany, P. *Yves Klein*, New York (1982).

## Kleophrades Painter
*fl. c500–470* BC

The Kleophrades Painter was the greatest Athenian painter of large vessels of his generation. He was the pupil of Euthymides, and was the last red-figure painter to use the black-figure technique with any proficiency. Some of his early works have subsidiary zones in black-figure. Like the Berlin Painter, he painted a series of prize Panathenaic *amphorae*.

Early in his mature period he painted the wonderful pointed *amphora* in Munich (Staatliche Antikensammlungen; Inv. 2344). There we see Dionysos surrounded by satyrs and maenads, huge figures filled with power and life. Two maenads on the reverse show the painter's great gift for "mood-figures". One dances ecstatically,

head flung back, feverishly pulling at her *thyrsos* rod, a raucous cry on her lips. In contrast, the other maenad sways gently, her expression detached and serene, her lips parted in transcendent joy.

A later piece of his mature years is the *hydria* showing the sack of Troy by the Greeks (Museo Archeologico Nazionale, Naples; Inv. 2422). Here despair and resistance, flight and ruthless violence fill the eye. The simplicity of the woman seated beneath the drooping palm and her companion in despair at the foot of Athena's statue rival Giotto's hooded mourners of Christ (*Mourning of Christ*, c1306; Capella dell'Arena, Padua). The quality of quiet grandeur and lofty seriousness in his figures seems not unlike that attributed to the famous Classical wall-painter Polygnotus.

His last pieces, however, show signs of fatigue. His style had burned itself out and his only follower, the Boot Painter, continued his late weak work on a series of rather poor cups.

## Klimt Gustav 1862–1918

The Austrian painter Gustav Klimt was born at Baumgarten, a suburb of Vienna, the son of an engraver. Between 1876 and 1883 he studied at the School of Decorative Arts in Vienna. His early large-scale decorative works were followed in 1894 by a commission to produce designs for a painted ceiling at the Vienna University Hall. Klimt presented his designs for *Philosophy*, *Jurisprudence*, and *Medicine* in 1896. Two years later he was asked to carry out the work in conjunction with Franz Matsch, who was to paint the centerpiece and *Theology*.

By this time Klimt had already been made president of the Vienna Secession. His art had undergone a radical change, partly as a result of his assimilation of *Jugendstil* and the work of the Munich painters. *Pallas Athene* (1898; Historisches Museum der Stadt Wien, Vienna), shown at the second Secession exhibition, marks this new style. It is characterized by frontality, interest in surface pattern, and the use of gold and other metal. Its inclusion of a tiny naked female figure in the lower left-hand part of the canvas looks forward to paintings and decorative schemes in which sexuality was a predominant theme—one that often caused offence. Klimt's use of a variety of exotic materials was an important device. His interest in ornament was

further stimulated by a visit to see the Byzantine mosaics at Ravenna in 1903; it reached a climax in the huge mosaic frieze Klimt designed for the Stoclet Palace, known as the Stoclet Frieze (1905–11; Palais Stoclet, Brussels; working drawing for the Stoclet Frieze in the Österreichisches Museum für Angewandte Kunst, Vienna).

*Philosophy* was exhibited in March 1900 at the Secession; it aroused great controversy amongst Viennese academics, the public, and the press. *Medicine* had a similar reception the following year. *Jurisprudence*, shown at the Secession's Klimt retrospective in 1903, was the most decorative of the three but also the most stylized and abstract in design. The influence of the Symbolist painter Jan Toorop is distinctly shown in this work. In 1905 Klimt resigned his commission for the University paintings.

His large allegorical frieze for the Secession's *Beethoven* exhibition of 1902 was as controversial as the University paintings, and accusations of pornography were leveled against it. The motif of the embracing couple was taken up again in *The Kiss* (1908; Österreichische Galerie, Vienna), probably his most famous work. This was exhibited at the first Kunstschau (1908), together with some fine landscapes and female portraits. Portraiture and landscape preoccupied Klimt after the second Kunstschau (1909): both genres show the artist adopting a simpler, more painterly style, devoid of dazzling ornamental effects. It was not until 1917 that his art appeared to be ready to make another stylistic turn—possibly influenced by his knowledge of Schiele's work. But Klimt did not live long enough to explore any new directions fully. He died in 1918.

**Further reading.** Bouillon, J.-P. *Klimt: Beethoven, Frieze for the Ninth Symphony*, New York (1987). Comini, A. *Gustav Klimt*, London (1975). Nebehay, C.M. *Gustav Klimt: Dokumentation*, Vienna (1969). Vergo, P. *Art in Vienna 1898–1918*, Oxford (1981).

## Kline Franz 1910–62

The American painter Franz Kline was born in Wilkes-Barre, Pennsylvania. He studied painting at Boston University (1931–5) and then in London, returning to New York in 1939. His earlier work, which includes landscapes, portraits, and

Franz Kline: Painting no. 7; oil on canvas; 146×208cm (57×82in); 1952. Solomon R. Guggenheim Museum, New York

was designed as a sequence of changing scales and viewpoints, creating dream worlds populated by nightmarish or surreal figures. His paintings included both decorative panels and large easel works. *The Judgment of Paris* (1885–7; Kunsthistorisches Museum, Vienna) combines the spatial unease and veiled symbolism of his engraving series with Klinger's growing interest in sculpture, to which he devoted himself almost exclusively after 1900.

## Koetsu Hon'ami 1558–1637

Calligrapher, potter, and designer, Hon 'ami Koetsu was the greatest all-round figure in Japanese art. He was a member of

murals (for the Bleeker Street Tavern, New York, 1940) was relatively traditional in character. But from 1947 onwards, Kline became increasingly preoccupied with abstraction. He is best known for his large black and white paintings, in which a rugged and powerful structure of black forms is imposed on a white ground. These are among the most distinguished productions of Abstract Expressionism (for example, *Mahoning*, 1956; Whitney Museum of American Art, New York).

## Klinger Max 1857–1920

Max Klinger was a German painter, printmaker, and sculptor. His pictorial images haunted the imaginations of Symbolists and Decadents, and his innovations in sculpture (for example the polychrome marble monument of a Jupiter-like *Beethoven*, 1902, which he left to the Museum der Bildenen Künste in Leipzig) paralleled those of Sir Alfred Gilbert, Fernand Knopff, and Sir George Frampton. Born in Leipzig, Klinger trained in Karlsruhe (1874), Berlin (1875), and briefly with Arnold Böcklin. He traveled extensively during his life (Brussels, Vienna, Paris, Rome, Leipzig), finally settling in Grossjena near Naumberg, where he died.

Success first came to Klinger through his engravings. Issued in series (such as *On Death*, 1889; *Brahms Phantasy Opus XII*, 1894) between 1879 and 1903, each set

Max Klinger: To Beauty, from the series of etchings "Of Death"; 41×32cm (16×13in); 1898. Graphische Sammlung Albertina, Vienna

Oskar Kokoschka: **The River Elbe near Dresden**; oil on canvas; 81×112cm (32×44in); 1919. Art Institute of Chicago

the Hon'ami family, who for generations had been appraisers of sword blades—the most astringent form of aesthetic appreciation in Japanese life. Like many artists of his time, he was an adherent of the nationalistic and practical Nichiren Buddhist sect.

Koetsu first came to notice in the early 17th century with his *Saga-bon*, sumptuously printed texts of *No* plays and old poetic anthologies done on high quality paper. His basic mission was to revive the arts of Kyoto's glorious past, and to make them better known to the merchant class to which he belonged. In this he partly resembled the 19th-century Englishman William Morris. Like Morris, Koetsu was very much a man of his age, as can be seen in his wonderfully liquid calligraphy. This recalls Heian *hiragana* works, but is done on top of motifs, either printed or painted, designed by the flamboyant artist Sotatsu.

In 1616 he was given land by the govern-ment at Takagamine in northwest Kyoto, and there set up a village of artists, potters, lacquerers, papermakers, and other crafts-men. He did designs for the lacquerers and papermakers, the most famous being his *Boat-Bridge* ink-box (Tokyo National Museum), inlaid with his calligraphy in mother-of-pearl. He also set up a pottery and produced powerfully astringent teabowls used in the tea ceremony, among them the very celebrated *Mount Fuji*. Through his association with Sotatsu he is often thought of as the founder of the *Rimpa* School, and his influence on later design was great.

## Kokan Shiba 1747–1818

Shiba Kokan was both artist and scientific writer. Born in Edo (Tokyo) he studied with a *Kano* artist; after the death of Harunobu in 1770 he spent a few years making prints in his style. He then studied with the Nagasaki School artist So Shiseki. He revived European copperplate engraving and pioneered etching, producing prints of Japanese scenes using Western shading and perspective, like the *Ryogoku Bridge* (British Museum, London). He also painted landscapes in imitation of European oils, using chalk pigments mixed with oil or wax. As a writer on European science he was very influential.

## Kokoschka Oskar 1888–1980

The Austrian painter Oskar Kokoschka was born at Pöchlarn on the Danube in Lower Austria. His father's family were goldsmiths from Prague. He studied at the Kunstgewerbeschule (School of Applied Art) in Vienna and in 1907 began working for the Wiener Werkstätte, designing fans and postcards. In 1908 a group of artists and architects, who had resigned from the Vienna Secession with Klimt three years earlier, put on a large and important exhibition, the Kunstschau. Here Kokoschka showed tapestry designs, illustrations for his Expressionist drama *Murderer, Hope of Women* and for his fairy-tale *The Dreaming Youths*, and a painted plaster bust—a savage self-portrait—which was bought by Adolf Loos. He also designed the poster for the exhibition.

It was Loos who persuaded Kokoschka to leave the Werkstätte and embark upon a painting career. His many portraits of this period, in which tactile, free brush strokes are used to convey intense emotion, are powerful examples of Expressionist art. They have a penetrating, analytical quality which has caused people to link the artist metaphorically with the name of Freud, Kokoschka's Viennese contemporary.

In 1910 Kokoschka went to Berlin where he was employed by Herwath Walden to draw for his avant-garde Expressionist periodical *Der Sturm*. During this period he also recorded his stormy relationship with the beautiful and seductive Alma Mahler (the widow of the composer Gustav Mahler and later the wife, in succession, of Walter Gropius and Franz Werfel) in two outstanding paintings: *Self-portrait with Alma Mahler* (1912; Horstmann Collection, Hamburg) and the great, symbolic *The Tempest* (1914; Öffentliche Kunstsammlung, Kunstmuseum Basel).

Kokoschka was severely wounded in the First World War. He settled in Dresden in 1917. The famous life-size doll that was specially made for him dates from this time: it became the model for the painting *Woman in Blue* (1919: Staatsgalerie, Stuttgart). Although it depicts an inanimate object, the painting is vibrant with color and pulsates with a life of its own. He continued to paint portraits of great intensity, including many self-portraits. His landscapes and townscapes of many of the great European cities were noted for their visionary power (for example, *Jerusalem*, 1929–30, Detroit Institute of Arts; *London, Large Thames View I*, 1926, Albright-Knox Art Gallery, Buffalo).

In 1934 Kokoschka emigrated to Prague. He painted a symbolical portrait of Tomás Masaryk, President of Czechoslovakia, a man with whose humanist views he felt he had much in common (completed 1936; Carnegie Institute, Pittsburgh). At the 1937 exhibition of "Degenerate Art" in Munich, organized by the Nazis, eight of Kokoschka's paintings were shown. His

Philips Koninck: An Extensive Landscape with a Road by a Ruin; oil on canvas; 137×168cm (54×66in); 1655. National Gallery, London

reply was to paint a large and tragic self-portrait which he called *Portrait of a "Degenerate Artist"* (1937; private collection).

He spent the years of the Second World War in England—years marked by a series of allegorical pictures, and by writings in which he fought for humanist principles. In 1953 he gave his first course at the International Summer School for the Visual Arts at Salzburg under the title "The School of Vision". He then settled in Switzerland. His autobiography—a fascinating story—was published in 1971.

**Further reading.** Hodin, J.P. *Kokoschka: the Artist and his Time*, London (1966). Kokoschka, O. *Der Expressionismus Edvard Munchs*, Munich and Vienna (1953). Whitford, F. *Oscar Kokoschka—a Life*, London (1986).

## Kollwitz Käthe 1867–1945

Born Käthe Schmidt, the German artist Käthe Kollwitz came from a nonconformist background and lived for most of her life in a poor district of Berlin. Her graphics and her sculpture—which resembles that of Barlach—are Expressionist; but her work is more concerned with objectifying social ills than with conveying an inner response. Her early etchings and lithographs are in an illustrative tradition, but her postwar woodcuts are in the ex-

pressive Gauguin-Munch technique of the Brücke group. In 1919 she was elected the first woman member of the Prussian academy, and in the 1920s depicted the social consequences of the First World War in an emotive, figurative idiom.

**Further reading.** Klein, A. and N. *Käthe Kollwitz: Life in Art*, New York (1975). Kollwitz, K. (ed. Kollwitz, H.) *The Diaries and Letters of Kaethe Kollwitz*, Chicago (1955). Nagel, O. *Kaethe Kollwitz*, New York (1971). Shikes, R.E. *The Indignant Eye: the Artist as Social Critic in Prints and Drawings*, Boston (1969).

## Koninck Philips 1619–88

The Dutch landscape painter Philips Aertsz. Koninck was a pupil of Rembrandt during the early 1640s. He initially modeled his work on his teacher's imaginary landscapes. Later he turned to more realistic views of Dutch scenes which have their origin in Rembrandt's drawings and etchings. Increasingly he developed a speciality in large, luminous panoramas seen from high vantage points, in which the sense of limitless space is heightened by the introduction of tiny figures. Dark cloud formations frequently scud across Koninck's skies, throwing immense patches of transparent shadow over fields, dunes, and winding rivers, and adding a note of melancholy to his work.

## Koninck Salomon 1609–56

The Dutch painter Salomon Koninck studied under David Colijns and Nicholas Moeyaert. Based in Amsterdam he was one of the most able imitators of Rembrandt's style. He specialized in biblical subjects, incorporating Oriental costumes and powerful facial types (for example, *The Idolatry of King Solomon*, 1644; Rijksmuseum, Amsterdam). He was also highly successful in his imitation of Rembrandt's effects of light and texture. The measure of his ability is reflected in the fact that Rembrandt's so-called Sobieski portrait in the Hermitage Museum, Leningrad, was once attributed to him.

Since Koninck excelled as an imitator, the limits of his oeuvre are difficult to define. There are signed works by him in Amsterdam, Dresden, Frankfurt, and Rotterdam.

## Kooning Willem de 1904–1997

The American Abstract Expressionist painter, Willem de Kooning was born in Rotterdam and apprenticed as a commercial painter and decorator. In 1926 he went to New York, initially with no idea of becoming an artist. There he met Arshile Gorky and John Graham, founding the nucleus of a Greenwich Village group of artists who experimented with and adapted all that they could learn of modern European art in the 1930s. De Kooning was painting extremely well by 1940. Unlike Pollock and Gorky, he made no radical break in the 1940s from his work of the previous decade.

De Kooning was interested in the separation and overlapping of objects and in emphasizing the space that contains them. These preoccupations are apparent in *Two Men Standing* (oil on board; c1938; private collection) in which the spatial ambiguity adds an element of disquiet to an otherwise straightforward figure study. *Seated Woman* (c1940; Collection of Mrs Albert Greenfield, Philadelphia) introduces a series of studies of women that, growing in intensity of expression and execution, characterizes de Kooning's work of the 1940s and 1950s and provides the perfect subject matter for the Abstract Expressionist technique (for example, *Woman I*, 1950–2; Museum of Modern Art, New

York). In *Pink Angels* (c1947; private collection) the human figure is dismembered, and any corporeal identity is blotted out by miscellaneous linear shapes and an almost ubiquitous pink: a color that was a leitmotiv of early Abstract Expressionist painting. The quality of blotting out is taken further in *Excavation* (oil on canvas; 1950; Art Institute of Chicago), a monumental statement of de Kooning's Abstract Expressionism, achieved after a period of severe retrenchment and study in black and white only. *Excavation* is built up of layers of overlapping forms. Fragments of dismembered sensuous shapes float against a cream background upon which shape is imposed by black lines and enlivened by patches of strong color.

The multiple interests of de Kooning as a painter were fused again in a further series of *Women* (mostly in private collections) in the 1950s. These were increasingly violent, becoming almost monstrous in physiognomy and crude physical reference. The vast scale, and the control of the slashing brush stroke nevertheless achieved the same sort of equilibrium that is found in the best of Pollock. The later works of de Kooning return to a landscape theme which emphasizes the ambiguity of intervening space, one of the painter's most enduring preoccupations.

De Kooning has painted far longer and with more consistently high-quality results than any other Abstract Expressionist painter.

Further reading. Butler, C. H. et al. *Willem de Kooning: Tracing the Figure*, Princeton, N.J. (2002). Stevens, M. and Swan, A. *De Kooning: an American Master*, New York (2004).

## Korin Ogata 1658–1716

The Japanese painter Ogata Korin was the second great master of the *Rimpa* School. He was the son of a rich Kyoto textile designer who had connections with Koetsu's artistic village at Takagamine, hence his interest in Sotatsu's work. But he trained in the *Kano* School, and did not become a professional painter until the ruin of the family fortunes in the 1690s. He moved to Edo (Tokyo) for a while, and developed a style based on the decorative work of Sotatsu, but less powerful and more elegant. His younger brother Kenzan (1663–1743) was a celebrated potter, and Korin painted sharply characteristic designs on some of his dishes.

Korin's monochrome ink style is strange and spiky, as in his twofold screens of plum and bamboo (private collection), where the blossoms are reduced to almost circular design-motifs, a habit which grew in the *Rimpa* School. These shapes appear in red and white in his famous *Red and White Plum Blossom* screens (Atami Art Museum). Here the distorted trees, their trunks covered with gold, green, and blue patches, their roots reduced to a horizontal line on the gold, flank the astonishing silver-and-brown river. This is perhaps the greatest example of the Japanese tendency to treat natural objects as pure decoration. The same can be seen in the *Waves* screens (Metropolitan Museum, New York).

Korin was also a master of the small, delicate fan-painting, based on the Kyoto traditions of the Heian court. There is a fine example of court nobles pasted on a box in the Yamato Bunkakan, Nara.

## Kossoff Leon 1926–

The English painter Leon Kossoff was born in London. He studied at St Martin's School of Art and in evenings with David Bomberg at the Borough Polytechnic from 1949 to 1953, and at the Royal College of Art, from 1953 to 1956. He taught at the Regent Street Polytechnic and Chelsea School of Art from 1959 to 1964, and at St Martin's School of Art from 1966 to 1969. Kossoff's Expressionist style, marked especially by very thick impasto, is directly related to Bomberg's teaching. His subject matter is restricted to figures in interiors and the London cityscape of excavations, demolition and building sites, and railways. His paintings are made very rapidly *alla prima*. Somber dense colors gave way to a brighter palette in 1975.

## Kosuth Joseph 1945–

The American Conceptual artist and theorist Joseph Kosuth was born in Toledo, Ohio. Combining analytical philosophy, aesthetics, and linguistics, Kosuth investigates the nature of the art object in relation to its context. While a student at the School of Visual Arts, New York (1965–7), and as a faculty member in 1968, he worked on his photoenlargements of dictionary definitions and words in neon. Later he used magazine and billboard advertisements to remove the work from the art context. From the early 1970s photocopies of his *Investigations* (begun in

Willem de Kooning: Woman and Bicycle; oil on canvas; 194×124cm (76×49in); 1952–3.
Whitney Museum of American Art, New York

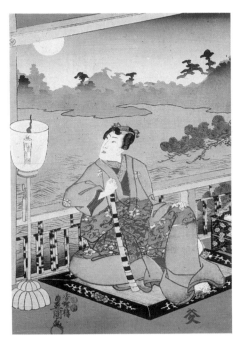

Utagawa Kunisada: Moonlight; woodblock print; each section 37×25cm (15×10in); 1857. British Museum, London

1966) have been displayed in special gallery installations. In 1971 and 1972 Kosuth studied philosophy and anthropology at the New School for Social Research, New York. He had a major retrospective exhibition in Lucerne in 1973 and one-man shows at the Leo Castelli Gallery, New York, from 1969 onwards.

Further reading. Kosuth, J. *Art After Philosophy and After: Collected Writing 1966–90*, Boston, Mass. (1991). Kosuth, J. *Guide to Contemporary Art*, Milan (2004). Oliveira, N. de *Installation Art*, London (1996).

## Ku K'ai-chih 345–406

The painter Ku K'ai-chih came from Chin Ling, Wu Hsi, and was the son of an official of the Chin State of East China. He became an official himself early in his life and died in office. His reputation, which was considerable in his own time, rested at least as much on his poetry as on his painting; indeed he is mentioned under the literati heading in the *Chin Shu* (Chin dynastic history) biography section. Amongst his poetry, of which little remains, his most famous work is the *Lightning and Thunder fu*. As a courtier the assessment of Ku K'ai-chih's success is problematical. He was notably skilled at getting along with sworn enemies and is reputed to have been naive to the point of

foolishness. It has been suggested that he may have acted the fool and thereby retained his position throughout a period of unrest, much as a court jester protects himself. His reputation as an eccentric is clearly not unkind and is a matter for admiration.

His fame as a painter rested in his own time largely on his portraiture, recorded as vivid and lifelike. His technique of "putting the highlights in the eyes last" is remarked upon with some wonder. He was a master of the "Red and Green" style, an old-fashioned style both rich and decorative. Our own experience of Ku K'ai-chih's painting, however, is of a different aspect. Although those works known to us today must be later copies of copies, we have three major works in the *Admonitions of a Preceptress to a Girl about to enter the Palace*, a hand scroll in the British Museum, London; another handscroll, *The Fairy of the Lo River*, now in the Freer Gallery of Art, Washington, D.C.; and the *Landscape* in the Royal Ontario Museum, Toronto. The last two scrolls, appearing in their copied form as somewhat stiff and lacking in life, retain a hint of the fascination the magical world of the Taoist had for Ku K'ai-chih. The fairies float above and into a delicate and simple landscape of groups of trees and trailing streams.

The *Admonitions* scroll, regarded as perhaps a 10th-century copy, is of separate figure-scenes. Each one represents a situa-

tion likely to be met by the young girl entering the palace as a concubine. The short script introducing each scene advises the girl on the proper attitude: to be kind to her children and get on well with her fellow palace women, to be dutiful to her husband, and so forth. The final scene of a huntsman in landscape seems to give a clue to the mountain landscapes which came into the painter's repertoire and were developed over the years to become his major art. Here the figures are lively and gracefully painted. Even in their copied state they retain something of the character with which Chinese genre painting at its most lively abounds.

While these works give us some hint of the late-4th-century landscape style, it is interesting to note also that Hsieh Ho in the *Ku Hua P'in Lu* rates Ku low among painters, regarding him as far from being the greatest artist of his day.

## Kunisada Utagawa 1786–1865

The Japanese print artist Utagawa Kunisada was a pupil of Utagawa Toyokuni. From 1844 he signed himself "Toyokuni", claiming to be the second of that name, though the true Toyokuni II was Toyoshige who died in 1835. Kunisada is therefore often called Toyokuni III. Kunisada's importance lies in his dominance of the figure print in the mid 19th century. He produced over 20,000 compositions and his long, rather ugly and tortured faces and his dark, hard colors became the standard for the period. In his youth, however, he had produced actor prints of some power in Toyokuni's tradition, and even a few sensitive landscapes. His prints are encountered more frequently than any other's.

## Kuo Hsi 1020–90

The Chinese painter Kuo Hsi was born in Honan; very little is known of his family. He was a Taoist. He was appointed early in his career to the Imperial Academy of painting of the Northern Sung, and became one of its most illustrious members, later becoming a member of the Imperial Council with various honorary offices. Kuo Hsi was a teacher in the Imperial Academy and was considered by his contemporaries to be the greatest master of landscape painting. As a court painter he undertook a wide variety of work, particularly fresco paintings. These have all perished with the palaces. The large landscape attributed to Kuo Hsi, *Early Spring* (National Palace Museum, Taipei, Taiwan) shows a masterly baroque composition, rich in detail and expressing great depth of distance and atmosphere. Clearly Kuo Hsi followed the styles of Li Ch'eng and Fan K'uan. But he added the dimension of his own breadth and articulation of form, to give his mountains not only the static grandeur of his predecessors' works, but also that quality of a landscape "in which one can take a walk" that his patrons and contemporaries so much admired.

## Kupezký Jan 1667–1740

Probably the greatest central European portrait painter of the early 18th century, Kupezký was Bohemian by birth, but worked all over Europe. He was trained in Vienna and was later active in Venice and Rome before returning to Vienna in 1709. However, he never felt secure in Catholic states, and he finally settled in Protestant Nuremberg in 1725. In his portraits Kupezký brought together Italian Baroque patterns and a Northern sharp eye for detail, often giving his sitters a brooding intensity and an extraordinary sense of immediacy. This psychological penetration was deepened further by the exploitation of still-life elements in sharp focus, which emphasized the personality of the sitter.

## Kupka Frank 1871–1957

The Czech painter Frank Kupka was born in Opocno in eastern Bohemia and studied in Prague and Vienna. He came to Paris in 1895 and worked there for the rest of his life. At first he made his living as an illustrator, his work for the satirical magazine *L'Assiette au Beurre* expressing his own anticlerical and anarchist beliefs.

The precise chronology of his development is difficult to establish, but it is certain that in the autumn of 1912 he exhibited one of the earliest nonfigurative paintings, his first entirely Abstract work, *Amorpha, Fugue for Two Colors* (1911–12; National Gallery, Prague). In this painting the arabesques created by intersecting arcs were the result of a process of abstraction from movement that Kupka had begun in 1908 with a naturalistic painting of his stepdaughter with a ball. Probably inspired by the multiexposure photographs of figures in motion made by Marey in the 1880s, Kupka made a series of drawings in which an abstract rhythm gradually replaces the subject. The movement of the ball acquires connotations of planetary orbits; it is likely that Kupka, who had a lifelong interest in the occult, believed he could depict an all-embracing cosmic motion.

The *Vertical Planes* (1913; National Gallery, Prague) exhibited in 1913 anticipate Malevich and Lissitzky in their depiction of floating rectangles. The emphasis on verticals stretching from top to bottom, destroying the opportunity to see a horizon, derives from a painting of piano keys of 1909. In drawings of the same year, the depiction of motion is aided by breaking up the surface continuity to suggest distinct moments of time.

Kupka has often been classed with Robert Delaunay as an "Orphist", although the opaque and labored handling of the Czech painter militates against the effects of space and light achieved by the Delaunays. After 1931, when he joined the *Abstraction-Création* group, his painting became absorbed into international geometric abstraction.

**Further reading.** Cassou, J. and Fedit, D. *Frank Kupka*, London (1965). Heath, A. *Abstract Painting: its Origin and Meaning*, London (1953). Mladek, M. and Rowell, M. *Frantisek Kupka: a Retrospective*, New York (1975).

# L

## Lachaise Gaston 1882–1935

The Franco-American sculptor Gaston Lachaise was born in Paris and studied there. He worked at the production of Art Nouveau objects for Réné Lalique. In 1906 he emigrated to the United States where he began work as an assistant to H.H. Kitson, a designer of military monuments. Lachaise quickly became a prominent sculptor whose vast bulbous women in bronze are in the tradition of Maillol and Matisse. Casts of his most famous work, *Standing Woman* (1912–17; Albright-Knox Art Gallery, Buffalo), are in galleries throughout America. Lachaise was also an accomplished portraitist whose subjects include notable American artists and writers such as Marianne Moore and e e cummings.

## Lafosse Charles de 1636–1716

The French painter Charles de Lafosse trained under Charles Lebrun. He spent the years from 1658 to 1663 in Italy, starting his studies in Rome where he examined the works of Pietro da Cortona, and spending three years in Venice where he studied the works of Paolo Veronese. He brought back to France a coloristic Venetian style, but was also much influenced by Rubens. Venetian and Flemish influences made him the leading *Rubéniste*, softening the classicism of Lebrun and preparing the way for the painterly grace of Watteau and the Rococo. He executed altarpieces and Baroque decorative schemes for the provinces, but worked mainly for projects in Paris (for example, the dome of the church of the Invalides, Paris, 1692) and for Versailles (mythological scenes for the Trianon, 1688). He was favored by the influential collector Pierre Crozat.

## Laguerre Louis 1663–1721

The French-born decorative painter Louis Laguerre was a pupil of Charles Lebrun. He came to England in 1684, and worked with Antonio Verrio at Windsor and Whitehall. He was also employed extensively in decorating the interiors of important country houses with grand illusionistic and allegorical mural and ceiling paintings.

Louis Laguerre: C. Dubosc's engraving after Laguerre's painting The Battle of Tanieres, near Mons, 1709, in Marlborough House, London; 48×73cm (19×29in); c1712–33. British Museum, London

Examples of these can be seen in Chatsworth House (1689–97) and Sudbury Hall (1691) in Derbyshire, at Burghley House in Lincolnshire (1698), and in various London houses. These schemes show the influence of Lebrun and Baroque decorative painting, tempered with a dull classicism. His masterpiece is the Saloon at Blenheim Palace, Oxfordshire (c1720), with its allegorical ceiling and illusionistic terraces on the walls crowded with the peoples of all nations. During the last decade of his life, his reputation was overshadowed by that of Sir James Thornhill.

## Lam Wifredo 1902–82

The Cuban painter Wifredo Lam (Wifredo Oscar de la Conception Lam y Castilla) was born in Sanga la Grande, Cuba, and studied first at the Havana School of Fine Arts (1920–3) and then in Madrid and Paris. In Paris in 1938 he met Picasso, André Breton, Max Ernst, and Victor Brauner. His first major one-man exhibition was in Paris at the Galerie Pierre in 1939. Lam fled from Europe in 1941 on the same boat as André Breton, André Masson, and Claude Lévi-Strauss. From

Wilfredo Lam: The Jungle; gouache on paper mounted on canvas; 239×230cm (94×91in); 1943. Museum of Modern Art, New York

1947 to 1952 he lived in Cuba, New York, and Paris, visiting Italy and England. In 1952 he left Cuba for Paris, where he has lived practically ever since. While Lam was never formally a member of the Surrealist group, his work—with its tortured human-like imagery (for example, *The Jungle*, 1943; Museum of Modern Art, New York)—indicates a close kinship with Surrealism and Cubism. (See also *Rumblings of the Earth*, oil on canvas; 1950; Solomon R. Guggenheim Museum, New York.)

**Further reading.** Jouffroy, A. *Lam*, Paris (1972). Lewis, M. *Wifredo Lam*, Milan (1970). Tarnaud, C. "Wifredo Lam et la Bestiaire Ambigu", *XXᵉ Siècle*, Paris (May, 1963).

## Lancret Nicolas 1690–1743

Nicolas Lancret was a French painter and draftsman. A student at the Académie de Peinture and of Claude Gillot, he was essentially a painter of *fêtes galantes*; as such, he was the chief follower of Watteau, continuing this mode into the 1740s. An early example of this is *Italian Comedians by a Fountain* (Wallace Collection, London), with colors less saturated than those of Watteau. A member of the Académie in 1719, he was soon established as a popular artist, particularly in court circles. As well as working for Versailles, he attracted many of Watteau's former patrons. His sense of observation was acute and often humorous, as in *The Cup of Chocolate* (National Gallery, London), shown at the Salon of 1742.

## Landseer Sir Edwin 1802–73

The sporting, genre, and portrait painter Sir Edwin Henry Landseer was born in London, the son of an engraver. He exhibited at the Royal Academy from 1815. He was taught by B.R. Haydon, beginning his studies by dissecting animals. Landseer became Royal Academician in 1831. It was on visits to the Scottish Highlands that he found his most popular subjects. Fine examples of his work include *The Hunted Stag* (c1833; Tate Gallery, London), *The Old Shepherd's Chief Mourner* (1837; Victoria and Albert Museum, London), *The Monarch of the Glen* (1851; Dewar House, London), and *Man Proposes, God Disposes* (1864; Royal Holloway College, London). He was admired by Queen Victoria, who employed him to paint royal

Nicolas Lancret: A Lady and Gentleman with Two Girls; oil on canvas; 89×98cm (35×39in); 1742. National Gallery, London

portraits and pets. He also modeled the lions for Trafalgar Square (1858–63), and was offered the presidency of the Royal Academy but turned it down because of failing health; he exhibited there for a total of 58 years.

## Lanfranco Giovanni 1582–1647

A painter of the transition from early to High Baroque, Giovanni Lanfranco was active mainly in Rome and Naples. Born in Parma, he was probably trained there by Agostino Carracci. In 1602 he went to Rome to work with Agostino's brother Annibale, perhaps as an assistant on the Farnese gallery; this experience is clearly reflected in his own ceiling of the Villa Borghese (1624–5). A brief return visit to his native town from 1610 to 1612 seems to have stimulated a new interest in Correggio, and in a work such as the *St*

Sir Edwin Landseer: Wild Cattle of Chillingham; oil on canvas; 229×155cm (90×61in); c1867. Laing Art Gallery and Museum, Newcastle upon Tyne

Giovanni Lanfranco: The Miracle of the Loaves and Fishes; oil on canvas; 229×426cm (90×168in); c1620–3. National Gallery of Ireland, Dublin

*Margaret of Cortona* (1618–20; Palazzo Pitti, Florence) the swirling movement, the flicker of light and shade, and the emotional expressiveness all anticipate the style of Bernini.

By this date Lanfranco's increasingly Baroque tendencies had already brought him into conflict with Domenichino, who was the leading representative of Bolognese classicism in Rome. The rivalry between the two artists was to reach a climax with their respective decorations in S. Andrea della Valle (1624–8). Lanfranco's illusionistically conceived *Assumption of the Virgin* in the dome, successfully updating Correggio's domes in Parma, and ingeniously exploiting the real light source of the lantern for dramatic effect, was to exert a profound influence on later Baroque dome decoration. By the mid 1630s, Lanfranco was beginning to lose his preeminent position in Rome to Pietro da Cortona. In 1634 he moved to Naples, where his many fresco decorations quickly established the High Baroque as the prevalent style. He returned to Rome in 1646 for the last year of his life.

## Lanyon Peter 1918–64

The English painter George Peter Lanyon was born at St Ives, Cornwall, where he lived all his life, though traveling widely. He studied with Borlase Smart at St Ives, at the Penzance School of Art in 1937, and at the Euston Road School in 1938. He died in 1964 after a gliding accident. Primarily a landscape painter, Lanyon's originality lay in his combination of a Cubist vision ordered by an Abstract Expressionist technique. Under the influence of Ben Nicholson and Naum Gabo, he spent a period making constructions. Later he returned to landscapes which were based on his subjective response to appearances rather than on overt description. After 1959, gliding added a further dimension to his style, especially in the use of brighter colors. Some of his paintings were preceded by studies in painted wood and collage.

Peter Lanyon: Thermal; oil on canvas; 183×152cm (72×60in); 1960. Tate Gallery, London

## Largillière Nicolas de 1656–1746

The French painter Nicolas de Largillière was born in Paris but trained in Antwerp. In 1674 he went to England, where he worked in the studio of Lely. Working in Paris from 1680, he was the leading portraitist outside court circles, where Rigaud was supreme. He was received into the Académie in 1686 with a portrait of *Charles Lebrun* (Louvre, Paris), a suitably grand and autocratic image of Louis XIV's chief painter. For the *Échevins* (magistrates) of Paris he made large group portraits in a somewhat Baroque manner, tempered by knowledge of Dutch corporation portraits. The masterpiece of this genre shows *The Échevins of Paris before St Geneviève* (1696; St Étienne-du-Mont, Paris), a cross betwen sober group portrait and Baroque altarpiece. He also painted still lifes and landscapes.

## Larionoff Michail 1881–1964

The Russian painter Michail Larionoff was born in Teraspol, Ukraine. His work at first went through Symbolist and Impressionist phases. In 1909 he adopted a "primitivist" manner based on Russian popular art. His paintings used strident and often bawdy imagery as a deliberate affront to Western pictorial conventions, an effect reinforced by the artist's unconventional behavior, designed to ruffle the complacency of the Moscow bourgeoisie. With his lifelong friend and associate Natalia Goncharova, he was the originator and principal exponent of Rayonism, a style that entailed the presentation of objects through reflected rays of light. By 1913, the schematic application of this method had led him to abstraction. He left Russia for Switzerland in 1915 to design for Diaghilev, and never returned.

## Lastman Pieter 1583–1633

Pieter Pietersz. Lastman was a Dutch painter of multifigure historical and mythological pictures. The dramatic impact of his glossy, sumptuously colored narratives—achieved largely by animated gestures and facial expression—tends to be diminished by distracting genre and still-life details. He is nowadays chiefly remembered as Rembrandt's teacher in Amsterdam for about six months c1624–5. Lastman worked in Italy in his youth, and it was through him that Rembrandt became acquainted with Italian Renaissance art.

Nicolas de Largillière: Self-portrait; oil on canvas; 79×63cm (31×25in); c1710. Musée Fabre, Montpellier

Michail Larionoff: Woman Walking on the Boulevard; oil on canvas; 116×86cm (46×34in); 1912. Private collection

## Latham John 1921–

The British artist John Latham was born on the Zambesi River in Mozambique in Africa. He trained at the Chelsea School of Art (1946–50). His infamous *Distillation* (1967; Museum of Modern Art, New York), a reduced and bottled copy of Greenberg's *Art and Culture*, led to his dismissal from St Martin's School of Art, London where he taught part-time (1966 to 1967). Latham has been a respected if poorly understood British avant-garde artist since the late 1950s when he produced his first book sculptures, which were seen at the time to be part of the Assemblage movement. His aesthetic theories developed over two decades are based on an interpretation of time, space, and events. They were published in a treatise, *Time-base and Determination in Events* (Düsseldorf, 1975), at the time of his major retrospective in the Kunsthalle in Düsseldorf. Since 1968 he has been active in the Artist Placement Group, of which he was a founder member, and through which he undertook several environmental projects in Scotland in the mid 1970s. In 1976 his work was shown at the Tate Gallery in London.

## La Tour Georges de 1593–1652

The son of a baker at Vic-sur-Seille in Lorraine, the French artist Georges de La Tour was of respectable but undistinguished origin. He is first recorded as a painter in Vic in his marriage contract of 1617. In 1620 he moved to his wife's town of Lunéville, where he remained for the rest of his life. La Tour's first known painting, probably dating from 1615–16, is a genre piece, *The Payment of Dues* (Lvov State Picture Gallery). It shows an interior scene, lit by a solitary candle, with figures gathered around a ledger while one man counts out money; its meaning is not wholly clear. The candlelit interior presages much of La Tour's later work. *The Fortune Teller*, in the Metropolitan Museum, New York, is known from its signature to have been painted in Lunéville, and with it may be associated *The Cheat with the Ace of Diamonds* (Louvre, Paris). In these pictures both the subject matter—with its covert sexuality and moral ambivalence—and the technique derive directly from Caravaggio; La Tour must have become familiar with his work, possibly through copies. However, the differences between the two artists are significant; in La Tour the earthiness and vigor of Caravaggio have become formalized, bland, and mysterious.

If La Tour declines to make a moral statement in these detailed depictions of conspiracy and deceit, he is more explicit in a series of mainly half-length figures of saints, some of which survive only through copies. In these paintings La Tour's minute realism is used to point a moral. His saints are bearded, compelling peasant figures, withdrawn in their concentration but no longer distant or frozen in some other world. The most important of the series is the *St Jerome* (1621–3; Musée de Peinture et de Sculpture, Grenoble). Here the aging Saint is shown almost naked, his thin wiry arms contrasting with his sagging old man's belly; the blood-caked knot of the rope with which he beats himself hangs from his hand, lying on the floor with sharp stones and a skull. Against this apparently dispassionate portrayal of the ravages of old age and the mortification of the flesh is set the absorbed concentration of the head as the Saint looks at the Cross clenched in his left hand.

The technique too has changed. The fluid luminous tones of *The Fortune Teller* have given way, most noticeably in the flesh areas, to a drier, almost clay-like handling; this probably derives from the artist's firsthand knowledge of the work of Hendrick Terbrugghen, a Dutch Caravag-

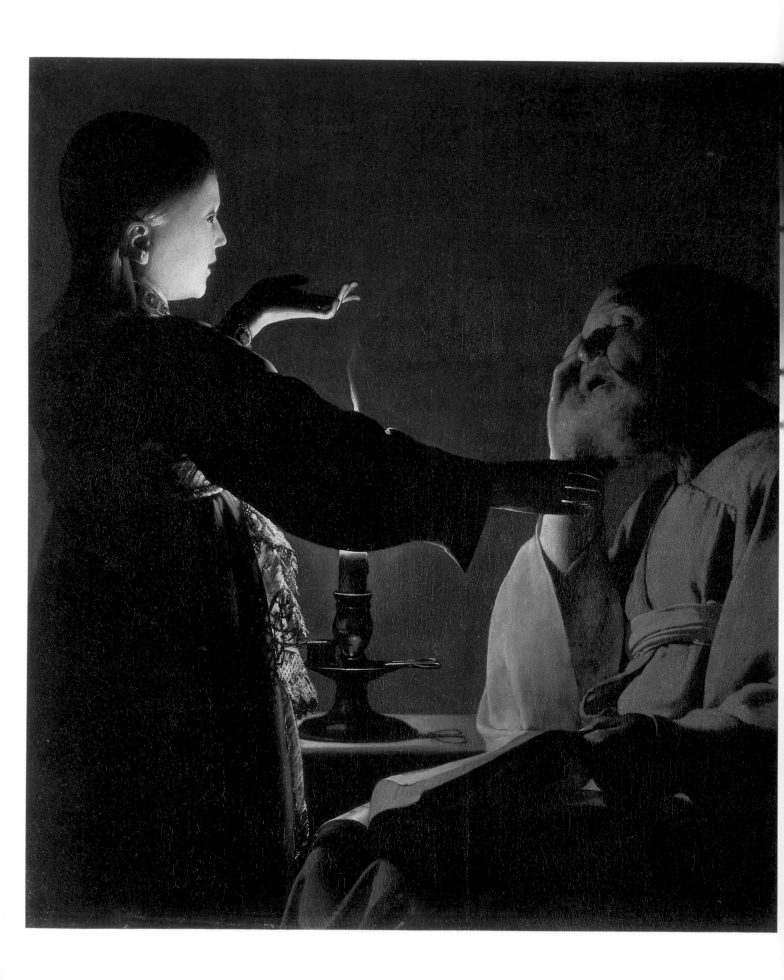

gesque working in Utrecht. Paralleled with the series of saints are a number of genre scenes, more loosely painted and more immediate than the earlier pictures. In these, beggars and musicians predominate, culminating in *The Beggars' Brawl* (c1627–30; J. Paul Getty Museum, Malibu), where the inaudible scream of the woman who looks out from the left of the picture gives the key to the viewer's response.

With *The Flea Catcher* (c1635; Musée Historique Lorrain, Nancy) La Tour reverts to the candlelit interior, a trick or perhaps an obsession that remains with him for the rest of his life. An extraordinary, intimate scene, the subject matter has parallels with "Susannah" subjects. But here, there is no sense of voyeurism; the figure is ungainly, self-absorbed, undressed rather than nude. A series of paintings of the Repentant Magdalene, datable to the late 1630s, shows possible evidence of a second visit to the Netherlands. In 1627 Terbrugghen had painted the *Magdalene Contemplating a Skull* (Schloss Weissenstein, Graf von Schönbornsche Kunstsammlungen, Pommersfelden) and the close parallels between this painting and La Tour's *Magdalene* are very close. They are alike in their candlelit interiors, in virtuoso effects of light and shade, and in their props: the mirror and the skull. They display a new, coppery tone which may derive from an acquaintance with the work of Honthorst.

Candlelit interiors of increasing virtuosity and religious intensity occasionally give way to genre scenes, such as *The Boy Blowing on a Charcoal Stick* (c1638–40; Musée des Beaux-Arts, Dijon). Despite the clear religious intensity of his work, there is substantial evidence that by this time La Tour had become an extremely difficult, aggressive, and conceited man, much given to self-aggrandisement. In 1639 he is referred to in a document as "Georges de La Tour Peintre Ordinaire du Roy", an honor that probably marked La Tour's presentation of a picture of St Sebastian to King Louis XIII.

In the paintings of the 1640s La Tour's technique becomes broader. Ostensibly simple, composition and lighting are in fact rigidly controlled; superfluous detail is

Georges de La Tour: The Dream of St Joseph; oil on canvas; 93×81cm (37×32in); c1640. Musée des Beaux-Arts, Nantes

eliminated, and forms reduced to almost geometrical terms. In the *St Sebastian Tended by St Irene*, painted for the church of Bois Anzeray in 1649 (Louvre, Paris), a variant of the painting presented to the King, this reduction to essentials of composition, lighting, form and gesture is clearly marked. The saint is transfixed by only one arrow, one drop of blood serving to indicate his martyrdom. St Sebastian is conventionally depicted bristling with arrows, running with blood, yet alive and radiant with faith; here he is seen motionless, apparently dead; the implicit violence and horror are replaced by an economy of movement, each figure expressing only one emotion: love, compassion, tears, and prayer.

His last years dogged by illness, La Tour died in 1652. His oldest surviving son had qualified as a painter in 1646 but he seems to have done little to prevent the almost total lapse into obscurity of the work and even the name of his father. Much of his work survived unrecognized, unidentified, or else ascribed to other artists. Many of his compositions exist in two or more versions, some autograph replicas, some copies. Few of his works are signed and fewer are securely datable. While much is known of La Tour's daily life in Lunéville, there survives no contemporary assessment of his work. The rediscovery of La Tour as a painter in 1915 and the gradual piecing together of his oeuvre has been described as a triumph of art history, but the triumph is not yet total. There remains much that is still guesswork.

**Further reading.** Arland, M. *Georges de la Tour*, Paris (1953). Nicolson, B. and Wright, C. *Georges de la Tour*, London (1974). Periset, G. *Georges de la Tour*, Paris (1948).

## La Tour Maurice de 1704–88

The French pastellist Maurice Quentin de La Tour was born in Saint-Quentin. After a visit to London, he settled in Paris. His first visit to the city had probably been in 1720–1, when he realized how he could benefit from the vogue for pastel portraits begun by Rosalba Carriera. He entered the Académie in 1737, and exhibited at the Salon that same year, achieving a success which was to be lasting. He specialized in portraits of the face alone, and made his sitters seem larger than life and very vivacious, with a twinkle in the eye and a direct

Maurice de La Tour: Portrait of Jean Restout; oil on canvas; 41×31cm (16×12in); c1738. Musée A. Lecuyer, St-Quentin

and open expression. His ability to make almost anyone seem attractive in spirit if not in face, and to grasp a sitter's character in that difficult yet sensitive medium, made his fortune.

## Lauber Diebold fl. 1427–69

Diebold Lauber was a German illuminator. Based at Hagenau in Alsace, he was the head of a large atelier of about 16 illuminators known as the Hagenau School. Although this workshop has a distinctive style, it is extremely difficult to identify the contributions of the individual members of the atelier. It seems to have specialized in large Bibles and popular treatises and chronicles. About 50 manuscripts from the Hagenau school are known, 12 of which are in the Library of Heidelberg University. The illuminations in these books are in general sketchily drawn and crudely colored. While they lack finish, they are often highly vivacious. Lauber worked for the Bishop of Strasbourg and for Count Ludwig IV of Heidelberg. He also produced manuscripts on his own account as speculative ventures for general sale. In this respect, his business practice foreshadows that of the later publishers of printed books.

## Laurana Francesco c1430–?c1502

The Italian sculptor Francesco Laurana was born in Vrana, Dalmatia. He is first

recorded in 1453 working on the Triumphal Arch of Alfonso I at Castelnuovo, Naples, where he is usually said to have carved the high-relief panel depicting Alfonso and his court. This shows a number of figures cramped beneath a loggia of classical design, with friezes of classically-inspired nereids, mermaids, and swag-bearing *putti* above and below. He also worked in Sicily (*c*1470) and in Provence from the 1460s, returning several times afterwards. There he produced medals for René d'Anjou and important work in Avignon and Marseilles (for example the Chapel of St Lazarus, Old Cathedral, Marseilles), demonstrating a peculiarly late-Gothic character. Apart from these excursions abroad, he worked mainly in Naples, where he produced several female bust portraits carved in smoothly polished marble with a calm and simple naturalism. Famous works are to be seen in the Kunsthistorisches Museum, Vienna, the Bargello in Florence, the Louvre in Paris, and in the Staatliche Museen, Berlin.

## Laurana Luciano 1420/5?–79

The Dalmatian architect Luciano Laurana was born at Zara. He was one of the most distinguished architectural designers of the 15th century in Italy. His most famous surviving work is at Urbino where he designed a considerable part of the existing Palazzo Ducale (*c*1465–72), in particular the main *cortile* and numerous doorways, chimneypieces, and other interior fittings. Laurana was much influenced by previous Florentine architectural practice; but his own work, with its clarity, precision, and restraint, has its own individual character. It seems likely that in the acquisition of this taste he was influenced by the work of the resident court painter, Piero della Francesca. Laurana also served as a military engineer in Naples; he was working on the fortification of Pesaro when he died.

## Laurencin Marie 1885–1956

Marie Laurencin was a French painter and theater designer. She was largely self-taught, but during the years 1908–12 was the mistress of Guillaume Apollinaire which enabled her to move in the Cubist

Francesco Laurana (attrib.): the Arch of Alfonso I, Castelnuovo, Naples; *c*1453

circles of the Bateau-Lavoir group, where she met Picasso and Braque. However, she never produced a Cubist picture herself; her *métier* was pictures of young, graceful girls, in subdued colors, living out their delicate idylls. She was much influenced by Rococo art and by Persian miniatures. She produced designs for Poiret and in the 1920s and 1930s, "Laurencin-girls" abounded; she answered a period need. She also designed Poulenc's ballet *Les Biches* for Diaghilev in 1924 and illustrated many books.

## Laurens Henri 1885–1954

The French sculptor Henri Laurens was born and died in Paris. He was originally trained as a decorative craftsman. Working and exhibiting in Cubist circles from 1911, he rapidly emerged as one of the most inventive Cubist sculptors: first in simple architectural stone pieces, then in a succession of polychrome constructions using a variety of improvised materials (for example, *Mask*, 1918; Museum of Modern Art, New York).

Henri Laurens: Clown; paint on wooden shapes; height 64cm (25in); 1915. Modern Museum, Stockholm

What they have in common with the great bronzes of his maturity (1920 onwards) is a generous sense of vitality and humor. "I aspire to ripeness of form", he said in 1951. His bronzes, usually of female nudes, and often with an aquatic theme, are characterized by a fruity opulence and sensuality. They have a natural skin-like surface, and they marry playful intimacy with a sense of the monumental. The largest collection is in the Musée National d'Art Moderne, Paris.

Laurens was also a fluent draftsman and worked extensively as a theater designer (for Diaghilev in the 1920s) and as an illustrator.

## Lawrence Thomas 1769–1830

The English portrait-painter Sir Thomas Lawrence was born in Bristol. His father, a bankrupted innkeeper, was not slow to exploit the boy's precocious natural facility, notably in Bath, where in his early teens he earned the main part of the family income making likenesses in pencil and pastel. In 1786 he moved to London, entering the Royal Academy Schools, and the following year sent seven oils to the Academy exhibition. Abundant official recognition lay ahead: succeeding Reynolds, he became Painter-in-Ordinary to the King in 1792; and at the Royal Academy he was elected Associate in 1791, full member in 1794, and President in 1820.

Seventeen hundred and ninety saw the exhibition of his *Queen Charlotte* (National Gallery, London). This glittering performance confirmed Lawrence's fashionable status, but he was disastrously tempted into accepting more commissions than he could well handle. His early career was thus something of an anticlimax, probably worsened by financial and emotional troubles. His works were criticized for their exaggerated highlighting effects and for their theatricality. Following ideas in Reynolds' *Discourses*, he believed that a painter's aspirations should lie beyond portraiture, in the realm of subject painting; but his most ambitious subject picture, the muscle-bound *Satan Summoning up his Legions* (1797; Royal Academy of Arts, London), lacks the romantic power of works such as the *Kemble as Hamlet* (1801; Tate Gallery, London), which bridge the gap between the two genres. The latter work also exemplifies Lawrence's fascination with the stage.

His declining reputation was revived by a

Thomas Lawrence: Charles William Lambton (The Red Boy); oil on canvas; 137×112cm (54×44in); first exhibited 1825. Private collection

strong showing at the Royal Academy exhibition of 1807, featuring the *Sir Francis Baring and his Associates* (Collection of Lord Northbrook, Winchester, Hampshire). This highly animated picture—the subjects are engaged in a business discussion—contrasts with the static Reynolds group portrait for which it was intended as a pendant, yet avoids the mannerisms to which the artist's style was prone.

Ceremonial or military costume lent itself especially well to the brilliance of Lawrence's treatment: *The Third Marquess of Londonderry* (1813; Marquess of Londonderry Collection, Cleveland) invites comparison with works by Gros and Géricault. In 1815, he was knighted as a prelude to undertaking an important royal commission to commemorate in portraits the sovereigns, soldiers, and statesmen associated with the overthrow of Napoleon: the Waterloo Chamber series at Windsor Castle. From 1818 to 1820 he worked

abroad from the sitters themselves—and thereby established an international reputation—leaving last touches for his return home. Some of the portraits in fact remained unfinished at the artist's death, when they were finally delivered up to George IV. The *Pius VII*, which alludes to the restoration to the Vatican of antique sculpture plundered by the French, is the most vital of the series. Lawrence seems to have been particularly attracted to the 77-year-old Pope, whose features, he felt, were "animated with benevolence and a sort of mild energy".

Lawrence's apparently dashing manner belies his careful working method; he always drew in features before painting. His work is nonetheless strikingly uneven in quality, owing partly to his use of assistants. This, and the glossy vulgarization of his style that became popular in the 1830s and 1840s, have provoked unjust defamations of his art.

## Lebrun Charles 1619–90

The French artist Charles Lebrun was the principal painter for much of the reign of Louis XIV. He created a style intended to glorify that monarch's prowess—a manner much imitated by the court painters of other European rulers and princelings with similarly absolutist ambitions.

Born in Paris, Lebrun received his training first from his father, Nicolas, a minor sculptor, and then from François Perrier and Simon Vouet. In 1643 he was sent by his patron, the Chancellor Séguier, to Rome; there he studied the works of Antiquity and of modern masters, and learned above all from the example and counsel of Nicolas Poussin. Returning to Paris in 1646 he received numerous commissions for altarpieces, designs for engravings, and ceiling paintings. Among the latter are those for the Hôtels de Nouveau (1650–1) and de la Rivière (1652–3), both now in the Musée Carnavalet, for the Hôtel Lambert, and for a room in the Louvre. From 1658 to 1661 he was employed by Nicolas Foucquet at his château of Vaux-le-Vicomte, not only on the decoration of the rooms, but also as a designer of sculpture for the park, of furniture, and of tapestries.

On the fall of Foucquet he passed into the service of the King, and for him he controlled the decoration of Versailles. He selected and in some cases guided the other painters, himself painted the Escalier des Ambassadeurs (1674–8) and the Galerie des Glaces with the Salons at either end (1678–87), provided drawings for sculpture, and directed the Gobelins factory which produced both furniture and tapestries.

In this work he had the support of Colbert, who was the *Surintendant des Bâtiments*. Colbert also favored the development of the Académie Royale de Peinture et de Sculpture, of which Lebrun had been a founder in 1648 and became Chancellor for Life from 1663. Lebrun used this forum to propound his ideal of narrative painting, in which the story was depicted by carefully studied facial expressions and gestures, supported by color. His lecture on the Expression of the Passions was his most influential single contribution. His approach, so important for the development of academic art in other countries and later centuries, is best exemplified by his painting of *Alexander at the Tent of Darius* (1660–1; Versailles).

After Colbert's death in 1683 Lebrun's

Charles Lebrun: Eberhard Jacob and his Family; oil on canvas; 275×325cm (108×128in); c1650. Formerly Kaiser Friedrich Museum, Berlin

power waned, and the failing economy of the court added to his troubles. His later years were devoted to producing smaller biblical paintings in a revived Poussinesque manner.

The traditional accusation that Lebrun exercised an artistic dictatorship is an exaggeration, and underestimates his tolerance of the variety of styles employed by his followers. Nonetheless, his influence was very considerable, and strongly affected many lesser talents, while the authority of his position ensured a basic unity in French court art of the period.

## Leck Bart van der 1876–1958

Bart Anthony van der Leck was a Dutch painter, book-illustrator, and designer. He studied at the State School for Decorative Arts, Utrecht. His early painting was in the tradition of the Hague landscape school. He was then influenced by the Dutch Monumentalists art movement, whose aim was to attain a simplified mural art. Gradually from 1912 his work, which was socially concerned, became more simplified and stylized, and extremely two dimensional: for example *The Tempest* (1916; Kröller-Müller Museum, Otterlo).

Reducing forms to rectangles, triangles, and their combinations, and using only primary colors, his stylization led to abstraction, exemplified in *Leaving the Factory* (Boymans—Van Beuningen Museum, Rotterdam). Leck's work influenced Mondrian, van Doesburg, and the artists of *De Stijl*. He joined the group in 1917 but soon left. His subsequent work became less abstract.

## Le Corbusier 1887–1965

The career of Charles-Édouard Jeanneret, known as Le Corbusier, is inextricably linked with the fate of 20th-century architecture; the same triumphs and defeats, the same hopes and frustrations were shared by both. To pin down this many-sided, controversial genius is as difficult as charting the twists and turns of a creative spirit like Picasso—an artist with whom Le Corbusier liked to be compared.

Born at La Chaux-de-Fonds in Switzerland, the son of an engraver of watches, Charles-Édouard Jeanneret was encouraged to take up architecture by his local art school teacher, Charles L'Eplattenier. The years from 1906 to 1912 were spent in self-education and travel. He made contact

with many of the pioneers of modern architecture: Josef Hoffmann and Adolf Loos in Vienna, Tony Garnier in Lyons, Auguste Perret in Paris, who taught him about reinforced concrete, and Peter Behrens in Berlin, then involved with industrial design. From his eye-opening tour of Greece and Turkey in 1911 he brought back some important sketches.

In 1917 he left Switzerland to settle in Paris, after the construction of his first major building, the Villa Schwob at La Chaux-de-Fonds (1916). Already the ideals of his later work are present: geometrical simplicity, perfect proportional harmony, a rational method of planning and construction, and an ability to sculpt fluid, plastic spaces.

In 1918 Le Corbusier and the painter Amadée Ozenfant launched the movement known as Purism. Le Corbusier began to paint, an activity he never gave up. In 1920, the year he adopted his pseudonym, they began publishing the magazine *L'Esprit Nouveau* in which he formulated his aesthetic and architectural ideas. These were collected in 1923 in what was to become the most influential book by any 20th-century architect, *Vers Une Architecture*.

In a series of private houses between 1923 and 1930 Le Corbusier put these ideas into practice. The Villa Savoye at Poissy (1927–31) was a poetic demonstration of the elements of the clean white cubic style first shown to the public at the Weissenhof Exhibition at Stuttgart (1927). It used a reinforced-concrete support system, developed from earlier projects for skeleton-framed, mass-produced housing (Dom-ino, 1914; Citrohan, 1921). It also abolished the load-bearing wall, permitting long uninterrupted strips of window, and fluid internal spaces that were often composed like the primary geometrical shapes of Purist painting, and were similarly colored. Thin columns ("pilotis") lift up the box-like living area, giving the house a weightless appearance. The roof is flat, with terrace or garden. The use of standard industrial components, given prominence in the Pavillon de l'Esprit Nouveau (1925), completes the streamlined, "machine aesthetic" finish.

In the early 1930s Le Corbusier worked on large-scale projects that were of great influence. Of the few actually built, the most important were the Salvation Army Hostel (1931; Paris) and the Pavillon Suisse (1932; Paris). Both works show their architect conceiving of a building in terms of a complex of interlocking but clearly defined parts, each with a different function, lending weight to his much-quoted proposition that "Architecture is the masterly, correct, and magnificent play of volumes assembled in light."

A crucially important but now largely discredited aspect of Le Corbusier's whole output, especially during the 1930s, was town planning, The smallest unit or cell of his many schemes for collective housing was the Immeuble-Villa (1923) or Pavillon de l'Esprit Nouveau, a flat on two floors with double-story living-room. His prototypes, the Contemporary City for three million (1922) and the Plan Voisin (1925), owed much to Sant'Elia's drawings for a Futurist New City (1914) and to Tony Garnier's Cité Industrielle (1901). Multilevel circulation, a cluster of enormous skyscrapers for business in the center, and multistory villas set in parkland, were the main features of these and numerous other designs for cities throughout the world.

In the 1930s Le Corbusier also renounced the somewhat inhuman, "precision-instrument" idiom of the previous decade; he began to incorporate solid, earthy materials—stone, brick, timber—and more willful forms into his buildings. The first hint of this came in the Pavillon Suisse, with its curved rubble wall; it was confirmed in a tiny, picturesque Maison de Weekend at La Celle-de-Saint-Cloud (1935). But it was not until the postwar, monumental Unité d'Habitation at Marseilles (1947–52) that crude concrete became an aesthetic end in itself, later to be imitated by the architects of Brutalism.

With the Unité, which was followed by others at Nantes and Berlin, Le Corbusier was at last able to put into effect his schemes for mass-housing, although even this was only one part of a proposed suburb made up of similar massive blocks. Some of the themes of his earlier work were taken up—giant "pilotis" (Pavillon Suisse) and sunbreaks (Salvation Army Hostel)—but the extraordinary sculpted roofscape was the most daring thing of its kind to date. The Unité was composed of 350 apartments in eight double-stories and based on a proportional system which Le Corbusier called "Modulor". In the two little Maisons Jaoul at Neuilly (1954–6) he continued his exploitation of rough concrete and natural materials; the brick walls and barrel vaults were again widely copied.

The pilgrimage church of Notre Dame du

Le Corbusier: Notre Dame du Haut, Ronchamp; 1950–4

Haut at Ronchamp (1950–4) was visually his most exciting postwar work and undoubtedly one of his masterpieces. Its shape suggests some huge bird poised for flight, a moving, living being. Every detail of this expressive, sculptural building appears arbitrary, but its irregularity is the result of a complete reassessment of the requirements of worship. It is a potent symbol of the wonder of religion; to visit it is a profoundly moving experience.

From 1951 Le Corbusier was busy with plans for the new city of Chandigarh, capital of the Punjab, where, in addition to designing the Law Courts and Secretariat, he was able to try out many of his solutions to problems of urban living. The Dominican convent of Sainte-Marie-de-la-Tourette at Eveux-sur-Arbreste (1957–60) was perhaps his strongest single statement in the years preceding his death. In stark contrast to the smooth white curves of Ronchamp, but no less dramatic, it is a predominantly rectilinear building in exposed concrete: it is rich in sculptural forms, with two identical strips of precast cells raised high on three sides above a central courtyard overlooking a valley.

Le Corbusier not only worked in Europe, he practiced on a world scale—in India, South America, North Africa, U.S.A., and Japan. Like Gropius and Mies van der Rohe, he helped to ensure the universal recognition of a new architectural language which he believed spoke for the rapidly changing patterns of 20th-century

life. He was the most internationally admired—and hated—of them all.

**Further reading.** Besset, M. *Who was Le Corbusier?*, Geneva (1968). Curtis, W. et al. *Le Corbusier, History of Architecture and Design 1890–1939*, Milton Keynes (1975). Jencks, C. *Le Corbusier and the Tragic View of Architecture*, Cambridge, Mass. (1974). Le Corbusier *The Complete Architectural Works*, London (1966).

## Ledoux Claude-Nicholas
### 1736–1806

The French architect Claude-Nicholas Ledoux was born at Dormans (Maine) and trained under J.F. Blondel. His first professional work was as a decorative designer, but by 1770 he had risen to fame with plans for several Parisian hotels. Although some of his early designs for churches and bridges foreshadow his mature work, he was best known before the French Revolution for his houses for the French nobility such as the château de Benouville (1768) and the Hotel Thélusson, Paris (1783).

In 1771 Ledoux was appointed *Inspecteur des Salines* for the saltworks at Arc-et-Senans, for which he drew up two projects: a design for the factory and workers' living accommodation, and the plan for an ideal city outside the saltworks. In the former elliptical plan, the rugged utilitarianism of the remaining buildings echoes the grandeur of Piranesi. For the city, Ledoux planned a wide range of buildings, in which the occupants' function was expressed by entirely original iconographic allusions: a woodcutter's house composed of a pile of logs, a cooper's house in the form of a barrel, and so forth. This visionary approach of *architecture parlante* was revalued in functional terms for civic schemes such as the Théâtre at Besançon, 1780 (destroyed in the 19th century).

In the 1780s Ledoux produced a number of plans, in many styles, for the new toll and guard houses encircling Paris; many of these *barrières* were destroyed during the Revolution. Ledoux's architectural theories were embodied in his treatise *L'Architecture considérée sous le rapport de l'Art, des Moeurs et de la Législation*, published in 1804, which, though badly written, had artistic and social significance.

## Léger Fernand 1881–1955

The French painter Fernand Léger was born of peasant stock at Argentan, Normandy. He first studied architecture at Caen in 1897 and then went to Paris where he worked as an architectural draftsman from 1900 to 1902. After military service he studied painting in the studios of Gêrome and Ferrier at the École des Arts Décoratifs in 1903, having failed to gain a place at the École des Beaux-Arts. Like many Parisian painters he was deeply affected by the Cézanne retrospective exhibition of 1907. His first major work, *The Seamstress* (1909; Kahnweiler Collection, Paris), demonstrates this influence in its boldly faceted relief, although its gray tones may derive from Douanier Rousseau.

After noticing from his studio window how billows of smoke enlivened the rooftop scenery, he painted *Smoke over the Roofs* (1910; R. Weil Collection, St Louis), in which large areas of pale grays bounded by taut curves are mingled with darker areas of small angular shapes, recognizable as roofs.

In the large canvas *Nudes in a Forest* (1909–11; Kröller-Müller Museum, Otterlo), Léger extended his explorations into the new Cubist forms, although his Cubism differs in significant respects from that of Picasso and Braque. This picture caused a stir at the first "Cubist" Salon des Indépendants, probably because in contrast to the flatness of much Cubist painting at the time it is made up almost entirely of cylindrical forms in aggressive relief. It also maintains the spacial integrity of a scene viewed from a single point, unlike the multiviewpoints and ambiguous shallow spaces implied in work of Picasso and Braque. The figures are merely geometricized, and the picture is still a scene rather than an object in its own right.

This anchor in reality is used by Léger as a dynamic quality. He begins to use the abstract pattern of smoke, first seen in *Smoke over the Roofs* and then developed in *The Smokers* (1911; Solomon R. Guggenheim Museum, New York), and *The Wedding* (1911–12; Musée National d'Art Moderne, Paris), as a contrast to the detailed areas containing references to reality such as faces, hands, and roofs. In *The Woman in Blue* (1912; Öffentliche Kunstsammlung, Kunstmuseum Basel), the large abstract shapes are distributed regularly over the surface, their edges as sharp as the cut paper inventions (*papier collés*) of Picasso and Braque, with the fragments of reality reduced to mere clues to the identity of the subject.

In 1913, the year in which Kahnweiler offered him a contract and bought the contents of his studio, Léger followed the logic of this development by producing a number of completely Abstract works. Called *Contrasts of Forms*, perhaps as a conscious parallel to Delaunay's ideas about color contrasts, these pictures maintain the fierce three-dimensional character of Léger's earlier works; thrusting cylinders and cones of roughly equal size are suggested by schematized reflections and shadows in crude primary colors and white. The rough, frequently incomplete, black outlines create a sense of restlessness by their repetition and diagonal orientation.

This phase did not last long, however, perhaps because Léger felt that the contrast between reality and abstraction was too dynamic to dismiss. *The Staircase* (1914; Öffentliche Kunstsammlung, Kunstmuseum Basel), returns to the depiction of the figure and its surroundings, but it is built out of the forms of the previous Abstract works.

Léger's military experience from 1914 to 1917 revealed to him the visual possibilities of machines as the representatives of modernity. His earlier style was predisposed to development along these lines, and he now used his cylindrical and geometrical forms to suggest a mechanized world. Unlike the Futurists he did not romanticize or worship machines; his preoccupation was to reconcile their hard, metallic, regular shapes to the organic forms of life, to build a humanistic vision.

Fernand Léger: The City; oil on canvas; 231×297cm (91×117in); 1919. Philadelphia Museum of Art

The horizontal *The City* (1919; Philadelphia Museum of Art), while being part of a general awareness of urban life shared by Delaunay, Mondrian, and the Futurists, differs from their work in its pragmatism, and also in the glimpse of the workers who have had a hand in the construction of the city.

As in his prewar paintings, Léger plays off large abstract forms against areas of detail; but now the detail is redolent of cogs and cranes, without actually depicting them, while the abstract forms tend to the geometrical. Frequently the contrast is made more poignant by the use of a landscape invaded by the man-made forms of buildings.

Léger was extraordinarily open to the stylistic developments of the 1920s and 1930s. Some of his paintings of these years bear the impressions of Kandinsky's more relaxed work, of the vertical and horizontal discipline of the *de Stijl* movement, and of Surrealism's juxtapositions of unlikely objects. His most characteristic works of this period, however, are figure-studies, from *The Mechanic* (1920; Louis Carré Gallery, Paris), to *The Beautiful Cyclists* (1943–8; Musée Fernand Léger, Biot), in which calm monumental, expressionless contemporary faces boldly confront the spectator.

He worked in many media, illustrating books, designing sets and costumes for ballet (including *The Creation of the World* in 1922), and contributing to sever-al films, before collaborating with Man Ray, Dudley Murphy, and G. Antheil to make *The Mechanical Ballet* in 1924. 1925 saw his first murals, at the Exhibition of Decorative Art in Paris, and he later designed his first mosaic, to decorate the facade of the church at Assy (1946–9), as well as various stained-glass windows. He visited the United States three times, in 1931, 1935, and 1938, before taking refuge there from 1940 to 1945 when he became a professor at Yale.

His lifelong allegiance to the people is demonstrated by his acceptance of large-scale public commissions, his attendance at the Wroclaw Peace Congress in 1948 and the Sokols Congress in Prague in 1955, but most of all by the ordinary working men and women who are the heroes of his art.

**Further reading.** Cooper, D. *Fernand Léger et le Nouvel Espace*, London and New York (1949). De Francia, P. *Fernand Léger*, New Haven (1983). Francis, P. de *Léger, the Great Parade*, London (1969). Kuh, K. *Léger*, Urbana, Ill. (1953).

## Lehmbruck Wilhelm 1881–1919

The German sculptor and printmaker Wilhelm Lehmbruck was born near Duisburg, the son of a miner. He trained at the School of Arts and Crafts, Düsseldorf, then visited Italy from 1905 to 1906 and again in 1912, and Paris in 1908. From 1910 to 1914 he lived in Paris, where he produced a series of larger-than-life-size statues in bronze and artificial stone (for example, *The Kneeling Woman*, 1911; Museum of Modern Art, New York). In his work, Expressionistic elongations were allied to an elegiac mood, conceivably influenced by medieval prototypes and also by Rodin. In 1914 he returned to Germany, his work becoming increasingly spare and tragic, and in 1919 he committed suicide.

**Further reading.** Hoff, A. *Wilhelm Lehmbruck*, New York (1969).

## Leibl Wilhelm 1844–1900

The German painter Wilhelm Maria Hubert Leibl studied at the Munich Academy (1864–9) where he concentrated on chiaroscuro portraiture. In 1869 he came under the influence of Courbet, whom he met in Munich, and he went to study in Paris (1869–70). Subsequently he became the head of a group of Realist artists in Munich known as the Leibl Circle, but in 1873 he moved to the Dachau moors. There he developed a flat, monumental Realism, based on a tight, detailed style and starkly silhouetted figures (for example, *Three Women in Church*, 1878–82; Hamburger Kunsthalle, Hamburg). Leibl was the first of many German artists to seek simple values in peasant communities.

## Leighton Frederic 1830–96

Frederic, 1st Baron Leighton, was the most esteemed English painter of the later 19th century. Born in Scarborough, Yorkshire, he spent much of his early life abroad, particularly in Frankfurt where he trained with the Nazarene Eduard Jakob von Steinle at the Städel Institute, and in Rome, where he executed his first major work, *Cimabue's celebrated Madonna is Carried in Procession through the Streets of Florence* (1855; Collection of H.M. Queen Elizabeth II). Widely acclaimed, its mixture of Italian Renaissance anecdote and contemporary German style, plus its high technical competence, made it an ideal antidote to the Pre-Raphaelites.

Moving to Paris, where he lived from 1855 to 1860, Leighton developed a heightened sense of coloring, based on contemporary French practice and 17th-century Italian masters. He displayed a preference for Classical subjects—at first emotionally tense and *mouvementé* (as in *Orpheus and*

Wilhelm Lehmbruck: Fallen Man; synthetic stone; 72×239cm (28×94in); 1915–16. Private collection

Frederic Leighton: Winding the Skein; oil on canvas; 100×161cm (39×63in); first exhibited 1878. Art Gallery of New South Wales, Sydney

*Eurydice*, 1864; Leighton House Art Gallery and Museum, London) but later more dispassionate.

In London from 1860, Leighton rapidly achieved a high position: Royal Academician in 1868, President of the Royal Academy in 1878, in 1896 he became the unique English painter-Peer. Though undoubtedly aided by tactful diplomacy and immense personal charm, Leighton's position owed much to consistent output of high-principled works. It is true he exhibited many seemingly slight studies of feminine beauty and charm (for example *Weaving the Wreath*, 1873; Sudley Art Gallery and Museum, Liverpool). But his serious works, their subject matter drawn from the Bible or Classical mythology, consisted of extended studies of form, composition, and color (for example, *The Return of Persephone*, 1891; City Art Gallery, Leeds). His masterpieces were vast; usually consisting of frieze-like arrangements of figure-groups in architectural and landscape settings, they embody a complex orchestration of the basic ele-

ments of painting (for example, *The Daphnephoria*, 1876; Lady Lever Art Gallery, Port Sunlight). Seeming too deliberate, these works lack the free handling and vital coloring of Leighton's sketches. But a sublimated color vibrancy remains, and the studied artistry is of permanent value, even though currently unfashionable.

**Further reading.** Newall, C. *The Art of Lord Leighton*, London (1990).

## Leinberger Hans *c*1480–*c*1535?

The sculptor Hans Leinberger was born in Landshut in southern Germany. His earliest works display the exaggerated pose of the figure and deeply-cut drapery style characteristic of the late Gothic. This is found both in his wood sculpture, such as the high altar for the collegiate church of Moosburg (1511–14) and in the armored bronze figure of *Albrecht von Hapsburg* for the funerary monument of the Emperor Maximilian in the Hofkirche, Innsbruck (1514–18). His awareness of contempor-

ary art, however, is evident, in the *Crucifixion* relief of 1516 (Bayerisches Nationalmuseum, Munich) which has affinities with the style of the Danube School.

## Lely Peter 1618–80

Sir Peter Lely was the foremost painter in England during the Commonwealth and Restoration. Born Pieter van der Faes in the town of Soest, Westphalia, Lely adopted a family nickname about the time that he became a student of Frans Pietersz. de Grebber in Haarlem, in 1637. Around 1641 he moved to London, where he remained most of his life. He practiced first as a history and landscape painter in the Dutch-Italianate manner of Cornelis van Poelenburgh, but receiving little encouragement for this type of picture he turned to portraiture. He modeled his early portrait style on that of van Dyck, although his vigorous handling of paint, strong local coloring, and richly atmospheric landscape settings were entirely his own. In 1661 Lely was made Principal Painter to Charles

II, and in 1668 he was knighted. His best known late pictures, the series of *Flagmen* (National Maritime Museum, Greenwich) and *Windsor Beauties* (Hampton Court Palace, London), evoke fully the swagger and voluptuousness of the second Caroline court.

## Lemercier Jacques c1585–1654

The son of a Parisian master mason, the French architect Jacques Lemercier studied in Rome from c1607 to 1614. With Louis Levau and Jules-Hardouin Mansart he may be credited with the formation of the French classical style. Less talented than they, his essential contribution was the introduction of the academic, Classical Roman tradition stemming from Giacomo della Porta (c1533–1602), although he himself was unable to fuse this successfully with his native tradition. Commissioned in 1624 by Louis XIII to extend the Louvre, his most significant contribution was the Pavillon de l'Horloge. For his principal patron, Cardinal Richelieu, he designed the château and church of Rueil, the château and town of Richelieu (begun 1631), the Sorbonne, Paris (begun 1626), and the Palais Cardinal (Palais Royal, begun 1633). He was an ingenious planner of townhouses and his Hotel de Liancourt (1623) was an influential prototype.

## Lemoyne François 1688–1737

The French decorative artist François Lemoyne was for a short time the master of François Boucher. He was received at the Académie Royale in 1718 and made First Painter to the King in 1736. He worked at Versailles, decorating the Salon de la Paix in 1736 with his highly praised ceiling, *The Apotheosis of Hercules*. He continued the 17th-century tradition of historical painting practiced by his predecessor, Charles Lebrun. Such classicism and love of allegory was still upheld by the Académie in preference to the gayer, more intimate approach of Watteau. Lemoyne was influenced by Veronese and Rubens. He killed himself, probably through overwork.

## Lemoyne Jean-Baptiste 1704–78

The French sculptor Jean-Baptiste Lemoyne was the son of the sculptor Jean-Louis Lemoyne. Born in Paris, he was the most distinguished member of a family of sculptors. In 1725 Lemoyne won the Prix de Rome; but, at his father's request, he never

Sir Peter Lely: Two Ladies of the Lake Family; oil on canvas; 127×180cm (50×71in); c1660. Tate Gallery, London

François Lemoyne: Perseus and Andromeda; oil on canvas; 184×151cm (72×59in); 1723. Wallace Collection, London

made the journey to Italy. Perhaps because of this, his art is quite untouched by classicism, and he is the great representative of Rococo in the French sculpture of his day. Lemoyne was the favorite sculptor of Louis XV. He produced some superb monumental sculpture, much of it mutilated or destroyed during the Revolution, but he is best remembered for his vividly expressive portrait busts.

# Lenain family
## 16th and 17th centuries

The French painters of the Lenain family were Antoine (c1588–1648), Louis (c1593–1648), and Mathieu (c1607–77). All three were born in Laon in northeast France close to what was then the frontier with Flanders. All three died in Paris. Their work was rediscovered in the middle of the 19th century by Champfleury and has been a source of continuous speculation. The whereabouts and extent of their artistic education is still unknown. Antoine was known to have specialized in small genre scenes while Louis concentrated on larger figure-compositions, some of which had a religious or mythological content. Mathieu is supposed to have been responsible for the rest, the portraits in particular.

Some 15 or so signed works survive. All the signatures take the form "Le Nain" and are sometimes followed by a date—usually in the 1640s. It would be absurd to suppose that all their surviving work dates from the 1640s and therefore even a tentative dating is difficult. The formation of their style, like their individual personalities, is a mystery. Their subject matter—peasant genre and down-to-earth religious scenes—conforms to the Netherlandish type, and their work has sometimes even been confused with that of Jan Molenaer.

Too little is known about the artistic context of the Paris of Louis XIII to say whether their work is typical of a general taste which does not happen to have survived, or whether they catered for a rather specialized patron familiar with Netherlandish art.

*Peasants at Supper* (c1642–5; Louvre, Paris) illustrates both the strengths and weaknesses of their style. There is an unerring eye in the observation of each figure, but there is a certain gaucheness in the composition. The artist is not always sure where to place the figures and is equally uncertain of their relationships with each other. This picture could almost be described as the seven ages of man, as each figure is clearly in a different age group.

In the *Charette* (1641; Louvre, Paris) the figures are integrated with some care into the landscape. It is this aspect of their art that has been neglected by many critics. French landscape is inevitably seen in terms of Claude and Poussin and the contribution of the Lenain brothers is often ignored. The *Group of Peasants* (Victoria and Albert Museum, London) shows figures both seated and standing with perfect naturalness in a flat (northeastern French?) landscape with a low line of hills in the distance. This landscape belongs to the tradition—or indeed is its beginning in France—of the observation of landscape without the intervention of theory or artifice. This approach is taken even further in the *Peasants in a Landscape* (Wadsworth Atheneum, Hartford, Conn.) where the picture is almost a landscape in its own right; it is painted in a direct manner which makes the work of many Dutch landscapists appear composed.

In their religious and mythological pictures the artists used conventional Baroque subject matter, but interpreted it in an original way. The *Venus at the Forge of Vulcan* (Musée des Beaux-Arts, Reims) is a strange mixture of heavy peasant realism and a none-too-happy Venus in a semiformal pose. The mythological element is eliminated in *The Forge* (Louvre, Paris) where the rapid brush strokes and direct vision make it difficult to conceive of such a work as the product of collaboration.

The religious pictures are equally varied.

Louis Lenain: The Donkey; oil on canvas; 51×59cm (20×23in); c1641. Hermitage Museum, St Petersburg

The *Nativity* (National Gallery, London) has a sentimental sweetness befitting the subject—indeed the artists did not seem to be at home with a subject they could not observe. This is particularly true of the *Birth of the Virgin* (Notre Dame, Paris) where St Anne in bed in the background seems perfectly observed from nature while much of the rest of the picture is composed in a conventional Baroque way.

It is to be hoped that one day the problem of the extent of the collaboration of the three brothers will be solved. They seem a little out of place in the context of the Paris of Vouet, Lesueur, and Philippe de Champaigne. Yet all three brothers were elected founder members of the Academy in 1648. Parisian art had not yet settled down to the conventions that were to inhibit individuality in the latter half of the century.

## Leochares 4th century BC

The Greek late Classical sculptor Leochares was probably Athenian. He collaborated with Scopas and Bryaxis in the Mausoleum, and with Lysippos in the bronze group of *Alexander's Lion Hunt* at Delphi. He also made portraits of the orator Isocrates in bronze and of the family of Philip of Macedon in ivory and gold. His bronze group of *Ganymedes Being Raised to Heaven by the Eagle of Zeus* is probably represented by a copy in the Vatican Museums, Rome; his *Apollo* in Athens by the striding *Apollo Belvedere* (Vatican Museums, Rome) which has fascinated European artists since the Renaissance. Leochares' style combines Attic grandeur with the elongated proportions, limbs moving into space, and restless stance first explored by Lysippos.

## Leonardo da Vinci 1452–1519

Leonardo da Vinci was a painter, sculptor, architect, engineer, and investigator of nature. He described painting as the "sole imitator of all the visible works of nature" and as "a subtle invention which with philosophy and clever speculation considers the natures of all forms". This elevated aspiration provided the basis for his claim that the painter was superior to the practitioners of all other disciplines, particularly the poets who were so highly respected in the court circles he frequented.

Most of the first 30 years of his life were spent around Vinci, the small Tuscan town near which he was born, the illegitimate son of a notary, and in Florence, largely under the care of the sculptor Andrea del Verrocchio. Leonardo's continued residence with his accomplished master, four years after his matriculation in 1472 as independent painter, suggests that the versatile studio provided a congenial environment.

His first dated work is a pen drawing of *The Arno Valley* (1473; Uffizi, Florence) which possesses a remarkable sense of atmosphere and flickering vitality. These qualities provide ample grounds for attributing to him the suggestive beauties of the distant landscape in Verrocchio's *Baptism* (Uffizi, Florence), in addition to the foreground angel ascribed to him in early accounts. The inner nervous life of this angel, the vibrant filaments of hair, and the naively obtrusive folds of angular drapery provide uneasy contrasts with the more orthodox modeling and conventional piety of Verrocchio's figures.

His earliest surviving painting, the *Annunciation* (c1472–3; Uffizi, Florence), contains splendid passages, but the overall organization is gauche, in spite of its pedantically correct perspective. The same combination of vivacious detail and stiff presentation characterizes his portrait of *Ginevra de' Benci* (c1474; National Gallery of Art, Washington, D.C.)

Greater compositional fluency first appeared in his drawings (for example, *Madonna, Child, and Cat*, c1480; British Museum, London). He developed a highly original technique of passionately energetic scribbling which both suggests new arrangements and captures complex movements in a spontaneous manner. His *Madonna with a Vase of Flowers* (c1476; Alte Pinakothek, Munich) and *Virgin and Child (Madonna Benois)* (c1478–80; Hermitage Museum, St Petersburg) are lively examples of his developing design methods. His growing reputation is reflected in his commissions in 1478 and 1481 for altarpieces in the Palazzo Vecchio (the Florentine seat of Government) and S. Donato a Scopeto. The former probably did not progress beyond the design stage, and the latter remained unfinished as the magnificent underpainting of the *Adoration of the Kings* (Uffizi, Florence). He has transformed the pageant spirit of Florentine Adorations into a crowd scene of disturbing urgency, in which awed figures gesticulate tumultuously around

Leonardo da Vinci:
Virgin and Child
(Madonna Benois);
wood transferred to
canvas; 50×31cm
(20×12in); c1478–80.
Hermitage Museum,
St Petersburg

Leonardo da Vinci: Self-portrait; red chalk; 33×21cm (13×8in); c1512. Royal Library, Turin.

the tranquil virgin, while in the background unbridled animal passions are given free rein in ruined architecture. In his interpretation, the replacement of the old world with the new was not to be an easy process of benign inevitability.

He moved to the Sforza court at Milan, probably in 1482. The draft of his introductory letter to Duke Ludovico indicates that he intended to establish himself as an engineer specializing in military matters. His range of activity at the court embraced the roles of architect, engineer, inventor, theatrical designer of court spectaculars, sculptor, musician, scientist, art theorist, pundit and painter; but little remains to show for his industry. His damaged Sala delle Asse (1498; Castello Sforzesco, Milan) gives some idea of the elegant inventiveness with which he fulfilled his court duties. From rock-embedded roots at the base of the wall painted tree trunks ascend on each side towards the vaults of the ceiling, where leafy branches interlace with a golden cord to form an incredibly complicated canopy.

In contrast to the witty conceit of transforming a room into a forest bower is the high spiritual seriousness of his contemporary *Last Supper* (c1497; S. Maria delle Grazie, Milan), in which Christ's terrible announcement of the impending betrayal, and the institution of the Eucharist provide profoundly interwoven themes. Within a

contrived and ambiguous space, which extends the end wall of the refectory, the figures are arranged behind the table with a cunning that conceals their crowding. The meaning is made fully apparent through his unrivalled command of expression and gesture. Judas is differentiated by psychological means—the guilty disciple is shocked rigid, not galvanized into innocent action—rather than by traditionally isolating him on the opposite side of the table.

Leonardo's scientific studies during the 1490s gave him an increasingly profound understanding of natural law as it was then understood. He demanded that painting should express the principles of light, space, anatomy, psychology, geology, and the other sciences, all of which he infused with his special sensitivity to nature as a living force. He filled his notebooks with variations upon medieval scientific themes; he also planned his treatise on painting, which was to contain uncompromising statements on art as the depiction of natural effects through an understanding of their causes.

His studies of light are reflected in the vivid modeling of the *Virgin of the Rocks* (c1483–6; Louvre, Paris) and the second version (finished 1508; National Gallery, London), which shows the meeting in the wilderness of the Virgin and Christ with the infant St John and the the archangel Uriel. The contours are softened, given the effect he called *sfumato* ("smoked") by means of softly veiling shadows, some of which he blended with his hands rather than with the brush. The progressive dominance of shadow over the individual colors created a new tonal unity, which is nowhere more apparent than in the pools of light and shade in his portrait of the Duke's mistress Cecilia Gallerani, *Lady with an Ermine* (c1483–4; Czartoryski Museum, Krakow). An ermine, the animal symbolic of purity, lies sinuously in her arms as she turns, smiling slightly, to greet an implied companion.

The major artistic project of his Milanese years, the huge equestrian statue of Ludovico's father, Francesco, became a victim of historical circumstance. Towards the beleaguered end of his reign the Duke could not afford the bronze for the horse, and when the French expelled him in 1499 they destroyed the full-scale clay model which had been unveiled in 1493. Leonardo left the city and wandered to Mantua and Venice before returning to Florence in 1500.

For two years he strove to reestablish himself, painting the *Madonna with a Yarnwinder* (lost, but known through drawings, copies, or studio versions) and completing a cartoon of the *Madonna, Child, and St Anne* (lost). These works introduced Florentines to a new narrative method of integrating symbols into Madonna compositions. The painting showed the young Christ surging across his mother's lap to grasp the cross-shaped yarnwinder (a reference to the future crucifixion), while the Virgin watches with anxious compassion. The lost cartoon was the distant prototype for the *Madonna, Child, and St Anne* in the Louvre, Paris (c1508–15). It involved a complex interplay of emotions between the child who innocently tried to play with a lamb (a sacrificial animal signifying the coming Passion), and the Virgin who restrained him as if wishing to forestall her son's fate; meanwhile, St Anne's expression knowingly implied that what must be, must be. The composition of the surviving painting, based upon a compelling diagonal, brilliantly conveys the ebb and flow of human relationships.

In 1502–3 he spent some months traveling as military engineer to Cesare Borgia, who was rampaging on the Pope's behalf in central Italy. Appropriately, when Leonardo returned to Florence he was commissioned to paint a scene of war, *The Battle of Anghiari*, in the Grand Council Hall of the Palazzo Vecchio. Michelangelo was to be asked soon afterwards for a companion piece, *The Battle of Cascina*. Leonardo began painting in 1504, but he seems to have run into difficulties with his experimental oil technique and the work was never completed. Copies and his own drawings assist in reconstructing the appearance of the central group, which consisted of a writhing knot of Florentine and Milanese cavalry. The interlocked motion set new standards in the depiction of violent action, which were to be as deeply respected by Rubens in the next century as they were influential upon Leonardo's contemporaries.

At the other extreme, during this period, he began his studies for *Leda and the Swan*, culminating in a lost painting of Leda in mutual embrace with the swan (Jupiter in disguise). The seductive curves of her serpentine pose provided a rhythmical counterpoint to the sinuous neck of the bird. Leonardo's fascination with the processes of generation, birth, growth, and motion pervaded the whole painting, from the total design to the smallest details—such as the springing spirals of Leda's hair, for which compelling drawings survive (Royal Library, Windsor Castle).

The Florentines, under pressure from the French king, Louis XII, were forced to grant Leonardo leave to visit Milan in 1506. None of his subsequent periods in Florence lasted as long as a year, and in July 1508 he resumed more or less permanent residence in Milan, in the service of the French governor. Shortly after his arrival he planned, but never executed, an equestrian statue of General Trivulzio.

Henceforth, he devoted much of his energy to scientific investigations, which gained new authority as he mastered medieval science and refined his methods. In his anatomy he aimed to discover a perfect functional explanation of every small facet of natural form. His studies of sight passed beyond painter's perspective and into the realms of illusions, distortions, and unstable variables. The more he investigated nature, the more he revered the complexity and subtlety of man and his world.

This awe is expressed in the background of the so-called *Mona Lisa* (Louvre, Paris), where rivers descend from high lakes, continuously and inexorably eroding the mountains. The sitter has not been satisfactorily identified, whatever popular myths and hopeful historians may have suggested to the contrary. The earliest reference (1517) records that it was "the portrait of a certain Florentine lady made at the request of the late Magnificent Giuliano de' Medici" (therefore finished in Rome after 1513 when he worked for Giuliano, rather than in 1503–4 as is generally assumed); but this is by no means definite. Never before had a portrait made such an open attempt to communicate with the spectator; but it is a consciously ambiguous communication, the elusive forms defying precise reading of her expression.

His conception of a portrait as an archetype of nature's inner power is utterly consistent with his transformation of *St John the Baptist* (c1509; Louvre, Paris) into an archetype of spiritual insight which is evocative of the creative forces behind and beyond the visible surfaces of forms. *St John*, disconcertingly bisexual in a way that may reflect Leonardo's homosexuality, looms from the shadows to mesmerize the spectator with his message of Christ's coming. The Saint's expression conveys the same ineffable knowingness as the *St Anne* and *Mona Lisa*.

After his move to Rome in 1513, he was increasingly concerned with the mathematics of nature in dynamic action. Sheets of geometrical conundrums are interspersed with beautiful demonstrations of nature in movement, whether it be the turbulence of blood in the heart, the spiraling flight of birds, or the destructive maelstroms of his *Deluge* drawings (c1515; Royal Library, Windsor Castle). In the *Deluges*, the vortex patterns which formed the basis of his hydrodynamic science have been reformed into terrifying visions of cosmological flux.

Alongside these largely private works, he continued his public career in the service of the Medici in Rome. After 1516 he lived in France under the patronage of François I, for whom he undertook many of the same court tasks he had performed in Milan. Honored in France as a venerable seer, he died at Amboise.

Only a small number of his relatively few finished paintings have survived. No extant sculpture or architecture can be definitely assigned to him, and none of his writings was published until 1651. But his impact upon almost every aspect of art was enormous. His immediate pupils were unworthy, but he found true successors in Raphael, Bramante, and even the apparently hostile Michangelo. His inventions became part of the standard currency of European art.

**Further reading.** Clark, K. *Leonardo da Vinci*, new ed. rev. by Kemp, M., Harmondsworth (1988, reissued 1993). Clayton, M. *Leonardo da Vinci: A Singular Vision*, New York (1996). Goldscheider, L. *Leonardo da Vinci, Landscapes and Plants*, London (1952). Goldscheider, L. *Leonardo, Paintings and Drawings*, London (1959). Heydenreich, L.A. *Leonardo da Vinci* (2 vols.), Basel and New York (1954). Kemp, M. *Leonardo da Vinci: the Marvellous Works of Nature and Man*, London (1981, reprinted 1989). McCurdy, E. *The Notebooks of Leonardo da Vinci* (2 vols.), London (1959, reissued 1977). O'Malley, C.D. (ed.) *Leonardo's Legacy: an International Symposium*, Berkeley (1969). Pedretti, C. *Leonardo*, London (1973). Pedretti, C. *The Literary Works of Leonardo: Commentary to Jean Paul Richter's Edition* (2 vols.), London (1977). Popham, A. *The Drawings of Leonardo da Vinci*, London (1946, reissued 1973). Reti, L. (ed.) *The Unknown Leonardo*, London (1974, reprinted 1990). Richter, J.P. (ed.) *The Literary Works of Leonardo da Vinci*, London (1970). Zubov, V.P. *Leonardo da Vinci*, Cambridge, Mass. (1968, reissued 1996).

## Leoni family 16th and 17th centuries

Leone Leoni (1509–90) and his son Pompeo (c1533–1608) were Italian sculptors. Born at Menaggio (Como) of Aretine stock, Leone Leoni is first known as a medalist at Padua in 1537 and was one of the most brilliant exponents of the art of the medal of his time. He seems to have come comparatively late in his career to sculpture, in which he perhaps had no formal training, and of which he became a highly idiosyncratic practitioner. Engraver at the Papal Mint in Rome from 1537 to 1540, he caused the imprisonment of Benvenuto Cellini in 1538, and was himself sent to the galleys in 1540 for a brutal assault on a colleague. Freed the following year, he became Master of the Imperial Mint in Milan in 1542, holding this post initially for three years, and then again from 1550 to 1589.

Although his finest work as a sculptor is the monument to Gian Giacomo de' Medici, Marquis of Melegnano, in Milan Cathedral (1560–3), he is best known for his great series of sculptures, mostly in bronze, for the house of Hapsburg (Prado, Madrid). These were the fruit of visits to the Court of the Emperor Charles V in Brussels in 1548–9 and 1556 and Augsburg in 1551. His collaborator in these was his son Pompeo.

Shortly after Charles V's abdication in 1556, Pompeo entered the service of the regent Juana of Austria in Madrid, later working for Philip II. Father and son collaborated on Pompeo's important commission of 1579 for 27 massive gilt-bronze statues for the high altar of the Escorial, cast in Milan between 1582 and 1589.

Pompeo's own most memorable achievements in sculpture are the splendid gilt-bronze monuments to Charles V and Philip II, commissioned by Philip in 1591 for the Escorial, and made entirely in Spain. Pompeo remained in Spain until his death in 1608; his many other works there prove him to have been a sculptor of great ability in his own right, who in the shadow of his brilliant father has never quite received the recognition he deserves.

## Le Parc Julio 1928–

The sculptor Julio Le Parc was born at Mendoza, Argentina, and studied in Buenos Aires. In 1958 he moved to Paris and in 1960 was a founder member of the *Groupe de Recherches d'Art Visuel* (*GRAV*, Paris 1960–8). He also took part in the activities fof the *Nouvelle Tendance* movement.

Le Parc's optical-kinetic constructions, made usually from polished metal, often exploit internal reflections. They rely upon air currents or the spectator's moving eye and body for their distorting, disorienting, and transient effects. As well as reliefs and mobiles (for example *Continuel Mobile, Continuel Lumière*, 1963; Tate Gallery, London) Le Parc has made light-reflecting machines, and works using mirrors and translucent plastic. He was awarded the first prize at the Venice Biennale in 1966.

## Lescot Pierre *c*1515–78

Unlike the master masons who preceded him, the French master mason Pierre Lescot came from a prosperous legal family and was a man of learning and liberal education. His reputation rests mainly on the rebuilding of the Louvre, Paris, begun under his direction in 1546. His other works are the Hotel Carnavalet (*c*1545–50), the Fontaine des Innocents (1547–9), and the screen at St Germain L'Auxerrois (1554), all in Paris. His buildings are striking in their classicism and accuracy of antique detail; but their lack of monumentality and their emphasis on surface decoration are both quite un-Italian: they are the antithesis of the work of his contemporary Philibert Delorme. In all his buildings, Lescot worked in close collaboration with Jean Goujon, the greatest sculptor of his day.

## Lesueur Eustache 1616/17–55

The French painter Eustache Lesueur was born in Paris. In 1632 he became a pupil of Simon Vouet, whose work at first greatly influenced him. He worked at the Hotel Lambert, on a *History of Cupid* for the Cabinet d'Amour (1646–7), and on paintings of the Muses for the *Cabinet des Muses* (1647–9). These works are markedly more independent than the commission

Leone Leoni: Ferrante Gonzaga Triumphant; bronze cast; 1564. Piazza Roma, Guastella for tapestry designs which Vouet had passed on to him *c*1637. Illustrating scenes from the *Hypnerotomachia Polifili*, an antiquarian love-story printed at Venice in 1499, these designs show the popularity of humanist themes in France at that time.

As Lesueur grew older, his style became more austere: the *Cabinet des Muses* paintings already suggest Raphael's work in the Villa Farnesina—if only by hindsight. Like his later series of *The Life of St Bruno* (for the Charterhouse at Paris, *c*1648; Louvre, Paris) they show a strong influence from Poussin, whom Lesueur may well have met during that master's visit to Paris from 1640 to 1642. Lesueur's late works show a reappraisal of Raphael, particularly Raphael's tapestry cartoons. Lesueur imitated these in works of grandeur, such as his *St Paul at Ephesus* (1649; Louvre, Paris).

## Le Sueur Hubert *fl. c*1610–51

Between 1610 and 1619, the sculptor Hubert Le Sueur was in the French royal service. By 1626 he was in England, making figures for the catafalque of James I. He executed a number of tombs, the only ones of real consequence being those of Sir Thomas Richardson and Lady Cottington, both at Westminster. From 1631 he was in the service of Charles I, for whom he designed his best-known work, the equestrian statue of the King at Charing Cross, London. He also made a series of busts of the monarch.

Although Le Sueur was a second-rate artist, he is important for introducing contemporary Continental ideas into English sculpture, helping to break the hold of the moribund style of the previous century.

## Le Tavernier Jean *fl.* 1434–67

The Flemish painter Jean Le Tavernier was one of the principal illuminators working for Philip the Good. A stylish and technically assured artist, he was not associated with any single publishing house; he presided over an independent illuminator's shop in Oudenaarde, near Ghent, where he is documented from 1454 until his death. The earliest extant work attributable to him is the Book of Hours for Philip of 1454 (Royal Library, The Hague; MS. 76. F. 2). His masterpiece is the *Chroniques de Charlemagne* (1458; Bibliothèque Royale Albert I, Brussels). Both are executed in grisaille, a medium in which the artist specialized. In his late period, exemplified by the *Miracles de Nostre-Dame* (Bibliothèque Nationale, Paris) made for Charles the Bold, his work shows the influence of the style associated with the name of Philippe de Mazerolles (*c*1420–79).

## Levau Louis 1612–70

The architect Louis Levau was a Parisian, and a contemporary of François Mansart. His career was, however, very different from that of Mansart—he was successful with his patrons, careless and impatient with the finer rules of classicism, and deeply committed to the Italian Baroque. His château at Vaux-le-Vicomte (1658–61), for the royal financier Fouquet, and his Parisian Hotel Lambert (1640–4) both show the full and dramatic use of that style. The gallery and staircase of the latter were remarkable for their ingenuity and magnificence. In the commissions that followed, the Collège des Quatres Nations (1662), the East Front of the Louvre (1667), and Versailles (begun in 1669), the lessons of these two buildings were repeated, with almost the same group of craftsmen in charge. At Versailles, the ingenuity with which Levau masked the old château of Louis XIII, and the lively grandeur he gave to his new garden facade, show him responding brilliantly to a problem that demanded both skill and imagination.

## Levine Jack 1915–

Jack Levine is an American painter, born in Boston. Brought up in the Depression and employed on W.P.A. (Works Progress Administration) mural projects, Levine became an artist of social protest, building on the legacy of the Ash Can School. His art is one of character exposure, in an Expressionistic technique that owes much to Daumier, Rouault, Soutine, and George Grosz. The objects of his satire are the gangsters, mobsters, and perverters of American justice. His paintings, such as *Gangster Funeral* (oil; 1952–3; Whitney Museum of American Art, New York) and *The Trial* (oil; 1953–4; Art Institute of Chicago), are elaborately worked out in both composition and symbolism.

## Levni 18th century

The Turkish artist known as Levni was court painter to the Ottoman Sultan Ahmet III (1703–30). His real name was Abdulcelil Chelebi. He was born in Edirne and brought to Istanbul by the Sultan in 1718. Here he enjoyed the Sultan's favor through the Tulip period of lavish patronage of the arts, especially the arts of the book. He directed the illustration of the *Sur-nama* of Vehbi with 137 miniatures (1720–1; Topkapi Saray Museum, Istanbul; A. 3593) and also a set of portraits of the Sultans to Ahmet III (A. 3109). These are icon-like and conservative; but he also drew a large set of single figures from life, including Europeans, in realistic style.

## Lewis Wyndham 1882–1957

The painter and writer Percy Wyndham Lewis was born at sea off Nova Scotia, Canada, son of an American father and a British mother. He moved to London with his mother, and studied at the Slade School of Fine Art from 1898 to 1901. From then until 1909 he often traveled and worked abroad, in particular in Paris and Munich. His companions included Spencer Gore, Augustus John, and Ambrose McEvoy. In 1909 and 1910 the influence of early Cubism and German Expressionism became apparent in his work, while his designs for the portfolio *Timon of Athens* exhibited at the Second Post-Impressionist Exhibition in 1912 revealed his assimilation of Futurist idioms, and the beginnings of a personal style.

In 1913 Lewis arrived at an original Abstract style derived from a synthesis of Expressionist, Cubist and Futurist ideas that was subsequently termed "Vorticism"; *Composition* (1913; Tate Gallery, London) and his folio of 20 drawings on modern life entitled *Timon of Athens* (1913) are typical works. His paintings of 1913 to 1915 were the first sustained body of Abstract work to be produced in England. In 1913 he also joined Roger Fry's Omega Workshops, but withdrew with others amidst controversy later in the year, to found the rival Rebel Art Center which became the seedbed of Vorticism. Most of the "rebels" contributed to the first issue of the Vorticist magazine *Blast* in 1914.

Lewis' verbal and visual concerns came together in this publication, not least in the aggressive typography and design. *Blast*, inspired by Futurist publications and intended to shake up the English art establishment, was very largely the expression of Lewis' attitudes. His were practically

Wyndham Lewis: A Battery Shelled; oil on canvas; 183×318cm (72×125in); 1919. Imperial War Museum, London

the only works illustrated in the magazine to match the strident prose; indeed Ezra Pound, a fellow-contributor, considered Vorticism itself to be "nine-tenths Lewis." His paintings of 1913 to 1915 were so individual and assertive and of such clarity and dynamism that it was inevitable that his work should shape the style of the other Vorticists.

By 1915 the conviction of his Abstract works began to wane. *Workshop* of 1915 (New York Public Library), for example, has lost much of the tightness and internal rhythm of the paintings of 1913 and 1914, such as *Man of War* and *Red Duet* (private collection). In 1916 Lewis joined the Army, and was seconded as a war artist in 1917. The paintings that resulted, such as *A Battery Shelled* (1919; Imperial War Museum, London), were figurative but tightly organized, and were some of the finest works of their kind. Apart from a brief episode in the early 1920s he never approached total abstraction again.

Lewis's linear gifts were subsequently evident in an increasing number of uncompromising portraits, both drawings and oils, from *Ezra Pound* (1914–15; now lost; 1938 version in the Tate Gallery, London) to *T.S. Eliot (II)* (1938; Durban Museum and Art Gallery). He also painted some rather unsuccessful literary and historical compositions in the 1930s.

The general tendency of his work after the crystalline Vorticist paintings was towards a more organic kind of composition. The latter can be linked with English neo-Romantic art of the Second World War. Lewis's vision deteriorated, and he finally went blind in 1950. Thereafter he concentrated all his energies upon writing, with which he had been engaged spasmodically for over 40 years. He died in London.

**Further reading.** Corbett, D. P. (ed.) *Wyndham Lewis and the Art of Modern War*, Cambridge (1998). Edwards, P. and Klein, J. *The Bone Beneath the Pulp: Drawings by Wyndham Lewis*, London (2005).

## LeWitt Sol 1928–

The American painter Sol LeWitt was born in Hartford, Connecticut. He attended Syracuse University from 1945 to 1949. In 1953 he moved to New York, where he worked as a graphic designer. From 1962 to 1965 LeWitt began to create abstract sculptures and reliefs in which he explored repeated square motifs and modular proportions. In the late 1960s he focused almost exclusively on open cubes made of wood or white enameled steel, combining them into various serial combinations and sometimes filling an entire gallery space. These arrangements were based on a predetermined system that could be executed by assistants, and the installations were eventually disassembled. This emphasis on process—at the expense of the artist's role or the final, collectable object—allied him to the Conceptual art movement, which he codified in his influential essay "Paragraphs on Conceptual Art" (1967). LeWitt extended these ideas to elaborate, systematic wall drawings consisting of combinations of straight, curved, or random lines. In the 1980s and '90s these became more expressive, with swirling bands of color creating a dazzling visual experience.

Sol LeWitt: untitled; etching; 18×17cm (7×6½in); 1971. Museum of Modern Art, New York

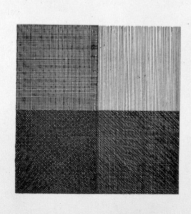

Liang K'ai: The Sixth Patrician Chopping Bamboo; hanging scroll, ink on paper; height 74cm (29in). Tokyo National Museum

## Liang K'ai *c1140–c1210*

The Chinese painter Liang K'ai came from Tung P'ing and started his career as a court painter of the late Southern Sung. He was therefore thoroughly trained in the Hsia-Ma School and his work bears all the qualities of skilled and controlled brushwork. Later in his life Liang K'ai retired to the Liu T'ung temple, although there is no evidence that he ever became a monk. It seems that he lived a retired but congenial life painting, drinking, and meeting friends. He was in sympathy with Ch'an painting, and was a fine exponent of the expressive style of direct and explosive brushwork which had already become as-sociated with the Ch'an artists.

Liang K'ai's name is often linked with that of Mu Ch'i; but from the evidence of the very few paintings attributed to him, Liang painted with a wry humor and witty brush. His two most famous works are of figures, each making a comment which is both succinct and good-humored. They each show the hand of a consummate draftsman used in a way quite unusual in Chinese figure-painting. Although Liang K'ai is an unusual genius in his treatment of his subject, he is one of the many elegant handlers of brush and ink working in the 12th and 13th centuries.

## Liberale da Verona *c1445–1526/9*

Liberale was, as his name indicates, a Veronese painter. Besides undertaking the usual commissions—altarpieces, fresco cycles, and devotional Madonnas— Liberale also displayed skills as a miniaturist. He worked in Tuscany from 1467 to 1476 illustrating graduals for Monte Oliveto Monastery (now at Chiusi Cathedral) and Siena Cathedral (Piccolomini Library, Siena), the latter with Girolamo da Cremona. His later work mainly centered around Verona; for example, the frescoes he painted in S. Anastasia. The dominant influence upon his style was Andrea Mantegna (1431–1506). Liberale used vivid coloring, particularly in his miniatures. He often gave his figures mournful eyes and pained expressions, such as those in the Berlin *Madonna and Saints* (1489; Staatliche Museen, Berlin).

Liberale da Verona: St Martin and the Beggar; a miniature on folio 76 of Graduale no. 12. Piccolomini Library, Siena

## Li Ch'eng *fl.* 940–67

The Chinese painter Li Ch'eng was a descendant of the T'ang royal house. Certainly educated in the Confucian scholarly tradition, he moved from Ch'ang An to Ying Ch'iu in Shantung Province. He is recorded to have been an overbearing and unsuccessful official who made a reputation as a landscape painter. However Mi Fei (1051–1107) records that Li Ch'eng's paintings were very rare by his time. He painted, in ink with slight color, winter landscapes of majestic mountains with bare trees which he depicted distinctively with "crab claw" branches. It is said that his brush strokes seem a thousand *li* away, emphasizing his skill in expressing distance. Although now a shadowy figure, he stands at the head of the school of great mountain painters, following the still more shadowy Kuan T'ung.

## Li K'o-jan 1907–89

The Chinese painter Li K'o-jan was born in Hsü-chou, Chiang-su Province. In 1923 he entered the Shanghai Academy of Fine Art, and in 1929 he began graduate studies at the National Academy of Art in Hang-chou, Chiang-su Province. During this period, Li was exposed to reformers who advocated integrating Western art techniques into Chinese art. In the 1930s Li began to make his renowned paintings of water buffalo and cowboys. While inspired by traditional Chinese subject matter and techniques, they hinted at a new, bolder approach. In the 1950s, Li began to explore landscapes, another Chinese tradition. In these works he found his mature style, characterized by condensed brush-

Roy Lichtenstein: Takka Takka; acrylic on canvas; 143×173cm (56×68in): 1962. Museum Ludwig, Cologne

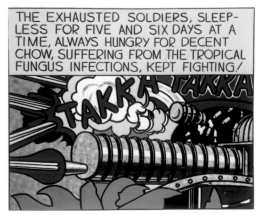

work and dark, dense ink washes applied in several layers; these paintings recalled abstract techniques in 20th-century Western art. Li taught at schools such as the Peking Academy of Art (1946–50) and the Central Academy of Art (1950–89), also in Peking.

## Lichtenstein Roy 1923–97

The American painter Roy Lichtenstein was born in New York. He studied under Reginald Marsh and at Ohio State College from 1940 to 1943. He served in the Second World War, taught at Ohio State College, and subsequently lived in Cleveland, Ohio (1951–7). During the 1950s, he worked in an Abstract Expressionist style; but after *c*1957, he became absorbed in imagery based on mass-market advertising and cheap comic strips, which he enlarged to heroic size. *Whaam!* (1962; Tate Gallery, London) is over 13 ft (3.96 m) wide. As well as incorporating wording, Lichtenstein imitates the dots that are part of the screened images from which comics were printed. This style was fully developed by the beginning of the 1960s and has remained the basis of his art. He has often applied it to more sophisticated sources, such as derivations from Cubism and Picasso, and views of Greek temples.

**Further reading.** Fitzpatrick, R. *Roy Lichtenstein: Interiors*, New York (1999).

## Liebermann Max 1847–1935

Max Liebermann was a German genre painter of the Realist school. He studied in Weimar and Paris from 1872 to 1878. He was influenced in his youth by Millet and Courbet and spent one important summer at Barbizon, in 1878. His Munich paintings depict daily life and people at work in interiors. After 1884 his works became increasingly Romantic, not only in their treatment of paint but also in choice of subject (for example, *The Parrot's Walk at the Amsterdam Zoo*, 1902; Kunsthalle Bremen). This reflected the later influence of the French Impressionists, who encouraged him to select open-air scenes, and to lighten his palette.

## Lievensz. Jan 1607–74

The Dutch painter and etcher Jan Lievensz. was born in Leiden, where he was first apprenticed. Later he became a pupil of

Max Liebermann: The Parrot's Walk at the Amsterdam Zoo; oil on canvas; 88×73cm (35×29in); 1902. Kunsthalle Bremen

Pieter Lastman in Amsterdam. He shared a studio with the slightly older but less precocious Rembrandt between 1625 and 1631. The two artists often collaborated on the same picture: the *Portrait of a Child* (Rijksmuseum, Amsterdam) is signed "Lievens retouched by Rembrandt". The early works of both painters exhibit a minute technique, dark tones, and dramatic mood (for example Lievens' somewhat theatrical *The Raising of Lazarus*, 1631; Art Gallery and Museum, Brighton); the attribution of paintings from their workshop is therefore sometimes a problem. Constantin Huygens, the Secretary of Prince Frederick Henry and a patron of both artists, regarded them as equals; he considered Rembrandt to be more emotionally expressive, but Lievensz. superior in "grandeur of invention and boldness".

The early pictures are genre scenes, religious subjects, and portraits. Lievensz. was in England between *c*1632 and 1634, and is reputed to have painted the Royal Family. On his return his portraits were influenced by the courtly style of van Dyck, while a small group of landscapes reveal his study of Rubens and Brouwer. Between 1644 and 1674 Lievensz lived mainly in Amsterdam as a popular portraitist and successful painter of large-scale historical and allegorical subjects, (such as his paintings from 1656 and 1661 for the new Amsterdam Town Hall).